From the Margins

Princeton Theological Monograph Series

K. C. Hanson and Charles M. Collier, Series Editors

Recent volumes in the series:

Ronald F. Satta
The Sacred Text: Biblical Authority in Nineteenth-Century America

Catherine L. Kelsey
*Schleiermacher's Preaching, Dogmatics, and Biblical Criticism:
The Interpretation of Jesus Christ in the Gospel of John*

Gabriel Andrew Msoka
*Basic Human Rights and the Humanitarian Crises
in Sub-Saharan Africa: Ethical Reflections*

T. David Beck
*The Holy Spirit and the Renewal of All Things:
Pneumatology in Paul and Jurgen Moltmann*

Trevor Dobbs
*Faith, Theology, and Psychoanalysis:
The Life and Thought of Harry S. Guntrip*

Paul S. Chung, Kim Kyoung-Jae, and Veli-Matti Kärkkäinen, editors
*Asian Contextual Theology for the Third Millennium:
A Theology of Minjung in Fourth-Eye Formation*

Bonnie L. Pattison
Poverty in the Theology of John Calvin

Anette Ejsing
A Theology of Anticipation: A Constructive Study of C. S. Peirce

Michael G. Cartwright
*Practices, Politics, and Performance:
Toward a Communal Hermeneutic for Christian Ethics*

Stephen Finlan and Vladimir Kharlamov, editors
Theōsis: Deification in Christian Theology

David A. Ackerman
Lo, I Tell You a Mystery: Cross, Resurrection, and Paraenesis in the Rhetoric of 1 Corinthians

John A. Vissers
The Neo-Orthodox Theology of W. W. Bryden

Sam Hamstra, editor
The Reformed Pastor by John Williamson Nevin

Byron C. Bangert
Consenting to God and Nature: Toward a Theocentric, Naturalistic, Theological Ethics

Richard Valantasis et al., editors
The Subjective Eye: Essays in Honor of Margaret Miles

Caryn Riswold
Coram Deo: Human Life in the Vision of God

Philip L. Mayo
"Those Who Call Themselves Jews": The Church and Judaism in the Apocalypse of John

Paul O. Ingram, editor
Constructing a Relational Cosmology

Edward J. Newell
"Education Has Nothing to Do with Theology": James Michael Lee's Social Science Religious Instruction

Mark A. Ellis, editor and translator
The Arminian Confession of 1621

Photograph taken by Loma Linda University; used by permission.

From the Margins
A Celebration of the Theological Work of Donald W. Dayton

EDITED BY
CHRISTIAN T. COLLINS WINN

Pickwick *Publications*
An imprint of *Wipf and Stock Publishers*
199 West 8th Avenue • Eugene OR 97401

FROM THE MARGINS
A Celebration of the Theological Work of Donald W. Dayton
Princeton Theological Monograph Series 75

Copyright © 2007 Wipf and Stock Publishers. All rights reserved. Except for brief quotations in critical articles or reviews, no part of this book may be reproduced in any manner without prior written permission from the publisher. Write: Permissions, Wipf and Stock Publishers, 199 W. 8th Ave., Suite 3, Eugene, OR 97401.

ISBN 13: 978-1-55635-135-8

Cataloging-in-Publication data:

From the margins : a celebration of the theological work of Donald W. Dayton / edited by Christian T. Collins Winn

Eugene, Ore.: Pickwick Publications, 2007
Princeton Theological Monograph Series 75

xxii + 434 p. ; 23 cm.

Includes bibliography

ISBN 13: 978-1-55635-135-8

1. Dayton, Donald W. 2. Dayton, Donald W.—Bibliography. 3. Evangelicalism. 4. Pentecostalism. 5. Methodism—History. 6. United States—Church history. I. Collins Winn, Christian T. II. Title. III. Series.

BR50 .F77 2007

Manufactured in the U.S.A.

For Don

The gospel of Christ knows of no religion, but social;
no holiness but social holiness.
"Faith working by love" is the length and breadth
and depth and height of Christian perfection.

—John Wesley, "Preface" to *Hymns and Sacred Poems* (1739)

Contents

Acknowledgements / xiii

Introduction by Christian T. Collins Winn / *xv*

1. Women's Studies / 1
   "A Neglected Tradition of Biblical Feminism" / 3
       —Donald W. Dayton
   Response by Nancy A. Hardesty / 21
   Response by S. Sue Horner / 25

2. The Social Role of the Church / 29
   "Piety and Radicalism: Ante-Bellum Social Evangelicalism in the U.S." / 31
       —Donald W. Dayton
   Response by Douglas M. Strong / 43
   Response by Jim Wallis / 49

3. The Theology of Wesley / 53
   "Law and Gospel in the Wesleyan Tradition" / 55
       —Donald W. Dayton
   Response by Howard Snyder / 67
   Response by William J. Abraham / 71

4. Methodist Studies / 75
   "'Good News to the Poor': The Methodist Experience after Wesley" / 77
       —Donald W. Dayton

5 The Holiness Movement / 109

"Pneumatological Issues in the Holiness Movement" / 111
  —*Donald W. Dayton*

Response by Melvin Easterday Dieter / 137
Response by David Bundy / 141

6 Pentecostal Studies / 147

"Revisiting the 'Baptism with the Holy Spirit' Controversy:
A Response to My Critics" / 149
  —*Donald W. Dayton*

Response by Bill Faupel / 175
Response by Amos Yong / 179

7 The Pietist Impulse / 191

"The Pietist Theological Critique of Biblical Inerrancy" / 193
  —*Donald W. Dayton*

Response by Frank D. Macchia / 207
Response by Scott Kisker / 221

8 American Popular Religious Culture / 225

"James Dean, Popular Culture and Popular Religion: With
Implications for the Study of American Evangelicalism" / 227
  —*Donald W. Dayton*

Response by Woodrow W. Whidden II / 243
Response by William Kostlevy / 249

9 Re-Thinking Evangelicalism / 253

"'The Search for the Historical Evangelicalism': George Marsden's
History of Fuller Seminary as a Case Study" / 255
  —*Donald W. Dayton*

Response by Robert K. Johnston / 281
Response by Clark H. Pinnock / 285

10 Toward a More Inclusive Ecumenism / 289
"Yet Another Layer of the Onion: Or, Opening up the Ecumenical Door to Let the Riffraff in" / 291
   —Donald W. Dayton
Response by Bother Jeff Gros, FSC / 323
Response by Cecil M. Robeck Jr. / 329

11 Interpreting Karl Barth / 335
"Karl Barth and the Wider Ecumenism" / 337
   —Donald W. Dayton
Response by Christian T. Collins Winn / 347
Response by James S. Nelson / 353

12 Re-Interpeting Christainity in Korea / 357
"The Four-Fold Gospel: Key to Trans-Pacific Continuities" / 359
   —Donald W. Dayton
Response by Myung Soo Park / 367
Response by Dawk-Mahn Bae / 371

13 Donald Dayton as Teacher / 377
   by Joel Scandrett

14 An Autobiographical Response / 383
   by Donald W. Dayton

Bibliography / 427

Contributors / 431

Acknowledgements

Like all works of scholarship, this one would not have been possible without the contributions of many hands. I would like to thank my editors at Wipf and Stock Publishers, K. C. Hanson and Charlie Collier, who walked me through the editorial process for the first time. Without their willingness to buy into the vision of the volume it is likely that it may never have seen the light of day.

During different points of the editorial process I have been assisted by a number of able teaching and research assistants, among whom are Breann Meierdirk, Gina Schulz, Tyler Gerdin, and Aaron Emery. I should also like to thank Young-Hoon Yoon whose bibliographic work on Dr. Dayton's corpus formed the basis for the select bibliography at the end of this volume. My colleague Juan Hernández Jr. also provided editorial comments that proved very helpful.

Thanks are also due to the contributors to the volume who worked with tight deadlines and somewhat amorphous parameters. Their patience, good humor and timeliness, as well as their enthusiasm for the project, gave hearty inspiration and encouragement as I labored over the volume.

Finally, thanks are due to Don Dayton. When I first joined Dr. Dayton at Drew University in 1999, I proposed to him the idea of editing a *Festschrift* in his honor. Over the course of the next few years, as I grew to understand and appreciate his work in more detail, the project morphed into the current form now before the reader. During this time, Dr. Dayton proved to be a teacher, mentor, and friend of the highest caliber. I hope that he will accept this humble volume as a small token of my thanks for all he has done and meant to me.

Chapters of this book appeared in an earlier form in various journals and books. The author and publisher gratefully acknowledge permission to reprint from these publications:

2. "Piety and Radicalism: Ante-Bellum Social Evangelicalism in the U.S." was first published in *Radical Religion* 3, no. 1 (1976) 36–40.

3. "Law and Gospel in the Wesleyan Tradition" was first published in *Grace Theological Journal* 12, no. 2 (1991) 233–43.

4. "'Good News to the Poor': the Methodist Experience after Wesley" was first published in *The Portion of the Poor: Good News to the Poor in Wesleyan Tradition*, edited by M. Douglas Meeks. Nashville, TN: Kingswood Books, 1995.

5. "Pneumatological Issues in the Holiness Movement" was first published in *Greek Orthodox Theological Review* 31, nos. 3–4 (1986) 361–87.

7. "The Pietist Theological Critique of Biblical Inerrancy" was taken from *Evangelicals & Scripture: Tradition, Authority and Hermeneutics*, edited by Vincent E. Bacote, Laura C. Miguélez, and Dennis L. Ockholm. Copyright © 2004 by Vincent E. Bacote, Laura C. Miguélez, and Dennis L. Ockholm. Used with permission of InterVarsity Press, PO Box 1400, Downers Grove, IL 60515. www.ivpress.com.

9. "'The Search for the Historical Evangelicalism': George Marsden's History of Fuller Seminary as a Case Study" was first published in *Christian Scholar's Review* 23, no. 1 (1993) 12–33. Copyright © 2003 by Christian Scholar's Review; reprinted with permission.

10. "Yet Another Layer of the Onion: Or, Opening up the Ecumenical Door to Let the Riffraff in" was originally published in *The Ecumenical Review* 40, no. 1 (1988) 87–110.

11. "Karl Barth and the Wider Ecumenism" was first published in *Christianity and the Wider Ecumenism*, edited by Peter Phan, 181–89. New York: Paragon House, 1990.

Introduction

Christian T. Collins Winn

For well over thirty-five years now, Donald W. Dayton's teaching, scholarship, and service have been contributing to and helping to reshape the discourse of multiple disciplines in the broad field of religious and theological studies. Many are the students, colleagues and friends whose thinking has been transformed through an encounter with Dayton. For those who have encountered him, Dayton has proven to be nothing less than a walking, talking bibliographic treasure trove. His mastery of the mainline traditions of Western Christianity is matched only by his vast knowledge of the lesser known, marginalized traditions and communities that have appeared throughout the history of the Christian churches, especially in the modern era. In fact, it is with these marginalized traditions that Dayton has often found himself allied. His identification with the ecclesial families associated with the Holiness movement, Pentecostalism, and others within the broader academy during the last thirty-five years has not come without controversy and, as some have observed, Dayton's ability to build bridges has not always meant that he could walk across them. Nonetheless, his work has provided scholars, pastors, and laypersons with alternative categories through which many have been able to make better sense of their experience and theology, while also being able to reconstruct their theological or ecclesial identity within the logic of their own tradition. It is for this reason that we gather to celebrate the body of work that Dayton has generated and given to the broader church.

Biography

Donald Dayton was born on July 25, 1942, in Chicago, Illinois. He is the eldest of four siblings. Dayton was reared in the Wesleyan Methodist branch of the Wesleyan Church. His father, Wilber Dayton, claimed to be the first theological ThD in the Wesleyan church and had an important impact on Dayton. After graduating from Houghton College in 1963 with a BA in philosophy and mathematics, Dayton attended Columbia

University as a pre-Woodrow Wilson Fellow, studying philosophy and history in preparation for graduate school. He matriculated at Yale Divinity School in 1964, graduating in 1969. In that same year he completed a Masters of Science in library science and bibliography from the University of Kentucky, which he had begun in 1967. In 1969, Dayton also married Lucille Sider, and later in 1976, the two celebrated the arrival of their son, Soren Charles Dayton.

Dayton received his PhD from the Divinity School at the University of Chicago in 1983, having written on Pentecostalism under the guidance of James Gustafson and Martin E. Marty. He has held teaching posts at Asbury Theological Seminary (1969–72), North Park Theological Seminary (1972–79), Northern Baptist Seminary (1979–97), Drew University (1997–2003) and Azusa Pacific University (2003–2005) and was a Visiting Professor at ISEDET (Instituto Superior Evangélico de Estudios Teológicos), in Buenos Aires, Argentina (1990). He has been invited to give lectures at over thirty-five institutions on seven continents and has taught classes at numerous institutions in North America, Europe, South America, Asia, and Australia. Throughout his career, Dayton has overseen countless dissertations and been a mentor to numerous students.

A number of key events in his life were decisive in shaping Dayton's academic career. Dayton has remarked that from early in his youth he had serious reservations about his own identification as a Christian. These reservations, which surfaced during his early secondary schooling, were intensified by debates with his father over the doctrine of inerrancy. Everyone told the young Dayton, including his father, that if the doctrine of inerrancy wasn't true, then the Christian faith was not tenable. While wrestling with this doctrine in his middle and high school years, Dayton concluded that the neo-evangelical articulation of inerrancy was not a tenable doctrine of biblical authority and therefore he could not be a Christian. Though he had come to this conviction, Dayton did not reveal his loss of faith to his family nor did he leave the church. Rather, he kept this knowledge to himself throughout high school and college. It was only while studying at Columbia University that Dayton rediscovered his faith. As he has noted on several occasions, while working his way through the works of Karl Barth and Søren Kierkegaard he found himself inside rather than outside the circle of faith. However, he was never able to accept the version of the doctrine of inerrancy associated with the Princeton School and venerated by mid-century neo-evangelicals and was even denied ordination in the Wesleyan Church because of it.

The experience of being forced to relinquish his faith, only to find it again, was formative for Dayton. In truth, he has been wrestling with the question of biblical authority and with what he has named the "pernicious effects" that certain doctrines can have within the Christian faith for much of his career. Through much struggle and with the help of Barth, Kierkegaard and the Pietists, Dayton was later able to find a way to articulate a non-inerrantist doctrine of biblical authority that he has often described as "Biblicist"—a position that has often pushed him to the margins of contemporary evangelicalism.

Another lifelong interest of Dayton's was also set in motion while attending the pre-Woodrow Wilson Program held at Columbia University. Aimed primarily at African-American students, the program was designed to give promising but socially marginalized students an opportunity to prepare themselves for graduate school at Columbia University. Dayton was the only white student in the program. This experience, as well as the race riots in New York City which broke out two blocks from his apartment on 118th street in upper Manhattan, was a crucible in which Dayton's commitment to the Civil Rights movement and other movements for social justice was initially formed. This commitment was further solidified in 1964, when Dayton worked with COFO, SNCC, and the Mississippi Freedom Democratic Party, canvassing African-American voters in Biloxi, Mississippi, in preparation for the '64 election.

Dayton's continuing commitment to the struggle for social justice has manifested itself in both his scholarly and service work. He has served on the boards of the Wesleyan Urban Coalition, the Urban Life Center, UMPS (Urban Ministry Program for Seminarians), SCUPE (Seminary Consortium for Urban Pastoral Education) and a number of other urban ministry programs that address issues of justice and equality in urban settings. In the 1970's Dayton was also involved in the creation of a series of journals all of which were attempting to recover an evangelical social witness. He was book editor for *The Post American* (now *Sojourners Magazine*), contributing editor for *The Other Side* and *The Epworth Pulpit*, and was intimately involved in the founding of the evangelical feminist magazine *Daughters of Sarah*. Dayton also played a key role in planning the meeting that produced the Chicago Declaration of Evangelical Social Concern that is widely hailed as one of the most important documents on social engagement to emerge from within the evangelical community. And anyone familiar with his body of scholarship knows that *Discovering an Evangelical Heritage*, in which Dayton recounts nineteenth century evangelical commitments to socially progressive movements, is no anomaly. Dayton has written widely on the socially progressive commitments of a wide range of figures and movements all in an attempt to call "evangelical Christianity" back to its roots.

Dayton's time at Yale was also marked by another formative experience. It was at Yale that he was first introduced to Pentecostalism. He matriculated not long after a famous Charismatic renewal had run its course on the campus, leaving in its wake many students who were burned out by the experience. During this time, Dayton became fascinated with the spiritual and theological dynamics that would produce such a phenomenon, a topic that he would later take up in his dissertation at the University of Chicago, *Theological Roots of Pentecostalism*.

We recount these experiences in particular because they illustrate that many of the historical and theological questions that have come to occupy Dayton's attention over his long career are rooted in life experiences and were not simply bequeathed to him by the academy or taken from a book. The connection of biography and theology also highlights Dayton's own characteristic style of theological writing. Often his pieces are a mixture of historical and theological analysis, critique, and memoir, filled with penetrating analysis, creative proposals and biographical reflection. This lends to Dayton's writings a humanity that is also evident in personal interactions with him. Dayton is one of the most genuinely empathetic scholars that many of the participants of this volume have ever had the pleasure to know. This empathy, at least in part, stems from Dayton's own existentially gained insight that scholarly questions are often more than simply intellectual puzzles that need to be solved. Rather, scholarly questions often reach into the lives of those who ask them, and the answers arrived at can have far-reaching consequences in lives of the inquirer.

Key Aspects of Dayton's Thought

Mapping the key themes in Dayton's work is not easy. Much like Karl Barth, one of his key theological influences, Dayton never thinks about methodological issues in abstraction from particular problems. Rather, it is only in the midst of reflecting on a particular problem or issue, or offering an alternative account of some phenomenon or other, that Dayton's major theological and methodological commitments become clear. Another major problem that confronts the interpreter of Dayton is trying to understand precisely what kind of a scholar he is. That is, is Dayton a historian or a theologian, or both? The truth is Dayton is in many respects, both, and not simply as a "historical theologian," though he may share some similarities with such a descriptor. Theological, historical, and historical theological themes and commitments inform his thought throughout. It may be precisely Dayton's unwillingness to identify himself as either explicitly one or the other (though he prefers to be identified as a theologian), which has given his thought such a creative edge.

Though these problems mean that Dayton's thought is not reducible to some simple set of principles, nonetheless, an outline can be given of some of the key themes that have informed Dayton's work and recur throughout his scholarship. I propose the following five key elements as axiomatic to his thought:

(1) *Phenomenological Analysis*: The first theme refers to Dayton's commitment to a phenomenological form of analysis, especially of what might be called historical or theological phenomena. From his initial attempts to recover the progressive origins of nineteenth-century evangelicalism, to his later account of Pentecostalism, Dayton has been concerned to make sense of the "phenomenon itself." That is, in his analysis he generally brackets questions of "truth", either in an ultimate sense or in the sense of the self-descriptions of those figures under question, in order to get at the nature and dynamics of the object in study. This concern reaches across theological and historical boundaries.

Theologically, Dayton seeks to understand the inner theo-logic of the phenomenon under observation, quite apart from questions as to theological validity or his own theological judgments of the phenomenon. Thus, his goal is to unearth and recover the original theological dynamics that gave birth to specific movements so that through a recovery of those dynamics a clearer picture of their development can be ascertained.

Furthermore, Dayton believes that understanding the theological dynamics of ecclesial movements goes a long way in explaining their particular historical trajectory. Thus, when he turns to understand and make sense of the historical development of certain traditions, he always has in mind the initial theological dynamics of that particular movement. To understand the later history in a phenomenological fashion, therefore, means to discern and clarify the ways in which the historical tangle of a movement have either distorted the original theo-logic of the movement, or have further developed it, or both. How does a particular movement begin with certain theological assumptions and later come to hold others? To unravel that puzzle is the goal of much of Dayton's scholarship.

(2) *A Theologically Informed Hermeneutic of Suspicion*: The second major theme works in tandem with the former. Dayton's work is marked by a theologically informed hermeneutic of suspicion. That is, much of

Dayton's historical and theological analysis begins with the important question: "who is telling the story and why are they telling it the way they are telling it?" A hermeneutic of suspicion questions the way that phenomena are described because the ways in which we describe certain phenomena are often over-determined by other commitments, whether conscious or unconscious, and these influences tend to distort the reality that we are trying to describe. This raises a problem, however. It would seem that our ability to divest ourselves of our prior commitments is not a possibility, nor is it really possible to describe phenomena without prior commitments. That is, getting at the "phenomenon itself" is almost impossible, given that all "phenomena" are always already encoded with certain interpretations. Here is where the theological roots of Dayton's hermeneutic become helpful.

Dayton's hermeneutic of suspicion is inspired less by the nineteenth-century masters of suspicion than by the theological conviction that the church is fallible. Built into this conviction however, is the belief that better theological and historical interpretations are both possible and demanded of the responsible scholar. One interrogates the received canons of interpretation of particular phenomena in the hopes of uncovering the suppressed, distorted, or forgotten aspects, not to fall into a sea of relativism, but rather in the hopes that by recovering the lost dimensions, the tradition or phenomenon in question will be liberated to be of service to the wider church by being able to be itself more fully. Dayton's work is almost universally marked by such interrogations, which is why he has been able to offer so many alternative theses and proposals for re-reading theological and historical phenomena, which much of the academy assumed was already fully understood.

(3) *The "Embourgeoisement" Thesis as Liberation Theology*: The third key element refers to the interconnection of the theological and the sociological that is embodied in Dayton's work. One of the more important contributions of Dayton has been to incorporate the insights of Liberation theology into the historical analysis of Methodism, Pentecostalism, and American evangelicalism. One of the key insights of Liberation theology that recurs in Dayton's analysis of these traditions is the basic assumption that social location often determines and distorts theological commitments. Thus, one of the key ways whereby Dayton is able to make sense of the developments within Methodism, for example, is to argue that as Methodism moved out of the lower strata of society it shed many of its key distinctives, not the least of which was Wesley's commitment to the poor. This sociological movement from the lower to the middle-class, then, helps

to explain the historical and theological development within Methodism, as opposed to trying to explain the shifts exclusively through theological categories. Dayton describes this sociological movement as the process of "embourgeoisement."

By highlighting this process, Dayton is arguing that quite often one of the forces that shape the development of vibrant religious movements as they evolve over time is a perceived need to negotiate a newfound social location and acceptability. For Dayton, however, this insight is of more than just historiographical value. Dayton often highlights this process of social distortion when analyzing movements in decline or when attempting to project the future of movements that are still vibrant but may shortly face the same fate. His motivation in both contexts, however, is not just descriptive, but ultimately prescriptive as his desire is to call the movements in question back to their theological roots. Rather than exchanging their theological and spiritual inheritance for the "fleshpots of Egypt," these movements ought to reconnect to their theological and spiritual roots and thereby renew their tradition. In this way, Dayton's historical work should also be seen as a Liberationist gesture meant to question the *embourgeoisement* of religious movements that originate out of the lower classes.

(4) *The Constitutive Relation of Theology and Ethics*: A fourth theological axiom that underlies Dayton work is his belief in the constitutive relation of theology and ethics. Theology and ethics are simultaneous and mutually constitutive for a proper and balanced knowledge of God. It is this conviction that unites many of the key sources that Dayton has drawn theological sustenance from: Karl Barth, Søren Kierkegaard, Anabaptism, John Howard Yoder, John Wesley, and the Holiness movement. Put in more recent theological jargon: justification and justice cannot be separated. This conviction illumines Dayton's extraordinary sensitivity to the social and political relevance of many different theological and ecclesial traditions.

Like Wesley, Kierkegaard and Bonhoeffer, Dayton is unwilling to grant faith the position of priority among the theological virtues. In fact, Dayton is fond of pointing out that for Wesley and others (including Paul), it is love that stands out as the primary theological virtue. This commitment allows for and produces in Dayton a profound intellectual and spiritual empathy for movements whose theological convictions he may question or even reject. However, by moving towards these movements primarily under the guise of love, Dayton is able to better understand these movements on their own terms rather than being forced to make them fit into a preconceived theological or intellectual grid. In this conviction, Dayton reveals his own Pietist colors.

(5) *A Theologian of Hope?* Finally, I raise the question of whether or not Dayton could be described as a "theologian of hope." I raise this question because it is evident that Dayton's scholarly and ecumenical work is oriented in a hopeful, even eschatological direction. That is, Dayton's serious and penetrating questions and critiques of the accepted canons of interpretation are ultimately not motivated by a sense of pessimism, but rather by the hope that by clarifying the real dynamics of particular theological traditions, those traditions will be freed to contribute to the life of the "whole household of God." It is his conviction that not only do marginalized religious movements have something to say to the wider Christian family, but that if given the chance what they have to say will be transformative for Christianity as a whole.

It is this conviction that I believe gives some coherence to Dayton's broad body of work. His engagement in the world of ecumenical dialogue is inspired by the same dynamic that has guided his criticisms of evangelical historiography, and his arguments for the recovery of Pietism. In each case, it is the conviction that the church, though torn by disagreement, is called to struggle in hope for a more faithful, fuller witness to the gospel of Jesus Christ.

Concluding Comments about This Volume

This *Festschrift* was motivated by three overarching concerns, all of which have influenced the final shape that the volume has taken. The first major concern was to highlight the vast contribution that Dayton has made to theological and historical scholarship for the past thirty-five years. To this end, I was able to draw together multiple respondents to varying aspects of Dayton's large body of work that highlights not only his scholarly, but also his personal contributions to other scholars and students in different and even disparate areas. A second major concern was a desire to show the coherence of what might at first glance be considered a rather disparate grouping of intellectual concerns. Dayton has written across a number of disciplines and made major contributions in fields that at first glance would seem to have no relation whatsoever. It was my conviction, however, that a closer inspection of Dayton's work in these different fields, and reflection on the various respondents would go a long way in dispelling this misconception. Finally, it was my conviction that Dayton's work deserved a fresh hearing.

The above concerns led me to consider the novel form that the present *Festschrift* has taken. I have organized the chapters according to broad headings of areas of research that Dayton has made a major contribution to. Each of the chapters consists of a key article or essay that is illustrative of Dayton's work and two responses, with the exceptions of chapters 4 and 13. I was unfortunately unable to secure respondents for the essay appearing as chapter 4, and chapter 13 is a concluding contribution by Joel Scandrett on Dayton's role as a teacher.

As the reader will find, overlapping themes and questions appear in Dayton's work across different disciplines or areas of study. In this way, readers are made aware of the inner-coherence of Dayton's work while simultaneously being exposed to the multiple areas where Dayton has brought his own revolutionary ways of thought to bear. Furthermore, there are several seminal essays reprinted here in combination with important unpublished pieces, thus giving Dayton a fresh hearing among friends and colleagues as well as younger scholars who have yet to encounter Dayton's work. In republishing these essays, some of which are almost thirty years old, I was faced with a dilemma: should I update the footnotes? For a variety of reasons, I have decided to leave the footnotes in their original published or unpublished format.

It should also be noted that I allowed for and encouraged a great deal of flexibility in the format and nature of the responses. Though I imagined that the responses would be oriented more towards the *Fest* side than the *Schrift*, the reader will find a nice mixture of the two scattered throughout the volume. Readers will also notice the difference in length, another element in which flexibility seemed appropriate. Finally, I should also note that some respondents chose to title their piece while others did not. Titles have been kept where given. In spite of the differences of format, I am confident that the reader will discern that in substance all of the respondents share a deep appreciation for the scholarly work and theological friendship they have found and a desire to celebrate the life and thought of a man whose work has come to shape many of us in deep and abiding ways.

I
Women's Studies

In 1995, Dayton was invited to participate in a session of the Society of Biblical Literature devoted to celebrating the centennial publication of *The Woman's Bible*—a project headed by the famous suffragist and feminist Elizabeth Cady Stanton. Dayton responded to the invitation with the plenary address "A Neglected Tradition of Biblical Feminism" here published for the first time.

This essay takes up a number of themes that Dayton had begun to explore early in his career with Lucille Sider and Nancy Hardesty as found in "Women in the Holiness Movement: Feminism in the Evangelical Tradition" in Rosemary Reuther and Eleanor McLaughlin's *Women of Spirit: Female Leadership in Religion, Past and Future* (New York: Simon and Schuster, 1978).

A Neglected Tradition of Biblical Feminism

Donald W. Dayton

Introduction

I have had some ambivalence about this assignment. I understand this session as part of a larger celebration of the centennial of *The Woman's Bible*, the first volume of which was published a century ago by Elizabeth Cady Stanton and colleagues. I have some fear, as a friend on the SBL program committee put it, that the invitation may have been an effort to avoid the appearance of "ladies day at the SBL." Even if this be the case, perhaps it is appropriate to thank the program committee for the honor of being a token male to break that pattern.

Many of my earliest scholarly articles might be considered contributions to the discipline of "women's studies." I began to back away from this work nearly two decades ago when I discovered that I was not particularly welcome in the "women's studies" group in the theological consortium in my city. It was clear there that "women's studies" was not defined by discipline but as a gender-specific caucus and support group. At that time, I concluded that my best contribution to "women's studies" might be made by withdrawing from the discipline, but I was delighted to receive this invitation as both an opportunity to pick back up this work and as a sign that in a new climate men may make a contribution to the discipline of "women's studies."

With regard to the role of this session in our larger commemoration of *The Woman's Bible*, I take my clues from the Divinity School of the University of Chicago where I was privileged to devote over a decade to my doctoral studies—a rather average period of time for that particular institution. It was part of the methodological commitment of the Divinity School, expressed in the requirements of the doctoral program, that a phenomenon could only be understood when put in a larger context, historically and culturally, and even more by comparison with related and contrasting phenomena of the same period. Before we proceeded to dissertations on a given figure we were required to pass doctoral exams on a contrasting figure from the same period. I think there was wisdom in this requirement, and in its light, I take it that the function of this session is to illumine the tradition of *The Woman's Bible* by holding it up to the mirror of contemporary movements whose feminist commitments took them in a distinctly different direction. It is this function that Evelyn and I hope to perform.

"Christianity" and "Feminism"

Before turning more directly to those currents of nineteenth century feminism that produced *The Woman's Bible*, we should perhaps make some more orienting comments about the complex nest of issues that cluster around any effort to understand the relation of the Christian tradition to a variety of "feminisms." This relationship is far too complicated to be reduced to any slogan or cliché.

I count as feminist any position that affirms the fundamental equality of women with men and I take it as a key sign of the integrity of such a position in a religious context the extent to which women are granted access to priestly and ministerial roles on an equal basis with men. Usually this is symbolized by ordination, though not always. Not all Christian churches practice ordination in this sense, and, as a "lay theologian," I have some affinity with those who make this case. But in what follows, I shall be primarily concerned with the question of a "biblical feminism" that has manifested itself in the practice of women's ministry and ordination.

Christianity may finally be one religion, but its rich tapestry of colors and nuances must be distinguished to understand the issues surrounding the ministry of women in the church. As I have reflected on these questions, it has seemed possible to distinguish several Christian currents that have been in the language of modern "computerese" particularly "women-friendly." Among these would be the following:

(1) Perhaps the strongest impulse to women's ministry has occurred in those more "pneumatically" oriented movements in the Christian church. An affirmation of the power of the Holy Spirit to call and bestow gifts independently of human claims to authority has often opened the way for the ministry of women—sometimes in the style of a prophetess, though history shows that this impulse may produce something approximating modern feminism as well. Montanism, for example, might illustrate the

role of the prophetess, and some forms of Quakerism the possibility of this dynamic moving in the direction of feminism. Pentecostalism has moved in both directions, but primarily in the former line.

(2) Experientially oriented traditions have often unwittingly created a situation in which women have felt compelled to testify to their religious experience and to take on a form of "teaching ministry." The conventicles of "Pietism" provided space for women's collegial ministry but shied away from ordination, while classical Methodism veered closer to a formal endorsement of the ministry of women and became an early advocate of ordination of women among "mainline American denominations."

(3) "Low church" traditions have often assimilated the ministry of women more easily than "high Church" ones—in part because the line between clergy and laity is already permeable, creating a situation in which women may more easily cross into formal roles of ministry. Thus if one arranges the Christian churches in order roughly according to "high Church" and "sacramental" orientation, one will approximate the relative difficulty each has had in adopting the ministry of women. Thus Catholic and Orthodox traditions still do not accept the practice, the Anglicans have only recently moved in this direction, not long after the churches of the "Magisterial Reformation" who followed the Methodists and the Baptists by a couple of decades, while it was the modern and more sectarian churches of the last century or so who pioneered the practice—the various Holiness and Pentecostal churches, in particular.

(4) Christian movements, like Methodism, that have been carriers of "perfectionism" have often given expression to this impulse in their powerful sense of a grace that is restoring the fallen creation to its pre-fallen state. In such traditions, which often saw women's subordination as a result of the "curse" of the Fall in Genesis, the church was being drawn forward to an eschatological vision that restored the Edenic equality of women, especially in the sphere of redemption in the church.

(5) The sectarian impulse has often supported the ministry of women, since only at the margins of a patriarchal society has it been possible for women to have major religious roles. Thus the nineteenth century saw many religious movements founded by women: from Mother Ann Lee of the Shakers who claimed to be a feminine incarnation to Mary Baker Eddy of the Christian Science Movement and Ellen White of the Adventists and finally to a variety of important women in the founding of the Holiness and Pentecostal movements within American Christianity—such as Phoebe Palmer, Hannah Whitall Smith, and Aimee Semple McPherson.

(6) One should also notice the role in the churches of a modern enlightenment-based "egalitarianism" devoted to the extension of "human rights" to an ever-increasing circle of those once denied them. Early eighteenth century feminism, largely outside the church, was largely rooted in this dynamic, which was incorporated into the churches in the nineteenth century in the Unitarian and Universalist churches that were early pioneers of feminism and the ministry of women.

This rough outline of "women friendly" currents in the Christian tradition has many exceptions and cannot be applied with too heavy a hand. But it does indicate the extent to which these issues are complex and must be so treated. I would also like to suggest that this analysis does illumine the history of women in the church and provides clues to understanding the emergence of a form of Christian and biblical feminism in the nineteenth century.

The Emergence of Nineteenth Century Christian Feminism

One of the remarkable features of the nineteenth century is the way in which these currents converged in a cumulative and reinforcing way to lay the foundation for the emergence of a Christian feminism. The enlightenment vision of progress and human rights provided the backdrop and helped lay the foundation for the optimism of the new nation and the social experiments that Alice Felt Tyler describes in her book *Freedom's Ferment*. Pietism and Methodism brought a new experiential orientation to American religion and initiated the "age of Methodism" in America—the century that ended with the First World War. By the Civil War Methodists had become the numerically dominant Protestant denomination and had convinced half the rest of Protestantism and some Catholics to act like Methodists. Presbyterian evangelist Charles Grandison Finney, for example, read the founders of Methodism and moved toward what came to be called "Oberlin Perfectionism." Methodism incarnated a "gospel egalitarianism" and a poor man's "optimism of grace" that reinforced enlightenment themes of progress and helped create the sense that one could start anew and carve new paths in history. The use of laity in Methodist patterns of ministry broke traditional patterns of clerical authority and opened doors to new roles through which lay women as well as lay men could walk.

This ferment was the womb of Christian feminism. It is probably still Alice Rossi who has made the closest study of the religious background of the nineteenth century feminists, including developing "sociograms" of the intimate relationships of the various players. Beverly Wildung Harrison comments on her work as follows:

> The fact is that the social origins of the woman's rights movement in America will not be fully or adequately understood, nor the early feminists rightly appreciated, until the connection is duly acknowledged between the woman's movement and left-wing Reformation evangelicalism in America. It is to Rossi's credit that she is one of the first contemporary feminists to identify the connection between the Second Great Awakening, in which Charles Finny himself was moved to support woman's right to pray and testify, and the woman's rights movement.[1]

I have never understood Harrison's use of the expression in this context of "left-wing Reformation evangelicalism"—unless it be playing to the galleries of the Southern Baptist journal in which her article was published. I believe it is possible to be both more precise and more radical in articulating her thesis about the social and religious origins of the nineteenth century feminist movement.

It is certainly astounding the number of key moments in the emergence of feminism that cluster around Finney and his institutions. As Harrison indicates, under Finney's ministry, women began to testify and pray in the mid 1820s. This practice became a major issue between Finney and the more conservative and "theocratic" evangelists of New England. And the New Lebanon Conference of 1827 called to negotiate this and other issues failed to resolve the issue or cause Finney to back away from the practice. Finney's Oberlin College founded in 1835 became the first co-educational college, probably the reason that a number of the early feminists chose Oberlin for their education. Among these feminists was Antoinette Brown from a Finney-influenced Congregational home; Brown studied theology at Oberlin (though not with everyone's approval) and became the first woman to be ordained. Theodore Weld, Finney's assistant under whom the women had begun to pray and testify, led the rebellion at Lane Seminary in Cincinnati that provided the abolitionist and radical student body at Oberlin—and later married Angelina Grimké, one of the famous feminist Grimké sisters.

For some reason Rossi sets Elizabeth Cady Stanton of *The Woman's Bible* outside the "revivalist" influence, perhaps because of her radical rejection of this tradition later. But as a fifteen year old girl she attended Finney's

---

1. "The Early Feminists and the Clergy: A Case Study in the Dynamics of Secularization," *Review and Expositor* 72 (Winter, 1975) 46. Rossi's work is in *The Feminist Papers* (New York: Columbia University Press, 1973—Bantam paperback 1975).

meetings for a six-week period and experienced a profound conversion under his ministry. And Henry Stanton, her husband, was a colleague of Weld's in the "Lane rebellion" and went to Oberlin for a period before moving on to become one of the famous "Seventy" abolitionist itinerant lecturers for the Anti-Slavery Society.

But Rossi's thesis can be extended and radicalized by attention to another strand in the period that has not been well understood, but is actually the same line as Oberlin and gives more weight to Rossi's thesis. I am speaking here of the Wesleyan Methodist Connection formed in 1843 out of the abolitionist Methodists who felt marginalized by Methodist bishops for their agitation of the slavery question. Rossi and other historians of the period do not seem to understand the significance of the fact that the first women's rights convention of 1848 was held in the Wesleyan Methodist chapel in Seneca Falls. And similarly, when Antoinette Brown was to be ordained in a Congregationalist Church in 1853, she had to turn outside her own denomination to find someone willing to preach her ordination sermon. She finally turned to Luther Lee, a radical abolitionist founder of the Wesleyan Church.

If Oberlin (and its theological expression as "Oberlin Perfectionism") represented a Methodistic and perfectionist wing of Presbyterian and Congregationalist revivalism, the Wesleyans represented the Oberlinite wing of Methodism, committed to the same values of "Oberlinism": abolitionists, peace activism, revivalism, health reform, etc. As later theological developments confirm, these lines were essentially the same movement and the fountainhead of those currents that produced the Holiness churches of the late nineteenth century. In their early years the Wesleyans modeled their colleges after Oberlin down to details of curriculum and used Oberlin as a sort of "finishing school" until their own schools evolved into four year collegiate institutions.

I apologize for some of this historiographical detail which must appear somewhat arcane to some of you, but I hope that you will see that I am arguing here a significant sub-thesis whose importance I hope will become increasingly clear. The unity of the Oberlinite and Wesleyan traditions becomes clear in the founding of Wheaton College just outside of Chicago. The Wesleyan founders of Illinois Institute stumbled financially after the Civil War as large segments of the new denomination reunited with mainstream Methodism with the "resolution" of the slavery issue that had brought them into existence. In an effort to stay afloat they reorganized the school and the board under joint control with a party of Congregationalists sympathetic to their cause and called as their president

Jonathan Blanchard, an Oberlin oriented Presbyterian. The Wesleyans continued to stumble financially and finally defaulted, allowing Wheaton to follow a trajectory through Congregational "independency" movements into a dispensational premillennialism that evolved into twentieth century fundamentalism and finally into the flagship collegiate institution of the post-fundamentalist "neo-evangelical" movement that took shape after World War II around the modern revivalism of evangelist Billy Graham. These matters are so little understood that a recent dissertation history of Wheaton reveals no sense of who the Wesleyans are (treating them as if they were a generic form of Methodism) and marveling at the ecumenical spirit revealed in Methodists calling a Presbyterian president. Blanchard's appointment was nothing of the sort; it was an in-house "denominational" appointment—if one can discern the shape of the informal "denomination" of "Oberlinism."

We are now back to Beverly Wildung Harrison's use of the expression "left-wing Reformation evangelicalism" to characterize the religious and cultural background of the early feminists. I am arguing that this background might better be characterized as "Oberlinism"—or the perfectionistic millennialist revivalism that dominated both Oberlin and Wheaton in the middle decades of the nineteenth century. One must wonder if these currents are well described as "Reformational," left-wing, or even as "evangelical" in the connotations that word usually carries today. But however we label this stream, it seems clear to me that it is the central axis along which nineteenth century Christian feminism emerged—along with the secondary axes provided by Quakerism and the enlightenment feminism of the Unitarian/Universalist traditions.

Oberlin and Wheaton are also useful paradigms for the unraveling of the subtle synthesis that lay behind the Christian feminism of the nineteenth century. Oberlin continued to some extent the social radicalism of its early years and suppressed the religious vision that had given birth to those currents. Most students and faculty today have little or no understanding of the piety of the founders for whom the early campus buildings are named (Finney, Tappan, etc.). Similarly, Wheaton, for a variety of reasons, has continued the piety of Finney but suppressed the social radicalism of the early Oberlinite vision. Today's Wheaton student and faculty have little sense of the Oberlinite vision expressed on plaques in Blanchard Hall.

The importance of rehearsing this history is that most of us take our clues for the understanding of history from the current realities around us. We bring to our historical study implicit assumptions about who does what and why that are really projections out of our contemporary experience. These preconceptions determine where we look to discover the history of feminism, how we arrange the results of our investigations, and so forth. Most of us cannot conceive of the mid-nineteenth century fusion of Oberlin and Wheaton, and it takes an unusual leap of historical imagination and empathy to transcend our own prejudices and discern the rather extraordinary religious culture that lay behind nineteenth century feminism.

Early Feminism and the Bible

We have already suggested that Oberlin and Wheaton Colleges provide a parable of the fragmentation of the nineteenth century conjunction of "revivalism" and "social reform." Similar dynamics are revealed when we turn our attention to the debates about the Bible that soon inundated the early feminist movement. These women (and their male supporters) were products of currents deeply shaped by the Bible and were deeply troubled by the growing awareness of the way in which the Bible was used by the traditional clergy in the church to block the women and their feminist agenda. This ferment was complicated by the way in which the energies of Finneyite revivalism tended to break its converts away from orthodox Calvinism and set them on trajectories toward, as in the case of Antoinette Brown and Theodore Weld, the heterodoxies of the Universalist and Unitarian traditions.

Very shortly after her ordination in 1853, Antoinette Brown was off to a women's rights convention in the line of the Seneca Falls meeting. At this meeting she engaged in debate for the continuing relevance of the "Bible Argument" for the continuing feminist agenda. Already a major fissure was opening up within the feminist movement. A more liberal party was becoming increasingly alienated from traditional Christianity and increasingly saw the Bible as a tool for the oppression of women. Others, like Antoinette Brown, maintained the importance of the biblical argument for their cause—some for strategic reasons, arguing that precisely because the Bible was so influential in the culture biblical counter arguments needed to be developed; others, for reasons of genuine piety, being unable to follow the feminist agenda unless convinced of its fundamental compatibility with Biblical teaching.

To make a long story as short as possible, by the end of the century this polarization had become quite profound. *The Woman's Bible* represents the left wing of this polarization. It is somewhat difficult to know how to categorize *The Woman's Bible* and to understand its original intent. It was presented in the guise of a "commentary" on the Bible and is often taken today as something of a "retrieval" of the biblical material in a feminist construal of biblical religion. It may well be, as we shall explore in our discussions of this work at this meeting, that it can function in this way today, but it is doubtful that this was the intention of Elizabeth Cady Stanton. Her correspondence at the time and even the introduction to the volume itself indicate the extent to which she saw her work not as a retrieval of the Bible but an attack on the Bible and the traditional churches of her time for the way in which they used the Bible to keep women confined to their special spheres of activity and influence. The last decade before the publication of her project was spent in close dialogue with Robert Ingersoll who enthralled and infuriated audiences with his making fun of the Bible. This side of *The Woman's Bible* is captured in the title given to Barbara Welter's 1974 reprint: *The Original Feminist Attack on the Bible* (Arno Press). This was certainly the way in which *The Woman's Bible* was received at the time. Antoinette Brown, by this time now a minister in the Universalist church, still felt compelled to refuse to participate in its production. And even the National-American Woman Suffrage Association, to which Elizabeth Cady Stanton had given so much of her life, felt compelled to disassociate itself from her project in a resolution that Susan B. Anthony tried mightily to deflect for the sake of her friend. But Stanton printed the resolution in the second volume of *The Woman's Bible* as a sort of "badge of courage."

I am not trying to denigrate *The Woman's Bible* or its value for our struggles to articulate a feminist reading of the Bible. The outrageous heterodoxies of one age can become the traditional commonplaces of a later age; and what was intended as an attack on the Bible might very well provide the clues for its reinterpretation in our own time. But *The Woman's Bible* cannot be fully understood without grasping this side of Stanton's agenda. And without seeing this side of her project we cannot understand the significance of those alternative trajectories out of the religious ferment of the nineteenth century that attempted to offer a feminist reading of the Bible while receiving it as a religious authority in much more traditional terms. These other trajectories are not well known and constitute a "neglected tradition of biblical feminism" that deserves more attention than it has received.

"The Neglected Tradition of Biblical Feminism"

Over against *The Woman's Bible* there developed an alternative tradition of biblical feminism that attempted to hold to a relatively traditional view of biblical authority and argue that rightly understood the Bible did not stand in the way of the feminist agenda—and even, if properly understood, was a sort of "Magna Carta" for women. These traditions stood in the direct line of Oberlin and attempted to keep the piety of Wheaton and the social radicalism of Oberlin intact. This was no easy task, and in the long run, this tradition fared no better than *The Woman's Bible* in terms of acceptance in the broader American culture. Just as *The Woman's Bible* was repudiated by the women's rights movement, this alternative tradition was also repudiated by the general culture and kept alive its vision in increasingly sectarian locations on the margins of society and in the lower classes away from the centers of established religion. For such reasons it has not surfaced often in the elite institutions of the dominant culture and raises some very profound questions about the implicit "classism" that infects our understanding of history and religious life.

I would like to survey this tradition and its development by distinguishing three lines of biblical interpretation that were adopted to sustain this biblical feminism. It is somewhat artificial to distinguish these subtraditions of interpretation. The various writings are often of mixed type appealing to the arguments of several traditions and building on their cumulative effect. But the arguments are distinguishable and doing so will illuminate the range of hermeneutical issues at stake and provide categories for analyzing the development of this tradition. In this tradition of interpretation the biggest problems were whether the Genesis "curse" as a result of the Fall required the eternal subordination of women and whether the Pauline (and deutero-Pauline) texts that were taken by some to prohibit the ministry of women must be so understood.

(1) The first hermeneutical stream I will label "abolitionist." This stream is most directly a product of "Oberlinism." Just as in the twentieth century the revival of feminism in the 60s and 70s was evoked by the Civil Rights revolution of the 1960s, so in the nineteenth century feminism emerged in the wake of abolitionism. There are several reasons for this. Abolitionist lecturers discovered that many of their arguments about slavery also applied to women (e.g., that their status as "property" prevented the full exercise of their religious duties to God). They discovered that the abolitionist hermeneutic that appealed to an anti-slavery "spirit" over against the "letter" that seemed to accept slavery provided the clues for

the development of a feminist hermeneutic. Even the key abolitionist text (Gal 3:28) seemed to conjoin the issues, insisting that "in Christ Jesus there is neither Jew nor Greek, slave nor free, male nor female." This text was made the hermeneutical key for the reading of the New Testament and other texts were read in conformity with this trajectory understood in a realistic and concrete way and not as a truth applicable to the "spiritual realm" *coram deo*.

These moves were facilitated by the deep structures of the perfectionist theology. Their optimism of grace allowed them to finesse the question of whether the curse implied a continuing subordination of women. Oriented to redemption rather than sin as the determinative norm for human life, they saw the "curse" as *descriptive* of the awful mess out of which we are being redeemed. This was opposed to those establishment theologians, like those at Princeton for example, who were more intrigued with sin and the precariousness of human existence in a way that make the "curse" of the Fall *prescriptive* for all of human life this side of the eschaton. The perfectionist traditions, on the other hand, saw a powerful transforming grace let loose in the world that was restoring Eden and elevating woman to her pre-Fall status as man's equal.

To make the same point by reference to eschatology, one must understand that this position was generally radically "post-millennial" in seeing the world on a trajectory of progress toward an imminent millennium. This presupposed that the Christian gospel had let loose in history a transformatory power that was changing history and the world in a way that meant that the Bible could not just be simplistically laid over our own age without some hermeneutical reinterpretation. Persons in this tradition generally argued that the Pauline prohibitions on the ministry of women had been misunderstood (that they referred to patterns of disruption of worship and not to forms of ministry), but even if they had not been misunderstood, they were probably not applicable to our day, in which in contrast to New Testament times, women are now educated and prepared to undertake that which might have been forbidden to them in an earlier age.

This line of argument is perhaps most clearly represented in Wesleyan Luther Lee's ordination sermon for Antoinette Brown, "Woman's Right to Preach the Gospel" (1853), in which Lee argues that Gal 3:28 requires the equal access of women to all roles of leadership in the church. This argument was extended later in the century by B. T. Roberts, the founder of a sister church, the Free Methodist Church, to include an egalitarian social agenda including egalitarian marriage on the model of a business partnership. The Free Methodists were founded about 1860 as an abolitionist denomination that advocated a preferential option for the poor in the face of the pew rentals that were used to finance the established churches. Roberts wrote *Ordaining Women* (1891) in response to the resistance of his denomination to follow his own radicalism on the question and in so doing produced probably the most egalitarian vision in this alternative tradition of biblical feminism.

(2) A second strand of "Oberlinite" feminist exegesis might be called "Pentecostal." In my book *Theological Roots of Pentecostalism* I have traced a gradual shift in the "Oberlinite" theology from the 1860s toward a more pneumatological orientation that finally eventuated in Pentecostalism at the turn of the century. This movement found expression in the reinterpretation of the event of Pentecost as an experience of "entire sanctification" in the Methodist tradition and the development of a doctrine of the "baptism of the Spirit" taught for half a century in a "Holiness" version before the question of speaking in tongues emerged to give the Pentecostal tradition its own distinct identity as a separate movement. These shifts were accompanied by a fascination with the language of the Pentecost account in the New Testament. And the radical egalitarianism and inclusivism of the Pentecost account—"in the latter days your sons and *daughters* shall prophesy"—gave perhaps the strongest impulse to women's ministry in the nineteenth century, an impulse that was on occasion extended as well into a full-blown feminism.

The fountainhead of innumerable defenses of the ministry of women was Phoebe Palmer's *The Promise of the Father* (1859). This volume was at the same time an early recasting of the "Oberlinite" theology in a pneumatological mode and a defense of the ministry of women, including her own rapidly expanding ministry. The wife of a physician husband and partner in ministry, Phoebe Palmer lived an advantaged life in New York and developed a "parlor" style of the Holiness theology that had great influence throughout the rest of the century. This "parlor" tradition shied away from the social radicalism of the "Oberlinites" and even the explicit advocacy of the ordination of women, though it released forces that went far beyond the sensitivities of Phoebe Palmer. Phoebe Palmer circulated in the elite circles of Methodism and her "Tuesday Meetings for the Promotion of Holiness" in her home attracted bishops, professors and other leaders of Methodism into circles that expanded through the century not only within Methodism—especially its camp-meeting tradition, but also in the formation by the end of the century of innumerable new denominations in the

Holiness tradition that have had great impact in the African-American community as well.

As suggested before, this pneumatological orientation defends the ministry of women in terms of the "prophetic" role—often identified with the preaching office"—suggested by the Pentecost account. This literature usually relies a great deal on the line of "prophetesses" throughout the Bible from Deborah and others to New Testament accounts of similar activity. It is argued that Paul is attempting to regulate but not forbid this activity. This tradition was ambivalent about the question of whether the "curse" required an on-going subordination of women and could live with some residual forms of subordination in the family and society while at the same time releasing women for extensive and often full ministry in the church. And, as I have indicated, this process often spilled over into a full-blown feminism.

This strand of exegesis also had an eschatological twist—one that was more compatible with the emerging premillennialism of the late nineteenth century. The subtitle of Phoebe Palmer's book was "a neglected specialty of the latter days" and anticipated what has come to be called the "latter rain" argument of Pentecostalism to justify the "revival" of unusual spiritual gifts in the church as a response to a felt eschatological urgency. This argument relied on a spiritualization of the pattern of rainfall in Palestine and uses hints in the book of Joel so influential in the shaping of the Pentecost account and the New Testament book of James. In Palestine there is an "early rain" just after the spring planting and a "latter rain" to prepare the crop for a fall harvest. This pattern was then identified with the special out pouring of Pentecost at the planting of the church and with the new spirit-oriented movements of the late nineteenth century whose function was to prepare the church for the return of Christ in the "latter days." The logic of this argument tended to justify "new" practices—whether the ministry of women or "speaking in tongues"—required by the eschatological urgency or preparation for that event. Such practices were then defended by a restorationist impulse that found these practices justified by the New Testament writings even when they had not been characteristic of the life of the church since.

We don't have the time or space to trace the complete development of this hermeneutical strand. I can only mention some of the more outstanding and influential illustrations. One of the most important of these is the influence of this tradition on the emergence of the Salvation Army in England and then later in the United States. Founder William Booth was converted under the ministry in England of Phoebe Palmer's pastor, and Catherine Mumford felt called to preach under the ministry of Phoebe Palmer in England during the Civil War years. Catherine refused to marry William until he changed his views of women in a more feminist direction. As a result the Army became surely the most explicitly feminist Christian movement of its time. Catherine herself authored an influential tract, "Female Ministry; or, Woman's Right to Preach the Gospel," that quoted Joel and the Pentecost account on the title page. Women were admitted to all ranks in the Army and eventually the office of General. The daughters hyphenated their last names long before the practice was common as symbols of both family pride and a form of feminism.

Most of the Holiness and Pentecostal denominations formed in the late nineteenth century were carriers of this tradition of women's ministry and the new emerging churches often had a third or more women ministers on their roles. Quaker Seth Cook Rees who played a major role in the founding of both the Church of the Nazarene and the Pilgrim Holiness Church argued in *The Ideal Pentecostal Church* (1897) that such a church is "without distinction as regard to sex." His wife Hulda, the "Pentecostal Prophetess," went so far as to advocate a form of ecclesiastical civil disobedience in the face of "man-made" rules restraining the ministry of women. Another wing of the Church of the Nazarene in Texas produced a fascinating volume, *Women Preachers* (1905) that presents not only a case for the practice but also the biographies of women called to ministry.

Perhaps the most unusual, and to modern consciousness ambiguous, illustrations of this line is to be found in the work of Alma White—the subject of a recent biography by Susie Stanley, *Feminist Pillar of Fire* (Pilgrim Press, 1993). White's Pentecostal Union evolved into the Pillar of Fire and has left behind a few remnants active today in a down-town Denver church and a communitarian movement in Zarephath, New Jersey. White was consecrated bishop in 1917, claiming to be the first female bishop in Christian history. Strongly anti-Pentecostal and anti-Catholic and pro-Klan in orientation, White was radically committed to women's rights and worked with the National Women's Party politically for suffrage and other elements of the feminist agenda. She edited for a number of years a magazine called *Woman's Chains*—founded in 1923 to support the Equal Rights Amendment. This magazine polemicized against "high-heeled shoes" as an invention of the devil and advocated the full participation of women in political life, including the presidency.

This "Pentecostal" argument for women's ministry also had great impact at the turn of the century in those fundamentalist circles taking shape around Moody Bible Institute and related institutions. Illustrative of these developments would be the tract "Prophesying Daughters" by Friedreich Franson who left behind more than a dozen mission organizations and denominations in the United States, Europe, and especially Scandinavia. In the United States he worked with Moody, the Christian and Missionary Alliance and in those circles that became the Evangelical Free Church perhaps best known through its seminary Trinity Evangelical Divinity School near Chicago.

(3) A final strand of biblical interpretation might be labeled "fundamentalist." This strand of feminist exegesis was equally leery of the hermeneutical maneuvering of the currents that we have just surveyed and of *The Woman's Bible* for its embracing of what appeared to be "destructive" forms of biblical criticism. This strand conceived of the task as "exegetical" rather than "hermeneutical" and attempted to argue that the Bible itself was radically egalitarian—and that impressions to the contrary were due to mistranslation or deliberate misinterpretation. Though not fitting the pattern exactly, the fountainhead of this tradition is Katherine Bushnell's *God's Word to Women*. Bushnell was the first female to graduate from Northwestern University's medical school and spent the early stages of her life working with issues of venereal disease among the prostitutes clustered around military camps in Asia. In the twentieth century she turned to the study of the bible in the original languages. She developed an argument that the doctrines of female subordination based on the curse of Genesis presupposed a misreading of that text in the rabbinical tradition of interpretation.

A similar line of argument may be found in *The Bible Status of Women* (1927) by Lee Anna Starr, a Methodist Protestant pastor of the college church at Adrian College—a school with close ties to Oberlin and the Wesleyan Methodists. This book deeply influenced Alma White who used it to defend her feminism and whose denomination has kept the book in print until today.

It would be profitable to explore other issues in these traditions, but time will not allow. But confirming the Biblical claim that there is nothing new under the sun is the fact that this literature speaks to many of the issues of feminist biblical interpretation today; sometimes in a quaintly pre-modern manner, but often in a way that strikingly anticipates modern issues. These figures debated, for example, issues of "inclusive language"— and it comes as a surprise to many that the first "inclusive language" translation of the New Testament came not from the more liberal centers of biblical interpretation but straight out of the heart of the most extreme forms of fundamentalist ultra-dispensationalism. There are discussions of the androgyny of Jesus and whether women can identify with a male savior. Hannah Whitall Smith, the major figure behind the Keswick variety of the Oberlinite theology that has been most influential in fundamentalist and evangelical circles, regularly gave Bible studies in the 1870s on "God as Our Mother," exploring female images for God. She also developed a theological argument for "universal restorationism" based on the experience of motherhood and her conviction that God like a loving mother would never abandon the children of the divine creation. Smith was the author of one of the most influential of American devotional books, *The Christian's Secret of a Happy Life*, which has sold millions of copies in both original editions and a modern paraphrase. Her pious fans in evangelical and fundamentalist circles would be astounded if they should ever understand the real Hannah Whitall Smith! I could go on, but these hints will have to suffice to suggest the interesting range of discussion of modern issues that can be found within this literature.

Some Conclusions

Finally, I would like to offer a few concluding reflections on this "neglected tradition of biblical feminism." The first issue is: what happened to this tradition and why are we not more aware of its discussion of issues that trouble the religious communities of today? Full exploration of this issue would require another paper. Suffice it to say that a variety of forces have conspired to suppress this tradition so that in most circles, even those that stood most directly in its line, have forgotten that such discussions had ever taken place. By the mid-twentieth century, the era of "father knows best" and the middle American celebration of traditional family life had overwhelmed these (and other feminist) efforts to call for a counter-cultural egalitarian vision.

The modern academy is not aware of these traditions in large part because these developments took place in sectarian locations and in social classes not taken seriously in the elite centers of religion (the "mainstream" religions) and culture (the university). As I have suggested above, our modern conceptual frameworks of historical and cultural analysis will not permit these currents even to exist—let alone direct our attention to these circles as centers of interesting discussion of feminist issues. These categories of thought create their own realities and train people who think they are religiously "conservative" to oppose "feminism" as the intrusion of "modernity" in the life of the churches. Thus the descendants of these traditions often unconsciously participate in a conspiracy to suppress these developments. Profound psychological and sociological forces toward assimilation into mainstream culture—abetted by the mainstream "cultured despisers" of these traditions—have eroded the feminist impulse of these traditions. The children of countercultural figures long to belong to the mainstream culture and unconsciously suppress the gaucheries of cultural dissent in their own search for identity and status. I have known in the fifties and sixties many children of women ministers who were deeply ashamed that they had come from such "disreputable" homes. It is only with the arrival at middle age in the context of a changed public consciousness of these issues that these friends have been able to celebrate the contributions of their mothers.

Another issue is the "retrievability" of these traditions and their ability to function today to support forms of feminist religious consciousness. Here the answer is somewhat ambiguous. These traditions are at times "modern" in their consciousness and at times pre-modern and precritical. This pre-modern side has contributed to their neglect in the "critical" circles of the academy. But the rise of post-critical and post-modern methodologies may permit them to be taken more seriously in the future.

But there is a sense in which these questions cannot be answered in the abstract. History may have the last word in helping us to understand whether these traditions will be retrieved and whether they can nurture women and support feminist consciousness. There are many signs that this is happening. Nearly every writing that I have mentioned in this paper remains in print and continues to nurture a significant community of women in their struggle for recognition and roles in the churches of our time. Would that our own scholarly productions could have such staying power!

The churches most in line of this tradition of biblical feminism are gradually acknowledging this history, and this fact is slowing the process of assimilation and abandonment of these distinctive positions. And pockets of women scholars and women ministers have gathered around this literature for nourishment in their own struggles. I think here of the various factions of the "evangelical women's caucus" and the work of Susie Stanley to gather the women of the Holiness churches in national gatherings to celebrate this heritage and be nurtured by it. And persons on all sides of this issue would probably be astonished by the extent to which this tradition has nurtured a small cluster of lesbian scholars. Several lesbian scholars have done dissertations in this area and have been nurtured spiritually by this form of women's piety.

It is not easy to discern the trajectories of this ferment—just as in the mid-nineteenth century it would have been impossible to predict that such trajectories would produce both *The Woman's Bible* and this "neglected tradition of Biblical feminism." History will have the final word about "retrievability." Our successors in the next century will be able to look back on our own century and tell us whether indeed this tradition was "retrieved." We still look through a glass darkly.

Response #1

Nancy A. Hardesty

I believe I met Don Dayton at a conference in the Chicago area in the summer of 1973. For the previous four years I had been teaching English composition at Trinity College in Deerfield, Illinois, and occasionally taking courses at Trinity Evangelical Divinity School. However, I had resigned that position and was about to return to the University of Chicago Divinity School to work on a PhD in the history of Christianity. I was thrilled to meet a fellow student. Don became my mentor, my friend, and of course my book dealer!

Both of us were students of Martin E. Marty, famed church historian. Both of us took Professor Jerold C. Brauer's course in American revivalism. We talked often and at length. I shared many enjoyable meals at the book-laden apartment he shared with his wife Lucille at North Park Theological Seminary, where he taught theology and served as a librarian. Lucille and I also developed a deep friendship, eventually sharing in the development of the feminist journal *Daughters of Sarah*.

I believe it was due to Don's connections and influence that I delivered my first academic paper at a conference in Evanston, Illinois, honoring Frances Willard, pioneer feminist and leader of the nineteenth-century Woman's Christian Temperance Union. He was also responsible for my only publication in the progressive evangelical journal the *Post-American*, which became *Sojourners*. Together, Don, Lucille, and I summarized our early research on evangelical women in an essay titled "Women in the Holiness Tradition: Feminism in the Evangelical Tradition" for the book *Women of Spirit: Female Leadership in the Jewish and Christian Traditions*, edited by Rosemary Ruether and Eleanor McLaughlin (1979).

When I came to the University of Chicago, it was somewhat of a foregone conclusion that I would write a dissertation on something about women, despite the fact that there were no women on the faculty at that time to guide me. I was already a committed feminist. Letha Dawson Scanzoni and I had completed the manuscript of *All We're Meant to Be: A Biblical Approach to Women's Liberation* (1974) and were searching for a publisher. Several possible dissertation topics crossed my mind, but in discussions with Don about revivalist Charles Grandison Finney, the Second Great Awakening, Oberlin College, the anti-slavery movement, and the Holiness movement, the names and work of women kept popping up: Mary Bosenquet Fletcher, Phoebe Palmer, Antoinette Brown, Lucy Stone, Elizabeth Cady Stanton, Frances Willard, and many more. Together we began to collect and read books from throughout the nineteenth century by and about the women and men of these movements.

When it came time to research and write my dissertation, the outlines were clear. Don had already laid the groundwork in a series of ten articles in the *Post American* from June 1974 through May 1975, titled "Recovering a Heritage." The essays were collected and published in *Discovering an Evangelical Heritage* (1976). What emerged from my research was "'Your Daughters Shall Prophesy': Revivalism and Feminism in the Age of Finney." I reworked it into the book *Women Called to Witness: Evangelical Feminism in the Nineteenth Century* (1984; 2d ed. 1999). It was also reprinted by Carlson Publishing under its original title in their University of Chicago dissertation reprint series (1991).

Even after I left Chicago, Don's and my life continued to intertwine. We both interviewed for a job in Methodist studies at Emory University's Candler School of Theology. It turned out that they were also looking for a woman and a feminist. So for four years I taught courses about John Wesley, American church history, and the Holiness movement.

Don stayed at the University of Chicago and at North Park Theological Seminary for a while longer. His dissertation was finally published as *The Theological Roots of Pentecostalism* (1987). One of the aspects of his research that fascinated me was the Holiness and Pentecostal movements' interest in divine healing. During my teen years I was a member of a Christian and Missionary Alliance church, founded by A. B. Simpson, a staunch advocate of healing. So Don and I often discussed that topic, and during my graduate study and for years afterward I continued to buy books on the subject from him and read them. And of course since Don had infected me with the habit of haunting used bookstores, I continued to search for such books on my own. But I always assumed that Don would be the one to write a definitive work on the topic. And he still may be. But when *The Theological Roots of Pentecostalism* came out, I was a bit sorry to see that healing was the subject of only one chapter.

So when I received my first sabbatical after finally becoming professor of religion at Clemson University, I gathered all of my books and my notes and wrote a book titled *Faith Cure: Divine Healing in the Holiness and Pentecostal Movements* (2003).

Now I am due for another sabbatical. And Don's influence continues. I was intrigued by his stories of Orange Scott, Luther Lee, Henry Stanton, Lucy Stone, and other nineteenth-century evangelical Christians who worked for abolition. He found for me a copy of Holiness advocate Amanda Berry Smith's autobiography: *The Story of the Lord's Dealings with Mrs. Amanda Smith, the Colored Evangelist.* He also introduced me to the story of William Seymour and the Azusa Street Revival. A few years ago I was asked and gladly accepted the challenge to develop a course at Clemson on African American religion. Providentially about the same time I was invited to participate in a Lilly Teaching Workshop titled "Mining the Motherlode of African American Religious Life." Out of that workshop and the course I developed there, I have a body of research on the history of black churches and other religious groups in the United States. During the next year I plan to complete a manuscript on the topic.

As I look back on my work as a historian of American Christianity, I owe a huge debt to Don Dayton. As my colleague, mentor, and friend in those formative graduate school years, he shaped and focused all of my subsequent work. I fell in love with the people he talked about. Lucille used to joke that when Don and I were talking, one never knew whether the people we talked about with such interest and affection were living or dead. In fact, most of them were from the communion of saints we have been blessed to come to know through our historical research and to share with others in our presentations and publications.

Response #2

S. Sue Horner

Becoming All We're Meant to Be: An Empowering Heritage

THE late 1960s and early 1970s was a time of new possibilities and the hope of a new age characterized by equality and peace. Change was evident in all aspects of society and culture. Some young men grew their hair and some young women shed undergarments and make-up—traditional symbols of female beauty and identity. In the church the identity of women as helpmeets, subject to men's authority was being challenged.

Vatican II brought significant changes to Catholic life, at the same time that theologies of liberation emerged within Latin American, African American, and women's liberation communities. Some fundamentalist evangelicals were reinventing themselves as signified by the term "neo-evangelical". In these circles a shift from cultural separatism to cultural engagement was observable. Young evangelicals began to choose mainline seminaries for theological and biblical studies and developed appreciation for historical critical methods of biblical interpretation. All these new Christian measures were attempts to integrate the message of faith with behaviors of love and justice and to be players in the larger culture.

Don Dayton, then a graduate student at the Divinity School of the University of Chicago, was a central figure in articulating these new ideas. Don early on had the ability to see what was left out—whether on issues of women's roles or definitions of evangelicalism. I recall reading in 1974, "Recovering a Heritage: (Part II) Evangelical Feminism" authored by Don and Lucille Sider Dayton. This *Post-American* (now *Sojourners*) article pointed to the emergence in the 19th century of biblical arguments to support the abolition of slavery and support of women's rights. The article demonstrated how Wesleyan, holiness traditions were central to women exercising leadership roles. Two years later Don published *Discovering an Evangelical Heritage*, which addressed this forgotten stream of evangelicalism and included the history of women who had claimed their gifts as ministers and articulated a biblical basis for their right to preach the Gospel.

In the early 1970s I was married with two children and struggling with the conflicting roles for women that society and the church were presenting. In college I had studied theology and Bible from evangelical men who were engaged in the new measures of that day. One had studied with theologian Karl Barth and another was an active leader in the renewal movement within the Episcopal Church. My personal sense of equality and fairness resonated with cultural changes and a new openness in this conservative Christian college I attended. Both during college years and in my early married days multiple progressive streams—the anti-war movement, the civil rights movement, the feminist movement and neo-evangelicalism—influenced how I understood the world and Christianity.

Don Dayton's work in Wesleyan historiography was indeed critical to my early interest in addressing feminist issues within the evangelical community. Learning about these early foremothers whetted my appetite for understanding how all this history had been lost or ignored. I read all I could find and by the mid 1970s I had finished my first graduate degree in library science. My thesis was a content analysis of over one hundred books written from 1965 to 1975 on women's roles in family, society and church from a Christian perspective. By the early 1980s I had started a women's center at Barrington College where I also functioned as the president's spouse and in 1987 completed a degree in theology from Harvard Divinity School where I focused on liberation and feminist theologies. I had classes with theologians that shaped feminist theology including Elizabeth Schüssler Fiorenza, Katie Cannon, Rosemary Radford Ruether, Diana Eck, Carter Heyward, Bernadette Brooten, Jane Smith, Mercy Amba Oduyoye, and even Mary Daly. Eventually I completed a doctorate at Northwestern University in the joint religion program with Garrett Evangelical Theological Seminary and studied with both Rosemary Skinner Keller and Rosemary Radford Ruether, who served as my doctoral advisor. My dissertation was a social history of the contemporary evangelical feminist movement—an analysis of the intersection of evangelicalism and second wave feminism beginning in the mid 1970s. Over the course of thirty years I had moved from arguing for biblical equality for women in church settings to encouraging my students to develop a hermeneutic of suspicion as they read theology and history.

It was not until the mid 1990s, during my doctoral studies, that I was privileged to both meet and study with Don Dayton, who was then teaching at Northern Baptist Seminary. I was keenly interested in his work on evangelicalism and used my work with him (as well as a course with Martin Marty) as the foundation for the chapter on evangelicalism in my dissertation. I was intrigued with Don's analysis of evangelicalism and in particular his debate with evangelical historian George M. Marsden at an American Academy of Religion workshop in 1988 on how to define evangelical. Specifically, Don critiqued Marsden for not including Wesleyan traditions in accountings of evangelical historiography.

In 1993 the *Christian Scholar's Review* devoted an entire issue to definitions of evangelicalism using the Dayton/Marsden debate as the center-point. Briefly stated, Dayton named the prevailing framework for interpreting evangelicalism, the "Presbyterian" paradigm. He suggested that this was the method of prominent evangelical scholars such as George M. Marsden, Bernard Ramm, Mark A. Noll, and Richard Quebedeaux. Essentially, this position placed evangelicalism in the "conservative" or anti-modernity frame, a view perceived by Dayton as too simplistic. Not only did it miss some of the "radical" behaviors of evangelicalism, but by situating the roots or the defining moment of evangelicalism in the fundamentalist/modernist controversies of the early decades of the 20th century, the "Presbyterian" paradigm missed the complexities of 19th century evangelicalism.

Dayton saw evangelicalism as multifaceted. It included revivalism, both New School Presbyterian and Wesleyan varieties, abolitionism and anti-abolitionism, pre- and post-millennialism, foreign and home missions, dispensationalism, inerrancy, women preaching and teaching, Bible institutes, holiness, and prophecy emphases. Evangelicalism had both "conservative" and "liberal" impulses. By defining evangelicalism as orthodox or conservative theology in reaction to modernity, the definition was partial. Such a description was missing huge pieces of the reforming or radical edges of the evangelical tradition.

Dayton proposed a "Pentecostal" paradigm, which took into account the varieties of evangelical beliefs and behaviors. It allowed for the dynamism and shifts between conservative and innovative behaviors. By using nomenclature descriptive of specific traditions, Dayton did not intend to suggest that evangelicalism was more like Pentecostalism than Presbyterianism. Instead he placed Wesleyan history under the rubric of innovation; Pentecostalism being the most recent radicalization. Ecclesiologically, Dayton linked Anglicanism, Methodism, Holiness and

Pentecostalism. Each historical reformation/transformation behaved in a sect-like manner. Methodism was a response to the sterility of Anglicanism. The Holiness movement focused on the power of the Holy Spirit. It did not matter if the "classical" tradition was Lutheran, Reformed or Anglican; what was significant was the innovative nature of the evangelical impulse. For Dayton, evangelicalism is a phenomenon that behaves more like radical sectarianism than a reaction to modernity.

This partial recounting of Dayton's challenge to "normative" understandings of evangelicalism demonstrates his longstanding ability to ask questions about what is missing and his passion for making the story of evangelicalism as complex and diverse as the lived realities. I deeply appreciate Don Dayton's academic contributions and his spirit of inclusion. His preference for a thick description resonated with my sensitivity to a similar phenomenon within feminist historiography and theology.

Just as evangelicalism is too often simplified in a desire for consistency, so is feminism. In my dissertation on evangelical feminism and subsequent writings I have attempted to bring a thick description to this movement. Christian feminism has not always been aware of feminist articulations within evangelical communities. In fact, Christian feminism of whatever stripe is often barely understood in Christian historiography or theology. It is also my experience that in the field of women's studies there is too often little attention to religious feminism and certainly in the broader culture very little is known of feminism, religious or not.

I agree with Don's concluding comments that retrieving history is key to nurturing women's awareness and abilities to become all they are meant to be. Certainly, the assembling of memory into historical narrative is a task never finished. One significant example of this task is the recently published three-volume *Encyclopedia of Women and Religion in North America* edited by Rosemary Skinner Keller and Rosemary Radford Ruether, published by Indiana University Press, 2006. This project was conceived in 1996 with the intention of offering in-depth essays on women's history through the lens of religious history. The editors gathered 147 authors representing an extraordinary diversity of expertise. My essay, co-authored with Reta Halteman Finger, longtime editor of Christian feminist magazine, *Daughters of Sarah*, tells the stories and theologies of the evangelical feminist movement. Yes, biblical/evangelical feminism is a neglected tradition and despite an increasing number of research projects we all still look through a glass darkly. Still, hope abounds and thanks are sincerely offered to Don Dayton for his early writings on women and his passion for justice—for all people.

2

The Social Role of the Church

This essay, which originally appeared in *Radical Religion* 3, no. 1 (1976) 34–40, is characteristic of Dayton's intense concern to find a social and political ethic that could engage contemporary concerns while also remaining faithful to his own Holiness roots. His concern was originally born out of his many experiences in the 1960's and early 1970's in the Civil Rights Movement and the protests against the Vietnam War, a more elaborate chronicling of which can be found in his *Discovering an Evangelical Heritage* (Grand Rapids: Hendrickson, 1976) 1–5.

In this essay, Dayton shows that contrary to contemporary perception both within the evangelical world and without, many of the leading figures of the 19th century Holiness movement were social progressives. Furthermore, and perhaps more importantly, the political radicalism of these early Holiness folk was animated by the central theological concerns of the 19th century Holiness movement, implying that in their conservative political orientation contemporary forms of evangelical and Holiness Christianity have strayed from their more radical theological roots.

Piety and Radicalism: Ante-Bellum Social Evangelicalism in the U.S.

Donald W. Dayton

"We believe there is sufficient piety and radicalism to entertain all who will attend."

—The Rev. George Pegler in a letter inviting delegates to Utica, New York, to organize a new abolitionist denomination in the Methodist tradition.

THE first issue of *Radical Religion* affirmed the need to "examine the relationship between politically active social Christianity and evangelical Christianity," while recognizing this task to be "no doubt a delicate issue, but one that must be addressed."[1]

Such a dialogue is not only "delicate" but also raises a number of difficult interpretive questions. Evangelical Christianity is not primarily a social movement and has not generally carried within it a developed social philosophy or political program—nor will it submit itself entirely to secular canons of validity. The social impact of Evangelicalism has been largely indirect, a byproduct of its search for Christian experience, for the fullest expression of Christian discipleship, for a "personal relationship" with God. When social positions have been taken, they have often had the character of absolutistic moralism—seemingly incapable of distinguishing central and structural issues from trivial and perhaps indifferent cultural mores.

The consequent problems of understanding can be seen in the very divergent interpretations of the social impact on British society of the Evangelical Revival of the eighteenth century. Some have argued that its influence was repressive and opposed to social change because of its orientation to personal morality and otherworldly goals.[2] Bernard Semmel,

---

1. "Introduction," *Radical Religion* 1 (Winter 1973) 4.

2. Cf. the writings of E. P. Thompson and J. L. and Barbara Hammond. Helpful literature surveys are included in Stuart Andrews, *Methodism and Society* (London: Longman,

on the other hand, has suggested that the Revival "might have been the English counterpart to the 'democratic revolutions of the eighteenth century.'"[3] More recently, Robert Hughes III has argued for "the Wesleyan Roots of Christian Socialism."[4]

To those whose acquaintance is primarily with modern—especially post-World War II—evangelicalism, these last two claims might seem preposterous. There is little question that modern evangelicalism has been largely allied with the status quo and has defended socially reactionary positions.[5] But we must not let the present character of Evangelicalism force the assumption that this form of Christianity has always taken—and will always take—a reactionary social stance. The fact of the matter is that the origins of many U.S. evangelical movements and institutions were in socially and politically active forms of Christianity that were quite "radical"—often more so than facets of the social gospel and other movements more usually taken as models of activist Christianity.[6]

Ironically, the existence of "radical evangelicalism" is not well known among either historians or evangelicals. Those interested in social Christianity have assumed evangelical history a strange place to seek activism; and modern evangelicals, whose historiography is often still primitive, have not been attuned to such themes. In fact, socially radical concerns have been so far from the minds of modern evangelicals that there has been a tendency—probably unconscious—to expurgate modern editions of classical texts.[7] "Rediscovery" of this heritage has most naturally taken place in the post-1960s evangelical consciousness, particularly among those figures and currents most closely identified with the "Chicago Declaration."[8]

1970) and in Bernard Semmel, *The Methodist Revolution* (New York: Basic, 1973).

3. Semmel, *The Methodist Revolution*, vii.

4. Cf. his essay by this title in *The Ecumenist* 13 (May–June 1975) 49–53.

5. Cf. Richard Pierard, *The Unequal Yoke* (Philadelphia: Lippincott, 1970) and a survey of the editorial positions of *Christianity Today* during the 1960s by John Oliver, "A Failure of Evangelical Conscience," *Post-American* 4 (May 1975), 26–30.

6. A popular and journalistic overview of this early evangelical radicalism is provided in my *Discovering an Evangelical Heritage*, a revised and expanded version of a series that appeared in the *Post American* under the general title "Recovering a Heritage" from June–July 1974 through May 1975.

7. Examples of such expurgation are given in chapters 2 and 10 of *Discovering an Evangelical Heritage*.

8. For this document and its context see Ronald J. Sider, editor, *The Chicago Declaration* (Carol Stream, IL: Creation House, 1974). Closest to the spirit of the earlier radical evangelicalism would be the modern manifestations found in *Sojourners* (formerly the *Post American*) and *The Other Side* (formerly *Freedom Now*).

Full analysis of the earlier radical evangelicalism or the dimensions of any "recovery" of some of its themes are beyond the limits of this study. This essay is simply one "case study" designed to sample the shape of pre-Civil War evangelical radicalism. It is hoped that this effort to determine how "radical" this movement became will facilitate comparison with other historical manifestations of socially active Christianity and make a contribution toward opening up the dialogue called for by *Radical Religion*

It is becoming increasingly clear that evangelical Christianity played its most creative role in the struggle to overthrow the institution of slavery. Roger Anstey has recently pitted his own economic analyses against those of economic determinists to argue that the emergence of the evangelical world-view played a decisive role in the emergence of anti-slavery thought and action in Britain.[9] Similar arguments have been made for the U.S. since Gilbert Barnes first claimed that U.S. abolitionism was largely rooted in the revivalism of the age.[10] Anne C. Loveland has furthered the discussion by pointing out an inner logical coherence between patterns of evangelical thought and those of the school of "immediate abolition."[11] John L. Hammond has provided empirical support for such claims in his computer-based analyses of pre-Civil War voting patterns in Ohio. He claims to have eliminated all independent variables except revivalism as explanatory factors for the emergence of anti-slavery politics.[12]

This essay, then, will focus on pre-Civil War evangelical abolitionism and particularly on the currents that lie most directly behind contemporary evangelicalism. This constellation of figures and movements will include Presbyterian/Congregationalist revivalist Charles G. Finney,[13] sometimes called the "father of modern revivalism"; Oberlin College,[14] the school he

---

9. *The Atlantic Slave Trade and British Abolition, 1760–1810* (Atlantic Highlands, NJ: Humanities, 1975).

10. *The Anti-Slavery Impulse, 1830–1844* (New York: Appleton-Century, 1933; also in modern edition with new introduction, Harbinger paperback).

11. "Evangelicalism and 'Immediate Emancipation' in American Anti-Slavery Thought," *Journal of Southern History* 32 (May 1966) 172–88.

12. "Revival Religion and Anti-slavery Politics," *American Sociological Review* (1974) 175–86.

13. The literature on Finney's role in the reform movements is largely in unpublished dissertations. In addition to Gilbert Barnes (note 10 above), cf. Garth M. Rosell, "Charles Grandison Finney and the Rise of the Benevolence Empire" (unpublished PhD dissertation, University of Minnesota, 1971) and Melvin L. Vulgamore, "Social Reform in the Theology of Charles Grandison Finney," (unpublished PhD dissertation, Boston University, 1963).

14. The detailed and definitive history of Oberlin College during this period is by Robert Fletcher, *A History of Oberlin College from its Foundation Through the Civil War*, 2

served as professor of theology and president; the closely related Wesleyan Methodist Church,[15] born as an abolitionist party within the Methodist Episcopal Church; and Congregationalist Jonathan Blanchard,[16] the founding president of Wheaton College, generally considered the most prestigious of today's evangelical "Christian Colleges." Within this configuration we shall examine four themes of interest to the modern discussions: racial attitudes, the role of women, the emergence of revolutionary themes, and the extent of class-consciousness.

I. Racial Attitudes

One of the disputed questions in the interpretation of pre-Civil War abolitionism is whether or not the movement was grounded in a broader egalitarian vision that actually broke through the racism of the era.[17] Robert and Pamela Allen, for example, have recently argued (and perhaps represent the emerging consensus) that abolitionism (as well as most other manifestations of U.S. reform) foundered on the question of racism.[18] Among the most explicitly Christian and evangelical of the abolitionists the issue takes a slightly different shape: whether the rise of the conviction of "immediate abolitionism" (that slave-holding was a sin to be immediately repented and repudiated) was rooted more in a self-serving concern for the purity of the church (and thus one's own contamination) or in a more altruistic concern for the slave grounded in a fundamentally egalitarian view of the human race.

The issue is complicated, and I am not yet prepared to make a final judgment, but I am more and more inclined to argue that the evangelical abolitionists came closer than most other abolitionists to breaking through

---

vols. (Oberlin: Oberlin College, 1943 and reprinted recently by Books for Libraries).

15. Although a new history is under preparation, there is no good single source. Cf. Donald C. Mathews, "Orange Scott: The Methodist Evangelist as Revolutionary" in *The Anti-slavery Vanguard*, edited by Martin Doberman (Princeton: Princeton University Press, 1965) and Donald W. Dayton, editor, *Five Sermons and a Tract* by Luther Lee.

16. Cf. Clyde Kilby, *Minority of One: The Biography of Jonathan Blanchard* (Grand Rapids: Eerdmans, 1959).

17. Cf. Louis Ruchames, "Race, Marriage and Abolition in Massachusetts," *Journal of Negro History* 40 (1955), 250–73 and William H. and Jane H. Pease, "Anti-slavery Ambivalence: Immediatism, Expediency, Race," *American Quarterly* 17 (1965) 686–95 for arguments on both sides of the question.

18. *Reluctant Reformers: Racism and Social Reform Movements in the United States* (Washington, D.C.: Howard University Press, 1974; also Anchor Paperback, 1975) chap. 2.

racist patterns. Evangelical religion carries within it a very strong impulse toward egalitarianism, one whose actual accomplishments may outrank more theoretical approaches to the problem of social and racial distinctions. This is most easily illustrated from the Evangelical Revival of the eighteenth century. A letter of the Duchess of Buckingham found the doctrines of the Calvinist Methodists

> most repulsive, and strongly tinctured with impertinence and disrespect toward their superiors, in perpetually endeavoring to level all ranks, and do away with all distinctions. It is monstrous to be told that you have a heart as sinful as the common wretches that crawl on the earth. This is highly offensive and insulting. . . . [a] sentiment so much at variance with high rank and good breeding.[19]

Besides John Brown, the Allens are inclined to exempt only the Grimké sisters from the charge of racism.[20] But Angelina Grimké married Theodore Weld,[21] the great evangelical abolitionist who served for a while as assistant to Evangelist Finney. Weld was the major force behind the events that moved Oberlin College into the abolitionist camp. In 1833 he entered the first class of Lane Theological Seminary with the express purpose of raising the slavery issue. His work converted most of the students to abolitionism, but it was student efforts at amelioration of the condition of Cincinnati's Blacks and their "carrying the doctrine of [social] intercourse into practical effect" that alarmed the community and led the trustees to forbid even the discussion of slavery.[22]

The radical students withdrew from Lane, formed their own "free seminary" and eventually most of them moved on to Oberlin College to constitute a large part of the first theological class there. Though it was not managed without controversy, Oberlin became one of the first colleges in

19. Aaron C. H. Seymour, *The Life and Times of Selina, Countess of Huntingdon* (London, 1844) I, 27. Compare the fact that early years of Pentecostalism saw widespread inter-racial worship in the South and early black leadership over whites as documented in H. Vinson Synan, *The Holiness-Pentecostal Movement* (Grand Rapids: Eerdmans, 1971).

20. Allen, *Reluctant Reformers*, 36.

21. The only biography is Benjamin P. Thomas, *Theodore Weld: Crusader for Freedom* (New Brunswick: Rutgers University Press, 1950; reprinted by Octagon Press), but his letters have been edited by Gilbert Barnes and Dwight Dumond, *Letters of Theodore Dwight Weld, Angelina Grimké Weld and Sarah Grimké, 1822–1844*, 2 vols. (New York: Appleton-Century, 1934; reprinted by Peter Smith). Cf. also Gilbert Barnes, *The Anti-slavery Impulses* (note 10 above) and chap. 3 in my *Discovering an Evangelical Heritage*.

22. These events are chronicled in Fletcher, *A History of Oberlin College* (note 14 above) and in chap. 4 of my *Discovering an Evangelical Heritage*.

the country to admit Blacks—and also women—and the school became "the hot bed of abolitionism and radicalism," while the colony became a haven for free Blacks. Though Oberlin apparently never produced an inter-racial marriage, there was seemingly no bar to other social relationships across the color line, and at least one report of inter-racial romance appears. Such openness was far in advance of the age.[23] Weld himself did not go on to Oberlin, though he apparently maintained throughout his life the doctrine and practice of "social intercourse."

The attitude of Finney himself may have been a little more ambivalent, though he was a major force behind the drive to open Oberlin to Blacks and his churches in New York City were in advance of other churches in bringing Blacks out of the "gallery" and onto the main floor. It is also clear that Finney's financial backers in New York City understood the slavery problem as one of the "hateful caste feeling that so extensively prevailed in the country"—though it is also true that they sometimes strategically avoided unloading all their convictions at once. Lewis Tappan wrote of his brother Arthur, that he believed "fully in the equality of all men in the sight of God" and that "he determined to evidence by his whole deportment that he despised caste."[24] That these convictions included some sensitivity to the more subtle and structural forms of racism is illustrated, for example, in the concern of the Tappans that Blacks were shut out of jury duty. This practice violated the fundamental right of "law and equity" that each person has a "right to be tried by his peers."[25]

Similar examples could be multiplied,[26] but these will suffice to demonstrate that on at least some points this constellation of evangelical abolitionists broke through the racism that permeated the culture and perhaps still infected much of the larger anti-slavery movement.

II. The Role of Women

Secular historians of the women's movement and those from the dominant religious traditions have noticed the interconnections between abolition-

23. Cf. Fletcher, *History of Oberlin College*.

24. For this material cf. Lewis Tappan, *The Life of Arthur Tappan* (New York: Hurd and Houghton, 1870; reprinted by Arno Press) 144–45 and the modern critical biography by Bertram Wyatt-Brown, *Lewis Tappan and the Evangelical War Against Slavery* (Cleveland: Case Western Reserve University, 1969; also Atheneum paper-pack).

25. Lewis Tappan, *Life of Arthur Tappan*, 192.

26. For another important advocate of equality and also intermarriage who reflects a later, reconstruction period manifestation of this same ethos, cf. William Gravely, *Gilbert Haven: Methodist Abolitionist* (Nashville: Abingdon Press, 1973).

ism and feminism, but almost none have bothered to observe the extent to which feminism may be said to be rooted in the evangelical and revivalist impulse.[27] Only recently have we begun to get judgments like that of Beverly Wildung Harrison of Union Theological Seminary in New York:

> The fact is that the social origins of the woman's rights movement in America will not be fully or adequately understood, nor the early feminists rightly appreciated, until the connection is duly acknowledged between the woman's movement and left-wing Reformation evangelicalism in America. It is to Rossi's credit that she is one of the first of contemporary feminists to identify the connection between the Second Great Awakening, in which Charles Finney himself was moved to support woman's right to pray and testify, and woman's rights movement.[28]

As Harrison suggests, the most controversial of Finney revivalistic "new measures" was the encouraging of women to speak, testify and pray "in promiscuous assemblies." Finney's assistant Theodore Weld was an ardent feminist who married Angelina Grimké, also a notorious feminist. Oberlin College was the first coeducational college; it graduated such feminists as Antoinette Brown, Betsy Cowles and Lucy Stone (though it must be admitted that these women sometimes still found Oberlin a little too stodgy on the issue).[29]

The first woman to be ordained to the Christian ministry (1853) was Antoinette Brown,[30] who attended theological classes (but was not given a degree) at Oberlin. The preacher at her ordination was Luther Lee, a founder of the Wesleyan Methodists, who preached on "Woman's Right to Preach the Gospel."[31] Though its significance is little recognized

---

27. I have argued this in an unpublished paper entitled "The Evangelical Roots of Feminism." Some of this material is summarized in chapter 8 of *Discovering an Evangelical Heritage*. Further proof of this thesis can be found in Nancy Hardesty's University of Chicago dissertation, now available as *Your Daughters Shall Prophesy: Revivalism and Feminism in the Age of Finney* (Brooklyn: Carlson, 1991).

28. "The Early Feminist and the Clergy: A Case Study in the Dynamics of Secularization," *Review and Expositor* 72 (Winter 1975) 46. The reference in the quote is to Alice Rossi, editor, *The Feminist Papers* (New York: Columbia University Press, 1973; also in Bantam paperback).

29. Cf. Robert Fletcher, *History of Oberlin College*, and for the broader interconnections, my unpublished paper on "Evangelical Roots of Feminism" (note 27 above).

30. The only biography of Antoinette Brown is fictionalized and superficial, cf. Laura Kerr, *Lady in the Pulpit* (New York: Women's Press, 1951). A new biography by Elizabeth Cazden will be released soon.

31. This sermon is reprinted in my *Five Sermons and a Tract* by Luther Lee.

by historians, it is also a fact that the first woman's rights convention of 1848 was held in the Wesleyan Methodist Church in Seneca Falls, New York. This denomination (whose present-day successor, The Wesleyan Church, is widely recognized as an "evangelical church" in the Methodist tradition and the founder of Wheaton College) began to ordain women in the 1860s, almost a century before the larger Methodist body from which it withdrew.

The churches that have most fully incorporated women into their life and ministry have not been the "liberal" or the "mainstream" churches, but instead those bodies that lie most directly in the wake of pre-Civil War abolitionist revivalism. These would be such groups as the Church of God (Anderson, Indiana), the Church of the Nazarene, the Pilgrim Holiness Church, the Salvation Army and the various Pentecostal churches. These groups have at various times in their history achieved as high as 20–40% women ministers, a phenomenal figure by the standards of what has been achieved elsewhere in Christendom.[32]

Admittedly, not all features of modern radical feminism would be found in such groups, but it remains a fact that early feminism in the U.S. was to a remarkable extent rooted in pre-Civil War revivalism and that the greatest incorporation of women into the Christian ministry took place in its wake.

III. Revolutionary Themes

The evangelical abolitionists we have been discussing understood the U.S. tradition to be explicitly a "revolutionary" tradition. This emphasis developed with striking parallels to the evolution of "radical" thought in the 1960s. The emergence of unpopular abolitionist doctrines in the early 1830s forced adherents to defend the right of "free speech" and "free press" in face of the anti-abolitionist mobs. The rise of the "underground railroad" and consequent deliberate disobedience of the state and federal fugitive slave laws required the further elaboration of a doctrine of "civil disobedience" based on the "supremacy of the divine law."[33] Evangelist Finney himself played a major role in developing this position.[34] These abolitionist struggles eventuated in the "Oberlin Wellington Rescue Case"

---

32. Cf. Lucille S. and Donald W. Dayton, "Your Daughters Shall Prophesy: Feminism in the Holiness Movement," *Methodist History* 14 (January 1976) 67–92.

33. These developments can be traced most easily in the sermons of Luther Lee.

34. Cf. Charles C. Cole, *The Social Ideas of the Northern Evangelists, 1826–1860* (New York: Columbia University Press, 1954).

in which Oberlinites were jailed and tried for rescuing slaves from the slave-catchers and authorities. Some have recognized in this case a major landmark in the development of U.S. civil liberties.[35]

But the climax of these developments came with John Brown's raid on Harper's Ferry, a clear case of revolutionary guerrilla warfare. Though Brown's hopes for a slave rebellion failed to materialize, he did have the evangelical abolitionists on his side. Two black residents of Oberlin participated in the raid; one died in the fight while the other was executed soon thereafter. The Oberlin bell tolled for an hour on Brown's execution. James A. Thome, member of Oberlin's Board of Trustees, esteemed him in a funeral sermon "the Wise Man of our times." At one of the student literary societies Brown was toasted as "the hero of Harper's Ferry—the true representative of the American idea."[36]

Luther Lee of the Wesleyan Methodists preached a memorial sermon entitled "Dying to the Glory of God." In it he argued that Brown's act was a biblically rooted witness against oppression. Lee insisted on the "right to resist wicked and oppressive laws"—if necessary "by force and arms" along the model of the "deeds of our revolutionary fathers, who drew swords and dashed upon the battle field to resist oppression."[37]

IV. Class Consciousness

A final interesting question to pursue is the extent to which evangelical radicalism broke through to any level of class awareness. In examining this point, we must remember that the period we are considering was largely before the emergence of sociology and preceded the earliest writings of Marx. In fact, the socialism of the period—with which the evangelical radicals had some affinities—was still pre-scientific and "utopian," to use Marx's own distinction. We should not expect either the sophistication or the categories of later class analysis.

Nonetheless there are some themes worth examining. Finney's churches in New York City (and those of related movements) were often designated "free churches" because they opposed the pew rental system that enforced seating along class and economic lines and tended to exclude

---

35. Cf. Edward H. Madden, *Civil Disobedience and Moral Law in Nineteenth-Century American Philosophy* (Seattle: University of Washington Press, 1968) and chap. 5 of my *Discovering an Evangelical Heritage*. A transcript of the trial appeared in Jacob R. Shipherd, *History of the Oberlin-Wellington Rescue* (Boston: Jewett, 1859; reprinted by DaCapo in their series "Civil Liberties in American History").

36. These facts are reported in Fletcher, *History of Oberlin College*, 414–15.

37. Reprinted in *Five Sermons and a Tract* by Luther Lee, 107–8.

the poor by embarrassment.[38] These "open churches" were often defended by explicit appeal to the Lukan theology requiring Christian identification with the "poor and oppressed" classes. This pattern would seem to be both an effort to break through class determination of church life and also a reflection of a tendency to identify more with the lower classes of society.

The abolitionist position was, of course, also constantly defended by appeal to those biblical passages about oppression, bondage and poverty that have helped give shape to the modern liberation theologies.[39] One can find a growing conviction that not only slavery but poverty required a major transformation of society. Though perhaps somewhat paternalistic and naive in tone, a deathbed statement of Orange Scott (1847), founder of the Wesleyan Methodist Church, indicates this movement:

> If I had lived to have carried out my plans, with the book concern, and seen another in my place, I should have gone into the work of impressing on the wealthy classes, their duty to the millions enduring poverty and toil. I feel deeply for that class, and would do my share in carrying forward a practical plan of reform, according to my means. The condition of the masses is wretched indeed, and a great change should be effected in the state of society.[40]

Even more striking is the position of Jonathan Blanchard, founder of Wheaton College, present-day bastion of conservative evangelicalism, in debate with N. L. Rice on whether slaveholding was in and of itself a sin.[41] Rice claimed to be an "abolitionist" who wished to see slavery overthrown, but insisted that Blanchard was too "radical" and pushing too hard. Blanchard's response was that Rice's position made his "religion . . . the religion of a privileged class" and closed the debate with the comment that he wished to be remembered only as "one who having humbly

---

38. Cf. Charles C. Cole, "The Free Church Movement in New York City," *New York History* 51 (July 1953) 284–97 and chap. 9 of my *Discovering an Evangelical Heritage*.

39. For examples of the evangelical attack on slavery, cf. Luther Lee, *Slavery Examined in the Light of the Bible* (Syracuse: Wesleyan Methodist Bookroom, 1855; reprinted by Negro History Press), LaRoy Sunderland (also a founder of the Wesleyan Methodists), *The Testimony of God Against Slavery* (Boston: Webster and Southard, 1835; reprinted by Scholarly Press) and Theodore Weld, *The Bible Against Slavery* (New York: American Antislavery Society, 1837; reprinted by Negro History Press).

40. Lucius Matlack, *The Life of Rev. Orange Scott* (New York: Cyrus Prindle and L. C. Natlack, 1847) 283.

41. Jonathan Blanchard and N. L. Rice, *A Debate on Slavery* (Cincinnati: Moore, 1846; reprinted by Arno Press, Negro History Press and Negro Universities Press).

striven in all things to follow his Lord, like him, also has been faithful to His poor."

The above comments constitute only a preliminary foray into a period of evangelical radicalism that needs further study and analysis. But this essay hopefully indicates that in this movement we have a manifestation of "politically active social Christianity" that deserves comparison with other manifestations. And perhaps my efforts to delineate the shape and limits of that evangelical radicalism may facilitate comparisons in such a way as to help lay the historical groundwork for further research and dialogue.

Response #1

Douglas M. Strong

Evangelical Piety and Radical Politics: No Longer an Oxymoron?

In 1975, Donald Dayton traveled to the "burned-over district"[1] of upstate New York to give a series of lectures at Houghton College, the Christian college that I was then attending and his *alma mater*. Don's father, Wilber T. Dayton, happened to be the college President at the time. But the substance of Don's lectures—which highlighted the nineteenth century correlation between evangelical revivalism and social justice advocacy—did not square with the conservative values held by his father and a number of other people at the college. By revealing the fact that the source of some of the hot-button, progressive concerns of the post-Watergate era, such as feminism, racial reconciliation, and the eradication of the root causes of poverty, were foundational to the evangelical tradition, including the denominational background of our college (Wesleyan Methodist), Donald Dayton challenged the too-easy linkage that had developed in the late twentieth century between evangelicalism and right-wing causes. Some folks at our school were threatened by the implications of Don's findings; others of us considered them to be liberating. As a practicing Christian and a budding historian of American church history, the content of Dayton's lectures—delivered in his inimitably rambling, but impassioned manner—electrified my interest. I knew straight away that my historical vocation had a new, and definitive, trajectory.

Not everyone had the advantage of hearing Donald Dayton in person in 1975, but the general contents of his lectures had appeared earlier in

---

1. The term "burned-over district," first used by nineteenth century revivalist Charles G. Finney, was popularized in the twentieth century by historian Whitney R. Cross, *The Burned-Over District: The Social and Intellectual History of Enthusiastic Religion in Western New York, 1800–1850* (Ithaca: Cornell University Press, 1950).

the journal *Post-American* (now called *Sojourners*) and were soon to be published in the book *Discovering an Evangelical Heritage*,[2] which provided a much larger stage for the expression of his ideas. That book became essential reading for the so-called "new" (or "young" or "progressive") evangelicals of that period. Additionally, his interpretation of nineteenth century evangelicalism had a great impact on a cadre of religious historians who continue to use these resources for teaching purposes and who, through them, have influenced a multitude of students.

In the same year (1976) that Dayton published *Discovering*, he wrote an article entitled "Piety and Radicalism: Ante-Bellum Social Evangelicalism in the U.S."[3] Both the book and the article, along with several other scholarly essays written at the same time, represent Dayton's initial forays into the academic field of Christian social engagement and, more particularly, the generally unexamined topic of the social impact of evangelicalism.[4] Dayton's thesis was straightforward: "the origins of many U.S. evangelical movements and institutions were in socially and politically active forms of Christianity that were quite radical."[5]

For most observers of American society—both in 1976 and today—the phrase "radical evangelicalism" seems almost ludicrously oxymoronic. The popular media, for instance, cannot comprehend the possibility that these two concepts could be combined—that an evangelical could be politically or socially radical. In his article, Dayton observed that the existence of radical evangelicalism was "not well known among either historians or evangelicals."[6] Unfortunately, many historians still do not know or appreciate the narrative of pre-Civil War religious activism. These historians do not wish to challenge their stereotyped presupposition that pietist movements are inextricably linked to otherworldliness and an unthinking defense of the *status quo*. Social historians, in particular, also have difficulty admitting that religious experience can be considered as an essential independent variable (let alone the *leading* independent variable) to help us to account for antebellum social reform.

Meanwhile, today's conservative [neo-]evangelicals are deeply uncomfortable with the notion that a predecessor movement that carried

2. Dayton, *Discovering an Evangelical Heritage*.

3. Donald W. Dayton, "Piety and Radicalism."

4. The topic of nineteenth century evangelical social reform was not completely unexamined. Timothy L Smith's *Revivalism and Social Reform* (New York: Abingdon, 1957) provided an early introduction to this subject, as did Cross, op. cit.

5. Dayton, "Piety and Radicalism," 36.

6. Ibid.

the treasured cognomen "evangelical" might be responsible for promoting women in ministry, affirmative action, and theology from a liberation perspective. Thus, both secular historians and the religious right have a vested interest in maintaining the usual caricatures regarding evangelical attitudes toward social concerns.

Nevertheless, some cultural historians who have written more recently agree with Dayton's argument. Richard Carwardine's writing echoes Dayton's, as does the work of John McKivigan and Paul Goodman.[7] Also, several church historians, such as Nancy Hardesty, William Kostlevy, and others have built on the scholarship that Dayton first introduced.[8]

Dayton's approach in the "Piety and Radicalism" article (as in *Discovering an Evangelical Heritage*) was to describe specific areas of study that were a "sampling of the shape of pre-Civil War evangelical radicalism."[9] The first question that he pursued in the article had to do with racial attitudes within the antislavery movement. Dayton challenged the persistent historiographical notion that abolitionism "foundered on the question of racism,"[10] by demonstrating that, although some abolitionists may have harbored racist attitudes, most *evangelical* abolitionists had a "very strong impulse toward egalitarianism."[11]

The second area of study that Dayton discussed in "Piety and Radicalism" was the expanding role of women in antebellum America, a topic about which he has consistently written and spoken over the years. In the article, Dayton contended that "early feminism in the U.S. was to a remarkable extent rooted in pre-Civil War revivalism" and that "the greatest incorporation of women into the Christian ministry took place

7. Richard Carwardine, *Evangelicals and Politics in Antebellum America* (New Haven: Yale University Press, 1993); John L. McKivigan, *The War Against Proslavery Religion: Abolitionism in the Northern Churches, 1830–1865* (Ithaca: Cornell University Press, 1984); Paul Goodman, *Of One Blood: Abolitionism and the Beginning of Racial Equality* (Berkeley: University of California Press, 1998).

8. Nancy A. Hardesty, *Women Called to Witness: Evangelical Feminism in the Nineteenth Century* (Nashville: Abingdon, 1984); William Kostlevy et al., *Poverty and Ecclesiology: Nineteenth Century Evangelicals in the Light of Liberation Theology* (Liturgical, 1992); Douglas M. Strong, *Perfectionist Politics: Abolitionism and the Religious Tensions of American Democracy* (Syracuse University Press, 1999) and *They Walked in the Spirit: Personal Faith and Social Action in America* (Louisville: Westminster John Knox, 1997).

9. Dayton, "Piety and Radicalism," 36.

10. The idea that white abolitionists were fundamentally and almost uniformly racist continues to be asserted by historians. See Beverly Eileen Mitchell, *Black Abolitionism: A Quest for Human Dignity* (Orbis, 2005).

11. Dayton, "Piety and Radicalism," 37–38. See also, Strong, *Perfectionist Politics*, 96, 101, 134, 162–63.

in its wake." He has argued in multiple venues that the extension of women's rights in the nineteenth century was one of the key indicators of the immense influence of anti-establishment, "free church" evangelical radicalism, particularly of the Holiness variety.[12]

Thirdly, Dayton wrote about the prevalence of "revolutionary themes"—or what might more commonly be termed civil disobedience—among evangelical abolitionists. Antebellum activists regularly defended their (illegal) behavior—by assisting fugitive slaves, for example—on the basis of their adherence to the "higher law" of God. Thus, antislavery advocates asserted the "supremacy of the divine law" over human-made legal statutes.[13]

The fourth subject developed by Dayton was the growing awareness of class-consciousness among mid-nineteenth century evangelical reformers, especially the abolitionists. Even though the mid-nineteenth century reform work of evangelical antislavery activists preceded the systemic class analysis of the social gospelers (such as Washington Gladden and Walter Rauschenbusch) in the late nineteenth and early twentieth centuries, Dayton asserts that the earlier evangelical expressions of social Christianity were often more determined and persevering "than facets of the social gospel . . . [that are] usually taken as models of activist Christianity."[14]

These four themes of interest that Dayton depicted in his article were illuminating examples of evangelical radicalism in the pre-Civil War period. He provided even more case studies in his book, *Discovering an Evangelical Heritage*. Nonetheless, Dayton admitted that the topic "needs further study and analysis."[15] Some of the areas that needed further analysis have been the focus of research in subsequent years,[16] while other areas of inquiry—such as the antebellum critique of militarism and the nineteenth century unease with the commodification of persons that occurs in

---

12. Dayton, "Piety and Radicalism," 38. See Dayton, *Discovering*, 85–98; "Your Daughters Shall Prophesy: Feminism in the Holiness Movement," *Methodist History* 14 (January 1976) 67–92. See also Hardesty, op. cit., and Susie Stanley, *Holy Boldness: Women Preachers' Autobiographies and the Sanctified Self* (Knoxville: University of Tennessee Press, 1994).

13. Dayton, "Piety and Radicalism," 38–39.

14. Ibid., 39, 36. On the connections between mid-nineteenth century evangelical reform and the later social gospel movement, see Strong, *Perfectionist Politics*, 131–32, 164–66 and Ronald C. White, Jr. and C. Howard Hopkins, *The Social Gospel: Religion and Reform in Changing America* (Philadelphia: Temple University Press, 1976), Part I.

15. Dayton, "Piety and Radicalism," 39.

16. For an analysis of antebellum evangelical critiques of the hierarchies of political power, both in the church and the state, see Strong, *Perfectionist Politics*.

a consumerist culture—are still waiting to be investigated. Also relatively unexplored is the question of what specific type of piety sustained the reformers' activism, that is, what kind of spirituality did evangelical radicals actually practice? What was at the heart of the religious experience of pre-Civil War evangelicals that led them to become socially engaged?

In the "Piety and Radicalism" article, Dayton mused that perhaps his "efforts to delineate the shape . . . of evangelical radicalism" might help to "lay the historical groundwork for further research and dialogue." Without question, his intention has been fulfilled, for his academic vision has borne fruit in a plenitude of articles, books, and dissertations. Perhaps more significantly, just as Dayton's original "rediscovery of this heritage" took place within the "post-1960s evangelical consciousness," now a new generation of progressive evangelicals on college campuses and within mainline, Holiness, and Pentecostal denominations has a renewed interest in such themes, thanks to his work.[17]

---

17. Dayton, "Piety and Radicalism," 39, 36.

Response #2

Jim Wallis

Donald Dayton: Helping Us Find Our Way Back Home

I have often said that at heart, I am a nineteenth-century evangelical; and was just born in the wrong century. In the 19th century, American religious revival was linked directly with the abolition of slavery and movements for social reform. Christians helped lead the abolitionist struggle, efforts to end child labor, projects to aid working people and establish unions, and even the battle to obtain voting rights for women. Here were evangelical Christians fighting for social justice, precisely because of what God had done for them—an activity that evangelicals have not been associated with in more recent times.

Leaders like evangelist Charles Finney didn't shy away from identifying the gospel with the antislavery cause. He was a revivalist and also an abolitionist. For him, the two went closely together. Finney has been called "the father of American evangelism," who directly linked revival and reform. That's the way it always is for revival—faith becomes life-changing, but rather than remaining restricted to personal issues and the inner life alone, it explodes into the world with a powerful force. And for Finney, taking a weak or wrong position on social justice was a "hindrance to revival."

I first learned about Finney and our other revivalist evangelical forefathers and mothers from Don Dayton. In the early years of the Sojourners community in Chicago, we quickly got to know Don. He was then a professor at North Park Seminary, and was doing seminal research on 19th century evangelicalism. As we were struggling to define a socially-engaged evangelicalism, Don was a wealth of historical information and personal encouragement.

I believed that the evangelical faith I had learned as a child naturally led to social engagement, and it was that impulse which led to the founding of Sojourners. But we were estranged from other, more conservative, evangelicals. When we met Don, he taught us that our concerns were not foreign to evangelicalism and, indeed, that others in earlier times and places had come to the same conclusion.

We published his ten-part series on the 19th century revival movement in the *Post-American* (now *Sojourners*) in 1974–75. The first article, in June 1974, began: "The current generation of evangelical Christians has been to a great extent deceived by a strange quirk of history. . . . The last half century or so of evangelical apathy on social issues is assumed to be characteristic of the whole history of evangelicalism. The calls to Christian discipleship, social involvement, and political engagement . . . are assumed to be a new emphasis. . . . This perspective is false to history and obscures a heritage that needs to be recovered." He then went on to tell the stories of Charles Finney, Jonathan Blanchard, Theodore Weld, and many others, including the role of women like the Grimké sisters and Lucy Stone in developing an evangelical feminism. The series then became the groundbreaking book, *Discovering an Evangelical Heritage*, in 1976.

Today, a new generation of evangelical students and pastors is coming of age. Their concerns are the slavery of poverty; the sexual trafficking of God's children; environmental "creation care"; human rights and the image of God in genocidal places like Darfur; and how the Prince of Peace might view our endless wars and conflicts. Whether they know it or not, they are really 19th century American evangelicals (or 18th century British evangelicals) for the 21st century. They are learning that the social mission of the church in the world will never be accomplished without the fire and passion that comes from personal faith. And the social gospel cannot be sustained without a personal experience of Jesus who brings the gospel good news.

I strongly believe that faith matters and can make a difference, not only in our personal lives but in our world. In fact, the church historians tell us that spiritual activity can't be called revival *until* it has changed something in a *society*. In other words spiritual renewal does not necessarily become spiritual revival without some decidedly social consequences. I believe the time is ripe for the kind of spiritual revival that leads to clear social consequences. When politics can't resolve problems, the role of social movements becomes more and more important. And the best social movements have spiritual foundations.

Revival is necessary, because just having a new and better political agenda will not be enough. Getting to the right issues isn't enough. Having the right message isn't enough. Finding the right program isn't enough. The real question is what will motivate and mobilize the kind of constituencies that will move politics to change. I believe that will require the energy, power, and hope that faith can bring. People acting out of their best ideas and values is a good thing; but people acting out of their deepest wells of faith can be a more powerful thing.

Don Dayton taught us our nineteenth century evangelical roots, we now need to rediscover their message for the twenty-first century. And on a more personal level, Don Dayton helped me to find myself in my own spiritual tradition after all. More than he knows, Donald Dayton helped me to find my way back home.

3

The Theology of Wesley

Dayton's concern with the social and political witness of modern neo-evangelicals has been accompanied by an attempt to recover the deeper theological dynamics of historic 19th century evangelicalism. The motivating factor for this recovery has been Dayton's judgment that the vast majority of neo-evangelicals are confused about their theological and historical identity. Instead of looking back to John Wesley and the eighteenth-century Evangelical Revival, they look back to Calvin and Luther. By so doing, modern neo-evangelicals are cut off from the real roots and animating vision that gave birth to their movement and thus have lost their connection to the vital traditions and sources that could continue to nurture and sustain their particular ecclesial traditions.

In this essay—originally published in *Grace Theological Journal* 12, no. 2 (1991) 233–43—Dayton takes up the classical Reformation question of the relationship between law and gospel. Dayton's thesis is that Wesley conceptualized the relationship between law and gospel in a fundamentally different way than Luther, and that Wesley's conception is better able to account for the key theological and spiritual characteristics within much of neo-evangelicalism, thus illuminating the real spiritual and theological dynamics of contemporary neo-evangelicalism.

Law and Gospel in the Wesleyan Tradition

Donald W. Dayton

ONE of the great puzzles about the literature interpreting modern "evangelicalism" is that the historical and theological experience of Methodism is hardly ever used to provide the categories of interpretation. Historically, this is very surprising because the Methodist movement, founded largely under the influence of John Wesley, has been the major continuing product of the "Evangelical Revival" of the 18th century that set the tone for what has become known as "evangelicalism." This is particularly relevant to the North American experience where the period from roughly 1820 to World War I has been interchangeably described by historians as the "age of Methodism" and the "age of evangelicalism." And if one turns attention to the modern progeny of Wesley—either to the children of Methodism (the Holiness movement) or to the grandchildren of Methodism (the Pentecostal movement), this neglect becomes even more obvious demographically because the vast majority of the membership of such groups as the National Association of Evangelicals or of the Christian College Consortium stands in this theological lineage. I am gratified therefore that the planners of this meeting have included the Wesleyan tradition among those whose understanding of "law and gospel" has an important contribution to make to the theological articulation of an "evangelical" perspective on this key issue.

Before turning directly to Wesley and his understanding of "law and gospel," I need to make a few preliminary comments about how to position Wesley in the larger Christian and evangelical panorama. One of the reasons for the neglect of the Wesleyan tradition in the larger interpretation of the "evangelical" experience is that there are strange quirks in the way that we use the label "evangelical"—and in the fact that behind the word is such basic confusion that we may speak of "evangelicalism" as such "an essentially contested concept," to use an expression more at home in the

British philosophical context. In several places[1] I have developed a typology of conflicting meanings of the word "evangelical" that roots each in various periods of conflict within the life of the church. The first meaning of "evangelical" derives its basic thrust from the Protestant Reformation and may be described theologically in terms of the great *solas* of Martin Luther: by *faith* alone, by *grace* alone, by *Christ* alone, and by *scripture* alone—a formulation of the gospel that makes the theme of "justification by faith" the organizing principle. The most recent experience giving rise to a set of connotations for the word "evangelical" has been the fundamentalist/modernist controversy, in which the basic thrust of the word "evangelical" has come to mean opposition to "modernity" and the "modern" reinterpretations of Christian faith that have emerged since the Enlightenment. In this sense "evangelical" conveys less of a theological position (with a particular perspective on the standard theological loci—that is, a particular doctrine of God, of human nature, of salvation, etc.) than a particular methodological stance with regard to Enlightenment "liberalism" that positions "evangelicalism" methodologically just to the right of "neo-orthodoxy" and just to the left of "fundamentalism" on some sort of spectrum that measures accommodation to the Enlightenment. I would contend that Wesley and classical Methodism constitute a third paradigm of what it means to be "evangelical"—one that I would call "classical evangelicalism." This position is a bit harder to describe theologically, but it brings the experience of conversion and regeneration to the fore in a way that organizes the gospel around themes of "sanctification" and the nature of the "Christian walk and life" that result from such an experience.

I want to suggest, then, that our dialogue about many issues is hampered by the fact that our use of the word "evangelical" today is largely determined by the conflicts of the 16th or the 20th centuries in such a way as to suppress the experience of the 18th century and lead us away from it and the determinative role of Methodism in the shaping of most modern forms of "evangelicalism." And the significant point for our discussion today is that the thought of John Wesley firmly resists being collapsed into the categories of either the 20th or the 16th century meanings of what it means to be "evangelical."

David Bebbington, speaking from the other side of the Atlantic, is about the only interpreter of "evangelicalism" that I have seen to notice the profound influence of the Enlightenment on the "evangelical" experience

---

1. Most recently in my essays in a volume I edited with Robert Johnston, *The Variety of American Evangelicalism.*

and its many continuities with it.[2] Another way of making this point is to remind ourselves of the fact that Methodism was the first major Christian movement after the Enlightenment and was to a remarkable extent radically contextualized to it and its categories of thought. This is clearly seen in the positive manner in which Wesley refers to "reason" in a way that is very foreign to both Luther and modern fundamentalist evangelicalism—a point which I shall demonstrate from Wesley momentarily.

Luther has become such a symbol of the Reformation and his categories of thought have become so determinative for all of Protestantism that we sometimes neglect the extent to which we cannot understand either Wesley or eighteenth century "evangelicalism" in this theological line. This is so true that I wonder if we may understand Wesleyanism as a form of Protestantism at all. Something like this was argued over half a century ago by French Catholic priest Maximin Piette in *John Wesley in the Evolution of Protestantism*,[3] in which it is suggested that Wesley constituted a sort of reversion to Catholicism within the Protestant tradition. We don't have the time to explore this thesis but, since it will be central to the case that I wish to make, I will point to a few provocative illustrations of this perspective that will help provide the context for understanding Wesley's doctrine of "law and gospel":

(1) Historically, we should remind ourselves that Wesley stands to a great extent outside the continental Reformation and remained to his death an Anglican priest who was influenced as much by Anglo-Catholicism as he was by his mother's Puritan and dissenting background. He stood in the tradition of Anglican "moralism" tempered by other influences as diverse as Moravian Pietism and Catholic mysticism.

(2) Epistemologically, it is doubtful whether Wesley may be interpreted in the categories of the *sola scriptura*. This is, of course, much disputed by parties who emphasize the priority of the bible in Wesley's thought against other interpreters of Wesley who emphasize the Wesleyan quadrilateral of the correlation of Scripture, reason, tradition and experience. However one resolves such debates, the fact that they exist testifies to the "catholic" character of Wesley's thought on the one side and the influence of the Enlightenment on the other.

---

2. Bebbington makes this point regularly, but most explicitly in his contribution to the recent festschrift for John Stott, "Evangelical Christianity and the Enlightenment," Martyn Eden and David F. Wells, editors, *The Gospel in the Modern World* (Downers Grove, IL: InterVarsity, 1991).

3. Maximin Piette, *John Wesley in the Evolution of Protestantism* (London: Sheed and Ward, 1937).

(3) Soteriologically, Wesley's turn to sanctification as the organizing motif of his theology may be interpreted as a reversion to Catholic themes. Certainly many of the implications of this move lead him toward themes that sound "catholic": the appropriation of virtue language, his understanding that righteousness is actually imparted to the Christian in a way foreign to the forensic language of "imputation" of the magisterial Reformation, and so on. A similar way of making the same point is to notice that magisterial Protestantism makes "faith" the central theological virtue, while Wesley is very clear that "love" is the central virtue and that faith is instrumental to love. This point is sufficiently important that I will quote directly from Wesley:

> . . . faith itself, even Christian faith, the faith of God's elect, the faith of the operation of God, still is only the handmaiden of love. As glorious and honorable as it is, it is not the end of the commandment. God hath given this honor to love alone. Love is the end of all the commandments of God. Love is the end, the sole end of every dispensation of God, from the beginning of the world to the consummation of all things. And it will endure when heaven and earth flee away; for 'love' alone 'never faileth'. Faith will totally fail; it will be swallowed up in sight, in the everlasting vision of God. (Sermon 36, "The Law Established by Faith," II, 1)[4]

Wesley makes the same point with other images—that faith is the door or the porch, while the house itself is love, and so forth. Indeed, one does not understand Wesley at all until one grasps the centrality of "love" in his thought—as the character of God in eternity, as the *imago dei* in creation, as lost in the fall, as restored in *regeneration* and sanctification, as the goal of "perfect love" in the Christian life, and as the fundamental characteristic of eternity when the need for faith has passed.

(4) And finally we need to make an explicit contrast between the thought of Wesley and that of Luther. I think it is fair to notice a "disjunctive" element in the thought of Luther that stands opposed to a "conjunctive" tendency in the thought of Wesley. By this I mean that Luther, perhaps in his reaction to Catholicism, tends to speak of faith *or* reason, gospel *or* law, scripture *or* tradition, faith *or* works, and so on, while Wesley speaks more naturally of faith *and* reason, gospel *and* law, scripture *and* tradition, faith *and* works, and so on. The same point may

---

4. The quotations by Wesley are cited informally and without reference to any particular edition in ways that will allow the citations to be found in various editions of the sermons and journals of Wesley—by sermon number, title and section (in the case of sermons) or by date (in the case of the journals).

be made in another way by noticing that Wesley is able to move from Galatians to James in the New Testament without feeling the tension that caused Luther to appropriate the former as the hermeneutical center of his theology while marginalizing the latter as "a right strawy epistle."

With these comments in the background it may now be possible to hear with new ears a statement from Wesley that picks up many of these themes and hopefully reveals how Wesley should be positioned with regard to them. Those who know only one thing about John Wesley probably know of his "Aldersgate" spiritual experience while hearing read in a Moravian meeting words from Luther's preface to the epistle to the Romans. Less well-known is Wesley's reaction to Luther when he got around to reading his commentary on Galatians. The following statement from his diary in 1741 (three years after Aldersgate) reveals how far his thought is from at least the Lutheran side of the continental Reformation:

> I . . . read over . . . that celebrated book, Martin Luther's Comment on the Epistle to the Galatians. I was utterly ashamed. How have I esteemed this book, only because I heard it so commended by others! Or, at best, because I had read some excellent sentences occasionally quoted from it! But what shall I say, now I judge for myself? Now I see with my own eyes? Why, not only that the author makes nothing out, clears up not one considerable difficulty; that he is quite shallow in his remarks on many passages, and muddy and confused almost on all; but that he is deeply tinctured with mysticism throughout, and hence often dangerously wrong. To instance only one or two points: How does he (almost in the words of Tauler) decry reason, right or wrong, as an irreconcilable enemy to the Gospel of Christ? Whereas, what is reason, (the faculty so called,) but the power of apprehending, judging and discoursing? Which power is not more to be condemned in the gross, than seeing, hearing, or feeling. Again, how blasphemously does he speak of good works and of the law of God; constantly coupling the law with sin, death, hell or the Devil! and teaching that Christ delivers us from them all alike. Whereas, it can no more be proved from Scripture, that "Christ delivers us from the law of God," than he delivers us "from holiness or from Heaven." Here (I apprehend) is the real spring of the ground of the error of the Moravians. They follow Luther for better or for worse. Hence their, "No works; no law; no commandments." But who art thou that "speakest evil of the law, and judgest the law?" (Wesley, *Journal*, Monday, June 15, 1741)

These comments of Wesley anticipate many of the themes which now follow. Let me attempt to unfold the Wesleyan understanding of "Gospel and Law" by providing a series of "thesis statements" with supporting quotations from Wesley that will indicate the major points that need to be made. We do not pursue each of these themes in detail, but together I think that they will indicate the basic shape of Wesley's thought.

(1) It is often assumed that anyone who puts as much weight as Wesley does on works and the law must be slipping into a form of "works righteousness" that qualifies the gratuity of grace and fundamentally compromises the gospel of "salvation by faith." But it was his preaching on "salvation by faith" that got Wesley into much trouble. The collections of the "standard sermons" that have become almost the doctrinal standards of the various strands of Methodism begin with his sermon on "Salvation by Faith" that was preached in St. Mary's of Oxford just a little over two weeks after his Aldersgate experience. Though perhaps still tinged with a Moravianism that he would later qualify—and still willing to laud Luther as the great champion of this theme, this sermon begins with the following ringing declaration of "salvation by grace":

> All the blessings which God hath bestowed upon man are of his mere grace, bounty, or favor: his free, undeserved favour, favour altogether undeserved, man having no claim to the least of his mercies. It was free grace that 'formed man of the dust of the ground, and breathed into him a living soul,' and stamped on that soul the image of God, and 'put all things under his feet.' The same free grace continues to us, at this day, life and breath, and all things. For there is nothing we are, or have, or do, which can deserve the least thing at God's hand. 'All our works thou, O God, hast wrought in us.' These therefore are so many more instances of free mercy: and whatever righteousness may be found in man, this also is the gift of God.

Wesley repeatedly goes on in this sermon and elsewhere to deny the possibility of any form of salvation on the basis of works or of any other human foundation.

(2) But perhaps Wesley's most characteristic move is to build on this protestant-sounding foundation a catholic doctrine of sainthood, to use the expression of the late Albert Outler, one of the most important of recent interpreters of Wesleyanism. Wesley uses the language of the "imputation" of the "righteousness of Christ" through "faith," but just as he makes faith instrumental to love, he makes this construct not the essence of "salvation," but the entrance to it so that the ultimate reality of salva-

tion is to be found in regeneration and sanctification. Another way of making the same point is to notice that Wesley's understanding of grace is more active and transformatory in character than that of the magisterial Reformers and especially that of Luther. Outler spoke of Wesley as having a "therapeutic" doctrine of grace—an understanding of grace that expects the "fixing" of the distortions of the fallen order in a way that picks up the theme of pardon and works it into the system in ways that lead beyond that theme to themes of restoration of the created order.[5] Still another way of making this point or a similar one is to speak of Wesley's use (like the Pietists before him) of biological metaphors of birth, regeneration, growth, fruits/roots, etc. rather than more forensic images of position or declaration in his understanding of salvation. The fundamental issue for Wesley is life rather than pardon. Thus he can say:

> It has been frequently supposed that the being born of God was one with the being justified; that the new birth and justification were only different expressions denoting the same thing . . . But though it be allowed that justification and the new birth are in point of time inseparable from each other, yet are they easily distinguished as being not the same, but things of a widely different nature. Justification implies only a relative, the new birth a real, change. God in justifying us does something *for* us: in begetting us again he does the work *in* us. The former changes our outward relation to God, so that of enemies we become children; by the latter our inmost souls are changed. The one restores us to the favor, the other to the image of God. (Sermon 19, "The Great Privilege of Those that are Born of God," 1, 2)

> . . . the new birth . . . is that great change which God works in the soul when he brings it into life: when he raises it from the death of sin to the life of righteousness. It is the change wrought in the whole soul by the almighty Spirit of God when it is 'created anew in Jesus Christ', when it is 'renewed after the image of God', 'in righteousness and true holiness', when the love of the world is changed into the love of God, pride into humility, passion into meekness; hatred, envy, malice, into a sincere, tender disinterested love for all mankind. In a word, it is that change whereby the 'earthly, sensual, devilish' mind is turned into 'the mind which was

---

5. Outler's important work on the interpretation of Wesley is scattered in various essays, but the kernel of his work may be found in his anthology, *John Wesley* (New York: Oxford University Press, 1964) and *Theology and the Wesleyan Spirit* (Nashville: Discipleship Resources, 1975).

in Christ'. This is the nature of the new birth. (Sermon 45, "The New Birth," II, 5)

(3) This consistently twofold character of salvation in Wesley (justification/new birth, justification/sanctification, salvation from the guilt of sin/salvation from the power of sin, what God does for us/what God does in us, and so on) means that he can talk about the law in two different moments of the Christian life. This is perhaps clearest in Wesley's famous sermon "On the Spirit of Bondage and of Adoption." This is a remarkable sermon in several of its key moves. In a manner reminiscent of Søren Kierkegaard's *Stages on Life's Way* and quite unlike much of modern evangelicalism, Wesley suggests that humankind be divided into three rather than two categories. Instead of sinners and saints, Wesley sees three stages: the natural, the legal, and the evangelical. In the first stage one is secure in one's own sleep—blissfully unaware of the issues of sin that become so troublesome in the second stage when one has been "awakened." This is the "legal" stage because it represents the experience "under the law"—the spirit of bondage. In this stage Wesley comes close to the Reformation language of the law as tutor to grace in that the law exposes and drives home our sinfulness. But Wesley differs somewhat in how he moves from this point. He maintains always a positive view of the law of God; for

> . . . sin, taking occasion by the commandment, deceived me, and by it slew me. It came upon me unawares, slew all my hopes, and plainly showed, in the midst of life I was in death. 'Wherefore the law is holy, and the commandment holy and just and good': I no longer lay the blame on this, but on the corruption of my own heart. I acknowledge that 'the law is spiritual; but I am carnal, sold under sin.' I now see both the spiritual nature of the law, and my own devilish heart, 'sold under sin', totally enslaved . . . (Sermon 9, "The Spirit of Bondage and of Adoption, II, 9)

(4) This brings us more fully to the point of Wesley's consistently positive attitude toward the law. Where other traditions speak of "freedom from the law," Wesley speaks always of "The Law Established Through Faith"—the title he gives to two key sermons. These two sermons follow another on "The Original, Nature, Properties, and Use of the Law." These three sermons are the *locus classicus* for understanding Wesley on the law. It may also be worth noting that these follow, in editions of either the forty-four or the fifty-three "standard" sermons of Wesley, thirteen discourses on the Sermon on the Mount where they seem to be placed deliberately to draw attention to that sermon as "law" to be followed by the Christian. In

these sermons Wesley makes a sharp distinction between the ceremonial and the moral law. It is the latter (i.e., the "moral law") that Wesley celebrates and almost hypostasizes in a sense in that the law seems to become for Wesley the "logos" or the fundamental ontological principle of the universe. This is especially clear in the first of these sermons (based on the text in Rom 7:12: "the law is holy"). This law is grounded in eternity—before Moses, Noah, or Enoch—"before the foundation of the world." At creation this law is engraved on human hearts by the finger of God. It is revealed more clearly to Moses where it is written on tablets of stone. When we see this law we see that it is "an incorruptible picture of the high and holy one that inhabiteth eternity." It is at times identified in language reminiscent of the "sophia" tradition of wisdom in the Old Testament and also with the "wisdom from above" of the book of James. Wesley speaks of the law as emanation from the essence of God and even drifts toward language that we more naturally use in a Christological context. The law "is 'the streaming forth' or outbeaming 'of his glory, the express image of his person'." Or, "yea, it is the fairest offspring of the Everlasting Father, the brightest efflux of his essential wisdom, the visible beauty of the Most High." Such language has caused such interpreters of Wesley as Kenneth Collins to speak of "Wesley's Platonic Conception of the Moral Law."[6]

(5) With this background we can now understand why Wesley can describe Luther as blasphemous in his treatment of the law. For Wesley the law is the gospel in a very profound sense. In Wesley gospel and law are brought together in a way that reminds us of the concept of "Torah" in Judaism at its best: the law is grace and through it we discover the good news of the way life is intended to be lived. In his fifth discourse on the Sermon on the Mount (on the text: "think not that I have come to destroy the law or the prophets: I am not come to destroy but to fulfill.") Wesley is quite explicit and self-conscious in taking this position:

> . . . there is no contrariety at all between the law and the gospel; . . . there is no need for the law to pass away in order to the establishing of the gospel. Indeed neither of them supersedes the other, but they agree perfectly well together. Yea, the very same words, considered in different respects, are parts both of the law and the gospel. If they are considered as commandments, they are parts of the law: if as promises, of the gospel. Thus, 'Thou shalt love the Lord the God with all thy heart,' when considered as a commandment, is a branch of the law; when regarded as a promise, is an

---

6. Kenneth Collins, "Wesley's Platonic Conception of the Moral Law," *Wesleyan Theological Journal* 21(1986) 116–28.

essential part of the gospel—the gospel being no other than the commands of the law proposed by way of promises. Accordingly poverty of spirit, purity of heart, and whatever else is enjoined in the holy law of God, are no other, when viewed in a gospel light, than so many great and precious promises.

3. There is therefore the closest connection that can be conceived between the law and the gospel. On the one hand the law continually makes way for and points us to the gospel; on the other the gospel continually leads us to a more exact fulfilling of the law. . . . We may yet further observe that every command in Holy Writ is only a covered promise. (Sermon 25, "Sermon on the Mount, V," II, 2, 3)

This then is at least the basic outline of the understanding of the "law and gospel in the Wesleyan tradition"—and something of an effort to position this understanding in the constellation of Christian traditions, most especially by contrast with the dominant traditions of the continental Reformation, at least on the more Lutheran side. In closing I would like to make a few suggestive points that I will not be able to develop in detail. But I need to make a few comments on the significance of what I have said for the interpretation of evangelicalism in general.

(1) Obviously, from what I have said above, I believe that the Wesleyan tradition has much at stake in those debates that are now revolutionizing our reading of Paul and the New Testament in general. I have in mind those efforts of persons like Krister Stendahl to wrest the New Testament from out from under structures of interpretation dictated by the spiritual struggle of Luther and continued even today in the majority of scholarship, especially that shaped by the German Lutheran experience. More recently, such debates have centered around the efforts of E. P. Sanders to reorient the interpretation of Paul by his revisionist readings of Palestinian Judaism. At the center of these discussions is the fact that traditional scholarship has not sufficiently accounted for the positive statements that Paul makes about the law, especially in the book of Romans—the texts that Wesley makes the foundation of his theology of the law. This is one of the key points being made by Methodist James Dunn in such essays as "The New Perspective on Paul"[7] and in his recent commentary on Romans. The

---

7. This essay is now available in *Jesus, Paul, and the Law* (Louisville, KY: Westminster John Knox, 1990). Useful surveys of the issue are John M. G. Barclay, "Paul and the Law: Observations on Some Recent Debates." *Themelios* 12 (September 1986) 5–15 and Thomas C. Geer, Jr., "Paul and the Law in Recent Discussion," *Restoration Quarterly* 31(1989) 93–107.

dust from these debates has not yet settled, but I suspect that, as it does, we shall take Wesleyanism more seriously theologically and find therein some significant clues for understanding both Paul and the gospel itself.

(2) I also find that the more I ponder the nature of "evangelicalism" in our context, the more I am convinced that it must be understood as standing largely in the line of Wesley. By this I mean that contemporary evangelicalism in its dominant "convertive" piety form is not primarily a Reformation product, but a later development with roots in Pietism and Puritanism that flowered in the "evangelical revivals" in the eighteenth century. Most forms of modern evangelicalism that emphasize the "new birth" are characterized by this later development rather than by the subtle dialectic of the Lutheran doctrine of "justification by faith" and the *simul justus et peccator*. If we are inclined to identify evangelicalism, for example, with modern revivalism of the last two centuries, we must notice that the founder of this tradition, Charles Grandison Finney, was characterized by a similar understanding of law (though perhaps a bit more Pelagian in tendency). One has only to notice the thesis expressed in David Weddle's book *The Law as Gospel: Revival and Reform in the Theology of Charles G. Finney*.[8] It is also becoming increasingly clear that more attention must be paid to the significance of Scottish Common Sense Realism for the interpretation of American evangelicalism. This philosophical school had a tendency to affirm the objective and immutable character of the moral law that was so a part of the ontological structure of reality that it could be discerned universally by common sense. Surely, it is the cumulative effect of such traditions that have given us modern controversies about "moral absolutes" and polemics against "situation ethics." Or how else am I to explain the many sermons that I grew up under that warned me against various sins which violated the moral law written in my heart—and warned that the pursuit of such would put me at odds with my essential nature.

(3) If such suggestions have any validity, we must rethink the nature of "evangelicalism" as we traditionally interpret it. If the Wesleyan tradition has a determinative role in the shaping of modern "evangelicalism," then it is not exactly a form of "traditional Protestantism." It is rather a protest and corrective to basic themes of the Reformation rather than a restatement of them. Indeed, if we think of the Reformation and the eighteenth century "evangelical revival" as dialectically related and mutually corrective, we may be able to avoid the "cheap grace" tendencies of the former and the "legalistic" tendencies of the latter. Søren Kierkegaard

---

8. David Weddle, *The Law as Gospel: Revival and Reform in the Theology of Charles G. Finney* (Metuchen, NJ: Scarecrow, 1985).

had much to say about the demonic tendencies that are manifested when correctives are isolated from that which they are intended to correct and made norms by themselves.

(4) If we grasp this dialectical and corrective struggle and notice how it is being played out in history, we might interpret the efforts of the last couple of generations of "evangelical scholarship" to reassert the classical traditions of the Reformation as a corrective to a popular (and populist) "evangelicalism" profoundly shaped by forms of Wesleyanism. Noticing such a dynamic might help explain the fact with which I began this paper —the massive suppression of the Wesleyan tradition in the historical and theological interpretation of modern "evangelicalism." This suppression has been so massive (no doubt for a variety of reasons) that most interpreters are not even aware of the Wesleyan tradition as a theological option. One of the most egregious illustrations of this is the book by Daniel P. Fuller, *Gospel and Law: Contrast or Continuum?*.[9] In this volume Fuller extends his earlier critique of dispensational hermeneutics to a similar critique of "covenant theology" for their emphasizing the contrast rather than the continuity of "gospel" and "law." But Fuller offers his solution as a new find, a discovery *de novo*, without any apparent awareness of antecedents to his position like the Wesleyan tradition. I am convinced that we need to reflect on such phenomena more than we do, because they reveal a sociological and cultural determination of our discussions that sometimes prevent us from hearing the gospel in its fullness.

---

9. Daniel P. Fuller, *Gospel and Law* (Grand Rapids: Eerdmans, 1980).

Response #1

Howard Snyder

Donald Dayton's Wesleyan Theology

DAYTON'S essay "Law and Gospel in the Wesleyan Tradition" shows how closely he has read Wesley and also his grasp of the larger historical and theological context in which Dayton has done his theological work. It is a brilliant paradigmatic piece that remains of abiding significance in the interpretation of the Wesleyan tradition and in understanding the nature of the gospel.

Dayton's decades-long insistence that the Wesleyan tradition and the holiness movement be understood on their own terms, rather than by alien paradigms, can at times appear a hobby or special pleading. We hear variations of the same speech repeatedly. The reason for the insistence, however, is that the Wesleyan tradition has been so massively misunderstood (if not caricatured) in much of the historiography and theological interpretation emanating from the United States.

I lift out two statements from Dayton's "Law and Gospel" essay as particularly suggestive: "One does not understand Wesley at all until one grasps the centrality of 'love' in his thought." And this: "I wonder if we may understand Wesleyanism as a form of Protestantism at all."

Law and Gospel

Dayton gives a lucid exposition of some of Wesley's deepest insights. Wesley was more soundly biblical on the law and gospel question than was Luther, despite Luther's profession of *sola scriptura*.

What enabled Wesley to have a more balanced view on the law than did Luther (not to mention much of contemporary evangelicalism!)? The answer is rather simple and has to do primarily with context, though also with personality and personal history. Luther struggled to break free from a medieval Catholicism that he experienced as salvation by works, by human effort. His breakthrough was naturally a reaction—biblically, an overreaction, as Dayton notes. *Justification* may be by faith alone, but *salvation* biblically understood is not solely by faith. It involves also works, "faith working by love." Here Wesley resists the Lutheran (and also typical contemporary evangelical) penchant for interpreting all Scripture through the lens of the book of Romans, rather than the other way around. This hermeneutical prioritizing of Romans easily distorts its meaning. We forget that Paul was doing precisely what Wesley insists in doing: interpreting all particular Scriptures in terms of the whole. The book of Romans needs the book of James (and vice versa). Otherwise we misinterpret both.

Wesley contrasts sharply with Luther here, as Dayton shows. Wesley's context was different from Luther's. Wesley inherited the Reformation tradition of salvation by grace alone, but he inherited it within the context of the Anglican *via media* and the Anglican triad of Scripture, reason, and tradition. He inherited it not only in the context of the early days of the Enlightenment, but also in a period of the Anglican rediscovery of the Eastern Orthodox tradition. Wesley's crucial discovery via the Moravians of the importance of personally experiencing the new birth thus came within this larger Anglican context. These dynamics, plus his own personality and family background, made Wesley more broadly biblical than either Luther or the so-called "Bible Christians" of Wesley's day.

This broad and varied Anglican context meant that, for Wesley, reason and tradition were not to be rejected but to be employed in the proper understanding and interpretation of Scripture. Divine love, not just faith (Luther) or God's decrees (Calvin) was to be the central category. Thus, the crucial importance of the image of God and of salvation as the full restoration of this image, of being conformed to the likeness of Jesus (Rom 8:29). Sanctification was more than just personal piety; it was both "inward and outward," enabling humans, like God, to exhibit "sincere, tender disinterested [i.e., impartial, selfless] love for all" humankind. "Real Christianity," as Wesley called it, meant Christ in us, not just Christ for us; a focus on the image of God as well as the word of God. This is what Dayton is pointing to in his key essay.

Wesley knew how to make corrections without over-correcting, as Dayton notes. His theology was "conjunctive" rather than "disjunctive." Thus the importance of Kierkegaard's insight, as Dayton puts it, on "the demonic tendencies that are manifested when correctives are isolated from that which they are intended to correct and made norms by themselves."

Wesleyanism and Evangelicalism

Does Dayton overstate the case when he says Wesley "stands to a great extent outside the continental reformation"? The key words here are "to a great extent." Wesley did see himself as standing in continuity with the Reformation—but also in continuity with early Eastern Christianity, many of the Roman Catholic saints (those who were not too "mystical"), many of the radical Protestants—in fact all who genuinely knew God through Jesus and lived a life of love, whatever their particular "opinions" (that is, doctrines).

It is here, especially, that Wesley so contrasts with U.S. evangelicalism (less so with many evangelicals elsewhere). Dayton is on target here, though his analysis in this particular essay is incomplete. He elsewhere points out additional factors that account for the peculiar, overly individualistic, overly otherworldly, and one-sidedly political nature of U.S. evangelicalism. A major part of the story is the rise of premillennialism a century after Wesley and the way popular dispensational premillennialism has been wedded to a nationalistic right-wing political agenda. Most Wesleyans in the U.S. seem oblivious to the fact that their understanding and experience of the Christian Faith today bears little resemblance to the faith and discipleship Wesley taught. Most purported Wesleyans today, including those in my own denomination, are unaware that they have collapsed the meaning of salvation into the doctrine of justification, becoming both unbiblical and un-Wesleyan.

It was the people Wesley dismissively called "Bible Christians" who most resemble today's U.S. evangelicals. Wesley today would no doubt make many of the same points he did in his day, for they're still relevant: law and gospel must be seen synergistically, not in opposition; salvation means much more than justification and is never simply "personal" in the sense of private and individualistic; God's plan for the salvation of his creation is as broad as his promises in both Testaments. Salvation means the "restoration of all things" (Acts 3:21); the creation healed.

A Personal Appreciation

Don Dayton has assisted me in my theology and writings in more ways than I can tell. From our initial animated conversation on an interurban train in the New York City area in 1966 to the present, he has been a kind of mentor, even though I am slightly older. He has helped me understand my own tradition, even when I haven't fully agreed with him. He has been a door into other larger discussions, such as Barthian theology. We both owe a profound debt to Gilbert M. James, the first Professor of the Church in Society at Asbury Theological Seminary and a pioneer in urban and interracial ministry.

From the time of *Discovering an Evangelical Heritage* in 1976 (which he said might better be called *Discovering a Holiness Heritage*), Dayton has often lifted up the historical and theological significance of Benjamin Titus Roberts (1823–1893), principal founder of the Free Methodist Church. Dayton's constant encouragement in my research on B. T. and Ellen Roberts, and his facilitating the publication of the biography that resulted, must especially be noted. Eerdmans published my *Populist Saints: B. T. and Ellen Roberts and the First Free Methodists* in 2006. The biography is not only the culmination of years of work; it is itself a tribute to the work of Donald Dayton.

Response #2

William J. Abraham

Donald Dayton is a walking, talking theological encyclopedia; his scholarly work represents one of the jewels of the evangelical tradition that should be a welcome addition to all future encyclopedias of Protestant theology. Dayton himself will probably be pleased at the first observation; but he'll baulk at the second.

I first got to know Professor Dayton when I was a student at Asbury Theological Seminary in the early nineteen seventies, and when he was honing his legendary bibliographical skills in the library. Even then he was an enigma wrapped in a mystery. He listened intently to what was happening all around him, was reserved in what he said publicly, and then from time to time would let loose with a torrent of informed insight that could take one's breath away. It was not easy to get a grip on the surprising, meandering journey he was on, but I knew that beneath the puzzling exterior there was an absolutely brilliant mind that would not be tamed by the routines of conventional scholarship. He had no ear for analytical philosophy (and readily confessed this, commenting that analytical philosophers seemed to have swallowed a dictionary and it had gotten stuck in their throats). He was ruthless in exposing the blind spots of his Wesleyan predecessors and their lapse into fundamentalism (as when he found that his father's generation had excised the radical parts of Finney's social ethics). He had worked his way through Barth and was uneasy with my sympathy for classical natural theology (yet he knew how contested his views were and had a reserved, if grudging, respect for the rigors of analytical philosophy). Much later I discovered he was very nervous about talk of the classical Christian tradition and edgy about interest in Eastern Orthodoxy (his Anabaptist underwear shone through at this point, but he had absorbed the core of the early tradition). When we met and talked, we would eye each other from a distance, unsure of what to do with each other's interests.

For my part, catching up with Dayton and what he was doing was like finding an oasis in the desert. The well never ran dry. His candor, his wit, and the natural flow of his discourse were a total delight. There was never enough time to absorb his sprawling commentary on the history of theology, or his perceptive normative review of the significance of his chosen topic of conversation, or his illuminating comments on contemporary theological bigwigs. No matter what my obsession at the time, I would gladly lay it aside to find out what new theological planet Dayton had lately discovered, scouted, and mapped with admirable clarity and depth. I always came away from a conversation having been superbly entertained and intellectually refreshed.

Professor Dayton's first love is clearly historical theology. History is his natural mode of thought and inquiry but theology is his passion. I first caught sight of this when I encountered his historical analysis of the evangelical tradition. He captured the core of the issues at stake in his incisive distinctions between the Reformation, the Evangelical Awakenings, and Conservative Evangelicalism. I made this part of my own mental furniture forthwith, dropping it into W. B. Gallie's incisive analysis of essentially contested concepts. On this score Dayton is happy to accept the friendly amendment from within the domain of analytical philosophy. He has restated his revolutionary discovery with typical flair in this essay on law and gospel.

Yet his interests and arguments are not woodenly historical; they are equally (but by no means exclusively) concerned with how best to conceptualize the best insights of evangelicalism across the ages for the current situation. On this score he strikes me as generally Barthian and Liberationist in orientation. However, there are no free intellectual lunches for these academically popular trajectories. He works on how best to absorb their treasures into the Christian tradition but does so with penetrating critical intelligence. His knowledge of Barth is simply mind-boggling; and his criticisms of establishment forms of Liberation theology can be both searing and hilarious. In and through this his work on Pentecostalism is extraordinary. Here he has been a generation ahead of the curve. All future theological work on Pentecostalism will have to come to terms with his groundbreaking interpretation of the early forms of this massive new arrival that everybody is now scrambling to identify and understand. His knowledge of the highways and byways of later developments, say, in Korea are detailed, discerning, and frequently full of surprises.

Dayton has never been a party animal. He is passionate but not partisan. He brings to bear on his normative vision his careful reading of the whole Christian tradition; and he is fearlessly committed to the truth whatever it costs. To crown it all he writes like an angel. His essays are in the league of Isaiah Berlin, Willard Van Orman Quine, and Albert Outler in their sheer beauty of word and organization.

His gifts are once again on display here. Consider the historical density in his treatment of evangelicalism, the nuanced contextualization of Wesley in the wider Christian tradition, the thorough knowledge of Wesley and his sources, the side glances at unresolved controversies (say, on scripture), the sharp recognition of mistaken readings of Methodism, and the carefully articulated and argued thesis on the shape of Wesley's thinking on law and gospel that is the heart of the paper. He rounds it off by connecting Wesley to the new interpretation of Paul (where he is exactly right on the resonance between Wesley and the new Paul), by relativizing once again contemporary forms of evangelicalism, and by insisting on correctives all around. He hints at but misses Wesley's fascinating attempt to go all the way to the bottom of the moral law in his efforts to solve Plato's famous queries in the *Euthyphro*. Wesley at this point is not a Platonist; he has gone beyond Plato in his own slapdash, amateurish way. Perhaps running down that rabbit trail does not fit with Dayton's audience; or perhaps it takes him too far into the epistemology and metaphysics of Wesley's moral realism.

It will only be a matter of time before old-line Methodism stumbles into Dayton's hidden den of treasures. I have seen student's minds turned inside out by his work. On this front he has been reticent to engage the discussion in the way he has interacted with the work of recent Reformed historians of evangelicalism. One senses that he is not entirely sure that mainline Methodists really are the children and grandchildren of Wesley too. They assuredly are. Their reception and development of the Wesleyan tradition is as important as the trajectory that Dayton traces from Wesley through the Holiness tradition to Pentecostalism. Their assimilation, corruption, and enrichment of the Wesleyan heritage have to be figured into any comprehensive assessment of the Wesleyan heritage. Dayton is rightly uneasy with their establishment triumphalism and beguiling ignorance, but his contribution on the whole sweep of the tradition will prove fruitful and invaluable to laborers in this vineyard. Once we touch one element in the historical developments all the others have to be refigured. Dayton's work in the Oxford Institute of Methodist Theological Studies for twenty-five years shows how important this side of the tradition was to him.

I noted earlier that Dayton would probably baulk at my identifying his scholarly work as a jewel of the evangelical tradition. At times he has wanted to be done with evangelicalism as a useful historical category; it has ceased to do any explanatory work; and his own theological sensibility as a Wesleyan is betrayed by its recent incarnation. I resonate with his unease and his arguments. Moreover, Dayton belongs to the whole Christian tradition, not to some narrow backwater. However, if Donald Dayton has taught us anything, it is that recent efforts to corral and contain evangelicalism are historically contingent and ineffective in the long haul. The tradition itself is not a monolithic edifice; it is a network of dwellings, each with its own architecture and ambience and each subject to constant repair and reconstruction. Dayton's reconstructive efforts have been magnificent. No doubt he will continue to contribute to this and other worthy projects for years to come.

4

Methodist Studies

The following essay may be one of the most important in this entire volume. The essay comprises a summary of Dayton's Wesleyan Theological Society Presidential Address, given in 1990. Dayton offers one of the most illuminating interpretations of Methodist history currently available by arguing that the historic splits within Methodism usually occur not because of disagreements over doctrine or theology, but over the continuing validity of Wesley's "preferential option for the poor." The essay was widely praised for offering a large "metanarrative" for the interpretation of the Methodist traditions. Its thesis was later debated among Chilean Methodists, as it suggests that it is Pentecostalism that continues this strand of Wesley rather than mainline Methodism, which adopted a more elitist mission strategy of founding schools to educate future leaders.

The essay also highlights Dayton's important contributions to the work of the Oxford Institutes of Methodist Theological Studies. Dayton has served on the core planning committee for a quarter of a century and was very influential in pushing the Institute to expand participation beyond the bounds of mainline Methodism. Along with W. R. Ward, Dayton was also responsible for co-founding and chairing the nineteenth-century studies group within the Institute, which served as an avenue for other Wesleyan traditions to be incorporated into the work of the Institute. The essay also contains an important sub-theme of Dayton's work: the "embourgeoisement" thesis. In this case, his argument is that Methodists, like other traditions, start among the poor and are more changed by moving into the middle classes than by other factors (such as the adoption of liberal theology, etc.). The essay was first published in *The Portion of the Poor: Good News to the Poor in Wesleyan Tradition*, edited by M. Douglas Meeks (Nashville: Abingdon Press, Kingswood Books, 1995).

Unfortunately, the invited respondents were unable to participate for different reasons. However, because of the importance of this essay, we have decided to include it here without responses in the hope that it will further illumine Dayton's contribution to the interpretation of Methodism.

"Good News to the Poor"
The Methodist Experience after Wesley

Donald W. Dayton

"To the poor the gospel is preached"—Which is the greatest mercy, and the greatest miracle of all.

—John Wesley, *Explanatory Notes on the New Testament,* commenting on the last phrase of Luke 7:22.

Introduction

In this essay I am taking on the nearly impossible task of tracing the theme "Good News to the Poor" through the "post-Wesley" history of the "Methodist" experience, including the great variety of Methodist traditions that derive from Wesley and now cluster themselves together in the World Methodist Council. I will be able to do this in the space available only by severe restrictions. I have chosen a more "cosmic" and illustrative, rather than detailed and comprehensive, method that will result in a more "broad stroke" analysis and interpretation.

I propose to deal with the topic in several steps. First, I will summarize my own reading of the theme in Wesley. Second, I will suggest that the theme "Good News to the Poor" provides a window of access into the very soul of Methodism as it struggles with an ambiguous legacy from Wesley—one in which the Methodist traditions are caught in a profoundly contradictory dialectic of countervailing forces. Third, though it has not often been so used, I will argue that the theme (and its explication in this manner) provides a "hermeneutical key" for a re-reading (*relectura*) of the Methodist tradition—a reading that we must confront more directly than we have generally done in our historical and theological work. Fourth, I will explore the manifestation of this theme in several key "flashpoints" of the larger Methodist tradition. And, finally, I will attempt a few closing observations.

It is, of course, "liberation theology," in its various manifestations but most particularly in its South American versions, that has taught the modern church to reflect on a dimension of "divine partiality," that is, the claim that the biblical witness clearly reveals a sort of "preferential option for the poor" that must be taken as an essential and not accidental aspect of the Gospel. The expression is modern, deriving from the title of one of the most controversial documents from the 1979 Puebla (Mexico) meeting of the Latin American Bishops' Conference (CELAM). This origin of the expression means that it often carries today a certain ideological and political freight that obscures the extent to which the basic question it raises has recurred again and again in the history of the church in a variety of ecclesiastical and cultural contexts. Indeed, Justo González has sought roots and antecedents of the idea in the early church and in the resistance to the "colonization" of South America in the wake of Columbus.[1] A forthcoming volume explores the parallels between liberation theology and a variety of nineteenth century radical protestant movements that had each articulated this theme in its own way.[2] In our own time the theme has found expression in such diverse locations as the "sectarian" ethics and theology of Mennonite John Howard Yoder (e. g., his *The Politics of Jesus*, which explores the biblical basis of this theme in the Gospel of Luke) and the "evangelical" social activism of Ronald J. Sider (e.g., *Rich Christians in an Age of Hunger: A Biblical Study*). When I use the expression "preferential option for the poor," I have a more general concept in mind than some; by it I mean little more than Karl Barth, who much earlier in this century said that,

> The church is witness of the fact that the Son of man came to seek and to save the lost. And this implies that—casting all false impartiality aside—the Church must concentrate first on the lower and lowest levels of human society. The poor, the socially and economically weak and threatened, will always be the object of its primary and particular concern. . . .[3]

---

1. See Justo L. González, *Faith and Wealth: A History of Early Christian Ideas on the Origin, Significance, and Use of Money* (San Francisco: Harper and Row, 1990) and his contribution to *Poverty and Ecclesiology: Nineteenth Century Evangelicals in the Light of Liberation*, ed. Anthony Dunnavant (Collegeville, MN: Liturgical /Michael Glazier, 1992).

2. See my Epilogue to Dunnavant, ed., *Poverty and Ecclesiology*.

3. Karl Barth, *Against the Stream: Shorter Post-War Writings*, 1946–52 (London: SCM, 1954) 36. This passage is in paragraph seventeen of Barth's famous essay on "The Christian Community and the Civil Community."

Barth's firm commitment to this theme is indicated in his willingness to draw as a correlate the conclusion: "We do not really know Jesus (the Jesus of the New Testament) if we do not know him as this poor man, as this (if we may risk the dangerous word) partisan of the poor. . . ."[4] It is in this sense that we may explore the significance of a "preferential option for the poor" in Wesley and the Methodist traditions without the fear of anachronism or of forcing our own modern categories on history.

The Wesleyan "Preferential Option for the Poor"

I have presented my interpretation of this theme in Wesley more fully in my November, 1990, presidential address to the Wesleyan Theological Society, the week of the publication of Theodore Jennings' book *Good News to the Poor: John Wesley's Evangelical Economics*,[5] with which I am generally in basic agreement. My fundamental reservation about that book is that, while we can probably agree with Jennings that "every aspect of Methodism was subjected to the criterion, how will this benefit the poor?" I am less convinced than Jennings that Wesley lifts this to the level of theological principle. His practice seems to make an option for the poor constitutive of the life of the church, but I am less clear how he would argue the theological grounding for this praxis.[6] It seems to me that one reason for the neglect of this theme in later generations is that Wesley did not ground his praxis sufficiently theologically to make the issue normative for those who would claim him as mentor in following centuries. No doubt we will be debating the various aspects of this question (Were the early Methodists really poor? Was this theme in Wesley an "accident" of the early years of Methodism? etc.) for some time to come. Meanwhile, however, let me summarize my own tentative and preliminary view of the matter.

---

4. Karl Barth, *Church Dogmatics*, IV/2 (Edinburgh: T & T Clark, 1958) 180. The German original was published in 1955.

5. I worked in advance with only Theodore W. Jennings, Jr., "Wesley's Preferential Option for the Poor," *Quarterly Review* 9 (1989) 16. This argument was then expanded in *Good News to the Poor: John Wesley's Evangelical Economics* (Nashville: Abingdon, 1990). My address, entitled "The Wesleyan Option for the Poor," has now been published in the *Wesleyan Theological Journal* 26/1 (Spring 1991) 7–22.

6. Perhaps I am influenced by the thorough-going and profoundly theological grounding of this principle in Barth (in the fundamental motifs of his Christology that lie at the heart of his Trinitarian doctrine of God–especially that we know no other God than that revealed in Jesus Christ by the nature of the incarnation as a form of "divine condescension" that provides the "direction" for our own life in the church) to expect something more of that sort. But this is perhaps a significant point for the successive history of Methodism.

First, anyone who has read at all in the *Journal* of Wesley will know that Wesley was systematic in his cultivation of the poor. He made it a regular practice from his Oxford student days to visit the sick, the poor, and those in prison, and he regularly insisted that his followers do likewise. He urged "a member of the society" in 1776 "frequently, nay, constantly to visit the poor, the widow, the sick, the fatherless, in their affliction."[7] Wesley's commitment to this practice is made clear in his sermon "On Visiting the Sick" based on the classic text of Matthew 25. In this sermon Wesley argued that the visiting of the poor is an absolute duty of the Christian without which one's "everlasting salvation" is endangered. Wesley built into the life of Methodism collections for the poor and on occasion went publicly begging for the poor.

Second, Wesley's struggle with and final acceptance of field preaching must surely also be related to this theme. It is no accident that his first major experience with this practice was a sermon based on Luke 4:18–19, a key text for "liberationist" readings of Scripture or any advocacy of a "preferential option for the poor." After a brief experience preaching in Nicolas Street on April 1, 1739, Wesley initiated the practice on the next day (a Monday):

> At four in the afternoon, I submitted to be more vile, and proclaimed in the highways the glad tidings of salvation, speaking from a little eminence in a ground adjoining to the city, to about three thousand people. The scripture on which I spoke was this, (is it possible any one should be ignorant, that it is fulfilled in every true minister of Christ?) "The Spirit of the Lord is upon me, because he hath anointed me to preach the Gospel to the poor. He hath sent me to heal the broken-hearted; to preach deliverance to the captives, and recovery of sight to the blind: to set at liberty them that are bruised, to proclaim the acceptable year of the Lord."[8]

Third, it is also possible to argue that Wesley's message was peculiarly adapted to the poor—that for some fundamental reasons "the poor heard him gladly." Robert D. Hughes III grounds this directly in Wesley's theology—in his "Arminian evangelicalism" with its "twin pillars of universalism and insistence on the role of man's free will in salvation."[9] These principles meant that *all* (even the poor and "disreputable") could come

---

7. *Works (J)* 12:302 ("Letter to a Member of the Society," February 26, 1776).

8. *Works (J)* 1:185 (April 1, 1739).

9. Robert D. Hughes III, "Wesleyan Roots of Christian Socialism," *The Ecumenist* 13 (May–June, 1975) 50.

and find acceptance in the Gospel and in the societies of Methodism. In *The Methodist Revolution* Bernard Semmel makes the same point through the doctrines of Christian Perfection and Assurance, "an experience more accessible to the humble and unsophisticated than to their better situated or better educated fellows."[10] Wesley's brand of Methodism affirmed the magisterial Reformation "pessimism of nature" but went on to profess an "optimism of grace" that offered the hope of change—both personally and socially. This is the revolutionary side of Methodism that offered hope to the poor.

Fourth, however we make the case, I think that it is clear that Wesley's theology and preaching tended toward a profound "gospel egalitarianism" that the poor found attractive. Wesley used the gospel radically to relativize a variety of factors that often sustain class structures and thus oppress the poor in various subtle and not so subtle ways: education, birth, social class, etc. As the Duchess of Buckingham wrote to the Countess of Huntingdon, significantly the patron George Whitefield and the "Calvinistic" wing of the Methodist movement:

> I thank your ladyship for the information concerning the Methodist preachers. Their doctrines are most repulsive, and strongly tinctured with impertinence and disrespect towards their superiors, in perpetually endeavoring to level all ranks, and do away with all distinctions. It is monstrous to be told that you have a heart as sinful as the common wretches that crawl on the earth. This is highly offensive and insulting, and I cannot but wonder that your ladyship should relish any sentiment so much at variance with high rank and good breeding.[11]

Fifth, no doubt the poor were also attracted to Wesley because he did not blame them for their poverty. "So wickedly, devilishly false is that common objection, 'They are poor, only because they are idle.'"[12] Wesley's favoritism for the poor was also revealed negatively by his hostility toward the rich, as evidenced in many of his sermons that we tend to neglect because they fall outside the "standard sermons" that we more usually consult: "The Danger of Riches" (#87); "On Riches" (#108); "The Rich Man and Lazarus" (#112); "On the Danger of Increasing Riches" (#126). If anything, Wesley became more cranky on this issue as he grew older

---

10. Bernard Semmel, *The Methodist Revolution* (New York: Basic, 1973) 17.

11. See Aaron C. H. Seymour, *The Life and Times of Selina, Countess of Huntingdon*, 2 vols. (1844) 1:27, as cited by Oscar Sherwin, *John Wesley: Friend of the People* (New York: Twayne, 1961) 40–41.

12. *Works (U)* 2:280 (February 9–10, 1753).

and more worried about the departure of Methodism from his principles. In this sense Wesley did not shirk, as do many modern advocates of a soft version of a "preferential option for the poor," from the "woes" against the rich that parallel the "beatitudes" that bless the poor (especially in Luke's version).

We could explore other aspects of Wesley's commitment to the poor: the role of his extensive publishing program in the education of the poor; his concern for health; Methodist structures for the relief of the poor; and so forth. But I must move on to the question of how Wesley grounded and defended his concern for the poor. I have hinted above that Wesley seems to have made visiting the sick and the poor a dimension of discipleship without which one's salvation is endangered. Very occasionally he appealed to the precedent of the life of Jesus and the Apostles.[13] Other times Wesley implies an egalitarianism based in the death of Jesus for all without distinction.[14] He also hints that the character of grace may be at stake: "Religion must not go from the greatest to the least, or the power would appear to be of men."[15] But as I have explored these passages, I do not think that I find a self-consciously theological articulation of the grounds for this "preferential option for the poor." In this lack of such a grounding, I believe that we see a major flaw in the Wesleyan articulation of this principle that contributed, along with other factors, to a profound ambiguity in the Wesleyan legacy on this question.

A Fundamental Ambiguity in the Wesleyan Legacy

Wesley himself was aware of the difficulty of sustaining the Methodist "preferential option for the poor" over time. Viewed from the perspective of this essay, his often-quoted words of warning to the Methodists gain a new poignancy:

> Does it not seem (and yet this cannot be) that Christianity, true Scriptural Christianity, has a tendency, in process of time, to undermine and destroy itself? For wherever true Christianity spreads, it must cause diligence and frugality, which, in the natural course of things, must beget riches! and riches naturally beget pride, love of this world and every temper that is destructive of Christianity.[16]

---

13. *Works (J)* 12:301 ("Letter to a Member of the Society," February 7, 1776).
14. *Works (J)* 12:302 ("Letter to a Member of the Society," February 26, 1776).
15. *Works (J)* 3:178 (May 21, 1764).
16. "Causes of the Inefficacy of Christianity," *Works (J)* 7:290.

Wesley pointed in this and other similar comments to the dynamic that "church growth" specialists call the "social uplift" effect of Christian movements that find new vitality in a turn toward the poor but are soon drawn away from the life of the poor by new disciplines and other factors that pull them toward the middle classes, a tendency that we may celebrate or regret depending on other commitments.

I often wonder how to interpret the epigraph from Wesley with which I began this paper. Why is it that the "greatest miracle of all" is that the "poor have the Gospel preached to them"? Could it be that sociological and cultural forces are so pitted against such a result that when it occurs it can only be a "miracle of grace"? And if a "preferential option for the poor" is a central theme of the Gospel and the biblical witness, should we move to think of those powers that pull us away from this task as the epitome of sin—as a form of "original sin" in which our desire for respectability and acceptance puts us in fundamental opposition to this basic theme?

Full analysis of this dynamic, this war within the soul of Methodism in which the movement is drawn both toward the poor and away from the poor, is beyond the purposes of this essay, but it would seem to have several layers. There is an obvious sociological dynamic in which Wesley seems to be pointing in the quotation above. Such movements, especially those with a rigorous and highly disciplined ethical standard and the expectation of a radically transformed life tinder grace, bring a new discipline and focus to life that provides a form of upward social mobility that draws the movement more and more into the bourgeois middle classes and forms of church life, a process that I have frequently called *embourgeoisement*.[17] But there is also a profound psychological dimension—a powerful urge to overcome the alienation from the culture caused by the marginalization of poverty and belonging to religious movements that are not carriers of central cultural values. This urge expresses itself most powerfully in the second and third generations among those who are reared from childhood within the life of such new movements. There is the powerful urge to "belong," to find a role at the center of the culture, and especially to move beyond the disreputable aspects of a "deprived background." The "liberationist" analysis has helped us to understand the extent to which oppression trains

---

17. I have become increasingly convinced that we need to give more attention to this issue in the life of Methodism than we have—and was pleased the hear from a friend that Albert Outler concurred in this judgment, citing my work, in a letter shortly before his death. I have developed this concept in a preliminary way in my essay, "Yet Another Layer of the Onion; Or, Opening the Ecumenical Door to Let the Riffraff In," *The Ecumenical Review* 40 (January, 1988) 87–110. This essay appears as chapter 10 in the present volume.

the oppressed to envy their oppressors and pattern their own lives after patterns of their own oppression.

As in most similar movements, there was in Wesley's legacy a profound ambiguity of countervailing forces. On the one hand, there was the model of Wesley in turning toward the poor—in field preaching; in planting churches among the lower middle classes, the working classes, and the poor; and so on. And, on the other hand, there were the profound sociological and psychological forces that pulled Methodism away from the poor—and back toward the more "respectable" established church and toward the center of the culture. These countervailing forces created a highly unstable Methodist mix that would shape the successive history of the Methodist traditions—and indeed the wider Christian world, since it is probably impossible to understand the life of Protestantism apart from Methodism. At times certain wings of Methodism would reassert, and on occasion even radicalize, the Wesleyan "preferential option for the poor." At other times certain other wings of Methodism, or the same wings in other times, would play out the other trajectory and move away from the poor. This fundamental ambiguity lies at the very heart of those currents that claim Wesley as a founder; Methodist history since Wesley must be interpreted in terms of this struggle in the very soul of our movements.

But to this constitutional instability of Methodism with regard to its relationship to the poor we must add a further dimension of theological and ecclesiastical instability in the life of Methodism. We see this conflict most sharply in the ongoing conflict between what I will somewhat reluctantly call the "high church" and the "low church" interpretations of Wesley and the Methodist experience. Perhaps the clearest illustration of what I mean here is to be found in the book *The Believers' Church: The History and Character of Radical Protestantism* by Donald F. Durnbaugh.[18] Though quite conscious of the difficulty of putting Methodism squarely in the category indicated in the title of his book, Durnbaugh does treat Methodism and provides an interesting analysis focused in the diagram on the following page.

This diagram is an effort to place the major Christian traditions in relationship to each other in a more sophisticated version of Troeltsch's sect/church typology. What is important for our purposes is that Durnbaugh puts the Methodists right in the center with arrows indicating that they may move in either a more radical or a more traditional direction de-

---

18. Donald F. Durnbaugh, *The Believers' Church: The History and Character of Radical Protestantism* (Scottdale, PA: Herald Press, 1985). This has become the classic interpretation of this strand of Christianity. The diagram is taken from p. 31.

pending on the historical circumstances and other factors in the life of Methodism in a given time. In Durnbaugh's words, "the middle ground is occupied by movements which are inherently unstable."[19] In this sense Methodism is constitutionally unstable, perhaps the most constitutionally unstable of all Christian movements, at least according to Durnbaugh.

I have analyzed further this theological "constitutional instability" of Wesleyanism in my book *Theological Roots of Pentecostalism*.[20] In one sense, I am suggesting little more than Albert Outler when he described Methodism as an "ecumenical bridge" tradition with points of contact with the whole range of Christian traditions, or when Colin Williams suggests that Wesley kept in balance Catholic, Magisterial Protestant, and Radical Protestant elements in a sort of "catholic" synthesis.[21] But the fundamental question is whether these diverse tendencies are held together in a principled matter in Methodism or whether in Wesley's time they were held together merely in the particularity of his own mind and personality, only to fragment in the age after Wesley. There is evidence on both sides of this question, and there is reason to celebrate the genius of Wesley and the Methodist tradition in attempting to hold these diverse elements together. But the point for us here is that Methodism is a highly complex and unstable synthesis in which the constituent parts are likely to fly apart into fragments, each of which has a genuine rootage in Wesley but yet has difficulty recognizing the Wesleyan dimension in the other. Thus the campmeeting tradition rooted in a sense in Wesley's field preaching has difficulty recognizing Wesley in the more traditional forms of church life rooted more in Wesley's high churchmanship, and vice versa.

Our present interests here are also more in the correlation of these two "instabilities," the theological and the sociological. Without trying to enforce a rigorous conformity to our paradigm and recognizing some counter evidence, I think it is nonetheless clear that there is a correlation between the countervailing movement toward the poor and away from them with the theological fragmentation of Methodism. It is the revivalist and campmeeting side of Methodism that has most faithfully preserved the Wesleyan "preferential option for the poor," cultivated the Wesleyan use of the laity, extended the Wesleyan openness to the ministry of women, and in general preserved a "low-church" reading of Wesley. It is the more classical and traditional side of Methodism that has brought Methodism

19. Durnbaugh, *Believer's Church*, 31.

20. Dayton, *Theological Roots of Pentecostalism*, chapter two.

21. Colin Williams, *John Wesley's Theology Today* (Nashville: Abingdon Press, 1960) chapter nine and appendix.

more into the cultural center, has pushed toward the professionalism of the ministry, has more faithfully preserved the complexity of Wesleyan thought with its classical and traditional tendencies, and in general been the carrier of a more "high-church" reading of Methodism.

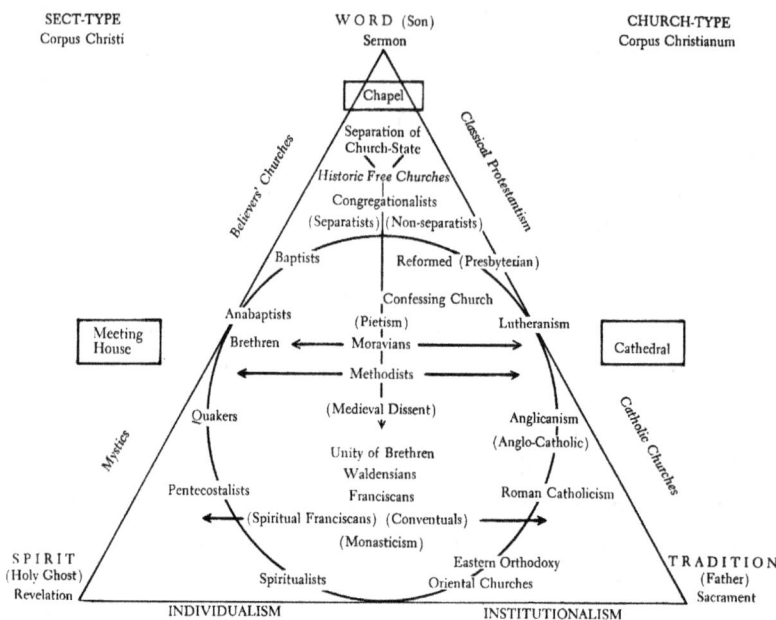

An Alternative Historiography?

In a modest sense we might find here a new "historiography" of the Methodist experience, one that would place this "war" of countervailing forces at the center of our focus to find a perspective that would revise many of our ways of reading that tradition. Such a reading might provide insight not only into the fate of our theme, the "preferential option for the poor," among Methodists, but also to wider dynamics in the life of Methodism.

I have come to many of these insights pursuing the history of the emergence of the ministry of women in the church in general, but especially in the Methodist traditions. This study has forced me radically to revise many inherited patterns of thought especially those that insist on dividing the world, especially the church world, into the categories of "liberal" and "conservative," a lens for viewing the world that seems almost unavoidable in the twentieth century and, perhaps especially in North

America, in the wake of the conflicts of the fundamentalist/modernist controversy. If we spread the Methodist traditions along such a spectrum, it is surprisingly the so-called "conservative" traditions that have been more open to the ministry of women while the "progressive" traditions have more often suppressed such a disreputable practice in their efforts to show that they belong in the center, at least until that point in the twentieth century when the basic tenets of feminism became generally accepted culturally and thus one of the elements that one needed to affirm to be accepted in the broader culture.

To understand such dynamics we need to use more subtle and complex paradigms of thinking to overcome the superficiality of the conservative/liberal spectrum. We should find other patterns of thought, perhaps in the diagram of Durnbaugh above, or in a dynamic of (perhaps alternating) centrifugal/centripetal movements away from and back toward the cultural center. Such ways of speaking would allow us more accurately to describe some of those movements within Methodism that we often label "conservative" as actually "radicalizations" of the Methodist impulse, sometimes in ways that go far beyond Wesley. The "campmeeting" traditions of Methodism, for example, are only in a few very specialized ways "conservative;" they more often are "radicalizations" of one side of Wesley that pull the Methodist tradition even further away from bourgeois church life, traditional views of the sacraments, classical theologies, "conservative" or "traditional" views of the ministry, and so on.

Such reorientations in my thinking have aided me in my attempts to offer more adequate interpretations of what constitutes the "evangelical" experience, the analysis of which consumes so much energy in our own time. "Liberal" is not a good antonym for "evangelical." This use of the words implies that "evangelicals" occupy the "center" of the Christian tradition now deserted by "liberals" who have left this space under the pressure of "modernity." This rather static analysis cannot explain the change in such movements over time, nor the rapid oscillation back and forth by such movements. Because the "conservative/liberal" paradigm helps us to analyze hardly anything historically, we should move beyond it in the analysis of Methodism itself.

With this preliminary call for new paradigms of analysis and perhaps even of a new "historiography" of Methodism, let us turn then to some historical illustrations of the playing out in history of this "constitutional" instability of the Wesleyan legacy.

The Challenge of Race Posed by the African American Methodists

Our first historical illustration is North American not only because of chronology but because it was in that context that Methodism most profoundly struggled with the question of race in the last decades of the eighteenth century. It may be part of the "epistemological advantage of the oppressed" that it was the African Americans who perhaps most clearly discerned this ambivalence of the Methodist tradition in its movement toward and away from the poor, and in many ways anticipated the historiographical perspective that I have suggested above.

It was no accident in the late eighteenth and early nineteenth centuries that African Americans moved toward the Methodist and Baptist traditions—or that the African American churches tend still today to be largely Methodist and Baptist, with the addition of the more recently formed Pentecostal tradition. Richard Allen, for example, was faithful to the Methodist tradition and thankful for its mediation of the gospel:

> The Methodists were the first people that brought glad tidings to the colored people. I feel thankful that I ever heard a Methodist preach. We are beholden to the Methodists, under God, for the light of the Gospel we enjoy; for all other denominations preached so high-flown that we were not able to comprehend their doctrine. Sure I am that reading sermons will never prove so beneficial to the colored people as spiritual or extempore preaching. I am well convinced that the Methodist has proved beneficial to thousands and ten times thousands. It is to be awfully feared that the simplicity of the Gospel that was among them fifty years ago, and that they conform more to the world and the fashions thereof, they would fare very little better than the people of the world. The discipline is altered considerably from what it was. We would ask for the good old way, and desire to walk therein.[22]

By the "semi-centenary" of the African Methodist Episcopal Church (1866) Bishop Daniel A. Payne, who became the first formal historian of the movement, had worked out an historiographical framework for the understanding of the impact of Methodism that almost exactly fits what we have developed above. At this point, however, we are less interested in his accuracy than his perspective, his experience of Methodism from the underside, so to speak. His jubilee interpretation struggled with the notion

---

22. Richard Allen, *The Life Experience and Gospel Labors of the Rt. Rev. Richard Allen* (Nashville: Abingdon, 1960) 30.

articulated by a Black clergyman at a recent General Assembly of the New School Presbyterians that "Methodism degrades the Negro." Payne's great concern in his book is to trace the "ennobling" and "uplifting" impact of Methodism on all that it touches. He takes it as a fundamental principle of history,

> that some men are apparently modest and good, while they are poor, but as soon as they become rich, their consequent influence begets pride and contempt, which lead them to acts of oppression against the weak, the poor and the defenseless.[23]

In Payne's view the Wesleys were raised up in response to the Church of England having fallen prey to such forces. The task for the Wesleys was "to convert the most vicious of the English peasantry," and to do so, "this apostolic band entered the public grounds, the alms-houses, the mines and the jails—expounding in simple speech the profound truths of Christianity. . . ." Interestingly, in Payne's view, they also "entered the mansions of the rich gentry and cultivated nobility, subjecting many of them to the *Rule of Jesus*." For Payne, Methodism is a double-edged sword, "a power exalting the lowly, humbling the powerful."[24] As successive African American interpreters have noticed, Payne's book at points reveals what seems at times to be an excessive reverence for education and something that might be called a naive doctrine of inevitable "progress." The ennobling impact of Methodism upon the "Anglo-Saxon" race is found in the production of literature, in the founding of schools and colleges, in the founding of Sunday-Schools, and finally in the support of Christian missions—in ways in each case that were particularly adapted to the poor.

Payne goes on to develop similarly the impact of Methodism on the "Anglo-American" race in a second section of the book before turning to the impact of Methodism on the Negroes. Here he repeats the observation of Allen that Blacks were attracted to Methodism: "Among the early *converts to Christ*, by the agency of Methodist preachers, were many Negroes" who "naturally joined the Methodist Episcopal Church."

> As long as this Church were in *number few*, and in *condition poor*, its colored members were *gladly received and kindly treated*, but as soon as it began to increase in numbers and wealth, so it became elevated in social position—with this increasing prosperity, the enslaved

---

23. Daniel A. Payne, *The Semi-Centenary and the Retrospection of the African Methodist Episcopal Church* (Baltimore: Sherwood, 1866; reprinted 1972 by "Books for Libraries") 6.

24 Ibid., 8.

and proscribed free Negro became contemptible in its eyes—this contempt culminated in such treatment of the colored members, as none but *men robbed of true manhood* could endure.[25]

This passage is followed by an extended quotation from the book of James about the honoring of the rich, a text that has always been a favorite of those advocating a "preferential option for the poor." In Payne's book the quotation ends with:

> hath not God chosen the poor of this world rich in faith, and heirs of the Kingdom which he hath promised to them that love him? But ye have despised the poor. Do not rich men oppress you, and draw you before the judgment seats? Do they not blaspheme that worthy name by which you are called? If ye fulfil the royal law according to the Scripture, *thou shalt love thy neighbor as thyself*, ye do well. But if ye have respect to persons, ye commit sin, and are convinced of the law as transgressors.[26]

I find it difficult to follow the logic of Payne in this section. He introduces it with a summary of the biblical argument for the equality of races, that God "hath made of *one blood* all nations of men." Payne then proceeds to argue that because of this unity of the race "Methodism" cannot "degrade the Negro"—or else "Methodism would cease to be Methodism."[27] Apparently it is certain "Methodists" rather than "Methodism" in general that have oppressed the African because Payne goes on to show how the African Methodist Episcopal Church itself has moved on to support the "education" and other forms of "social uplift" for the African American that he has celebrated among the "Anglo-Saxons" and the "Anglo-Americans." We must assume then, at least in the view of Payne, that the line of "true Methodism" moves from the first generation of the Wesleys through the first generation of the American Methodism to the emergence of the African Methodist Episcopal Church. We are left to wonder about the fate of Methodism in the next generation.

African American interpreters of Payne have not been too kind to him. No doubt Payne's reading of history is on one level naive and over-simplified, especially in its apparent commitment to education as a panacea for the evils and sins of the human race. Some of Payne's Black critics suggest that his own classism was revealed when he later felt impelled to resist the influx of the ex-slave preachers who were not quite

25. Ibid., 20.
26. Ibid., 21.
27. Ibid., 20.

up to his own standards of "respectability." Even the African American tradition in one sense experienced the limits of toleration to challenges to its own self-interest that qualified its own commitment to a "preferential option for the poor" that would reach beyond its own boundaries! But in this, it is no different than any of the traditions we will examine. We are not left with the freedom to dismiss entirely his historiography, for Payne clearly discerned this fundamental conflict at the heart of Methodism. And it is clear that race constituted one of the most fundamental challenges to Methodism, especially in North America, and that by and large Methodism failed the test. If the Wesleyan "preferential option for the poor" is an essential ingredient of Methodism or of the biblical gospel then, then Daniel Payne may be correct in his tracing of a line of "true Methodism" that finds it difficult to sustain itself over generations.

The Growing Fragmentation of Methodism: The Primitive Methodists

Race was not the only factor that led to the fragmentation of Methodism and the formation of various traditions of Methodism. The theological and ecclesiastical instability of Methodism also manifested itself on both sides of the Atlantic in the decades after Wesley's death. Some branches of Methodism played out the trajectory of the more radical side of Wesley while others drew back toward the more classical tradition and toward a more "respectable" style of church life. Methodism got caught up in the tensions produced by the spread of a democratic egalitarianism, which only exacerbated the inner struggle of Methodism between its radical push toward a "gospel egalitarianism" and the drawing back toward more traditional styles of church life and organization. On both sides of the Atlantic profound struggles emerged that led to splits over a variety of divisive issues: the extent to which democratic structures of government ought to prevail within the life of Methodism, the role of the laity in church governance, the even more radical question of the role of women in ministry, the nature of ministry and ordination in general, the value and necessity of an educated ministry, the nature of Methodist worship, the use of the prayer book and formal liturgy, the status of the sacraments in Methodist worship, congregational singing versus the use of musical instruments and the propriety of professional musicians, the structuring of the church in general, modes of financing church life, whether the "pew rental" system was an appropriate way of financing church life, the appropriateness of "field preaching," the accountability of independent evangelists to larger church structures, camp-meetings and their role in the life of the church, revivalism in general as a reading of Wesley and the heart of the Methodist impulse, and so forth.

We could take any of a number of examples of the splits over such issues. I have chosen to look at the emergence of Primitive Methodism and its conflicts with the more dominant Wesleyan Methodism to illustrate the dynamics in this period. Any selection of a case study during this period has its pros and cons. Primitive Methodism was in part (though only in part) a product of the American influence of Lorenzo Dow and his importation of the "camp-meeting" tradition from North America. This fact may confuse the matter, and divert our discussion into a debate about "revivalism," but it also illustrates the transatlantic character of most of the conflicts of this era. I have chosen this illustration primarily to move us back across the Atlantic again to the nation of Wesley, and to pick up the largest and most powerful of the divisions within British Methodism. We could approach the analysis of this division in a number of ways. Let me briefly suggest some dimensions.

On a superficial level we might be inclined to interpret the rise of Primitive Methodism primarily in terms of the conflicts between powerful personalities. There is something to be said for this perspective. Much ink has already been spilt in the analysis of the role of Jabez Bunting in the period after Wesley. Bunting dominated the development of the Wesleyan branch of Methodism so much that he became known as the "Methodist Pope." Though earlier in his life more committed to at least some forms of "revivalism" and an advocate of the nondenominational "Sunday Schools," Bunting moved eventually to resist the influence of revivalism and the camp meetings traditions, to bring the Sunday Schools and other educational efforts under denominational control, to push strongly for the value of theological education and an educated ministry, to defend a form of clerical authority against the claims of the laity, and in general to centralize authority against those like Hugh Bourne and William Clowes who in many ways represented a free spirit that resisted such moves and found themselves expelled by the Wesleyans. Bourne and Clowes moved to found the Primitive Methodists and in the polarization to emphasize the opposite side of these tensions, commitment to the ministry of the laity and their role in church governance, freedom to employ women in ministry, dedication to the structures of the camp meeting and the spirit of "revivalism" in general, and so forth.

John Kent, Reginald Ward, and others have analyzed these conflicts as a struggle between a "high church" and a "low church" Methodism.[28] At the time the polemics were often cast between "primitive" and "modern" Methodism. David Hempton summarizes the position of Ward, himself a product of "Primitive Methodism," as follows:

> Professor Ward's analysis of Methodism and revivalism has stood up well . . . The crude informality of the provincial revivalists challenged the respectable ecclesiastical ambitions of a Wesleyan elite based on wealth, connexions and education. This elite responded to revivalistic enthusiasm with the attitude that "what was needed was less revival and more denominational drill"; less expansion and more consolidation. Thus, Ranterism, which challenged Wesleyanism hard where it "teetered between form and formalism," encouraged the very thing it was reacting against–a more rigid denominationalism.[29]

This fundamental conflict was then played out in terms not only of style but also in more theological terms of visions of the church, the nature of ministry, forms of worship, and so forth.

But it is also clear that such issues, as is hinted at in the above quotation from Ward, had their roots in social class conflict. Again, one cannot absolutize such claims in the face of some contrary evidence, but most interpreters agree that the Primitives tended to find success in a level of society lower than that of the Wesleyans. This is the regular conclusion of observers both at the time and in the more recent scholarship, for example, Julia Stewart Werner, who comments:

> Where Wesleyan Methodism was deeply rooted and the Wesleyan itinerants both encouraged revivalism and permitted a greater than usual degree of lay involvement, Primitive Methodism prospered least. In circuits like Manchester and Bolton, however, whose Wesleyan and New Connexion preachers aligned themselves with

---

28. See W. R. Ward, *Religion and Society in England 1790–1850* (New York: Schocken, 1973) and various writings of John Kent, especially *Jabez Bunting: The Last Wesleyan* (London: Epworth, 1955) and chapter four in *The Age of Disunity* (London: Epworth, 1966).

29. David Hempton, *Methodism and Politics in British Society, 1750–1850* (Stanford: Stanford University Press, 1984) 92.

the middle class and stifled lay initiative, disenchanted Methodists were eager to embrace the sectarian alternative of Ranterism.[30]

In summary, she says:

> . . . the conversion tactics of the new sect, its fostering of lay enterprise, and the sense of community that characterized its societies fulfilled needs increasingly felt among the lower classes as they moved from a dependent and traditional pattern of life into the new ways of a rapidly evolving urban industrial nation. Primitive Methodism preempted a significant role that Wesleyan Methodism failed to play, and it undertook this mission precisely at the time when opportunities were greatest. In consequence, the Primitive Methodist Connexion ultimately became the preferred affiliation for many working class Methodists.[31]

In the Primitive Methodist literature that I have examined I have not found a full, self-conscious articulation of a "preferential option for the poor," but the kernel of the idea is clearly in the literature. John Petty's history describes the significance of the name as a call to "cultivate the simplicity and zeal, the faith and piety, by which the first Methodists were distinguished"—in part by "regular open-air preaching"—and to "preserve the life and fervour of apostolic Christianity; to maintain plain, pointed, and energetic preaching; to 'condescend to men of low estate.' . . . "[32] Or again, and more fully:

> It has been mindful of the apostolical admonition, 'Mind not high things, but condescend to men of low estate.' It has usually left the wealthy and the polished classes of society to the care of the older denominations, while it has sought the enlightenment and elevation of the poor.[33]

Similar themes and perspectives are projected back on the early Christian church, where the apostles were "'unlearned and ignorant,' or home-bred, possessing no extraordinary talents, and retaining much of their rough Galilean dialect and rusticity of manners."[34]

---

30. Julia Stewart Werner, *The Primitive Methodist Connexion: Its Background and Early History* (Madison: The University of Wisconsin Press, 1984) 133.

31. Ibid., xi–xii.

32. John Petty, *The History of the Primitive Methodist Connexion*. I have used the new edition of James Macpherson (London: John Dickinson, 1880) 51.

33. Ibid., 575.

34. Ibid., 2.

However one understands all of this, it is important to notice that Primitive Methodism played an important role in the emergence of the labor movement in Britain. A movement toward the poor often reshapes one's politics, even if, in some cases, it becomes a simple case of self-interest. This more radical branch of Methodism was a carrier of a more radical social tradition than the Wesleyan wing. As John Munsey Turner put it,

> Primitive Methodism brought into the union of Methodists in 1932 men and women who combined a simple, almost Quakerly style, a deep concern for social justice brought out of the struggles for workers' rights in mining and in the agricultural struggles. Certainly a deep fissure had developed between religion and labour politics which has widened since. Primitive Methodism, even if seen as an interim faith, played a role in the painful birth of modern English socialism out of all proportion to its numerical size.[35]

The Free Methodists in North America

One of the sharpest and most profound articulations of the "preferential option for the poor" emerged in North America, in upstate New York, under the ministry of B. T. Roberts, the primary founder of the Free Methodist Church. For Roberts, the equivalent of Jabez Bunting was probably Bishop Matthew Simpson, who was a symbol of the new *embourgeoisement* of the Methodist Episcopal Church. Simpson was the editor of *The Cyclopedia of Methodism,* which surely must be understood, at least in part, as an effort to put Methodism more clearly on the ecclesiastical map. Simpson was a leader in advocating theological education and other efforts to lead American Methodism toward more traditional church life. Some of this was rooted in his travels in Europe and his respect for European culture and more traditional church buildings and music. He was in many ways a symbol of the *embourgeoisement* of Methodism in the generation before the Civil War in the United States. One can almost hear the collective sigh of relief of American Methodists at having finally arrived culturally when Bishop Simpson was asked to participate in the various funeral services of assassinated President Abraham Lincoln.

This new denomination of "Free Methodists" focused many of the issues that troubled Methodism on both sides of the Atlantic in the nineteenth century. The emerging church rejected the episcopacy and affirmed

---

35. John Munsey Turner, *Conflict and Reconciliation: Studies in Methodism and Ecumenism in England, 1740–1982* (London: Epworth, 1985) 88.

the equal representation of the laity in church governance. Roberts himself was deeply committed to the ministry of women, and was profoundly disturbed when his denomination failed to support him on this point toward the end of the century. The "free" in "Free Methodism" carried a great deal of freight. It signaled the new denomination's commitment to abolitionism, a concern to "free" the slaves (the one Free Methodist change in the "general rules" was to forbid the holding of slaves). It expressed a concern to articulate a version of the Wesleyan doctrine of "Christian Perfection" that enabled the Christian to live "free" from sin. It identified a style of worship that was congregational in style and "free" in spirit, as well as being "free" from musical instruments, paid professionals, and other innovations that turned worshippers into an audience of observers. It referred to the reaffirmation of a pattern of dress that would be "free from the outward ornaments of pride." There were other connotations to the word "free," including freedom from secret societies (a response to controversies over Free Masonry), but the primary meaning of "free" was a polemic against "pew rentals" and an assertion of commitment to a system of "free pews." This commitment to "free pews" was symbolic of a larger commitment to a church that would serve the poor and structure church life on their behalf.

This "free pews" theme permeates the writings of Roberts but his thinking on the question is epitomized in the lead article in the first issue of *The Earnest Christian* (January 1860), the heart of which was reprinted as the introduction to early *Disciplines* of the Church. This article is preceded by a description of the "object and scope" of the magazine, including that,

> *The claims of the neglected poor*, the class to which Christ and the Apostles belonged, the class for whose special benefit the Gospel was designed, to all the ordinances of Christianity, will be advocated with all the candor and ability we can command.

The key article is entitled "free churches." B. T. Roberts argues that "*Free Churches are essential to reach the masses.*" In making this case Roberts carefully balances both the universality of the gospel and its particular commitment to the poor. "The provisions of the gospel are for all . . . to civilized and savage, black and white, the ignorant and the learned, is freely offered the great salvation." But Roberts goes on to ask, "*for whose benefit are special efforts to be put forth?*" In answering this question Roberts makes an interesting appeal to Luke 7, where he links his answer directly to the messianic office of Jesus:

Jesus settles this question . . . When John sent to know who he was, Christ charged the messengers to return and show John the things which they had seen and heard. "The blind receive their sight, and the lame walk, the lepers are cleansed, and the deaf hear, the dead are raised up," and if all this would be insufficient to satisfy John of the validity of his claims, he adds, "AND THE POOR HAVE THE GOSPEL PREACHED TO THEM." This was the crowning proof that He was the One that should come. It does not appear that after this John ever had any doubts of the Messiahship of Christ. He that cared for the poor must be from God.

Roberts goes on to make this theme decisive for the church and the disciples of Jesus: "In this respect the Church must follow in the footsteps of Jesus. She must see to it, that the gospel is preached to the poor." This fact is grounded in the plan of God, who "hath chosen the foolish things of the world to confound the wise." But Roberts takes another step and moves on to make this theme defining of the nature of the church:

> There are hot controversies about the true Church. What constitutes it, what is essential to it, what vitiates it? These may be important questions but there are more important ones. It may be that there cannot be a Church without a bishop, or that there can. There can be none without a gospel, and a gospel for the poor. Does a church preach the gospel to the poor–preach it effectively? Does it convert and sanctify the people? Are its preaching its forms, its doctrines, adapted *specially* to these results? If not, we need not take the trouble of asking any more questions about it. It has missed the main matter. It does not do what Jesus did, what the Apostles did.[36]

This strikes me as a very remarkable theology and a very radical position. B. T. Roberts seems to be arguing that a "preferential option for the poor" is *defining* of the true church, that it belongs to its *esse* rather than to its *bene esse*. As such Roberts has more than any other in the Wesleyan tradition (at least that I have read) clearly articulated the Wesleyan "preferential option for the poor," grounding it theologically in the messianic office of Jesus and making it defining of the church, thus raising it to the level of the *status confessionis* of more confessional traditions.

It is worth noting also the way in which the "pew rental" theme and its correlate "preferential option for the poor" was the organizing principle of Roberts' theology and church practice. The early Free Methodist commitment to "plain dress" was *not* just a form of legalism, but was firmly

---

36. B. T. Roberts, "Free Churches," *The Earnest Christian* 1 (January, 1860) 6–10.

grounded in a larger missional vision that said that all should dress to make the poor feel comfortable in their midst. Consistent Free Methodists "dress *down*" to go to church! Similarly, their commitment to "prohibition" and the Prohibition Party (for many years the Prohibition Party candidate for President in the United States was a Free Methodist) was not so much a campaign against alcohol as an issue of *personal* vice as such but rose out of a conviction of Free Methodists that alcohol oppressed the poor. Prohibition was a "social vision" that worked for a new society through the political process—and occasionally outside it, as in the axe wielding of Carrie Nation who was also associated with the Free Methodists. This commitment to the poor led to a range of political activity that one might not expect: a radical critique of capitalism, including an occasional tendency to favor a sort of "Christian socialism"; critiques of monopolies and emerging economic structures like the stock market; advocacy of the poor farmers, including forms of political activism on their behalf, and so on. And, at least in theory, there was a push to move beyond a patronizing view of the poor to a real vision of solidarity. As Roberts put it,

> A Christian goes among the poor–not with the condescending air of a patron–but with the feeling of a brother . . . In the Christian congregation the rich and poor meet together on terms of equality, and no preference is given to a man on account of his riches, or his gay and costly apparel.[37]

It is not clear that Free Methodism has sustained this commitment any better than mainstream Methodism, but it has managed to produce some important advocates of a "preferential option for the poor." Free Methodism may also demonstrate that even a profound theological grounding of the principle may not serve to sustain the theme in the face of the forces that would erode it. Nonetheless it remains true that B. T. Roberts of the Free Methodist tradition was, at least historically, one of the clearest of the Methodist articulators of a "preferential option for the poor."

---

37. *The Earnest Christian* (March, 1871) 160, as cited by William Kostlevy, "A Preference for the Poor: Benjamin Titus Roberts and the Preferential Option for the Poor in the Early Free Methodist Church," in Dunnavant, ed., *Poverty and Ecclesiology*. See also my unpublished essay that circulates among Free Methodists under the title, "Reclaiming our Roots: The Social Vision of B. T. Roberts." On Roberts in general, see Clarence Howard Zahniser, *Earnest Christian: Life and Works of Benjamin Titus Roberts* (privately published, 1957).

The Salvation Army as a Radicalization of Methodism

Many of us generally do not naturally consider the Salvation Army a branch of the Methodist tradition, but I think that it is clear that we should. Both William Booth and his wife Catherine had roots in the Reform traditions of Methodism, and William served New Connexion churches before his break. One famous picture in the Salvation Army literature shows William Booth waving to his Catherine in the gallery of a Methodist church. Booth was calling his wife to meet him at the door in a symbolic departure in impatience with church bureaucracy in meeting the needs of the poor. This symbolic shaking of Methodist dust off his feet led William Booth out of the Methodist tradition in a formal sense, but the movement continued to reveal the influence of especially the Holiness tradition of theology, perpetuated still today in the "Holiness meetings" and doctrines of the Army, particularly perhaps in the United States.

This is no accident; the Army reflects again the transatlantic character of many of these movements in that William Booth was converted under the preaching of James Caughey, the American Methodist evangelist with revivalist and holiness leanings, and in that Catherine felt called to ministry and preaching during the "four years in the old world" of Phoebe Palmer, often considered the founder of the Holiness movement. This influence of Phoebe Palmer probably led Catherine Booth to push William on the question of the ministry of women, a pressure that made the Army one of the most consistently feminist religious organizations in the nineteenth century.

The Army was more the praxeological incarnation of the Wesleyan "preferential option for the poor" than a theological articulation of the principle. By such measures as the adoption of the military style of dress and organization it managed to freeze its commitment to the poor into a "permanent sect" that gives us some continuing reflection of what many Holiness churches were in earlier years. Early Army literature is filled with polemic against the "respectable churches" and the claim to be the true followers of Christ, "who though he was rich, yet for our sakes became poor, that we, through his poverty, might become rich, and who had left us an example that we should follow in his steps."[38] Similar rhetoric appears throughout the Army literature, though not, so far as I have seen, with the same regular and systematic development of a "preferential op-

---

38. I trace some of these themes in *Discovering an Evangelical Heritage* (San Francisco: Harper and Row, 1976; reprinted with a new preface, Peabody, MA: Hendrickson, 1988) chapter nine, 116–49.

tion for the poor" as I have suggested appears, for example, among the Free Methodists.

There exist many parallels in the Army to the radical side of Methodist preaching. Booth remarks in his book *In Darkest England and the Way Out* that,

> The Scheme of Social Salvation is not worth discussing which is not as wide as the Scheme of Eternal Salvation set forth in the Gospel. The Glad Tidings must be to every creature, not merely to an elect few who are to be saved . . . It is now time to fling down the false idol, and proclaim a Temporal Salvation as full, free and universal, and with no other limitations than the "Whosoever will," of the Gospel.[39]

Here one finds many of the Wesleyan themes of a personal "gospel egalitarianism" overflowing into a social vision for the poor, though perhaps not with the same theological sophistication but with the same anti-Calvinistic polemic.

One also finds many of the same issues as the Salvation Army struggled with its status over against the churches. Was it to be like Wesley's Methodist movement before the separation, a movement of renewal and revitalization that met outside the "church hours" and so declined to become a church? Is this how, for example, we are to understand the Army tendency to avoid the use of the sacraments? Or was there a theological issue at stake, as David Rightmire argues, that the Army was a radicalization of the Holiness movement away from traditional church life and a parallel radicalization of the Holiness theological tendency to subordinate ecclesiology to pneumatology and thus reconceive the whole logic of Christian faith?[40] Such is but a recasting of the issues that Methodism struggled with after Wesley's death.

From a modern view point we often see the Army as a traditional and sentimental view of charity, typified by the food-basket at Christmas. We forget what a threat the Army posed to the dominant culture by its "turn to the poor." In one twelve-month period around 1880, 669 Salvationists were reported "knocked down, kicked, or brutally assaulted," 56 Army buildings were stormed, and 86 Salvationists imprisoned. We forget what a threat it was to conventional morality to have William Booth argue that

---

39. This quotation is found on page 44 of the "Social Services Centenary Edition" of William Booth, *In Darkest England and the Way Out* (Atlanta: Salvation Army, 1984).

40. *Sacraments and the Salvation Army: Pneumatological Foundations*, Studies in Evangelicalism10 (Metuchen, NJ: Scarecrow, 1990).

prostitution was not caused by lack of virtue but was the product of such social forces as low wages that could not support young women flocking to London or to reject the double standard of sexual morality on profoundly feminist grounds. We forget that the mere movement toward the poor to identify with the poor is often so profound a move that it threatens the whole culture and appears to be "subversive." W. T. Stead in a biography described Catherine Booth as a "socialist and something more" because she was "in complete revolt against the existing order."[41] And many of our modern day forms of social ministry have not advanced far beyond the scheme of "social salvation" of Booth with its credit unions, day care centers, shelters for the homeless and abused, legal assistance, and so forth, not to mention the various campaigns of political advocacy in which the Army engaged.

The Church of the Nazarene: A "Preferential Option for the Poor"

The Church of the Nazarene was the major denominational product of the "Holiness revival" in the United States. This revival had many sources, from the Finneyite revivalism that emerged in the increasing "Arminianizing" of New England Theology after Jonathan Edwards, through the cultural optimism of the age that was ready to receive Methodist perfectionist egalitarianism as a support for the emerging "democratic" vision in the new nation, to the Tuesday Meetings for the Promotion of Holiness in which Methodist laywoman Phoebe Palmer led many Methodists and others into a form of the Methodist experience of "entire sanctification." The American Holiness Movement emerged out of the amalgamation of such currents, gathered force during the century, found expression in the National Campmeeting Association for the Promotion of Holiness (which has evolved into the present-day Christian Holiness Association), went through a period of fragmentation at the end of the century into local Holiness associations and eventually into an agglutinative process that began to produce at the turn of the century a variety of new Holiness denominations claiming fidelity to a sort of "campmeeting" version of the Wesleyan tradition.

There is a strong tendency to describe this movement (both within and without its boundaries) as a "conservative" or "evangelical" version of the Methodist tradition. I am more and more convinced that this is a superficial reading of the situation along the lines described above in

41. See *Discovering an Evangelical Heritage*, 118.

our historiographical discussion. This movement is better described as a reaction to the nineteenth-century embourgeoisement of Methodism in North America. It is more a radicalization of the Wesleyan tradition than a "conservative" version of it, though it often identifies itself as a reaction to a perceived "liberalization" of the Methodist tradition. There is no doubt some element of truth to that perception, but I find issues of class conflict more explanatory of many phenomena than the conservative/liberal paradigm.

However one sorts out such questions, it is clear that most wings of the Holiness Movement continued some commitment to a "preferential option for the poor" with varying degrees of clarity and radicality. Charles G. Finney, the Presbyterian/Congregationalist evangelist who was so influenced by Methodism that his theology was called "Oberlin Perfectionism" and became a major source of Holiness thinking, was so committed to "free pews" that his followers founded a separate Presbytery committed to the principle. Even Phoebe Palmer, whose "parlor holiness" so shunned controversy over political issues like slavery that Free Methodist B. T. Roberts disassociated himself from her in spite of having felt her influence spiritually, was known for her involvement in the "Old Brewery," an early antecedent of the "rescue mission" and "settlement house" movements. It was explicitly acknowledged in the emerging National Campmeeting Association that a major motive was to cultivate the masses. The campmeeting was the vehicle designed for this purpose. The close affinity of the Holiness Movement with the Salvation Army (today a member of the Christian Holiness Association) is to be explained not only in terms of the shared commitment to the "Holiness" version of Wesleyan theology but also in a shared polemic against high steeple churches that neglected the poor and the masses. Similar dynamics were present in the founding of the Pilgrim Holiness Church and Holiness movements that emerged from other denominations (especially the Christian and Missionary Alliance under the influence of Presbyterian turned Holiness preacher A. B. Simpson); both churches boasted of their commitment to the poor and neglected, especially of the cities. In a sermon based on Luke 4:18–19, A. B. Simpson announced his departure from his east side Manhattan church to work among poor immigrants. But let us turn to the Church of the Nazarene to indicate a particular focusing of this theme within the Holiness Movement.[42]

---

42. I have traced some of these currents in *Discovering an Evangelical Heritage*, especially chapter nine.

Phineas Bresee was a successful Methodist pastor who precipitated a crisis in California Methodism when he requested "location" to work with a rescue mission in the face of the concern of Methodist Episcopal Church leadership who wished him to continue founding and leading successful and substantial churches that contributed more to the advance of Methodism and its financial success. It was this issue, more than "theology" or "conservatism" as such, that precipitated the crisis that led to the founding of a major new denomination in the Wesleyan tradition. The very name of the Church of the Nazarene was chosen to signal a "preferential option for the poor"; it was meant to express the commitment of the church to the mission of the "lowly Jesus of Nazareth." The first stationery of the Church quoted Jesus, "Inasmuch as you have done it unto the least of these my brethren, ye have done it unto me." And the preface to the first Articles of Faith and General Rules of the new church in 1895 clearly alluded to work among the poor.[43] Bresee was quite explicit about these commitments:

> The first miracle after the baptism of the Holy Ghost was wrought upon a beggar. It means that the first service of a Holy Ghost baptized church is to the poor; that its ministry is to those that are lowest down; that its gifts are for those that need them the most. As the Spirit was upon Jesus to preach the gospel to the poor, so His Spirit is upon his servants for the same purpose.[44]

Bresee developed from this position a polemic against elaborate and expensive church buildings and other features of the Holiness "preferential option for the poor." But such sentiments were not Bresee's alone. They pervaded the life of the early church of the Nazarene. One paper started in Texas in 1906 was called *Highways and Hedges* and boldly proclaimed that "the respectable have had this call and rushed madly on after the things of this world" and claimed that "steeple-house church people are busy chasing dollars." This paper vowed to "open up a chain of missions in all of our large cities where real mission and slum work is pushed; and the poor and destitute looked after."[45]

---

43. These developments are described in Timothy Lee Smith, *Called Unto Holiness* (Kansas City: Nazarene, 1962) 110–15, and in Donald P. Brickley, *Man of the Morning: The Life and Work of Phineas F. Bresee* (Kansas City: Nazarene, 1960) 135–64.

44. This is taken from the Messenger (September 12, 1901) as quoted in Harold Ivan Smith, *The Quotable Bresee* (Kansas City: Beacon Hill, 1983) 167.

45. I trace more of this theme in *Discovering an Evangelical Heritage*, chapter nine, especially 113–14.

Again, of course, it was very difficult to sustain these early commitments. Like the Free Methodists, the Nazarenes, again with some significant exceptions, have found ways to avoid and suppress this theme in their lives and churches. Certain wings of the church, like the organization of philanthropic agencies and some forms of urban ministry, still appeal to this history and rhetoric, but it is difficult to avoid the impression that this theme is no longer vitally alive in the church.

Latin American Pentecostalism Viewed in the Same Line

Where in the twentieth century is this centrifugal motion of a Wesleyan preferential option for the poor" being played out? There might be several answers to this question. The *embourgeoisement* of the various Holiness churches is producing its own powerful but little noticed reaction in a variety of places. One might also point to various social movements over the last century or so that have revitalized in new modes the Wesleyan "preferential option for the poor," but I am convinced that the place where the original dynamic of Methodism is being played out most clearly is in the rise of Pentecostalism in our century. We are not accustomed to thinking in these categories, but I am again convinced that we must. We do not understand the full range of Methodist experience, or Methodism itself, in a sense, without attending to this phenomenon. In many ways Pentecostalism is the radicalization of the holiness impulse within the Methodist traditions, or perhaps more recently a reaction to the *embourgeoisement* of the Holiness churches. The historical linkages between Methodism and Pentecostalism have been traced by H. Vinson Synan[46] and I have extended this argument on the theological level in my *Theological Roots of Pentecostalism*.[47]

The way in which this Methodist dynamic is being played out in our time is perhaps best seen in the South American country of Chile, where Pentecostalism is most firmly rooted in the Methodist tradition and is threatening to become the dominant religious force in the country to the point of challenging the Roman Catholic Church. Chilean Methodism has its roots in the early visits of William Taylor, the maverick missionary Bishop of American Methodism, who planted a fiercely independent form of Methodism around the world (Africa, Asia, South America, espe-

---

46. H. Vinson Synan, *The Holiness-Pentecostal Movement in the United States* (Grand Rapids: Eerdmans, 1971).

47. Various editions as cited above in note 20.

cially–after years of street preaching in the California "gold rush" at mid-century). The Methodism that Taylor planted was very close to the Holiness Movement that gave him much support and named Taylor University after him, and the "self-supporting" missions that Taylor founded were also unique and largely outside the control of "official" Methodist mission boards. Taylor's plan raised the laity to new roles, placed the missionaries and nationals on a more equal footing financially, encouraged structures of "self-support" that provided for a dimension of independence, and was so demanding that it appealed only to the "less cultured revivalist fringe of the Methodist church in the United States."[48] This naturally gave the Methodism of Chile a "Holiness" tinge and laid the foundation for the emergence of Pentecostalism in this context.

The early twentieth century brought new Methodist missionaries to Chile more in the tradition of the modern rejection of revivalism. According to John Kessler this precipitated a conflict between North American missionaries bringing a more middle class and modern orientation into a context in which the more traditional revivalism was more effective where Methodism was still located primarily among the working classes. The first decade of this century led to a number of conflicts that included the emergence of Pentecostalism under the ministry of a North American, Willis C. Hoover, pastor of a large Methodist Church in Valparaiso. Hoover was, however, so indigenized and acculturated that he was accepted as a "national," and to this day it is difficult to get Chilean Pentecostals to admit that the movement is in any way dependent on the North American scene and not totally an indigenous movement. At any rate, Chilean Pentecostalism arose rather spontaneously among Methodists at the end of the first decade of this century and from those beginnings has grown to about fifteen percent of the population, enough to compete with the number of "practicing Catholics," to use that unhappy term. Missionaries from classical Pentecostal denominations did not begin to have major impact until mid-century.

The Methodist influence is still predominant in the names of denominations, in the preservation of infant baptism, episcopal church government, doctrine, and hymns. Chilean Pentecostals often see their most characteristic practice to be "street preaching" which they understand to be in the "apostolic" line of the "field preaching" practiced by John Wesley (generally ignorant of William Taylor as a significant carrier of the

---

48. See the analysis of Jean B. A. Kessler, Jr., *A Study of the Older Protestant Missions and Churches in Peru and Chile* (Goes, Holland: Oosterbaan & Le Cointre, 1967) 103–5 and passim.

practice). My examination of the rather limited literature that I have available to me on Chilean Pentecostalism does not reveal any self-conscious articulation of a "Wesleyan preferential option for the poor," but there can be little doubt that in practice there was the equivalent. Studies of Chilean Pentecostalism tend to see the growth of the movement as a result of its turn to the flood of poor workers from the country to the city. And in this and other features, John Kessler judges that "Hoover maintained the essence of the Wesleyan tradition more faithfully than the Methodist missionaries who opposed him, and this has come to be recognized increasingly by the Methodists themselves."[49]

In this context we need also to think of the recent book by David Martin, now an Anglican but with Methodist roots. In *Tongues of Fire: The Explosion of Protestantism in Latin America*, Martin argues that we must see the rise of Pentecostalism in Latin America as the third great wave of the Methodist impulse that flowered in Great Britain in the eighteenth century, in North America in the nineteenth century, and now in Latin America in the twentieth century. Martin uses the categories of his Methodist background to provide one of the most powerful and useful interpretations of Pentecostalism to date.[50]

Such suggestions bring pause to our usual interpretations of Pentecostalism, but they suggest that to predict the future of Latin American Pentecostalism in the next century, we need to look at North American Methodism in this century. What now appears as a somewhat otherworldly movement of the disenfranchised may prove to have a powerful social impact. There are already some signs of unexpected developments.[51] It is from the Chilean Pentecostals that the majority of Pentecostal members of the World Council of Churches have come, and the indigenous character of the Chilean Pentecostal churches may give them freedom to move in new directions apart from the influence of North America. On a recent visit to Chile I was privileged to visit a congregation of the "Mision Wesleyana Nacional" whose founder had served on the *junta* of the Socialist Party of Chile in part out of his formation in the southern mining district of

49. Ibid., 308.

50. David Martin, *Tongues of Fire: The Explosion of Protestantism in Latin America* (Oxford and Cambridge, MA: Basil Blackwell, 1990).

51. For an illustration of the growing minority of ecumenically minded and socially engaged Pentecostals, see the recent publication edited by Carmelo Alvarez, *Pentecostalismo y Liberación: Una Experiencia Latinoamericana* (San José: DEI, 1992). This volume, which came out of several conferences, including one that I attended in Chile, is part of the DEI "relectura" project of the various Latin American Protestant traditions that produced the volume that so many of us have found help on the Methodist tradition.

Chile.[52] Shades of early Methodism, the Primitive Methodists, and other brands of the Methodist tradition that have often broken into a form of social radicalism rooted in a "Wesleyan preferential option for the poor"!

Some Concluding Observations

I am aware of the limitations and modest results of this study, which has in many ways been narrowly focused on one strand of a Methodist "preferential option for the poor." I have not dealt with a more modern form of such a concern as would be expressed in the nineteenth-century move toward a more holistic social analysis as expressed in the social gospel, the "social principles" of the modern ecumenical movement, or more recently the questions raised by the theologies of liberation. This is not to deny their significance, nor to suggest that there is not much to learn from them. Such currents have often had significant roots in the Methodist traditions. I would welcome such study but have felt that such was beyond the limits of my own essay. But, in this concluding section, I would like to suggest something of what I have intended here.

(1) I have suggested that there is buried in the Methodist tradition a very significant and profound history of a "Wesleyan preferential option for the poor" that deserves study and pondering. It does not answer all the questions that we have about this theme in the Methodist experience, but I believe that it speaks more profoundly to them than we might suppose. While not primarily political in the first sense, it has often given impulse to political currents and raised significant political questions, both within the movements that it has generated and in the social radicalization that has come as persons have responded to a "preferential option for the poor" and shifted social location enough to gain a real sympathy for the poor.

(2) I have intended to unsettle our thinking by celebrating the "underside" of the Methodist experience, the side that most of us find somewhat disreputable and from which many of us are in various ways fleeing, and I have on occasion deliberately used provocative language to drive this point home. For a variety of reasons we scholars are all trained to read the Methodist tradition through the lens of the dominant and "higher" Methodist traditions, but we also need to reverse this lens and read the Methodist experience from the bottom up as well. Only by doing

---

52. See on this tradition, see Manuel Ossa, *Espiritualidad Popular y Acción Politica: El Pastor Victor Mora y la Misión Nacional* (Santiago: Ediciones Rehue, 1990).

so will we ever really understand the internal dynamic of Methodism and the profound social influence that it has had.

(3) I have also tried to suggest that our readings of Methodist history might be informed by a "new historiography" more rooted in this "underside" of Methodist history, and that we may find here many clues not only about the social impact of Methodism but about the soul and fundamental intention of Methodism, issues that I am convinced remain unresolved in the life of our traditions.

(4) It should be clear that I have had an ecumenical intention in this essay. I have tried to put the "disreputable" traditions of Methodism at the table with the more traditional forms of Methodism in a way to open up a new dialogue about the nature of Methodism. I am convinced that we will understand Methodism fully only when such a dialogue takes place at a table of equals.

(5) It should also be clear that I have had a theological agenda as well. I have tried to suggest that Wesley bequeathed us a subtle synthesis, too subtle and complex (and perhaps idiosyncratic) to be kept together in one piece by the minds and cultural experiences that followed him. I am convinced that most of our traditions serve as carriers of only certain fragments of the tradition that disenfranchise and excommunicate each other as reflections of themes that cannot be genuinely "Wesleyan." We have hope of recovering the "historical Wesley" (and perhaps the spiritual inner dynamic of the Wesleyan tradition) only as we bring those pieces back together in the dynamic interaction that they had in Wesley.

(6) I have also sought to extend our view of what constitutes the broader Wesleyan tradition. For this reason I have included the Salvation Army and Chilean Pentecostalism as illustrations of the Wesleyan tradition, and particularly of the power of its "preferential option for the poor." I am convinced that we will not fully understand the full range of the Methodist experience and power until we find a way to do this.

5
The Holiness Movement

Though Dayton has been concerned with the history and theology of modern neo-evangelicalism for much of his career, his first love has always been the Holiness movement. This essay—originally published in *Greek Orthodox Theological Review* 31, nos. 3–4 (1986) 361–87—represents the fruit of Dayton's involvement in ecumenical discussions surrounding the Holiness movement and the doctrine of the Holy Spirit.

Pneumatological Issues in the Holiness Movement

Donald W. Dayton

Lost as it is between the better understood evangelical and Pentecostal traditions (between which it is the historical and theological bridge), the "Holiness movement" was one of the most influential religious movements in nineteenth century America and has produced in the twentieth century a cluster of denominations and institutions which, with the products of their missions and other forms of international impact, constitute one of the more recent "world confessional communions" to emerge on the Christian landscape. This "Holiness movement" is basically a variation within Methodism, but has in this century evolved into a distinct ecclesiastical and theological tradition represented by its interdenominational "ecumenical" agency, the Christian Holiness Association, and the related Wesleyan Theological Society. Since this movement is not well known in wider church circles and is not yet well chronicled in the studies of American religion, it is necessary to preface this study with a more extensive introduction to the movement whose pneumatology is described in this paper.

Like the evangelical revival before it and the Pentecostal movement that it spawned, the Holiness movement has been a complex spiritual movement with many subsidiary currents and eddies that make it difficult to describe simply. It was born in the 1830s in the confluence of recently imported Methodism and the older American revivalist traditions as they were finding current expression in the evangelism of Charles G. Finney, the so-called "father of modern revivalism." The motivating force was a reassertion of a variation on the doctrine of "Christian perfection" or "entire sanctification" that had been articulated by John Wesley in the preceding century. Essentially it was a spiritual movement that involved a search for a deeper spirituality or a "higher Christian life" that took on many characteristics of the more recent charismatic movement. Within its broader emphasis on process and growth within sanctification, this movement expected generally a second "crisis" or "blessing" following conversion in which a high degree of consecration and sanctification took place so that the believer was lifted to a new plane of spirituality and purity of intention that permitted a life of "victory" over sin. In the formative years before the Civil War this movement gathered force, especially in the revival of 1857–58, and, like the charismatic movement of today, broke the boundaries of Methodism to become an interdenominational spiritual revival that had wide impact among Presbyterians, Congregationalists, Episcopalians, Baptists, Quakers, and others. This interdenominational impact and growing tensions within Methodism led eventually to new sect formation and a process of realignment and new denominational configurations still in the process of taking shape.

The vanguard of this new configuration was in two splits within Methodism during the antebellum period. Both groups antedated the denominational formation of the Holiness movement proper, but both were efforts to preserve themes of original Methodism (or at least current perceptions of what constituted the themes of primitive Methodism). Such efforts to preserve original Methodism led naturally to an emphasis on Wesley's teachings on Christian Perfection (though one must, of course, notice a nuancing provided by the optimistic—and thus perfectionist—impulse of the American antebellum experience). The Wesleyan Methodist Connection (now the Wesleyan Church by virtue of a 1968 merger with the Pilgrim Holiness Church) was founded in protest against the Methodist Episcopal compromise of Wesley's anti-slavery convictions and developed a reformist platform combined with a congregationalism that reflected a corrective to a conservative episcopacy that had tried to suppress Wesleyan dissent and abolitionist activity. Similarly the Free Methodist Church emerged as a protest against the *embourgeoisement* of classical Methodism and its assimilation into traditional church life, especially the adoption of the "pew rental" system that Free Methodists felt hampered Methodism's historic relationship to the poor and forms of worship that minimized congregational participation in music and liturgy—as well as the concern shared with the Wesleyans about Methodist compromise on slavery. Both churches, as we have suggested, emphasized doctrines of "Christian perfection" and with the rise of the Holiness movement proper and under its influence moved toward identification with the larger movement.

The Holiness movement proper, especially in its more Methodistic wings, tends to look back to the work of Phoebe Palmer and her doctor husband Walter C. Palmer. Phoebe was known especially for her widely imitated "Tuesday Meeting for the Promotion of Holiness" that took the shape of a parlor "house church" meeting somewhat akin to some facets of the more recent charismatic movement. This movement had wide impact among the leadership of Methodism and eventually broadened its impact as church leaders and educators in a number of denominations came into the experience of "entire sanctification." Methodist preachers identified with the movement founded just after the Civil War a National Campmeeting Association for the Promotion of Christian Holiness, the precursor of today's Christian Holiness Association. The movement spread through independent camp meeting associations, local and state "Holiness" associations, independent mission societies carrying the message, innumerable rescue missions, and various other institutions spread across the continent and around the world in a very loose but identifiable network. By the end of the century tensions with Methodism had increased with the traditionalists accusing the Holiness folk of a new "specialty" or "hobby" that upset the delicate balance of classical Methodism while the Holiness advocates accused the Methodists of losing touch with both the teachings (especially the Wesleyan emphasis on sanctification but also more generally a broader defection from classical Christianity) and disciplines of early Methodism. The expulsion/departure of holiness advocates from Methodism, the increasing interdenominalization of the movement, and a weakening of national Holiness leadership producing a form of scattered seeding in which the fragments of the Holiness network were spread across the North American continent to contribute to the rise of innumerable new denominations.

The first of these denominations to emerge in the wake of the Holiness revival was the Church of God (Anderson, Indiana), which in the early 1880s combined the Wesleyan/Holiness soteriology with a Campbellite ecclesiology that hoped to transcend the sects and denominations as the new "Church of God." Like the Cambellite Disciples of Christ, this vision led in some cases to an ecumenical concern illustrated in the extended involvement of the late John Smith in the NCCC Faith and Order Commission. Its distinctive ecclesiology, however, led the Church of God to stand aloof from other denominations and thus interdenominational agencies like the Christian Holiness Association with which it nonetheless cooperates.

More typical of the Holiness movement and its largest denominational product has been the Church of the Nazarene which took shape at the turn of the century in an agglutinative process by which various fragments of the broader Holiness movement have coalesced to form a new denomination. This denomination, while proud of its interdenominational origins, has felt the strongest loyalty to the more conservative and more Methodistic leaders of the National Campmeeting Association and reveals in its life and ethos the profound influence of the campmeeting culture. At the same time the radicals of the period (here so-called because of their affinity with doctrines of divine healing and the rising tide of premillennialism—topics forbidden on the platform of the National Campmeeting Association) tended by a similar process to gather into what became the Pilgrim Holiness Church, a major tributary of the present Wesleyan Church. Many other similar groups were also founded at the turn of the century, but some of these moved on into Pentecostalism and others have tended to maintain a more isolated existence.

Perhaps the best known product of the Holiness movement has been the Salvation Army. William Booth was converted under the evangelistic ministry in England of Phoebe Palmer's pastor, and his wife-to-be Catherine Mumford felt called into public ministry under the influence and example of Phoebe Palmer during her several years of evangelistic tours of England in the wake of the Revival of 1857–58. In a pattern reminiscent of similar developments in America, the Booth's concern for the disenfranchised and the downtrodden led to tensions with a Methodism rapidly moving into the middle class and a separate organization incarnating the polemic against bourgeois church life. The identification of the Salvation Army with the Holiness movement has been particularly strong in the United States where the army has been active in the Christian Holiness Association and has produced in the twentieth century spiritual teachers of broad influence within the larger Holiness movement.

The intense piety and disciplined Christian lives of the holiness advocates had a special affinity with the Anabaptist and Quakers of the nineteenth century, especially those groups that felt the influence of revivalism. Holiness revivalism had great impact on certain yearly meetings of Quakers (especially in Ohio, Kansas, the Rocky Mountains, and the Pacific Northwest). These Holiness Quakers have recently come together in the Evangelical Friends Alliance and many of them have found identity in the broader Holiness movement. Similarly the Mennonites and "Dunkers" felt the influence of the Holiness revival, especially among the various antecedents of the present Missionary Church and the Brethren in Christ with their roots among the "Dunkers."

The twentieth century has also seen the emergence of a certain dynamic which has swelled the ranks of the Christian Holiness Association with new denominations that have found a "Holiness" identity without being strictly products of the Holiness revival as such. Along the lines of the fundamentalist/modernist controversy that has divided many Protestant denominations along more conservative and more liberal lines, there have emerged in the present century various conservative Methodist bodies who by their appeal to a form of classical Methodism have often preserved original Wesleyan teachings on sanctification and have thus tended to identify with the Holiness churches. Illustrative of this current would be the Evangelical Methodist Church and more recently the Evangelical Church of North America which represents largely congregations of the old Evangelical United Brethren who refused to join the 1968 merger to form the United Methodist Church. Other examples could be given.

In addition to these separate denominational groupings, one needs to give attention to the large pockets of the Holiness movement that have remained within the United Methodist Church. The most influential of the these would be the circles dominated by Asbury College and Asbury Theological Seminary (both in Wilmore, KY), but one could speak of other colleges, innumerable local campmeetings, the vestiges of various local Holiness associations, independent Holiness oriented missionary societies and the like that have had great impact within United Methodism. A similar pattern would exist in England with the role of Cliff College within Methodism in that context.

The Holiness spirituality has also had a diffusion through many other denominational contexts, especially in a more moderate form known as the "Keswick" or "victorious Christian life" piety. American holiness teachers like Asa Mahan and Hannah Whitall Smith were determinitive in the Oxford and Brighton Holiness Conventions that climaxed in the annual summer conferences held in Keswick in England's lake district. Keswick spirituality had been profoundly influential among Anglican Evangelicals and was reintroduced into America in close association with the revivals of D. L. Moody. Because of the impact of evangelists Finney and Moody American revivalism has been largely suffused with holiness teachings—so much so that holiness spirituality of the Keswick variety is the dominant piety of American revivalistic evangelicalism and the various "faith" missions associated with it from the China Inland Mission to the present. The extent to which this is still true is clear in the writings of such evangelists as Billy Graham and Bill Bright, as well as in the books on the Holy Spirit by such prominent evangelicals as Harold Lindsell and Harold John Ockenga.

One other facet of the holiness constellation deserves mention. As already hinted above, the Pentecostal movement is best understood as an offshoot of the radical wing of the Holiness movement; from the Holiness perspective it was in a sense a "holiness heresy" that was largely repudiated by the Holiness movement in spite of its paternity. As a result of this relationship, many themes of the Holiness movement and its piety and spirituality are carried along into Pentecostalism. A large block of the Pentecostal movement is also decidedly Holiness in doctrine and piety while most of the rest advocates the more moderate Keswick form of the Holiness spirituality. More attention will be given to this question below, but Pentecostalism needs to be clearly listed here as one of the currents arising from the Holiness revival.

As can be seen from the above effort to delineate the major products of the Holiness revival, the movement is very complex and includes many facets that make easy generalization very difficult. In this paper I am attempting to speak in general for as much of the movement as possible, though I will speak most directly out of that aspect of the tradition which has found identification with the Christian Holiness Association. This perspective sets both the Keswick spirituality and Pentecostalism somewhat off to the side as related but not strictly "Holiness" traditions.

The Holiness Movement and the Filioque Controversy

The assignment for this paper includes the reviewing of the WCC discussions on the *filioque* controversy as reported in Faith and Order paper No. 103 edited by Lukas Vischer under the title *Spirit of God, Spirit of Christ*. This is very difficult to do from the perspective of the Holiness movement—for a variety of reasons, but basically because I have not been able to find much literature that speaks directly to this issue. The collected works of Wesley reveal no comment on the *filioque* issue and only a couple of casual references to Nicea, basically in the context of Wesley's Anglican affinity with the church fathers and a special fondness for the Ante-Nicene fathers which he considered especially authoritative in view of his conviction of a radical decline in apostolic faith and piety after Constantine.

On the other hand, it seems clear that Wesley would have followed the Western tradition and affirmed the *filioque*. His abridgement of the Anglican thirty-nine articles of religion into the Methodist twenty-five includes 4) "Of the Holy Ghost": "The Holy Ghost, proceeding from the Father and the Son, is of one Substance, Majesty and Glory, with the Father and the Son, very and eternal God." One is not sure what to make of this appropriation of traditional language, but Wesley's commitment to the *filioque* is made clear in his *Explanatory Notes on the New Testament*. In commenting on John 15:16, he suggests,

> that he [the Holy Spirit] proceeds from the Son, as well as from the Father, may be fairly argued from His being called the "Spirit of Christ" (1 Peter 1:11), and from His being here said to be sent by Christ from the Father, as well as sent by the Father in His name.

But the situation is complicated interestingly enough by the fact that Wesley dropped the Nicene Creed from the Anglican communion service when he revised it for the American Methodists. It is not known whether Wesley had any reason for this excision other than the fact that the morning prayer service, which he expected to be used with the communion service, already included the Apostles' Creed. Wesley surely used the Nicene Creed regularly in his own Anglican worship, and as far as I know, made no critique of its use. At any rate, the Nicene Creed was not restored to American Methodist worship until the twentieth century merger of the Northern and Southern churches, long after the Holiness departures from Methodism.

A similar situation obtains for the classical systematic theologies of Methodism that the Holiness movement has treasured and the twentieth century expositions of holiness theology. These include occasional references to the *filioque* controversy, but typically in historical sections on the development of the doctrine of the trinity without entering into any discussion of the issues as a live debate. They seem satisfied to live within the Western tradition confessionally.

Within the Holiness movement proper the question does not rise with regard to the use of the creed because of the accentuating of the Methodist tendency away from creeds and confessions as normative for church life or a usual part of the liturgy. It is not common for even the Apostles' Creed to be used in holiness worship, though this is changing in some contexts, and the Apostles' Creed is contained, for example, in the Nazarene hymnal and in the latest (1976) revision of the joint hymnal of the Wesleyan and Free Methodist Churches. But the use of the Nicene Creed would be as far as I know unheard of.

It could be argued that this reluctance to use the creed is a principial, at least in the holiness ethos, which has, if anything, amplified Wesley's tendency to find continuity with "apostolic faith" in terms of spirituality and piety. For Wesley, the "apostolic faith" is to be lived and experienced rather than confessed; it is a matter of the "heart" rather than the mind and propositions. On the other hand, it could be argued that because of the "classical" and "orthodox" character of Wesleyan and Holiness thought, it has no real objection to the Nicene Creed and could well accommodate it into theology and worship. From this angle the "soteriological" focus of Wesleyan and Holiness thought shifts attention away from speculation about the internal life of the Trinity to the *opera ad extra*, especially the work of redemption, and views the Holy Spirit primarily in that context. From this perspective one could argue that holiness thought assumes and applies classical Trinitarian formulations—that its contribution to Trinitarian reflection is practical rather than speculative.

This difficulty could lead one in several directions. One might affirm the continuity of Wesley and the Holiness tradition with the classical Western tradition and suggest that it so far has no significant contribution to make to Trinitarian reflection. Or one might argue that its contribution to the discussion is to raise the fundamental question of whether the "apostolic faith" is basically a matter to be "confessed"—whether in the Nicene Creed or otherwise. Or one might argue, somewhat along the lines of Rahner, that one cannot separate the immanent and economic trinities, and that in the practical and soteriological focus of the Wesleyan tradition certain moves are made that when raised to the level of theological articulation do have implications for the discussion at hand. I have the feeling that when these issues are fully sorted out, elements of all three of these positions will find a place in the discussion, but since I myself am new to these issues and have no history of textual discussion on which to rely, I am reluctant at this point to speculate about what might emerge as a normative position on the issues raised in *Spirit of God, Spirit of Christ*, especially with regard to the *filioque* controversy directly.

On another level, however, the Wesleyan and Holiness tradition finds itself drawn into the wider issues of the discussion as they go beyond the question of the *filioque* clause itself. Here we enter debated territory where I am not competent to make an independent judgment, though I am inclined with Yves Congar and others not to attribute the major differences between East and West so exclusively as some to the *filioque* difference. But *if* there is any truth to the thesis of Vladimir Lossky, a surprising result emerges with regard to the Holiness movement. In *Spirit of God, Spirit of Christ* Andre De Halleaux summarizes the supposedly fatal consequences for Western ecclesiology of the *filioque*—as discerned by Lossky: "the subordination of charisma to the institution, of freedom to power, of the prophetic to the legalistic, of mysticism to scholasticism, of the laity to the clergy" (71–72). Again, *if* there is truth in this thesis, there would be a strong tendency in the Wesleyan and Holiness tradition toward the "eastern" tradition in spite of apparent acceptance of the "western" *filioque* formulations.

If so, this might be another illustration of the Wesleyan and Holiness tradition tendency to break the usual categories of interpretation. It has been a common observation that Wesley attempted a synthesis of the Protestant doctrine of grace with the Catholic vision of sainthood. Albert Outler has argued repeatedly what Wesley represents a sort of "third alternative" to Protestantism and Catholicism:

> a Protestant doctrine of original sin minus most of the other elements in classical Protestant soteriology, *plus* a catholic doctrine of perfection *without* its full panoply of priesthood and priestcraft.[1]

This argument can be continued in the way that Wesley has affinities as well with the disciplines of the radical reformation and its critique of the magisterial reformation while remaining within the "catholic" Anglican tradition.[2] The point is that Wesley was so "catholic" in his sources that he represents a subtle synthesis that breaks most categories of interpretation. He was both Catholic and Protestant, established and radical in his view of the church, and so on. In a similar way he transcended some of the differences between East and West.

It is clear that the Wesleyan and Holiness traditions are deeply dependent on sources outside the Western experience. The Wesleyan tradition has always been profoundly ambivalent about the Augustinian tradition of the West. While it has its affinities (especially in the doctrine of original sin), it has always resisted the implications for election and soteriology as they were mediated by the reformed tradition within Protestantism. Wesley, moreover, thought Pelagius a great saint much maligned by Augustine. A close examination of Wesley's sources (often abridged in his extended *Christian Library*) reveals that among the most determinitive were Makarios the Egyptian, Ephraim of Syria (for Wesley the "most awakened" of the early church), Clement of Alexandria, and interestingly the Cappadocians, especially Gregory of Nyssa, according to Outler the most significant source of Wesley's theology of perfection so often misinterpreted because it has been read in the Western rather than the Eastern context.[3]

---

1. Albert C. Outler, *Theology in the Wesleyan Spirit* (Nashville: Tidings, 1975) 33.

2. Cf. Howard Snyder, *The Radical Wesley and patterns for Church Renewal* (Grand Rapids, MI: Zondervan, 1980).

3. Cf. the famous, provocative footnote 26 in Albert Outler, ed. *John Wesley* (New York: Oxford University Press, 1964) 9–11.

As far as I know, these connections have not been pursued as fully as they deserve. They remain one of the highest priorities on the agenda of holiness scholarship. A start has been made in the most recent study of the Wesleyan sources by Paul Bassett of the Church of the Nazarene. He suggests that the holiness views of perfection came close to finding full expression in Gregory of Nyssa, but that the Wesleyan position is essentially a "unique fusion of a genuinely Augustinian perspective with the perspective of Eastern Christianity in the unique context of the thought and worship of the Church of England."[4] If these undeveloped hints are correct, and I am inclined to think that they are, then perhaps the Wesleyan tradition will find itself at the center of broader efforts to reconcile the Eastern and Western perspectives—if not precisely at the point of the *filioque* controversy—and we may find in the Wesleyan tradition a significant ecumenical bridge between them.

One final point deserves comment. The "Memorandum" produced by the WCC dialogue suggests that the relevance of the *filioque* is to be found in two "warnings": the danger of separating the Spirit from Christ in such a way as to allow a "Christologically uncontrolled 'charismatic enthusiasm'" on the one hand and the danger of too radical a subordination of the Spirit to Christ on the other so that the Spirit becomes a mere "power" or "instrument." If this is to be understood as the meaning of the *filioque* controversy, then we are immediately into the most essential and profound question of the Holiness movement—and the greatest ambiguity in its pneumatology. This question will be developed more fully in the next section.

Holiness Pneumatology

Here we are immediately beset with difficulties that need some mention. As will already be clear in the earlier part of this essay, there is a fundamental ambiguity in the Holiness movement that makes it difficult to determine what might constitute its normative expression. It has two formative moments—the eighteenth century evangelical revival expressed in the work and teachings of John Wesley and the nineteenth century holiness revival expressed in a variety of strands and teachings. In an earlier era the nineteenth century Holiness reading of Wesley was accepted within the movement uncritically. With the more sophisticated scholarship of the last couple of decades the differences between the eighteenth and nineteenth

---

4. Paul M. Bassett and William M. Greathouse, *Exploring Christian Holiness*, vol. 2: *The Historical Development* (Kansas City: Beacon Hill, 1985) 108.

centuries have become more apparent. As a result the Holiness movement is now engaged in a very complex theological and hermeneutical struggle at precisely this point: will Wesley be interpreted through the nineteenth century developments or will Wesley be allowed to correct the nineteenth century? The pneumatological issues are at the center of this struggle, and the final results are not in. I am, moreover, a partisan in these theological debates with some preference for the formulations of the eighteenth century, and readers may wish to take account of this possible bias.

A second problem is the difficulty of interpreting Wesley. His thought is so "catholic" (some might say eclectic) and so subtle a synthesis of apparent opposites (or at least having a tendency to conjunctively relate what many other traditions have disjunctively separated) that few of his successors and interpreters have maintained the same balance and catholicity. Wesley, moreover, has become something of a mirror, in which many interpreters have found enough of their own concern in Wesley that in pursuing that theme have ultimately given a reading of Wesley that reflects back the image of the interpreter. Thus Wesley has been claimed by both sacramentalist and campmeeting preacher, Protestant and Catholic, liberal and conservative, etc. Wesley cannot be all of these; yet he has something in common with each.

I myself am inclined to interpret Wesley as basically a soteriologically and practically oriented theologian. His thought includes, of course, other communal, world-transforming elements and so forth, but these are organized around and rooted in an individual soteriology. This, of course, can be said of much of Protestantism, especially the more "evangelical" versions of that tradition, but there are significant differences in Wesley that deserve attention. In the first place, it should be noticed that Wesley's soteriology works with organic and therapeutic metaphors. That is, the intention of God is to put the world back together, and Wesley is rather optimistic about the extent to which this can be done under grace within history—both personally and socially. The Wesleyan traditions of theology are as a result very leery of the Protestant traditions that cultivate too exclusively "forensic" categories of justification and salvation that do not include "actual" or empirically verifiable transformation. While Wesley learned much from Luther, for example, and incorporated much of his thought on justification into his own thinking, he insisted on pushing beyond these themes to a genuine doctrine on sanctification that becomes in many ways the organizing principle of his thought.

Another way of making the same point is to notice the moral/ethical axis around which Wesley's thought revolves. Wesleyan theology shares much of the critique of Protestantism—that the radical reformation, Catholicism and other critics have made at various points the danger of "cheap grace." For Wesley love rather than faith is the chief theological virtue; faith for him was clearly instrumental to love. Wesley's thought often seems to be organized around the motif of "love." What was lost in the fall is the ability to love, the essence of sin is the lack of love, what is restored by grace is the ability to love, the goal of the Christian life is "perfect love," and so on. This shift of emphasis is crucial, I believe, to understanding the inner dynamic of the Wesleyan tradition and the shape of its theological reflection. It is no accident that the magisterial reformation left great confessions of faith as its major legacy to the Christian world and the Wesleyan tradition has left instead a trail of acts of mercy and love, including great campaigns against social evil.

Such a position obviously leads to the questions and problems of "perfectionism." At this point Wesley is often described as having a "pessimism of nature and an optimism of grace" that brings into this life what other traditions have reserved to life beyond the grave. From one angle Wesley has a form of "realized eschatology" that conceives of "salvation" primarily in terms of what it means for this world—or perhaps better, that whatever salvation may be in the other world is continuation of the processes begun, and to a great extent achieved, in this world. This may be seen by contrasting Wesley's thought with the Puritanism of his time by which he was so deeply influenced. Both had elaborate schemes of the *ordo salutis* that detailed the progress of the soul from the first promptings of grace through conversion, justification, sanctification, and the Christian life to eschatological themes of glorification. Both traditions agreed on the necessity of "entire sanctification," but Puritanism reserved this for the moment of death and made it a part of "glorification." Wesley wondered why this experience could not be a part of human life and take place this side of the grave. This leads eventually to the claim that "entire sanctification" was a blessing to be expected in this life.

But the doctrine of "entire sanctification" must be seen in this larger context, as a point along the long and continuous path toward glorification. It is both preceded and followed by growth in grace and continued sanctification. It is not "sinless perfection" in the strong sense if by that one means being beyond the possibility of sinning. It is a perfecting of the ability to love according to one's capacities at a given point in one's life pilgrimage—a purifying of intentions and a focusing of the will. The Wesleyan tradition has all too often been interpreted by those assuming and importing into the discussion a foreign concept of an absolute "perfection." Here is the significance of interpreting Wesley in terms of the Eastern tradition rather than the Western tradition. It is also possible to discern in these teachings of Wesley certain echoes of the Eastern doctrine of *theōsis*.

Wesleyan pneumatology needs this background because for Wesley the Holy Spirit is to be understood primarily as the instrument by which this whole process of salvation and sanctification is achieved. Though this perspective would be disputed by some, I am inclined to read Wesley very much at this point in the classical Protestant tradition in which the Holy Spirit is the spirit of Christ. I think that it is striking that Wesley does not devote extended attention to the Spirit as such. His treatments are buried in larger discussions, and are, at least according to my reading, very Christocentric in character. For example, Wesley's sermon on "Scriptural Christianity," based significantly on the text "and they were all filled with the Holy Ghost" (Acts 4:31), describes the purpose of the coming of the Spirit in these terms:

> It was, to give them (what none can deny to be essential to Christians in all ages) the mind which was in Christ, those holy fruits of the Spirit, which whosoever hath not, is none of His; to fill them with 'love, joy, peace, long–suffering, gentleness, goodness' (Gal 5:22–24); to endue them with faith (perhaps it might be rendered, fidelity), with meekness and temperance; to enable them to crucify the flesh, with its affections and lusts, its passions and desires; and in consequence of that inward change, to fulfil all outward righteousness; to 'walk as Christ also walked,' in the 'work of faith, in the patience of hope, the labour of love' (1 Thes 1:3).[5]

The tendency of Wesley to conceive of the work of the Spirit in almost exclusively sanctification terms is also seen in perhaps his clearest short summary of his teaching on the Holy Spirit, found in his letter "to a Roman Catholic":

> I believe the infinite and eternal Spirit of God, equal with the Father and the Son, to be not only perfectly holy in Himself, but the immediate cause of all holiness in us; enlightening our understandings, rectifying our wills and affections, renewing our natures, uniting our persons to Christ, assuring us of the adoption of sons, leading us in our actions, purifying and sanctifying our souls and bodies, to a full and eternal enjoyment of God.[6]

5. Wesley, "Spiritual Christianity," preface, section 4.
6. Wesley, *Letters*, Vol. 8; also cited in Robert Burtner and Robert E. Chiles, *A Compendium of Wesley's Theology* (Nashville: Abingdon, 1954) 91.

But there is in Wesley another theme that breaks this pattern to a certain extent. It was his doctrine of "assurance" or "the witness of the Spirit" that so often got him into trouble and caused the epithet of enthusiast to be applied to him in his own time and since. Twenty years later Wesley quotes himself and indicates that he has no reason for retracting his definition of this experience:

> by the testimony of the Spirit, I mean, an inward impression on the soul, whereby the Spirit of God immediately and directly witnesses to my spirit, that I am a child of God; that Jesus Christ hath loved me, and given himself for me; that all my sins are blotted out, and I, even I, am reconciled to God.[7]

I have not studied the role of this doctrine within Methodism in any detail, but some have attached great importance to it as the real key to the growth and impact of Methodism. On the other hand it has had less consistent cultivation in the Wesleyan and Holiness traditions than the doctrine of sanctification. It has not been a major theme in my experience of the Holiness movement, though I must remain open to correction at this point.

At any rate, these two themes (a Christologically oriented doctrine of sanctification and a more directly pneumatologically oriented doctrine of assurance) indicate some of the ambiguity in Wesley's thought. The issue can be focused somewhat by raising the question of in what sense Wesley might be appropriately called a "theologian of the spirit." Many have made this claim. For example, Clare Weakley paraphrased some key texts of Wesley under the title *The Holy Spirit and Power*[8] for modern Charismatics. But the title does not sound like Wesley to me; the language is more characteristic of the charismatic movement than the Wesleyan tradition. And the content of the book is primarily about the experience of salvation and includes little direct exposition of teachings about the Holy Spirit. There are similar problems in a thesis by Norman Kellett on "John Wesley and the Restoration of the Doctrine of the Holy Spirit to the Church of England in the 18th Century" (Ph. D dissertation, Brandeis University, 1975). Upon closer examination it appears that this is actually a study of Wesley's orientation to Christian experience. It may be that any heightening of Christian experience involves an intensification of a pneumatological orientation, but I am still inclined to argue that one may

---

7. Wesley, "The Witness of the Spirit, Discourse 2," part 2, section 2.

8. Weakley Clare, *The Holy Spirit and Power* (Plainfield, NJ: Logos International, 1977).

be experientially oriented in both a Christological mode and a pneumatological mode. If this distinction can be sustained, then I think it is quite clear that Wesley falls in the former camp, though one must grant that this impulse toward a stronger pneumatological orientation is always present in the Wesleyan tradition. Again, at least in my reading, Wesley maintains here a delicate balance that was not always sustained by his followers. The work of the Spirit is firmly rooted for Wesley in the work of Christ and is essentially the application of his benefits to the human soul, but this is a real and active application through the Holy Spirit that cannot be reduced or naturalized to a mere "influence."

This question, however, sets up the problematic that would trouble the next century within Methodism and the Holiness movement, and the issue was raised even within Wesley's time by a proposal by the man that Wesley hoped would succeed him as the leader of Methodism, but who unfortunately died before Wesley, the saintly John Fletcher. By the 1770s the pattern of expecting the "second blessing" of "entire sanctification" was well established, and several figures around Trevecca College (the center of the Calvinistic wing of Methodism under the Countess of Huntingdon) began to speak of this moment as a "baptism of the Spirit" to be understood along the line of Pentecost. Fletcher especially was inclined to see in the Scriptures a pattern of history that he felt should be replicated in the life of each believer. This involved a Trinitarian division of history into the ages of the Father (basically the Old Testament era), the age of the Son (the Messianic age of the presence of Christ), and the age of the Spirit (basically the age of the church, ushered in by Pentecost and climaxed in the return of Christ). This corresponded quite well to the division of the Christian life into three stages that was emerging in the Wesleyan tradition. Fletcher suggested that pre-Christian existence corresponded to the state of the race in Old Testament times, that Christian discipleship before entire sanctification corresponded to the ambiguous status of the disciples of Christ before the full empowerment of Pentecost, and that Pentecost should be understood as the moment of entire sanctification of the disciples. It seems to me, at least, that this scheme of Fletcher involves something of a revision of the classical Protestant pattern. In the older way of thinking we remain in the "dispensation" or "covenant" of Christ—though administered by the Holy Spirit. In the new scheme there is a heightened emphasis on the Holy Spirit—we are now in an age of the Holy Spirit that is a different "dispensation" (Fletcher's term) from that of Christ. But whatever we are to make of Fletcher's thought, it is clear that Wesley objected to this scheme on the grounds that it tended to separate the bestowal of the Spirit from conversion or the beginning of the second stage. In this concern Wesley clearly expresses his identification with the classical Protestant tradition on this question, and by force of his leadership managed to suppress Fletcher's position within Methodism—though it always remained in the background and Wesley and Fletcher remained always conscious of this difference in their thinking.

More was at stake in this difference than either realized. During the period of early Methodism, especially in the British context, Fletcher's exposition of Wesleyan soteriology continued to carry the Christocentric and moral transformatory themes of the Wesleyan exposition. But it had the potential of moving in the direction that Wesley feared—to give more autonomy to the Holy Spirit in such a way as to separate the work of the Spirit from the work of Christ and to separate the coming of the Spirit in the life of the individual from initiation into Christian life. At the very least it involved a subtle shift of axis for theological thinking. This can be seen most clearly in the nineteenth century writings of Asa Mahan, the first president of Oberlin College, who wrote books articulating the holiness doctrine in both the style of Wesley and the style of Fletcher. In *The Scripture Doctrine of Christian Perfection* Mahan was careful to insist that the Holy Spirit was merely the administrator of the work of Christ. In the *Baptism of the Holy Ghost* the orientation had so shifted that he was anxious to make the point that even Christ was dependent upon the Holy Spirit, the great facilitator of all spiritual life.[9] This shift in theological axis also involved a subtle shift in exegetical foundations. Wesley had tended to ground his doctrines of soteriology and sanctification in the Johannine and Pauline texts of the New Testament. Fletcher's scheme worked better as an exposition of the Lukan texts, especially the book of Acts. But the Lukan texts lead more naturally to an understanding of the "baptism of the Spirit" in terms of empowerment for witness, service, prophecy and even miracles in a way that moves away front the distinctively Wesleyan soteriology. This struggle was played out in the background of Methodism over the next century.

Wesley's patterns of thought dominated early Methodism in America. There is a debate about whether themes of entire sanctification tended to be suppressed during this period before the Holiness revival. I am inclined to think so. It is also clear that the writings of Fletcher, however, began to gain circulation during this period—and his formulations were also in

---

9. I am preparing an edition of these two texts by Asa Mahan which will appear (in 1987) in the new series, "Sources of American Spirituality," being published by Paulist Press.

the background. They tended to surface briefly in the late 1830s among the theologians of early Oberlin College, the Congregationalist center of Finney's revivalism that by this time had adopted essentially Methodist theology with regard to sanctification. The American Holiness reformulation of entire sanctification tended to mechanize the process of its reception and move the event from goal to precondition of the Christian life. These tendencies accentuated the event-like character of "entire sanctification" and moved in the direction of Fletcher's formulation. Fletcher's formulation gained acceptance especially in the years just before and after the Civil War. After the Civil War, the Holiness movement increasingly moved in the direction of the doctrine of the "baptism of the Spirit" as the way in which to articulate Wesleyan themes of "entire sanctification" while Methodism more and more despaired of the whole issue and tended to move away from the themes of perfection that were so fascinating the Holiness movement.[10]

The Holiness Movement and Pentecostalism

It should be obvious by now that we are now discussing the theological history that led to the emergence of Pentecostalism. The interpretation of Pentecostalism has often so focused on the distinctive practice of speaking in tongues that the underlying theological substructure has been obscured. My own analysis of early Pentecostal documents has led me to the conclusion that Pentecostalism is best described as a gestalt of four regularly recurring theological themes: conversion (as understood in the revivalist tradition); baptism in the spirit with the evidence of speaking in tongues (the evidence aspect of this doctrine is diluted in the charismatic movement and is debated now within classical Pentecostalism); divine healing; and an emphasis on the second coming of Christ. Late nineteenth century Holiness theology had moved in all of these directions. The primary shift is the pneumatological one that we described above toward the formulations of Fletcher and the doctrine of the "baptism with the Holy Spirit." This led to a series of new themes—an increased emphasis on the "empowerment" of the Holy Spirit (and the consequent theological problem of how to relate this to the themes of sanctification that had been the hallmark of the Holiness movement); a greater emphasis on "prophecy"

---

10. These developments are treated in much more detail in my dissertation, "Theological Roots of Pentecostalism" (PhD dissertation, University of Chicago Divinity School, 1983), to be published as *Theological Roots of Pentcostalism*, forthcoming (1987) in the series "Studies in Evangelicalism," published by Scarecrow Press and Zondervan.

and speaking under the influence of the Holy Spirit, increased concern about "impressions" (or direct dealings with the Holy Spirit in guidance, etc.). By the late nineteenth century the Holiness movement was immersed in these themes, had adopted doctrines of divine healing and had shifted from a post- millennial eschatology to a premillennial eschatology. All that was needed for the emergence of Pentecostalism was the addition of the evidence doctrine. This might well be seen as a resurfacing of the Wesleyan doctrine of "assurance" which had served the same function in the preceding century. At any rate a biblical search for the evidence of the "baptism of the Spirit" in the book of Acts in a small Bible College outside of Topeka Kansas led to the final articulation of Pentecostal theology and the separation of the Holiness movement into those who resisted the practice of *glossolalia* and attempted to freeze the theology of this trajectory at its pre-Pentecostal stage and those who followed out the trajectory and became the Pentecostal movement.

This split led to a tremendous struggle in which the Holiness movement built strong barriers to Pentecostalism and became probably the strongest critic of Pentecostalism in the Christian world. On one level this antipathy must be seen in terms of a struggle over turf. Large segments of the Holiness movement were torn down the middle by the struggle; whole conferences were swept out of Holiness churches and into Pentecostalism. The Holiness movement (and large segments of revivalistic evangelicalism in the Keswick tradition) repudiated Pentecostalism and moved to disassociate itself from the new movement. One of the most striking signs of this was the movement in the (then) Pentecostal Church of the Nazarene to strike the word "Pentecostal" from the name of the church to avoid any confusion. And the Church of God (Anderson, Indiana) began to emphasize in its name the location of its headquarters so that on all church signs it would be clear that this group was not Pentecostal in contradistinction to the many Pentecostal denominations bearing the name "Church of God." This historical position of the Holiness movement has been largely maintained into the present. Entering into charismatic experience (especially speaking in tongues) has meant more or less instant excommunication in many Holiness denominations, particularly for the clergy, though in some cases closeted Charismatics or sympathizers have found a role in holiness leadership.

This phobia of Pentecostalism has had its impact theologically and exegetically on the Holiness movement. Most exegetes in the Holiness movement deny that *glossolalia*, as it exists in modern Pentecostal and charismatic experience, can be grounded in the New Testament. They tend to take the Pentecost account as normative and use it to interpret Paul to claim that "speaking in tongues" is a supernatural "missionary gift" of speaking in other "unlearned" (but not "unknown") tongues for the purpose of witness to the gospel. Similarly there is in the Holiness movement a certain ambivalence about any stress on the "gifts of the Spirit." When the theme is addressed, it is often with great warnings and caution about the dangers of this emphasis. The popular way of expressing the holiness position is to say that the Holiness movement places the emphasis on the "fruits" of the Spirit rather than the "gifts" of the Spirit—and that this is basically the thrust of Paul in 1 Corinthians 12–14. This basic line is, however, not without its dissenters. Howard Snyder, for example, has argued that these concerns have distorted Holiness ecclesiology so that the movement has difficulty recognizing the appropriate senses in which the church must be understood to be "charismatic" and in which one may appropriately speak of "gifts of the Spirit."

Genuine theological issues are, of course, at stake in this discussion—ones that have troubled the Holiness movement for a century now. I reveal my own sympathies with the classical Holiness movement when I prefer the sanctification motifs and the holiness emphasis on "fruits" and "love"—an emphasis which I believe best captures the thrust of the Wesleyan tradition and the concern of Paul in the key text in Corinthians. The major question that the Holiness movement faces theologically, in my view, is whether these themes can be preserved in the late nineteenth century "Pentecostal" formulations. I am inclined to think that the Pentecostals do a better job of reading the key Lukan texts than recent holiness exegesis and more appropriately work out the logic of a pneumatological orientation theologically. But I am, of course, strongly opposed in these positions, and the questions are intensely debated within the movement at the present time. Only time will tell what the final resolution will be, and hopefully what will emerge from these discussions is a new and more subtle synthesis of all the biblical themes that need attention.

Social Holiness and Political Concern

These theological debates within the Holiness movement have implications as well for the shape of social Holiness and political witness. History reveals a very complex intertwining of themes that cannot be fully explored here. But it is very significant—and deserving, I believe, of wider ecumenical notice—the extent to which the Holiness traditions have been carriers of a quite profound and consistent witness on a series of important social questions that have bedeviled the church over the last century and a half. In fact, nearly every facet of the Holiness movement has had a significant social issue at the heart of its emergence, though this has not received the attention that it deserves from outside the movement and has often been forgotten inside the movement. I have tried to explore this in more detail in *Discovering an Evangelical Heritage*, a study of the social witness of American evangelical traditions when they were more under the sway of the holiness ethos. Let me merely mention three themes of this history of social witness and attempt to make pneumatological correlations wherever possible.

(1) Deeply influenced by the civil rights movement during my college years in the 1960s, I have been fascinated with and explored more fully the question of the interrelationship between the Holiness movement and abolitionism in the antebellum era in the United States. Wesley, of course, had been profoundly opposed to slavery and had great impact on Wilberforce and the British abolitionist movement. Early Methodism in the United States attempted at first to maintain his anti-slavery witness, but soon gradually qualified it when it began to hinder growth, especially in the South. The early antebellum vanguard of the Holiness movement—in part by virtue of its claim represent the "original" thrust of Methodism—was largely abolitionist and may even be said to have intensified this original thrust of Methodism. The American optimism of a new nation born in the midst of enlightenment visions of human perfectability led to much social experimentation in this period—and Holiness themes of perfection were easily assimilated into this larger vision and led to a broad-based "reform" platform within the early years of the Holiness movement. Such reform (abolitionist, temperance, peace activism, etc.) was seen to play a role in the inauguration of the millennium whose imminence was widely contemplated in the period. (The rise and fall of this reform vision is closely tied to the rise of an intense "postmillennial" eschatology during this period before a decline under the rising influence of the fundamentalist premillennialism). Even the perhaps excessive moral scrupulosity of the Holiness movement heightened the stakes by denying the classical doctrine of the *adiaphora*—the morally neutral practices that for some Reformed theologians of the time included not only smoking and drinking, but also slavery and political despotism. For the Holiness folk nothing was morally neutral; a determination had to be made about everything, including slavery; and if a practice was determined to be sinful, it had to be immediately denounced and put away—thus immediate abolitionism. The cumulative effect of these factors was an intense abolitionism that appears among the

Wesleyans, the Frees, at early Oberlin College under Evangelist Finney and President Mahan, and within Methodism among the early editors of *The Guide to Christian Perfection.*

It is fascinating to read this literature after a century and a half. Contrary to what many would expect, this abolitionist vision was grounded in an intensification of piety rather than in its dilution. Finney was to argue that resistance to reforms was a sign of a vapid piety and to insist that taking the wrong position on a question of civil rights was a "hindrance to revival" that could stop the work of the Spirit in a church or community. The Wesleyans were proud of the conjunction of "piety and radicalism" in their midst. In fact, I have become increasingly fascinated with the parallels between these movements and contemporary liberation theologies. Some of these are on the structural and methodological level: the Methodist praxeological and ethical orientation; the expectation of a form of salvation within history; the similar function of perfectionism and millennialism in the earlier period and utopianism (whether Marxist or not) in the more recent movements; the consequent impatience with "realist" thinking in both periods, and so on. Other parallels relate to a common content: a preferential option for the poor that characterized Wesley and much of the Holiness movement; the understanding of God as a deliverer of the oppressed, and so on. The struggle against slavery led in some similar paths of radicalization. What began as a sympathy for the slave and a conviction that slavery was a sin led to acts of civil disobedience through the underground railroad and other acts of resistance to fugitive slave laws and finally to a defense of a form of "just revolution" that defended John Brown's raid on Harper's Ferry and the impending Civil War. These parallels are just beginning to be studied and understood, but there is surprising receptiveness to making many of these connections in the modern Holiness movement.[11]

(2) As has always been suggested, Methodism has always had a special relationship to the poor. Much of the power of early Methodism was its turn to the unchurched poor more or less untouched by the Church of England. Wesley's own struggles with field preaching and his own turn to the miners and other workers required a profound resocialization for this

---

11. A significant beginning to such discussions may be found in Theodore Runyon (ed.), *Sanctification & Liberation* (Nashville: Abingdon, 1981), the proceedings of the sixth Oxford Institute of Methodist Theological Studies, July 18–27, 1977, which was also noteworthy for bringing together in a common arena theologians of both the holiness movement and classical Methodism. Articles arguing that Wesley was a sort of "liberation theologian" may be found a short-lived periodical *The Epworth Pulpit* founded largely by students and faculty of the Nazarene Theological Seminary in Kansas City.

Oxford don. But Wesley came to understand that Methodism was called to the poor and argued that her spiritual vitality was bound up in keeping this task at the center of her vision. Historians are still trying to sort out the role of the Methodism in the modernizing of English society and the rise of the trade unions in the nineteenth century. The Holiness movement arose in the period of Methodism's emergence into the middle class and into traditional church life—and largely in response to that dynamic. It is becoming clearer that nearly every facet of the Holiness movement incarnated in its origins some form of a "preferential option for the poor." In antebellum America this was closely tied up with the anti-slavery struggle. The Free Methodist Church was especially articulate about this theme in its struggle against the pew rental system that was increasingly adopted within Methodism to finance the more expensive churches that were being built. Founder B. T. Roberts proclaimed these principles in the founding editorial of his journal *The Earnest Christian*, arguing from the Lukan texts that are so much used today that Christ's own turn to the poor was the crowning proof of his messiahship and that following the model of Christ was of the *esse* rather than the *bene esse* of the church. In his words, "There are hot controversies about the true church. . . . It may be that there cannot be a church without a bishop, or that there can. There can be none without a gospel, and a gospel for the poor."

Phoebe Palmer, who represents in many ways the mid-century dilution of social reform in the Holiness movement (especially the more radical anti-slavery struggle) and a turn to a more privatized and experiential "parlor" version of sanctification, was nonetheless also a carrier of this theme. She was deeply involved with the "ladies of the mission" in transforming the "Old Brewery" into an inner-city mission that became the model for much Protestant urban ministry in New York City. Part of the explicit rationale for the adoption of the "campmeeting" in mid-nineteenth century was that it was a form adapted to maintaining contact with the "masses" that Methodism was perceived to be losing touch with. The Salvation Army is, of course, the epitome of this impulse and a continuing symbol of the churches' identification with the poor. Similar themes dominated the formation of late nineteenth century Holiness churches. In early years many of these churches were little more than a loosely affiliated string of rescue missions in various American cities. The event that precipitated the founding of the Church of the Nazarene was the request of Phineas Bresee that he be "located" so that he could work with an inner city mission in the Los Angeles area while the Methodists were anxious to have his skills in building large churches. The founders of the Pilgrim

Holiness Church were proud of the fact that they were willing to go into the "darkest jungles" as missionaries and into the heart of the cities as mission workers. The illustrations could be multiplied indefinitely—as could the appeals to the fourth chapter of Luke so popular today in defending a "preferential option for the poor."

This theme deserves further analysis. In the later era of the Holiness movement the call to "preach good news to the poor" was especially attractive because of its pneumatological grounding in Luke 4:18 ("The Spirit of the Lord is upon me, because he has anointed me to preach good news to the poor") and took primarily the form of evangelism—but an evangelism that breaks many of our stereotypes. While it was not a direct form of political and social action, it often led in that direction. The act of moving to be with the poor often led to a new awareness of their physical condition and often a political radicalization. It is too easy today to overlook the radical side of even the temperance movement with its effort to transform the debilitating environment in which too many poor people were reared. And the tendency to see the Salvation Army today as illustrative of the forms of Christian "relief" that need to be transcended by direct political action fail to understand the broader political commitments of the Army in the profundity of its holistic involvement and fail to grasp the radicality of its vision in its own time. Obviously these issues need fuller exploration than can be given here. My basic purpose at this point is to draw attention to a significant witness to a form of a biblically grounded "preferential option for the poor."

(3) In view of the debates about the question in the churches today, it is perhaps worth noting the consistency with which the Holiness movement has been committed to the ordination and the ministry of women. Again this practice was foreshadowed in Wesley's time by his openness to a more informal ministry of women. Methodism in America struggled with the question throughout the nineteenth century but did not proceed with the full ordination of women until the middle of the twentieth century. It is, however, the Holiness movement that competes with Unitarianism perhaps for the honor of first opening up the ordained ministry to women. It is amazing the number of events in the rise of feminism and the ministry of women that are associated with facets of the Holiness movement; so much so that the history of this question will never be fully understood until this fact is taken into account—and much current historiography on this question is vitiated by its failure to do so.

The first woman to be ordained was Antoinette Brown, who though she later became a Unitarian was originally a follower of Finney and educated at Oberlin College. Oberlin was the first co-educational college and for that reason educated many of the leaders of the nineteenth century feminist movement. The preacher of Antoinette Brown's ordination sermon was Luther Lee, a founder of the Wesleyan Methodist Church. The first Woman's Rights Convention in 1848 was held in the Wesleyan Church in Seneca Falls. Antoinette Brown was ordained in 1853 and the Wesleyans began the practice of ordaining women soon thereafter. B. T. Roberts, founder of the Free Methodist Church, wrote *Ordaining Women* (1891) and other defenses of the practice, but his church did not follow his advice until the mid–twentieth century. Many agitators for the ministry of women in other contexts, such as Frances Willard within the Methodist Episcopal Church, were persons who had fallen under the influence of the Holiness movement during this period.

Historians have noticed the close linking of abolitionism and feminism in the nineteenth century and the civil rights movement and feminism in the twentieth. In the last century it was natural to extend the anti-slavery hermeneutic to women, and Galatians 3:18 seemed to provide an obvious rationale for doing so. The Holiness commitment to abolitionism led many to take this path and defend in the antebellum period a strong doctrine of sexual equality that was supported by other Holiness theological themes. While some traditions found in Genesis 3:16 a curse that prescriptively determined an inferior status of women for all time, the Holiness movement was more inclined to see a description of the sinful state out of which we are being redeemed. As grace effects its transformation of persons and the world, women are restored to equality with men as the new "Eve." And even if Paul may be proved to have opposed the ministry of women (a doubtful claim in the first place to much of the Holiness movement), grace is so much at work that this is not the same world, and what may have been inappropriate then might very well be appropriate now. And as has often been the case, the turn to religious experience in Methodism and the Holiness movement proved to be a great leveler that took religious authority out of the hands of the privileged and the educated and put it in the hearts of those who respond to the grace of God.

This openness to the ministry of women was, if anything, radicalized by the Holiness turn to pneumatological orientation in the late nineteenth century. After all, the account of Pentecost proclaimed that "in the latter days . . . your sons and your daughters shall prophesy." And if one were not convinced by the antebellum arguments for the ministry of women, it was now clear that this new practice as a sign of the "latter day" outpouring of the Spirit of which the Holiness movement was the harbinger.

Very significantly Phoebe Palmer's book, *The Promise of the Father* (1859) was both one of the first to fully adopt the pneumatological exposition of "entire sanctification" and also essentially a defense of the ministry of women—required, of course, by her own practice. We have indicated the impression that Phoebe Palmer made on Catherine Booth about this time, but one result was that the Salvation Army became arguably the most consistently egalitarian Christian organization to date. At any rate, with the rise of the pneumatological language came increasing commitment to the ministry of women—so that by the end of the century the practice was a hallmark of the movement. In some groups, such as the Church of the Nazarene and the Pilgrim Holiness Church, the percentage of women achieved was about one third earlier in this century. Interestingly enough, with the not unexpected decline of intense pneumatological focus and the twentieth century *embourgeoisement* and assimilation of the Holiness churches to more traditional forms of church life, the ministry of women, while still largely accepted, has declined—though there is renewed commitment today to the practice as a hallmark of the Holiness movement.

Other illustrations of the resulting social commitment of the Holiness movement could be given, but these illustrations should suffice to indicate something of the subtle interaction of the Wesleyan soteriology and Holiness pneumatology with these issues to produce, so it seems to me, a series of models of Christian social witness worth much more exploration.

Response #1

Melvin Easterday Dieter

Don Dayton and I have enjoyed more than thirty-five years of academic collegiality and personal friendship which have issued in a complex web of shared-in-common experiences: conferences, travel, maniacal bibliophilia, committee meetings, preaching, teaching, writing, lecturing, planning, debating, etc. There are many incidents in that mix that merit mention here, but the limits of this format and the continuing complexities of the issues Don addressed and their importance for Wesleyan and related studies will allow no meaningful comment on the content of the paper itself. Consequently what is said is couched more in the spirit of interpersonal "fest" than in extended scholarly "schrift."

One observation will have to suffice in relation to the whole historiography of explications such as this of the relationship of Wesley, pneumatology, and Wesleyan related movements. In the paper Don recognizes its importance, but it is worth reiterating here because of its centrality to Wesleyan studies as a whole. The struggle to establish an authentic Wesleyanism follows a pattern reaching back into Methodism's history long before Don gave it more contemporary focus and now extends itself with increasing complexity throughout an increasingly pluralistic Wesleyan community. Let me use an analogy to give it further illustration. Some readers will remember the format of the once popular television series "To Tell the Truth." Contestants did their best to present proof of a certain personal identity. A panel of judges probed their claims and defenses, but there came the point when all arguments of the claimants, and all answers to the questions of the inquiring judges, were laid bare by the truth when the master of ceremonies asked, "Will the real (John Wesley shall we say) please stand up?"

Numerous politically, ecclesiastically and critically conditioned "Wesleys" have been giving their stories and credentials, making every effort to prove their propositions. But, unfortunately the "real Mr. Wesley" cannot stand up and the production cannot end. Like any influential historic figure, who he really was and is is always subject to new historical evidence, the most recent in this case being some newly researched testimony by his cohort and friend John Fletcher. Hopefully, as the testimony continues we will have a clearer picture of who the "real" John Wesley was, with the fervent hope that in the process the Wesley we find will not again be laid aside for an unfit peer not worthy of a place in our dialogue as he was by a host of his followers for almost fifty years at the turn the nineteenth century.

The other line of reflection prompted by the review of this article has to do with the setting in which this paper was given. Don was using his presence on this occasion not only to present his thesis propositions on the significance of the doctrine of the Holy Spirit but also to promote his efforts to challenge the Wesleyan/Holiness movement to move its story beyond its parochial concerns into broader ecumenical settings, even with traditions who historically and currently have been mutually suspicious of one another. At the same time he was inviting the wider religious and theological circles to give representatives of the holiness tradition a voice in a variety of inter-faith dialogues. This was his milieu and was representative of one of his most important contributions to all of us, in short, his persistent ecumenical instincts.

I became aware of Don's ecumenical bent with our first personal and academic contacts around 1970. He and I were attending the annual graduate student consultations sponsored by the Free Methodist's department of higher education at the Wainright House in Rye, New York. There, under the leadership of Dr. Arthur Zahniser, the Free Methodist's denominational secretary for higher education, the church's young doctoral candidates in religious and philosophical studies, together with a few graduate students from related holiness churches such as Don (a Wesleyan Methodist), joined selected faculty members of the religion departments of the Free Methodist Colleges, and the Free Methodist Foundation Seminary Foundation at Asbury Seminary, for a weekend of community dialogue and spiritual renewal. Art Zahniser generously opened the annual Rye Consultations to full Wesleyan participation and eventual co-sponsorship. "Rye" proved to be a unique ecumenical setting for initiating better dialogue and understanding between the two Wesleyan/Holiness denominations and a whole generation of their up-and-coming academics, retaining many of them for the denominations at a critical stage in Wesleyan/Holiness denominational and educational development. I believe Don may have been the person who once suggested that the Wesleyans really were accepted into this select group of Free Methodists as much for the popularity and continuing significance of the annual Saturday night pizza party which they sponsored as for any other meaningful contribution to the event.

The fact that Don was already actively involved in the Free Methodist's "Rye" circle when his fellow Wesleyans showed up was only one of many indicators of the ecumenical bent, which has marked his commitments and involvements throughout his academic life. In the mid seventies our paths met again in another ecumenical setting. Vincent Synan invited both of us as representatives from the Wesleyan/Holiness academic community to take part in a symposium on the historical roots of Pentecostalism held at the Church of God School of Theology in Cleveland, TN. It was a meeting with multiple pioneer ecumenical undercurrents. The direct engagement of Pentecostal and Wesleyan historians and theologians was still a rare event in itself. Don presented a paper that incorporated his thesis on the development of Pentecostal themes in the nineteenth century holiness revival that would later be more fully explicated in his *Theological Roots of Pentecostalism*. The Catholic secretary of the Pentecostal-Catholic interfaith dialogue group was there along with Pentecostal ecumenist David Duplessis. At the time, the Church of God (Cleveland, TN) was looking forward to its one-hundredth anniversary and many of its younger scholars were renewing the church's interest in its Wesleyan/Holiness roots.

During much of this period Don's position as promotional secretary of the Wesleyan Theological Society served his ecumenical interests well. He wrote numerous articles introducing the broader American religious society to the significance of the Wesleyan/Holiness revival movement and churches in American history and culture. His feedback as promotional secretary to the WTS community also shaped the outreach and influence of the society. He and other members of the society became regular participants in the Ecumenical and Cultural Institute at St. Cloud, Minnesota along with Catholic, Lutheran and other mainline traditions.

As already indicated, the presentation of the paper at hand at a consultation on the Holy Spirit sponsored by the Faith and Order Commission was the most significant fruit of his ecumenical activities on behalf of the Wesleyan/Holiness tradition. Through his personal efforts and with the encouragement of Wesleyan Theological Society he became a regular representative/participant for the society in the ongoing affairs of the commission.

Finally, I could never conclude any personal comments on Don's contributions to Wesleyan and Holiness scholarship without expressing again my own personal gratitude to him and his co-editor Ken Rowe for choosing to publish my history of the nineteenth century holiness revival as the inaugural volume for a new series of proposed publications (1980) on Wesleyan evangelicalism. Their interest moved that work into the mainstream of nineteenth century religious studies and led to many of the good things that have come along and continue to engage my academic life and ministry in ways that have helped to keep me only semi-retired over these past sixteen years.

Response #2

David Bundy

The Holiness Traditions and Orthodoxy

DON Dayton has devoted himself to the study of theology and to its practical implications for the life of Christian communities around the world. He has cast his net widely as the essays collected in this volume reveal. Dayton, like his mentors John Wesley and Karl Barth, is a very learned man who has drawn upon the resources of biblical and Christian literature to understand the Christian faith and to present it to the world.

It was in the summer of 1970 when I arrived at Asbury Theological Seminary as a new student that I met Don Dayton. He had a Masters of Divinity from Yale and was working as Collection Development Librarian at the B. L. Fisher Library. It was an ideal position for his wide ranging bibliographical knowledge. One of his colleagues at the Library was D. William (Bill) Faupel who was working on his M.L.S. at the University of Kentucky. Susan Schultz was the director of the Library. I began working in the Library as a work-study student that August. Over lunches and occasional conversations, we came to know each other and a friendship was formed that has lasted through the decades. One of my first jobs was to write the first drafts for entries in a small volume entitled *Resources for Research* that was edited by Dayton.[1]

At the time I met Don, he was planning to move on to write a dissertation on Karl Barth. He was invited by Susan Schultz to write his *The American Holiness Movement: A Bibliographical Introduction* (1971). Faupel followed with *The American Pentecostal Movement: A Bibliographical Introduction* (1972) and I tagged along with *Keswick: A Bibliographic Introduction to the Higher Life Movements* (1975). Those essays brought us all into interaction with the larger Wesleyan/Holiness/Pentecostal tradi-

---

1. Donald W. Dayton, *Resources for Research* (Wilmore, KY: B. L. Fisher Library, 1971).

tions. Dayton went to the University of Chicago to produce *The Theological Roots of Pentecostalism*.[2] Faupel went to Birmingham and I to Louvain. Don visited me in Louvain on various occasions and we trouped across Europe visiting bookstores. Indeed, we have visited bookstores together on three continents!

The essay on "Pneumatological Issues in the Holiness Movement"[3] ties together a number of Dayton's interests. It is *multo in parvo*. For years he thought and wrote about the uses of the Holy Spirit and Holy Spirit related language in Wesleyan, Holiness and Pentecostal theology.[4] He has also been a committed active ecumenist and has been a longtime participant in Faith and Order where the relationships of Orthodoxy and the various streams of Western Christian thought have been a constant matter of concern. This essay works to place the Holiness traditions within the ecumenical structures of the Christian tradition, using the activist pneumatology of the tradition as a focus for his reflection.

Don Dayton, as indeed many have been, was influenced by the suggestions of Albert Outler who first called attention to the importance of Eastern Christian theologians for Wesley's thought. It was Outler who first suggested that the source connections might have implications for ecumenical discussions between these Christian traditions.[5] Don has also been interested in the relationships of Orthodoxy and the various streams of Wesleyan thought. Wesley drew upon a variety of sources to think about theology. One of the groups of writers used by Wesley was a group that can be described as early eastern Christian writers. These writers wrote in Syriac or Greek. They wrote in Alexandria, Asia Minor and Syria. They shared a perspective that Wesley found compatible with his own: the

2. Donald Dayton, *The Theological Roots of Pentecostalism* (Studies in Evangelicalism, 5; Metuchen: Scarecrow, 1987).

3. Donald Dayton, "Pneumatological Issues in the Holiness Movement" *Greek Orthodox Theological Review* 31(1986) 361-387.

4. See one of his early studies: Donald W. Dayton, "The doctrine of the Baptism of the Holy Spirit: its emergence and significance," *Wesleyan Theological Journal* 13 (1978) 114-126.

5. Albert Outler, *John Wesley* (Oxford: Oxford University Press, 1964) 9, note 26. It was this footnote that led to my initial interest in early Eastern Christianity. See the more developed discussion in Albert C. Outler, "The Place of Wesley in the Christian tradition," in *The Place of Wesley in the Christian Tradition: essays delivered at Drew University in celebration of the commencement of the publication of the Oxford edition of the Works of John Wesley*, ed. Kenneth Rowe (Metuchen: Scarecrow, 1976), and Albert Outler, "John Wesley's Interest in the Early Fathers of the Church," in *The Bulletin published by the committee on archives and history of the United Church of Canada in collaboration with Victoria University* 29 (1980–1982) 5-17.

vision that sanctification, or *theosis*, is the goal of the Christian life. They had reflected intensely on the restoration of the image of God to fallen humanity. Wesley found them mentors in his own quest and he recommended them to others!

Following Outler, attention has been paid to the issue of Orthodoxy and the Methodist family. Authors have attempted to establish and define the historical connection with varying degrees of sophistication. The work of Ted Campbell was an important, careful and sophisticated contribution toward identifying ways in which Wesley understood himself to have appropriated materials from the church of "antiquity."[6]

Others, including this author, have insisted that the appropriation by Wesley of the insights of Orthodox writers needs to be understood in light of their mediation through the English Anglican tradition of scholarship on early Christian history and texts.[7] Randy Maddox has demonstrated that a number of Eastern Christian theological themes pervade Wesleyan theology.[8] Others wrote arguing for a direct and simple connection between Wesley and his Eastern Christian Sources; their tendency was to treat the complex historiographical questions of influence very simplistically.[9] These essays did not generally address issues of the ecumenical identity of the Holiness and Pentecostal movements.

6. Ted A. Campbell, *John Wesley and Christian Antiquity: Religious Vision and Cultural Change* (Nashville: Kingswood, 1991). Campbell's approach contrasts with the discounting of those influences by Henry D. Rack, *Reasonable Enthusiast; John Wesley and the Rise of Methodism* (2 ed.; Nashville: Abingdon, 1992).

7. Four essays were published in the *Wesleyan Theological Journal* 36 (1991) including my "Christian Virtue: John Wesley and the Alexandrian Tradition," *Wesleyan Theological Journal* 26(1991) 139–63. A few years ago an essay of mine, "Approaches to Theosis: Orthodox, Holiness and Pentecostal" was presented in my absence to a ecumenical gathering in Prague by Don Dayton. A few years later I presented as my Wesleyan Theological Society Presidential address, "Visions of Sanctification: Orthodox Themes in the Methodist, Holiness and Pentecostal Traditions," *Wesleyan Theological Journal* 39 (2004) 104–36.

8. Randy Maddox, *Responsibility and Grace: John Wesley's Practical Theology* (Nashville: Kingswood, 1994); see especially, *idem*, "John Wesley and Eastern Orthodoxy: Influences, Convergences and Divergences," *Asbury Theological Journal* 45:2 (1990) 29–53.

9. Thomas E. Brigden, "Wesley and the Homilies of Macarius," *Proceedings of the Wesley Historical Society* 8 (March 1911) 6–7; G. S. Wakefield, "La littérature du Désert chez John Wesley," *Irenikon* 51 (1978) 155–70, David D. Ford, "Saint Makarios of Egypt and John Wesley: Variations on the Theme of Sanctification," *Greek Orthodox Theological Review* 33 (1988) 285–312 (this essay is an anti-Holiness and anti-Pentecostal apologetic), Howard A. Snyder, "John Wesley and Macarius the Egyptian," *Asbury Theological Journal* 45 (1990) 55–60. See especially, Ernst Benz, *Die protestantische Thebais: Zur Nachwirkung Makarios des Ägypters im Protestantismus der 16. und 17. Jahrhunderts in Europa und Amerika* (Wiesbaden: Verlag der Akademie der Wissenschaften und der Literatur, 1963).

The ecumenical question is crucial for the future. One of the pressing issues for the Holiness and Pentecostal movements is to establish their identities with regard to the larger Christian world. There have been assertions that these two interconnected religious movements constitute a fourth way of Christianity in parallel with the older Orthodox, (Roman) Catholic, and Protestant traditions. Others have argued that both are thoroughly rooted in Reformation Protestantism and Pietism with minimal influence from other sources.[10] Another scholarly tradition has insisted that the Holiness and Pentecostal movements are an expression of American Fundamentalism.[11] Míguez Bonino has suggested that this is the new face of Protestantism.[12] Others want to see the Holiness and Pentecostal traditions as expressions of the Anglican tradition that were corrupted during their nineteenth century American experience.

Dayton has realized that there are no simple answers to the historical and ecumenical questions. He notes the ambiguities of the Methodist and Holiness traditions toward the Western Augustinian traditions as transmitted through the Catholic and Anglican theologians, but has also observed that they are quite Western in their modes of theological reflection and in their commitments to the "*filioque*" of the Western Church. He suggests that pneumatology and soteriology may be better places for beginning an ecumenical discussion between Holiness and Orthodox than the creeds. He has celebrated that Holiness Movement's appropriation of Wesleyan theological impulses and the activist social tradition that was central to the identity of that movement. His summary of the Holiness history and theology places that social activism directly within the theological structures of Wesley and the nineteenth century American Holiness theologians, arguing that the logic of their pneumatology and soteriology compelled them toward their social agendas.

It is here that the proposal of ecumenical discussions between Orthodox and Holiness traditions may have another point of difficulty. The Orthodox, until their recent experiences in England, the Americas, and Africa, have relied on the power of the State to maintain discipline

---

10. For example: Karla Poewe, "Introduction: the Nature, Globality, and History of Charismatic Christianity," in *Charismatic Christianity as a Global Culture*, ed. Karla Poewe (Studies in Comparative Religion; Columbia, SC: University of South Carolina Press, 1994).

11. For example: Steve Brouwer, Paul Gifford and Susan D. Rose, *Exporting the American Gospel: Global Christian Fundamentalism* (New York, London: Routledge, 1996).

12. José Míguez Bonino, *Rostos del protestantismo latinoamericano* (Buenos Aires: Nueva Creación, 1995).

and a monopoly of religious power (as did Catholics and European State Churches until recently). The Holiness and Pentecostal Churches have never relied on the power of the State; indeed, they have generally found themselves at odds with the powers of the State, a condition that continues in many places in the world. These ecclesiological issues become central, it would appear, to any ecumenical conversations. It will be interesting to see if the foci of ecumenical discussion suggested by Dayton can work. If they do, it will be because Orthodox and Holiness/Pentecostal theologians find a way to address meaningfully the very sensitive issues of ecclesiology and state as theologians deliberate on the meaning of *theosis* for the totality Christian life.

Donald Dayton has contributed significantly to that possibility in this essay which deservedly has been selected from among his many to present his lifetime of scholarly reflection. It is an important essay the implications of which will take generations of theologians to fulfill.

6
Pentecostal Studies

Dayton's groundbreaking study, *Theological Roots of Pentecostalism*, made explicit a thesis he had been developing for over ten years in various essays and conference presentations. Throughout that time, and especially after the publication of *Theological Roots of Pentecostalism*, Dayton has been at the center of a debate about the origins and nature of Pentecostalism.

The following previously unpublished essay was given at the Wesleyan Theological Society in 2000 and is Dayton's response to criticisms from various camps regarding his theses about the origins and theological "gestalt" of Pentecostalism. The essay sheds more light on Dayton's work by revealing some of his key methodological assumptions and recounting the history of reception of his work both before and after *Theological Roots of Pentecostalism* was published. It also highlights an ongoing debate between Dayton and Larry Wood on the interpretation of John Wesley and John Fletcher that has been carried on in the pages of *Pneuma: The Journal of the Society for Pentecostal Studies*.

Revisiting the "Baptism with the Holy Spirit" Controversy

A Response to My Critics

Donald W. Dayton

Introduction

Two factors make this an appropriate occasion to revisit the "baptism with the Holy Spirit" controversy that troubled this society in the 1970s and 1980s. In the first place, it seems that we are entering a new phase of the controversy in the work of Larry Wood of Asbury Theological Seminary. His plenary paper at our Cleveland, Tennessee meeting, and the special issue of the *Asbury Theological Journal* (Spring, 1998) that he made available there, argued that John Fletcher's doctrines of "dispensations" and "Pentecostal sanctification" were appropriate extensions of the thought of Wesley and even approved by him. Though Larry Wood did not make my work the centerpiece of his critique, it was obvious to many in the audience that the work that culminated in my *Theological Roots of Pentecostalism* was under challenge—so much so that I was asked in that session to respond and was later offered the chance to respond formally at the next meeting or in the *Wesleyan Theological Journal*. I demurred at the time, not wishing to undertake such debate. Since then the discussion has heated up with the recent exchange of Randy Maddox and Larry Wood in the *WTJ* (Fall, 1999) and with the anticipated publication with Oxford University Press of a 500-page manuscript by Larry Wood expanding these articles. It is already being reported to me from various circles that this book constitutes a definitive refutation of several aspects of my work. In light of such claims I have felt it incumbent on me to make some sort of response. In preparation for this paper I spent a month in Bristol, England, at the Charles Wesley Heritage Center, currently directed by one of my doctoral students, to test again my understanding of the Wesleyan sources. I then taught my way through the material in a doctoral seminar at Drew, where I asked the students to test my reading in the light of the available materials from Larry Wood. So far I have not seen reason to change my reading and need to account for that conclusion.

Secondly, I have always been frustrated that the substantial and theological issues raised in my book (as opposed to the historical questions) have not been discussed as much as I had wished. This occasion provides the opportunity to attempt to redirect the discussion. Since these issues are to a great extent Trinitarian, this meeting provides an appropriate context in which to highlight such issues.

The Context and Origins of My Work

Theological Roots of Pentecostalism is, of course, with only minor revisions my 1983 dissertation at the University of Chicago. It began as a "contextual" (in other schools a "minor") in the department of Christian theology. I chose American church history and proposed to study my own denomination, the Wesleyan Methodist branch of the current Wesleyan Church. This was vetoed by Martin Marty on the grounds that I should not do denominational history in an exercise intended to expand my horizons. My sociopathological tendencies often take such limits as challenges to subvert them, and I chose instead "Oberlin Perfectionism," the Presbyterian/Congregationalist counterpart to the Wesleyans and a very close parallel. Out of this work came my *Discovering an Evangelical Heritage* exploring the conjunction of "revivalism and social reform" that found its most radical expression in the Wesleyans and at Oberlin.

Here I encountered Asa Mahan, first president of Oberlin, drawn increasingly into the Holiness movement and the Wesleyan Methodist church whose Adrian College he served as president. I was intrigued by two of his books, the *Scripture Doctrine of Christian Perfection* written at Oberlin as a Congregationalist and his later *Baptism of the Holy Ghost* written at Adrian as a Wesleyan. I had begun my studies at Chicago just a few years after the merger of the Wesleyan Methodists with the Pilgrim Holiness Church to form in 1968 the current Wesleyan Church. The two books of Mahan seemed to reflect the original dominant ethos of each of these two tributaries that had been brought into somewhat uneasy unity in the new church—and provided another way of smuggling denominational history into my "contextual." Though Mahan in his autobiographies (he wrote two) seemed to equate these books and the experiences they represented, they seemed to me to represent quite different worlds of thought, and I took on this question as the center of my contextual study. A version of that paper won the student essay contest of the Society for Pentecostal Studies and resulted in an invitation to present the results of my work at its Cleveland, Tennessee, meeting, as an illustration of the developments in Holiness theology that moved in the direction of Pentecostalism. Another version of the paper was given to the WTS, using Mahan to *illustrate* and analyze a major shift in Holiness theology in the nineteenth century. Both papers gave attention to theological issues and the differences I discerned between the two books of Mahan–though response to the papers has centered on the historical questions.

About the same time the WTS began to explore, especially through a paper by British Nazarene Herbert McGonigle, the apparent reluctance of the Wesley brothers to use Pentecostal imagery and especially the developed doctrine of "Pentecostal sanctification" that dominated the late nineteenth century and became codified in the Nazarene articles of religion, among other places. As I engaged this discussion, I realized that the issues in Mahan had their roots in tensions between the thought of John Wesley and John Fletcher. My growing interest in this question led to a dissertation on these questions when James Gustafson vetoed a study of Karl Barth's doctrine of sanctification because the topic had been preempted by Stanley Hauerwas. Under these pressures I began the exploration that consumed a decade and resulted in *Theological Roots of Pentecostalism*, offered as a study in both the origins of Pentecostalism and the development of Holiness theology in the nineteenth century.

Some Methodological Issues

The dissertation/book consists of two different intellectual exercises, the second (a history of the "roots" of Pentecostalism in the Holiness movement and related currents) made possible by the successful completion of the first (a non-reductionistic "theological" analysis of the themes of Pentecostal thought). Because some of the issues in the recent debate are shaped by underlying methodological choices, I should describe some of the intellectual streams in which I understood myself to be working—without claiming to have been bound fully to any of them.

A Phenomenological Analysis of Pentecostalism

In college, I was deeply influenced by a reading of Husserl's *Phenomenology* and especially his suggestion that one should radically "bracket" one's own presuppositions (including whether a phenomenon actually even exists!)

to reveal or unpack the inner logic of the object of study. In seminary I found a certain similarity between this idea and the theological method of Barth, who had attempted to set aside modern questions to penetrate into and unfold the inner logic of Christian faith. I was also intrigued with Barth's refusal to be bound to any one methodology, resulting in a more eclectic approach that used tools from a variety of sources as needed and demanded by the nature of the phenomenon under study. I appropriated some of these ideas, and attempted what might be described as an interdisciplinary phenomenological effort to describe the inner *theological* logic of Pentecostalism, though I was not explicit at the time about the intellectual streams in which I was working.

Those of you who know the book will know that I have argued that most, if not all, streams of the Pentecostal and charismatic movements find expression in four basic themes epitomized in the "foursquare gospel" of Aimee Semple McPherson: Jesus is "Savior," "Baptizer with the Holy Spirit," "Healer," and "Coming King." These themes appear individually elsewhere, but come together in a distinctive "gestalt" in Pentecostalism held together by a distinctive inner logic. In one of the sections of the book of which I am perhaps most proud I expounded this inner logic in an exploration of the meaning of three early names of the movement: the "Pentecostal," the "apostolic faith," and the "latter rain" movement. In this process I purposely "bracketed" the most distinctive practice of Pentecostalism ("speaking in tongues") to discern the underlying theological themes that provided the context in which that practice was to be understood. This step also made clear that these themes and logic had taken shape in the larger Holiness context of the late nineteenth century.

Some have suggested that my book constituted a major advance in the study of Pentecostalism, and its analysis has been widely accepted. The Spanish translation of the book provides in Latin America the major sympathetic *theological* analysis of Pentecostalism (as opposed to the more truncated and hostile analysis of James Dunn and the less systematic treatment of Walter Hollenweger) that has enabled a maturing influential movement to begin its own theological articulation, to find a hitherto obscured theological lineage, and enter the ecumenical arena with a deeper sense of its own location in the larger Christian tradition. Similarly the Korean translation, which has gone through several printings, has been well-received and has found similar functions, where it has been useful in clarifying the relationships between the Pentecostal and Holiness Movements, especially since the Holiness Movement in Korea is largely a product of the missionary work of the Oriental Missionary Society (OMS), which has its roots in the more radical wing of the Holiness movement at God's Bible School where the Holiness message was articulated in terms of the "fourfold gospel" (Jesus as savior, sanctifier, healer and coming king).

In offering this analysis I have deliberately bracketed my own questions and reservations about Pentecostalism (which are several—about the practice of speaking in tongues, the claims of "faith healing" and "exorcism," and so on) for the sake of this positive role of the book within the Pentecostal movement. I have often been reassured (and occasionally amused) when Pentecostal students (for example, in Mexico City) find that I seem to understand the inner logic of Pentecostalism better than they but have not become personally a Pentecostal. I take this as evidence that I have achieved some success in my effort to find an "objective" phenomenological description of Pentecostal theology. And the book would not be able to play the positive role that it has if I had been more explicit about some of my own concerns—though these are not entirely absent in the book.

This analysis, however, has not been without its critics, though mostly of the nature of what I would call "friendly dialogue." Representative of these would be the following:

(1) Some, such as Baptist (originally Pentecostal) Roger Olson in *Christianity Today* (12 August 1988) have felt I have underplayed "tongues" as the distinctive theme of Pentecostalism. I have acknowledged that this is the most distinctive feature of Pentecostalism and bracketed it for the purpose of finding the deeper meaning of this practice—and would argue that the advantages of this move outweigh the disadvantages.

(2) Roman Catholic charismatic Peter Hocken described the book in *The Ecumenical Review* (October, 1989) as "magisterial" and deserving to become the "standard" interpretation of the "self-understanding" of Pentecostalism. His concerns, however, are shared by many of the students of Hollenweger: that my analysis is too "white" and obscures the African-American themes in Pentecostalism (which I in turn find overstated by them, though I am sympathetic to their theological and social commitments) and that, in a related manner, I have underplayed the non-theological and physical (or "bodily") dimensions of the movement in my effort at a *theological* analysis.

(3) Bill Faupel of Asbury Theological Seminary has argued in his Birmingham dissertation (excerpted in *The Everlasting Gospel*) that eschatology is the organizing theme of Pentecostal thought. He largely accepts my analysis while giving greater emphasis to one theme. My book acknowledges this possibility (as argued, for example, by Bloch-Hoell in

Norway and in Faupel's work emerging as I was writing), but argues more for a model of mutual interpenetration of the themes. I might give priority to the "healing" theme if forced to chose, but am reluctant to make the eschatology central and definitive—in part because for sociological reasons it is often the first to drop into the background (through its importance and integrality is revealed in its tendency to be reasserted in such movements as the "latter rain" movement that is at the center of Faupel's concern).

(4) And finally, my friends in Cleveland, Tennessee, would argue for a "five-fold" gospel that would incorporate the Holiness theme of "entire sanctification" into the defining center of Pentecostalism. I am sympathetic to their concerns; in a sense this might be seen as the whole point of the book, but to do so would get in the way of the wider applicability of the analysis to the non-Holiness wings of Pentecostalism and the charismatic movement in general. It appears to me that they have essentially granted the validity of my analysis in the way in which they have used the "four/five-fold" analysis in their teaching of systematic theology and related efforts.

The Implications of a Typological and Motif-Analysis Method

It is, however, the "pre-history" of Pentecostal thought in the Holiness movement that has generated the most controversy, and here again certain methodological points need to be made. As indicated above, I was in my doctoral program a student of James Gustafson, the student, collaborator and successor to H. Richard Niebuhr at Yale. Niebuhr was in turn fascinated with the work of Troeltsch (some interpreters see him as attempting in a sense to reconcile the work of Barth and Troeltsch) and especially some of the efforts at "typological" analysis that are found in Troeltsch's work under the influence of sociologist Max Weber. This stream of thought has produced the much debated church/sect typology utilized by Niebuhr, the classic *Christ and Culture* by Niebuhr, Gustafson's own *Christ and the Moral Life* and other imitators. I have always been fascinated with this intellectual stream and often use such materials in my teaching to help students discern fundamental options in Christian thought.

At the same time at Yale I was introduced, again through Barth (*Church Dogmatics*, IV/2), to the work of Anders Nygren in *Agape and Eros*. This classic study is perhaps the major product of the Swedish Lundensian theology and its method of "motif analysis" which analyzes theological history in terms of fundamental and characteristic "motifs." Nygren analyzed the Greek concept of love in terms of "eros" and the NT concept of love in terms of "agape" and then traces their synthesis in the Augustinian concept of "caritas" before the NT idea of agape was recovered in Luther. I have always been fascinated with this method and taught at a Swedish seminary (North Park) while writing—a fact that kept the method before my eyes.

Also at Yale I studied with Brevard Childs, whom I consider to have been my greatest teacher. He characteristically offered courses that took OT texts (selected Psalms, for example) and studied the original Hebrew, Septuagint translation, Targums and rabbinic interpretation before tracing such texts through Christian history. He was a genius in the discernment of how subtle shifts in translation or a new historical context can give a new meaning to older texts that gain a new life and meaning perhaps unintended within "authorial intent." I was deeply influenced by my work with Childs—and these other streams of thought at Yale—and fragments of these methods may be said to be found in my work in the historical latter part of my book.

All of these intellectual currents share certain strengths and weaknesses—as I tell my students when we talk about such matters. The search for distinctive motifs or typological differences involves a certain abstraction from historical reality for the sake of analytical clarity. The process also has a tendency to overstate differences and neglect commonalities—as has always been recognized in the sociological literature on typological analysis since Weber (see, for example, the work of Georg Semmel). I alluded to these issues indirectly in my book, indicating for example the common elements between Wesley and Fletcher that underlie the differences in characteristic ways of speaking or fundamental motifs—nuances that in another time and place could grow into more fundamental differences.

Within these methodological parameters, I see no major corrections required by the discussion since. It is no refutation of my work to find in Wesley use of Pentecostal imagery in the discussion of sanctification, references to the "sanctifying Spirit of Pentecost," or a text or two in which Wesley seems to speak of a "Pentecostal sanctification." What is required is an argument that such expressions are Wesley's *characteristic* way of speaking and the *fundamental* "motifs" of his thought. I still find that Wesley's thought is *more* fundamentally Christological (and classically Protestant) than Fletcher's more pneumatological orientation. We shall return to these issues later.

The Pentecostal Critique

I have indicated above some of the minor reservations about my "phenomenological" analysis of Pentecostal thought. There has also been a great deal of "dis-ease" about my work in certain other Pentecostal circles. The more important discussion, already alluded to above, is about whether my work underplays the importance of the African American influence in the origins of Pentecostalism through the work of W. J. Seymour and the Azusa Street Revival. That discussion is somewhat outside the logic of this paper. More to the point here are the criticisms that my book is too narrowly focused on Holiness sources.

The major critic from this perspective is probably Edith Waldvogel Blumhofer. There is a sense in which our respective dissertations constitute mutual critiques (refutations) of each other. Her Harvard dissertation was an exploration of the "Reformed Evangelical Roots of Pentecostalism" and was completed before mine with full knowledge of my emerging work. Full discussion of the issues here is impossible, but I would like to make a few general comments:

(1) It has always seemed to me that Edith's work is part of a larger "evangelicalizing" agenda that has found its strongest force in the Assemblies of God to support its desire to finds its identity in the fundamentalist/evangelical world of the National Association of Evangelicals. This stream of thought (and ecclesiastical politics!) finds it opportune to suppress the historical and theological connections with the Holiness movement for the sake of a "generic evangelical" identity—in spite of the fact that the "fundamental truths" of the Assemblies of God commit it to "entire sanctification" (modified in mid-century in the direction of a more Baptistic form of "evangelicalism").

(2) Part of the issue is semantic and has to do with the definition of the Holiness movement. I have worked with a broader definition that includes the Keswick tradition and have seen the latter as directly dependent on the American Holiness tradition (contra the historiography of George Marsden and others who emphasize the independence of Keswick as a British import). Edith works with a more narrow definition that limits it to the eradicationist stream with distinctively Wesleyan roots. Thus she interprets A. B. Simpson, erstwhile Presbyterian founder of the Christian and Missionary Alliance, as a "reformed evangelical" while I am more inclined to see him as a central figure in the Holiness movement broadly conceived.

(3) I have always felt that Edith's Harvard dissertation has a major methodological defect in its tendency to stop working backward just at the points at which the Holiness roots would become manifestly clear. Thus she discusses evangelist D. L. Moody's "empowerment for service" understanding of the "baptism with the Holy Spirit" but neglects to mention that his experience was prompted by the entreaties of two Free Methodist ladies, to explore the extent to which such themes were at issue in the Holiness movement, or to recognize that stream of historiography that would speak of Moody himself in a Holiness stream.

(4) Similarly, I have always felt that the crowning argument in my book for the Holiness origins of Pentecostalism is the chapter on the healing movement where I make the *theological* argument that "faith healing" is grounded in a radicalization of Holiness soteriology. I show that both theological articulations and personal biographies demonstrate that the healing movement arose as various figures asked if they could be healed of the "effects of sin" (in a moment?) as they had of the guilt of sin and the power of sin ("entire sanctification"?). This is clear for A. B. Simpson, who significantly learned the doctrine of "faith healing" from holiness Episcopalian doctor Charles Cullis whose biography shows a similar development. A similar trajectory takes place in the life of Presbyterian William Boardman, author of the influential *The Higher Christian Life*.

(5) I do wish that my claims could be more directly confronted. Edith, for example, only indirectly treats me in her two-volume history of the Assemblies of God when she is analyzing Pentecostal roots, but does refer to me in other contexts to which my work is less relevant, with the result that I am made to look a little foolish. But this sort of issue brings me more directly to my Holiness critics.

The Holiness Critique

As Melvin Dieter has often commented, my book is as much a history of the development of Holiness theology in the nineteenth century as it is a study of Pentecostalism. I have always responded, only partially tongue in cheek, that it is more marketable as a "prehistory" of Pentecostal theology. But as such, it has prompted as much or more response within the Holiness Movement—and often a much more intense and radical critique because of its implication that in many ways late nineteenth century Holiness thought is closer to Pentecostalism than to Wesley. This claim of discontinuities within the stream of Holiness theology has been a major threat in several contexts, where either personal convictions or denominational articles of faith have been committed to an understanding of seamless continuity. It has also flown in the face of the "pyrophobia" (the label of B. H. Irwin of the turn of the last century "three blessing heresy") rooted in the anti-Pentecostal animus of the Holiness movement that dates back to conflicts over turf as Pentecostalism began to separate from the Holiness movement. I cannot here offer a definitive response to all my critics; I will limit myself to some more general comments in response to three of the most vigorous and influential interlocutors: Charles W. Carter, Timothy L. Smith, and Laurence W. Wood.

Charles W. Carter

I knew that I was taking up delicate issues in this book, but I was unprepared for the vehemence of the response. I was soon to learn that I had scraped a very sensitive nerve. The first blast came from Charles W. Carter, who on a sabbatical in Taiwan was reading the proofs of *The Person and Work of the Holy Spirit: A Wesleyan Perspective* (Baker, 1974) when he received the 1974 *WTJ* containing my early study of Mahan and inserted into his book at the last minute an extensive footnote (188–89 in the original hardback edition, but dropped in the paperback edition).

Carter's book, though subtitled a "Wesleyan Perspective," stands firmly in the Fletcherian or late nineteenth century "Pentecostal" reading of Holiness theology and carries the "full endorsement" of Thomas Hermiz, executive director of the Christian Holiness Association, as a "fair, scholarly, and exhaustive exposition . . . within the Wesleyan interpretation of the Holy Spirit." My timing could not have been worse; my work appeared to be a direct challenge to this self-understanding.

Carter's footnote is more a bellow of protest, but he does do me the honor of engaging me in more detail than some other of my critics—such as responding to my comments about the canonical role of the book of Acts. His book had already attacked Vinson Synan and Dale Brunner for their "unreliable historical position" that the roots of Pentecostalism are to be found in Methodism and the Holiness movement. This, as for Timothy Smith later, was a profoundly disquieting thesis that must be refuted. I was, therefore, critiqued for perpetuating this "unreliable" thesis. I take it, however, that history has vindicated my position so that even those who would not like the association are bound to recognize its historical accuracy. This new orientation is evidenced by the fact that joint meetings of the WTS and the SPS (in Cleveland, Tennessee, and at the AAR, etc.) now take place in recognition of this sibling and historical relationship.

I am accused of making Mahan the *cause* of the shift rather than seeing him as being *illustrative* as I had intended—perhaps an understandable confusion as I was just beginning to be aware of the rootedness of these issues in Wesley and Fletcher. More substantially, I am accused in my typological "motif" analysis of a "practical, though not necessarily doctrinal, denial of the divine trinity." I will pick up these issues again later, but it does seem to be important in the light of the positions of Timothy Smith and Larry Wood, to notice that Carter does struggle mightily in his book with what he calls "the problem of neglected emphasis upon the baptism of the Holy Spirit" (176–86) in Wesley (and also in Fletcher!). At least Carter, in contrast to certain other critics, recognized the problem in the classical Wesleyan sources to which I was pointing.

Before moving on, I should perhaps mention that this interchange had profound political implications for the WTS and the CHA. In what might be a decidedly un-Wesleyan display of unsanctified "carnality," I followed the slogan: "Don't get mad, get even." I reviewed Carter's book in *Christianity Today* (January 16, 1976), pointing out the irony of his anti-Pentecostal animus while representing a Fletcherian or late-nineteenth century interpretation of the Holiness message that was in some ways closer to Pentecostalism than to Wesley. This review, which now seems, at least to me, to be gracious and tame, proved explosive. Timothy Smith made an impassioned personal plea to me to lay-off for the sake of the Holiness movement.

I was told this interchange precipitated behind the scene meetings with Carter, Thomas Heriniz and Timothy Smith to find ways to protect the Holiness movement from me. I was understood to be taking a battering ram to the Holiness defenses against Pentecostalism. The irony is that if I had an agenda for the Holiness movement it was the opposite—to suggest that it move back toward more classically Wesleyan patterns of thought. I do take it as a compliment to my efforts at "objective" description that the book has often been misunderstood in this way.

This interchange also marks a key turning point in the life of the WTS. Charles Carter had been the promotional secretary of the WTS. I was elected to replace him during his two year sabbatical in Asia. Upon his return, somewhat against the will of the WTS executive, I suggested that he be made the chair of the nominating committee. The slate he brought in nominated himself as promotional secretary. Mildred Bangs Wynkoop insisted that I be restored to the ballot to run against him. I was elected in a secret ballot in a very tense meeting, and I believe I am correct in saying that Carter never again attended the WTS.

I have always been intrigued by the fact that the footnote attacking me was dropped in the paperback edition, though I have never known why and have always wondered whether this reflected a change of position on the part of Carter or a backing away from the tone of it—or perhaps a graciousness rooted in personal relationships. Carter was a major influence in my father's life and lived a block or two away from us in Marion, Indiana, in a house that I served as paperboy.

Timothy Smith

My most persistent critic was perhaps Timothy Smith who in most years of a decade or so proposed a WTS paper hacking away at my work long before the book appeared. I have become convinced that I was a large part of the force that propelled Smith to devote the last decade or two of his life to classical Wesleyan sources, buying a cottage in the Cotswalds from which to pursue his research in the British materials. He shared much of the agenda that has since resurfaced in the work of Larry Wood; so some of my response to Smith also has applicability to Wood.

I was again shocked to discover the depth of feeling over the issues involved. I soon discovered that I would have to endure the systematic efforts of Smith to dismantle me. This became clear when he gave a paper at a meeting of the SPS in Ann Arbor, Michigan. In the middle of his presentation, I suddenly realized that one of my papers was being critiqued point by point in the order in which I had made them—without any explicit or public reference to me. I sank in my seat behind members of the audience, hoping as a mere graduate student to avoid a direct confrontation with the "master" of Holiness studies. This effort was undermined when after the paper Vinson Synan stood to his feet and commented that it appeared that Smith did not agree with the thesis that I was beginning to elaborate. Smith dismissed my work with a snort and the comment that all he had seen was an elaborate hypothesis. I was put on a panel to respond to this address that was later to be published as his critique of the irrational practice of "speaking in tongues" over against the "rationality" of the Wesleyan/Holiness tradition—and the struggle that would go on for a decade or two was launched.

I have always had difficulty in knowing how to respond to this "crusade" of Timothy Smith. Several factors made me feel invisible, subliminal factors were driving it, and there was no way that I could engage him on the levels of academic discourse. Though it usually appeared to me and others that Smith was after me, he almost never mentioned me by name or dealt directly with my text in an explicit way. In Ann Arbor, for example, I asked to see his paper, and even though both Vinson Synan and I recognized it as an attack on my work, I was, as I remember it, not mentioned in the footnotes. This created some difficulty in knowing how to respond, especially when this indirection resulted in a style of response whose target was a straw man that I did not always recognize. I sometimes felt that Tim Smith was not prepared to engage a mere graduate student and honor him by direct interaction. And I sometimes wondered if he felt some pique in this indirect challenge to his role as the authoritative spokesperson for the Holiness movement on such issues. As a result of such dynamics I avoided interaction—not because I felt that he had the better part of the argument.

It is not possible to respond in detail here to all of Smith's essays. His most substantial attacks were expressed in two books that he published: *The Promise of the Spirit* (Bethany, 1980), a collection of essays by Finney from the *Oberlin Evangelist* (1839–40), and *The Pentecost Hymns of John and Charles Wesley* (Beacon Hill, 1982), a reprint with comments of the Whitsunday hymns of John and Charles Wesley originally published as *Hymns of Petition and Thanksgiving for the Promise of the Father* (1746).

In the former Smith seems to be arguing for the role of Finney in establishing the doctrine that entire sanctification comes through the baptism of the Holy Spirit. I, of course, had read this material (including the *Oberlin Evangelist* and the writings of all the faculty members at Oberlin on these questions) and had not considered that their work moved so fully in this direction, though Henry Cowles and John Morgan came closer, as I indicate in my book. Part of the issue is the one that Randy Maddox clarifies in his recent exchange with Larry Wood. I was looking for the explicit connection of Pentecost and "entire sanctification" in the doctrine of "Pentecostal sanctification." It still seems to me that Finney falls short of this, arguing that the "sanctifying Spirit" comes at Pentecost without suggesting that Pentecost is the "entire sanctification" of the disciples—or that a personal Pentecost or baptism of the Spirit is the way in which "entire sanctification" is achieved. It is also noteworthy that only one lecture (#17 "The Holy Spirit of Promise") is explicitly devoted to the topic indicated in Smith's title, and this is the lecture containing the presumed doctrine of "Pentecostal sanctification." It has also always seemed to me significant in this discussion that A. M. Hills, the Congregationalist first theologian of the Church of the Nazarene who had studied with Finney at Oberlin, was convinced that Finney did not make this connection, as he mentions in his biography of Finney. There he laments that "Finney failed to connect the obtaining of sanctification with the baptism of the Holy Ghost"— "though sometimes he almost got the truth" (my book, 71–72).

A major purpose for my trip to Bristol last summer[1] was to read in Charles Wesley to test whether the hymns of Charles Wesley disproved what I had said. So far, I remain unconvinced. The "promise of the father hymns" are of course written for liturgical use in connection with Pentecost Sunday, for which reason they speak of the Holy Spirit and even of the work of the Spirit as "sanctifying." But I am unable to find in these hymns the doctrine of "Pentecostal sanctification." The related *Hymns on the Trinity* by Charles Wesley also has a section on hymns to the Holy Spirit, but these are even less related to our discussions in that their point is to speak to Arian controversies of the time in an effort to defend the "divinity" of both Christ and the Holy Spirit. There is a subtle methodological point to be made here, one that I first noticed in reading John Dreschner's *Wesley's Christology* (SMU, 1960). There Deschner argues for the classical character of Wesley's theology by appeal to his writings that are most derivative and dependent on the tradition (the twenty-five articles, for example), rather than making his case on the texts that would reveal the most characteristic patterns of thought (perhaps the sermons and the letters). So, too, there may be problems in seeking the most characteristic patterns of thought in hymns written for use on Pentecost Sunday. But it seems even odder to seek the doctrine of "Pentecostal sanctification" in Charles Wesley, who most scholars agree had major reservations about his brother John's tendency to speak of entire sanctification in a "moment" of "crisis." The doctrine of "Pentecostal sanctification" by definition puts the emphasis on the moment of entire sanctification—Pentecost is after all an event rather than a process. While in Bristol, I discussed these matters with S. T. Kimbrough, Jr., until recently the president of the Charles Wesley Society, to confirm my reading. He concurred. This would seem also to be the position of John R. Tyson in his Drew dissertation published as *Charles Wesley on Sanctification* (Zondervan, 1986), which discusses this and the matters at debate in the larger discussion—and finds, contra Smith, Charles as well as John fundamentally "Christocentric" in his thought.

We cannot work through all of Smith's texts in this context. My book contains analyses of what he had published up to 1983. But I hope that I have indicated something of the reasons that I continue to resist his reading of the issues—as others have done. I sometimes refer in class to Ken Grider's 1980 *WTJ* essay as his "I wish to God Timothy Smith were right,

---

1. Editor's Note: This refers to a trip Dayton took in the summer of 1999.

but he isn't" essay. I comfort myself with the fact that I suppose that Tim now has a better and more generous understanding of these issues and hope that I shall someday have the chance to discuss them with him under more appropriate circumstances!

Laurence W. Wood

This brings us to the work of Larry Wood and new discussions that are opening. Again several factors make it difficult to know how to proceed. For one thing, I have not had access to the forthcoming Oxford manuscript. I was asked by Oxford to read this manuscript, but since I was already getting reports from Asbury that Larry considered this book a refutation of my claims, I suppressed my curiosity and declined, feeling as a partisan in the debate I ought not to participate in the process of judging its fitness for publication. Larry at one point volunteered to send me a copy for the use of my seminar last fall, but the manuscript never arrived, in spite of several efforts on my part to get these materials for my class. Finally, late in the process of composing this paper, I received from Larry a few pages with explicit reference to me, once he had received the WTS program and saw that I intended to respond to my critics. He presumed that he was one of these! My comments are based on the earlier materials: his ATJ essay, his WTS paper later published in the *WTJ* and the recent *WTJ* exchange with Randy Maddox. On the basis of these materials I have not yet seen that I need to make any significant retractions of what I have said in my book.

With regard to another issue of difficulty in knowing how to respond to Larry, I do not wish to presume that his work is directed primarily at me. Even though his work has been represented to me as such, he is very sparing in actual references to my work, his most substantial allusion to my work being a paragraph in an extended two-page footnote in his WTS paper (*WTJ*, 28–29). I have not discussed this issue directly with Larry, but it was reported to me via an Asbury colleague that he did not quote me more extensively to save me embarrassment. It remains to be seen who will be embarrassed in all of this, but here I find the same difficulty that I regularly had with Smith. If something is supposedly a critique of my work, then I have the right, if I am to take it seriously, to see a more careful analysis of what I am actually saying. I have the strong impression that Larry has not read me carefully. I think my own account is much more nuanced than I am given credit for. I am constantly surprised, if I correctly read between the lines, to have qualifications that I made to my argument thrown out as refutations of it, to hear claims that I do not think could be made if my book had been carefully read, and so forth.

Larry, for example, claims that no one until the WTS dialogues of the 1970s questioned whether Fletcher's doctrine of dispensations was the natural and appropriate extension of Wesley's thought that Wesley approved and incorporated into his own thinking. I'm not sure what Larry would count as disproving this claim, but it is certainly true that it has been a staple of Wesley scholarship to either celebrate or lament the fact that Wesley did not link entire sanctification with the "baptism of the Holy Spirit." I cite much of this literature in my book. Carter's treatment of Wesley's reluctance to move in this direction was written independently of the post-McGonigle discussion and refers to earlier Holiness literature struggling with the same issue: Mildred Bangs Wynkoop and Robert Mattke, for example. Leo Cox struggled with this problem in his 1959 Iowa dissertation published as *John Wesley's Concept of Perfection* (Beacon Hill, 1964). W. E. Sangster noted Wesley's failure to link sanctification sufficiently with the Holy Spirit in *The Path to Perfection* (1943). And so on. Especially important for our purposes is the Methodist literature at the turn of the last century. James Mudge in his *Growth in Holiness Toward Perfection or Progressive Sanctification* (1895), a book that Larry Wood cites on several occasions, includes a chapter on the "baptism with the Holy Ghost" in which Mudge cites journal entries and letters in which Wesley "had the occasion in which to rebuke this very error" (that is, the identification of the "baptism with the Holy Spirit" with "entire sanctification"). In my book, I make much of the writings of R. C. Homer, a Canadian Methodist (his writings were published often by the Methodist Publishing House in Canada) who played a major role in the founding of three Holiness groups in Canada. Horner was an advocate of the so-called "three-blessing heresy" at the turn of the last century that provided the "missing link" between the Holiness movement and Pentecostalism, especially in its Holiness variety. In his book *PENTECOST* (1891), which I reprinted in *From the Altar to the Upper Room* in my series "The Higher Christian Life," Homer laments that "most professors of religion know no difference between the blessing of entire sanctification and the baptism of the Holy Ghost" (131) and proceeds to sharply distinguish the two in a "History of the Doctrine." It was his awareness that Wesley did not speak of a baptism of the Spirit that was in part responsible for his distinguishing two subsequent experiences: entire sanctification (Wesley) and baptism with the Holy Ghost (Fletcher?—though for empowerment and not attributed directly to him). There is a sense in which millions of

Holiness/Pentecostal folk are a testimony to the difficulty of reconciling Wesley and Fletcher. Yet this tradition of objection to his thesis seems to be conveniently overlooked in Larry's work.

The thrust of Larry Wood's argument seems to be that Wesley's thought was continued in Fletcher and that Holiness theology continued this synthesis virtually unchanged since then, whether in mainline Methodism or the Holiness subculture. He explicitly attacks my efforts to identify a change in the mid-nineteenth century in which the Fletcher, Benson, etc. articulation became influential through the writings of Phoebe Palmer, Asa Mahan, and others and dominated the late nineteenth-century Holiness circles. To sustain this argument Larry seems to me to be forced to make highly speculative and improbable arguments that occasionally border on the bizarre.

I cite C. I. Scofield's judgment in *Plain Papers on the Doctrine of the Holy Spirit* (1899) that in the preceding twenty years more books had been published on the Holy Spirit than in the eighteen centuries before that—a similar judgment has been made by modern critical scholars as well (e.g., Grant Wacker). In more than one place, including the new Oxford book, Larry argues that any such increase in emphasis on the Holy Spirit is to be attributed to the demographic growth of Methodism; there are so many more books on the Holy Spirit because there are so many more Methodists writing them in continuity with the Fletcherian interpretation of Wesley. I struggle to take this argument seriously. In the first place his demographic analysis is exaggerated if in the late nineteenth century we are focusing on those Methodists (largely in the Holiness wings) who were inclined to use Fletcher. Secondly, I have not seen any evidence that Larry has sufficiently internalized the range of developments in the late nineteenth century to make a nuanced judgment about what did happen there. And how does he explain those outside of Methodism? And his speculative demographic suggestion cannot explain those who shifted ground (Asa Mahan in the 1860s, A. B. Simpson in the 1890s) or those like Daniel Steele who reported their own change in language (1874). Nor do such demographics explain the change in title to the *Guide to Holiness* in 1897 when *And the Pentecostal Life* was added. I once asked Timothy Smith how he could sustain his position of unchanged continuity in light of this change and the radical shift in rhetoric that followed it. He admitted to me that he had not read the *Guide* for the 1890s, and I rather suspect that Larry has not done so either and so is really not in a position to refute my work when he has not really examined the evidence, apparently even not as I have summarized it in my book.

The major burden of Larry's work, however, is to assert that Wesley approved of Fletcher's articulation and moved in that direction, especially in the last twenty years of his life. This is a very complicated discussion that is further complicated by Larry's interest in liturgical reform in Methodism, in which he sees Fletcher as an ally in preserving certain themes having to do with confirmation. Larry argues that this remained a constant feature of Methodist theology through the nineteenth century and into the Holiness movement. I cannot respond in detail to every feature of this argument. Fortunately, Randy Maddox has made an extensive reply to Larry in a recent issue of the *WTJ*. A key issue in this debate is whether any reference to the Holy Spirit or even the "sanctifying Spirit" constitutes the doctrine of "Pentecostal sanctification" whose rise I traced in my book. It is possible to attribute the working out of sanctification to a work of the Holy Spirit that came at Pentecost without arguing that Pentecost was the entire sanctification of the disciples and that entire sanctification is to be equated with a personal Pentecost of the Baptism with the Holy Spirit. It is a subtle but important difference that marks one in the classical tradition of Pentecost as the historical experience of the church and since that time Christ and the Spirit are united in our reception of them or in the Pentecostal tradition of seeing the separation of conversion to Christ and the reception of the Spirit as two stages in a personal pilgrimage explicitly perpetuating the pattern of the NT. These are all points that I regularly make in my book, and go far to explain the differences in the readings that I offer and that of Larry.

There are other issues of documentation and argument that I think vitiate Larry's argument. He regularly over-reads his sources. A single reference to the Spirit becomes a basic theme of the writer. A reference to the "sanctifying Spirit" becomes the full-blown doctrine of "Pentecostal sanctification." A commendatory comment of Wesley about Fletcher's doctrine of dispensations becomes total approval of every feature of it. And so on. I urge you to read his footnotes very carefully and make your own independent judgment before you accept the conclusions that he offers. This we attempted to do in my seminar, and we discovered many problems in his documentation; so much so that it became a continuing joke in the class. I was able to use his documentation for many lessons in how not to write doctoral dissertations. A few examples of this will have to suffice.

On occasion we could not figure out the relevance of the citations to the point being made, and often when we saw the connection we were not convinced that the note proved the point at hand. Take, for example, the long lists of early nineteenth-century Methodist figures that supposedly regularly taught "Pentecostal sanctification." I took Joseph Pilmore, regularly cited by Larry and a text I had read in preparing my dissertation and book, to check his claim that Pilmore preached on the baptism with the Holy Spirit. I looked at the diary edited by Frank Baterman Stanger and could find only that Pilmore had preached a Pentecost sermon in which he spoke of the Holy Spirit, but I could find no evidence of the doctrine of "Pentecostal sanctification." In fact, I could only find two references to Christian Perfection, cases in which Pilmore was pressed on the possibility of "sinless perfection," a question which he apparently attempted to duck, responding, in very Wesleyan language, that he contended for nothing more than the loving of God and neighbor with all one's body, soul and spirit. I still take it, then, that Pilmore, properly read, supports my position rather than Larry's. I have not reread all the early American Methodist sources that I read for my dissertation, but I rather expect to come to the same conclusions if I should. To double-check my perception about this I have tested my conclusions in a couple of conversations with Lester Ruth of Yale Divinity School (though about to move to Asbury) who has extensive computer files of the recorded testimonies to conversion and sanctification of early Methodists in revivals and camp meetings. He was astounded at my questions and could not think of a single case in which early experiences of sanctification were expressed in terms of a baptism of the Spirit. Obviously there is much more work to be done in this area, but so far I have not seen convincing evidence that shakes my earlier conclusions.

Elsewhere, one can see the point Larry is making, but he seems not to take seriously other explanations of the material than the one he assumes. One key text for Larry is Wesley's letter of January 17, 1775, to Elizabeth Ritchie commending Fletcher's doctrine of dispensations. Larry takes this commendation to include all aspects of Fletcher's doctrine including the understanding of "Pentecostal sanctification" and the "baptism with the Holy Spirit." It seems to me that Wesley was attracted to Fletcher's teaching because it gave him language in which to discuss "stages" in the Christian life, a central issue for both Wesley and Fletcher over against classical Protestantism, especially Lutheranism, which has difficulty assimilating such ideas. I find such a reading of Wesley also natural in other contexts in which he commends Fletcher.

This last issue seems to me to be crucial in the face of Larry's tendency to argue from silence because his own reading *must* be true. There are texts in which both Wesley and Fletcher describe their differences on this issue. There are the texts surrounding the controversies at Trevecca in 1770–71.

Larry argues that these are attributable largely to a misunderstanding that soon cleared up and later Wesley unambiguously accepted the whole of Fletcher's teachings. Yet four to five years later Wesley wrote to Fletcher (March 22, 1775) "our views on Christian Perfection are a little different, though not opposite," finding the difference to be "that every babe in Christ has received the Holy Ghost" but he "has not obtained Christian Perfection." And three *years* later Fletcher is more explicit about the difference in a letter to Mary Bosanquet (later his wife, March 7, 1778) "I would distinguish more exactly between the believer baptized with the Pentecostal power of the Holy Ghost, and the believer who, like the Apostles after our Lord's ascension, is not yet filled with that power." It seems to me quite clear that Wesley and Fletcher continued to be aware of their differences long after the Trevecca controversies, and it seems to me questionable to argue that these texts should not be taken seriously. Yet Larry regularly argues from silence: Surely Wesley would not have designated Fletcher his successor if he had not accepted every feature of Fletcher's thought including his doctrine of "Pentecostal sanctification"; Wesley would not have commended his doctrine of dispensations if he had not approved of this particular feature; and so on. I prefer to trust the explicit comments of Wesley and Fletcher to speculations that they could not have really meant what they say in these quotations.

This is obviously not a definitive response to Larry Wood. There remains much to be discussed, and perhaps the discussion can continue after the publication of Larry's book. But I hope that I have said enough to indicate that I have substantial reasons for not backing down.

The Larger and More Substantial Issues

I have indicated above my disappointment that some of the larger substantial issues that I thought my book raised have not been at the center of the discussion. Let me illustrate.

There is first a major Trinitarian issue. I have always been puzzled at the response to my contrasting motif analysis of Wesley and Fletcher, especially those like Carter and Smith who have accused me of driving a wedge between Christ and the Spirit. It seemed to me that I was affirming Wesley's critique of Fletcher that his formulation had precisely this tendency—to separate the reception of the Spirit from the reception of Christ. It has always seemed to me to be at the same time both profoundly Christological and profoundly Trinitarian. I take Barth as an illustration of this. He is perhaps the most profoundly Christological theologian in the history of the tradition while at the same time profoundly Trinitarian and probably responsible more than anyone for the renewal of Trinitarian theology in the twentieth century. Here obviously we are dealing with the issues of the *filioque*, which I, following Barth, am inclined to defend (against the current "ecumenical political correctness"). I am very leery of a Spirit that does not also proceed from the Son, as if there were a God-ness not revealed in Christ to which we need access. And I am a little nervous that its neglect might open the way for an understanding of God based in Greek philosophy rather than biblical categories. Perhaps I am on the edge of whatever it is in Barth that sometimes evokes the charge of "modalism," but I understand this more in terms of a commitment to the classical Trinitarian slogan *opera trinitatis ad extra indivisa sunt*.

Let me illustrate this concretely. One of the issues at debate in the late nineteenth century was the fuzziness of the content of "baptism with the Holy Spirit." Some were afraid that this language of "experience of the Holy Spirit" might lose the concretion of the Christological orientation. I have always appreciated the way in which Wesley defines the content of Christian Perfection in Christological terms: it is "to have the mind of Christ in you," to "walk in the way Jesus walked," to love God and neighbor as Jesus taught, to live out the teachings of Jesus in the Sermon on the Mount as empowered by the Holy Spirit, and so on. The point for me is precisely the unity of Christ and the Spirit and the role of the Spirit to mediate the presence of Christ—as defined by the concretion of Christ found in the historical Jesus of the New Testament and his teachings. One of the great problems of Protestantism since the reformation is the separation of soteriological categories from the figure of Jesus in the NT. In both Barth and Wesley I find profound allies in attempting to keep these together in unity.

I also thought I perceived a certain theological and exegetical instability in late nineteenth century Holiness theology as it shifted from Wesley to Fletcher. By this I have in mind that Wesleyan theology was developed, if we are to trust the analysis of W. E. Sangster, on the basis of first Johannine texts and then Pauline texts. In his analysis the book of Acts is conspicuous by its absence. The instability was rooted in the late nineteenth century effort to preach Johannine theology through Lukan texts less amenable to those themes. That is to say that I think Pentecostalism has always done a better job of exegeting the Lukan texts with their emphasis on the empowering and supernatural work of the Holy Spirit. Only one text in Acts 15 ("purifying their hearts by faith") moves in the Wesleyan direction. Once the Pentecostal framework was adopted by Wesleyans it was only a matter of time before the Lukan themes would overwhelm the Wesleyan ones and produce Pentecostalism. It may be that there are certain themes in Acts (and Pentecostalism!) that need to be incorporated into the Wesleyan understanding, but it is also important to maintain the Wesleyan themes that were gradually lost in the late nineteenth century—and I'm convinced that Pentecostalism needs our witness to the original Wesleyan themes of the primacy of love and the graces/fruits of the Spirit rather than the gifts.

One of the most troublesome problems in Holiness theology has been how to preserve the crisis in process understanding of original Wesleyan theology. Most recognize that Holiness theology has tended to underplay the process for the crisis and in the language of David Cubie (*WTJ*, 1976) make "entire sanctification" inaugural rather than teleological as it tended to be in Wesley. Various explanations have been offered for this development: changes in Wesley, post-Wesleyan figures like Adam Clarke, and the role of Finney and Phoebe Palmer in "mechanizing" the appropriation of sanctification so that Palmer is to Wesley on sanctification as Finney is to Edwards on conversion. But it seems to me that the most obvious explanation for both of these developments is the adoption of Fletcher. In his thought entire sanctification is instantaneous; Pentecost is, after all, an event, a point in time rather than a process. It is much harder in Fletcher's framework to maintain the process that was integral to Wesley's framework. And ironically it seems to me that he was originally attracted to Fletcher's thought because it gave him the vocabulary to speak developmentally of stages in the Christian life—first the bud and then the flower; first the babe, then the young man, then the mature man; and so on.

I do not blame all of this on Fletcher, but as his formulation moved out from under Wesley and the context of original Methodism, I think it had the tendency to take on a life of its own and prepare the way for fundamentalism in the Holiness movement. This would involve a complicated argument that I can only sketch here, but it would involve the following elements:

(1) Much (if not all) depends on the definition of fundamentalism that one assumes. I am drawn more and more to the thesis of Ernest Sandeen that fundamentalism must be understood "fundamentally" in terms of the rise of "dispensational premillennialism" and that more features of the movement are explicable in this than other paradigms: from the resistance to evolution, to a hyper-supernaturalism that rends asunder earlier more synergistic patterns of thought, to a literalistic view of Scripture, to cultural disengagement, to the "great reversal" that abandoned "social reform," to the curriculum of the bible colleges, and so on. I am convinced that

Fletcher's doctrine of dispensations helped open the door to this. I know that this will at first seem improbable to many. But it is worth noticing that Arnold Ehlert's *Bibliographic History of Dispensationalism* starts with Fletcher. And I think that this hypothesis gains credibility when one notices how often in the late nineteenth century the adoption of the Fletcherian framework antedated the adoption of "dispenational premillennialism" by about a decade.

(2) These hints gain force when one notices how Fletcher's position placed greater weight on the return of Christ as the "blessed hope" in contrast to Wesley's tendency to speak of eschatological matters in terms of the Puritan tradition of "holy living and holy dying." In a similar manner, Fletcher's position heightened the "prophetic" categories of the interpretation of the Bible, especially the OT. Attention is shifted to Joel's prophecy of the outpouring of the Holy Spirit in a way that makes more problematic direct appropriation of OT models of piety. For Wesley Noah walked perfect before the Lord, something that was more difficult in the Fletcher construct.

(3) There is a certain biblicism in Fletcher (in his appeal to Acts, etc.) that undercuts Wesley's more Catholic appeal to the normativity of the first three centuries of the early church.

Many of these issues have behind them an ethical concern. Much of my work still puzzles over the eclipse of the "revivalism and social reform" celebrated by Tim Smith. I am convinced that keys to this are to be found in the synergism of Wesley's thought, in the postmillennialism that I see as a natural extension of Wesley's thought, and so on. I see the Fletcher formulation (as it developed in the late nineteenth century) undercutting many of the themes at the root of the antebellum reform experience. The matter is disputed because Wesley was so soteriologically oriented that he neglected a developed eschatology, but I see postmillennialism as the social correlate of Wesley's doctrine of Christian Perfection: postmillennialism stands for a certain vanquishing of sin in the social order as Christian perfection does in the individual Christian. Similarly baptism with the Holy Spirit finds its social correlate in premillennialisrn. Both have a certain apocalyptic tone—both come in a more "zap" paradigm in which the dominant motif is to "tarry and wait" for the visitation from on high. This apocalyptic focus rends asunder the more synergistic constructs of Wesley and makes human effort less relevant both personally and socially.

These suggestions need more debate, but I would hope that they could be moved more to the center of the discussion. I think such a move would lift the level of our debates on this topic.

Bibliography on the Wesley/Fletcher Question in the Wesleyan Theological Journal: "Sanctification as Perfecting Process or Personal Pentecost?"[2]

Histories of the Debate

Merritt, John G. "Fellowship in Ferment: A History of the Wesleyan Theological Society, 1965–84." 21 (1986) 197–99, 203.

Dayton, Donald W. "Thirtieth Anniversary of the Wesleyan Theological Society, Recollections by Decade: Society's Second Decade (1975–1984)." 30:1 (Spring 1995) 222–26.

Bundy, David. "The Histiography of the Wesleyan-Holiness Tradition." 30:1 (Spring 1995) 55–77.

[See also Donald W. Dayton, *Theological Roots of Pentecostalism* (Metuchen, NJ: Hendrickson, 1996) 183–86.]

Chronology of the Debate

Mattke, Robert A. "The Baptism of the Holy Spirit as Related to the Work of Entire Sanctification." 5:1 (Spring 1970) 22–32. [Note: John Merritt (see above) views this article as foundational for the scholarly exchange.]

McGonigle, Herbert. "Pneumatological Nomenclature in Early Methodism." 8 (Spring 1973) 61–72.

Rose, Delbert R. "Distinguishing the Things that Matter." 9 (Spring 1974) 5–14.

Hamilton, James E. "Academic Orthodoxy and the Arminianizing of American Theology." 9 (Spring 1974) 52–59.

Dayton, Donald W. "Asa Mahan and the Development of American Holiness Theology." 9 (Spring 1974) 60–69.

Smith, John W. V. "Holiness and Unity." 10 (Spring 1975) 24–37.

Cubie, David L. "Perfection in Wesley and Fletcher: Inaugural or Teleological?" 11 (Spring 1976) 22–37.

Knight, John A. "John Fletcher's Influence on the Development of Wesleyan Theology in America." 13 (Spring 1978) 13–33.

Coppedge, Allan. "Entire Sanctification in Early American Methodism: 1812–1835." 13 (Spring 1978) 34–50.

Hamilton, James E. "Nineteenth Century Philosophy arid Holiness Theology: A Study in the Thought of Asa Mahan." 13 (Spring 1978) 51–64.

Smith, Timothy L. "The Doctrine of the Sanctifying Spirit: Charles G. Finney's Synthesis of Wesleyan and Covenant Theology." 13 (Spring 1978) 92–113.

---

2. Editor's Note: Dayton appended the following bibliographic history of the debate, which this paper both assumed and was responding to, with the following remarks: "I have appended to this paper a copy of a bibliography of the WTJ articles relevant to the discussion. This was originally prepared by Timothy Salo, a member of my fall seminar who is as a member of the WTS and the Wesleyan Church present here at this meeting."

Dayton, Donald W. "The Doctrine of the Baptism of the Holy Spirit: Its Emergence and Significance." 13 (Spring 1978) 114–26.

Lyon, Robert W. "Baptism and Spirit-Baptism in the New Testament." 14:1 (Spring 1979) 14–26.

Deasley, Alex R. G. "Entire Sanctification and the Baptism with the Holy Spirit: Perspectives on the Biblical View of the Relationship." 14:1 (Spring 1979) 27–44.

Turner, George Allen. "The Baptism of the Holy Spirit in the Wesleyan Tradition." 14:1 (Spring 1979) 60–76.

Wynkoop, Mildred Bangs. "Theological Roots of the Wesleyan Understanding of the Holy Spirit." 14:1 (Spring 1979) 77–98.

Agnew, Milton S. "Baptized with the Spirit." 14:2 (Fall 1979) 7–14. [Note: The Journal editor described this article as applicable to the ongoing debate of the time.]

Arnett, William M. "The Role of the Holy Spirit in Entire Sanctification in the Writings of John Wesley." 14:2 (Fall 1979) 15–30.

Grider, J. Kenneth. "Spirit-Baptism, the Means of Entire Sanctification." 14:2 (Fall 1979) 31–50.

Wood, Laurence W. "Exegetical-Theological Reflections on the Baptism with the Holy Spirit." 14:2 (Fall 1979) 51–63.

Aikens, Alden. "Wesleyan Theology and the Use of Models." 14:2 (Fall 1979) 70.

Smith, Timothy L. "How John Fletcher Became the Theologian of Wesleyan Perfectionism." 15:1 (Spring 1980) 68–87.

Wood, Laurence W. "Thoughts upon the Wesleyan Doctrine of Entire Sanctification with Special Reference to some Similarities with the Roman Catholic Doctrine of Confirmation." 15:1 (Spring 1980) 88–99.

Grider, J. Kenneth. "Evaluation of Timothy Smith's Interpretation of Wesley." 15:2 (Fall 1980) 64–69.

Lyon, Robert W. "The Baptism of the Spirit-Continued." 15:2 (Fall 1980) 70–79.

Smith, Timothy L. "Notes on the Exegesis of John Wesley's Explanatory Notes upon the New Testament." 16:1 (Spring 1981) 107–13

Smith, Timothy L. "The Holy Spirit in the Hymns of the Wesleys." 16:2 (Fall 1981) 20–47.

Mitchell, T. Crichton. "Response to Dr. Timothy Smith on the Wesleys' Hymns." 16:2 (Fall 1981) 48–57.

Dunning, H. Ray. "Systematic Theology in a Wesleyan Mode." 17:1 (Spring 1982) 15–22.

Bible, Ken. "The Wesleys' Hymns on Full Redemption and Pentecost: A Brief Comparison." 17:2 (Fall 1982) 79–87.

Smith, Timothy L. "A Chronological List of Wesley's Sermons and Doctrinal Essays." 17:2 (Fall 1982) 88–110. [Note: This is a list helpful for scholarly research.]

Maddox, Randy L. "Responsible Grace: The Systematic Perspective of Wesleyan Theology."19:2 (Fall 1984) 7–22.

Berg, Daniel N. "The Theological Context of American Wesleyanism." 20:1 (Spring 1985) 45–60.

Dieter, Melvin E. "The Development of Holiness Theology in Nineteenth Century America." 20:1 (Spring 1985) 6 1–77.

Smith, Timothy L. "John Wesley and the Second Blessing." 21(1986) 137–158.

Dayton, Donald W. "The Holiness Witness in the Ecumenical Church." 23 (1988) 92–106.

White, Charles Edward. "Phoebe Palmer and the Development of Pentecostal Pneumatology." 23 (1988) 198–212.

Snyder, Howard A. "Presidential Address: The Holy Reign of God." 24 (1989) 74–90.

Bundy, David. "Christian Virtue: John Wesley and the Alexandrian Tradition." 26 (1991) 139–63.

Lennox, Stephen I. "The Eschatology of George D. Watson." 29 (1994) 111–126.

Dieter, Melvin E. "Primitivism in the American Holiness Tradition." 30:1 (Spring 1995) 78–91.

Jones, Charles E. "Reading the Text in Methodist-Holiness and Pentecostal Spirituality." 30:2 (Fall 1995) 164–81.

Truesdale, Al. "Reification of the Experience of Entire Sanctification in the American Holiness Movement." 31:2 (Fall 1996) 95–119.

Jones, Charles E. "The Inverted Shadow of Phoebe Palmer." 31:2 (Fall 1996) 120–31. [Note: Designated by the editor to be applicable to the theme of Sanctification and the American Holiness Movement.)

Reasoner, Victor P. "The American Holiness Movement's Paradigm Shift Concerning Holiness." 31:2 (Fall 1996) 132–146.

Maddox, Randy L. "Reconnecting the Means to the End: A Wesleyan Prescription for the Holiness Movement." 33:2 (Fall 1998) 29–66.

Wood, Laurence W. "Pentecostal Sanctification in John Wesley and Early Methodism." 34:1 (Spring 1999) 24–63.

Land, Steven J. "The Triune Center: Wesleyans and Pentecostals Together in Mission." 34:1 (Spring 1999) 83–100.

Response #1

Bill Faupel

Don's interest in Pentecostalism came about by accident in 1970. Receiving a BD degree from Yale he accepted the position of Acquisition's Librarian at Asbury Theological Seminary before pursuing a PhD in Barthian studies. An unexpected invitation changed the course of his career, and subsequently, mine as well.

One of Asbury's professors, who had been asked by the American Theological Library Association to prepare a bibliographic essay on the most significant literature of the American Holiness Movement for their annual meeting, had to drop out. Don was asked to write the essay instead. It proved to be a cathartic experience, enabling him to embrace his theological roots from which he had become alienated. As he expressed it in his first monograph, it was a process of *Discovering an Evangelical Heritage*.

To his great surprise, Don discovered that the American Holiness movement was born in the midst of a great struggle to achieve social reform—abolition, women's suffrage, greater equity between labor and management. What puzzled him was why had a movement with such a progressive start been transformed into the inward looking conservative, fundamentalist, and somewhat reactionary tradition he had experienced growing up in the mid-twentieth century. He also wondered why this early history was not part of the received tradition. Thus, when he left Asbury to pursue his doctoral studies at the University of Chicago, his intention to explore some aspect of Barth's theology had been replaced by these burning questions.

He soon discovered that the Holiness movement underwent a paradigm shift following the Civil War. As he tells the story it began with the movement's central doctrine, entire sanctification. John Wesley had articulated the doctrine primarily in terms of "Christian Perfection." Using primarily Pauline categories and Matthew's presentation of Jesus' Sermon on the Mouth, Wesley spoke in terms of a life-time quest of "going on to perfection." Following the war between the States, Holiness leaders tended to articulate the doctrine in terms of Baptism of the Holy Spirit, using concepts taken from Luke-Acts and understanding the doctrine in terms of a second existential crisis to be sought and experienced subsequent to conversion.

This shift in the central doctrine was followed within a couple of decades by a shift of worldview and mission finding primary expression in the movement's eschatology, namely moving from a postmillennial understanding of Christ's return, to a premillennial point of view. As Don has stated many times, this shift was far more than stating that Christ's second coming would inaugurate a thousand-year reign, rather than coming at the end of this period. It also changed the focus of the movement's understanding of its mission. Postmillennialist Wesleyans, following their founder's lead, understood the mission to "spread Scripture holiness across these lands." By this they meant both converting the peoples of all nations to Christ and transforming all institutions to functioning in a manner consistent with a Christian ethic. Premillennialist Wesleyans, on the other hand saw their mission as giving witness of Christ's claims to the nations and calling the church, Christ's bride, to put on her bridal garments to prepare for the coming of Christ the bridegroom. This study, of course, culminated in Don's doctoral dissertation and subsequent monograph, *Theological Roots of Pentecostalism*.

This work of Don's has raised significant and interrelated issues for Pentecostalism, Wesleyanism, and Evangelicalism. For Pentecostalism, *Roots* did theologically what Vinson Synan's *The Holiness-Pentecostal Movement*[1] did historically. It showed conclusively that Pentecostalism emerged out of a Wesleyan context. It raised two challenges for Pentecostals. First, on the surface it seemed to suggest that most Pentecostals, especially those that adopted William Durham's "Finished Work" doctrine of sanctification, had abandoned a dimension that was at the heart of Pentecostal theology. In truth, however, Don was arguing the exact opposite. The Pentecostal understanding of Spirit-baptism as "empowerment for service" rather than as "cleansing from sin" was a far more faithful articulation of Luke-Acts categories. For Dayton, Pentecostalism was the logical consequence and legitimate heir of the paradigm shift that took place within the nineteenth century Holiness movement.

The second challenge was the more serious one. It called into serious question a historiography that interpreted Pentecostalism as essentially a wing of the emerging Fundamentalism that was rooted in the Princeton theology of Hodge and Warfield and that sought to resist a growing lib-

---

1. (Grand Rapids, MI: Eerdmans, 1971).

eralism. Rather, Dayton's analysis suggests that Pentecostalism is rooted in a Wesleyan pietism that is historically much more closely aligned with classic theological liberalism.

As Don's article to which this commentary is a response makes clear, his dissertation has prompted a more forceful response within the Wesleyan/Holiness tradition than it has within Pentecostalism. Struck by a fear that Don's analysis suggested that the shift from Christological categories to Pneumatological ones in the mid-nineteenth century resulted in a holiness theology more closely related to Pentecostalism than to John Wesley's distinctive message of entire sanctification, critics responded by arguing that the Luke-Acts formulation was built on the dispensational theology of John Fletcher, Wesley's designated successor. They contended that since Wesley endorsed Fletcher, this theological articulation was a natural and legitimate extension. Dayton has countered that Wesley felt uncomfortable with Fletcher's articulation and after Fletcher's death, clearly refuted the position in a series of letters to Joseph Benson, Fletcher's biographer:

> If they like to call this 'receiving the Holy Ghost,' they may; only the phrase in that sense is not scriptural and not quite proper; for they all 'received the Holy Ghost when they were justified . . .
>
> . . . Likewise, think whether you can abstain from speaking of Mr. Fletcher's late discovery. The Methodist in general could not bear this. It would create huge debate and confusion.[2]

The latest and most sustained response to Don's articulation is found in Laurence W. Wood's monograph: *The Meaning of Pentecost in Early Methodism: John Fletcher as Wesley's Vindicator and Designated Successor*.[3] In this work, Wood argues that Fletcher's "late discovery" referred to receiving "the witness of the Spirit" rather than equating entire sanctification with Spirit-baptism and that during the last twenty years of his life, Wesley articulated the doctrine in Spirit-baptism categories.[4] In the present article, Don responded to Wood without having had the opportunity to read the manuscript that was in preparation for publication. Since that time they

---

2. J. Telford (ed.), *The Letters of the Rev. John Wesley*, V (London: Epworth, 1931) 214, 228. Likewise, Fletcher acknowledged this difference in understanding. In a letter to his future wife, Mary Bosanquet dated March 7, 1778, he wrote: "I would distinguish more exactly between the believers baptized with the Pentecostal power of the Holy Ghost and the believer, who like the Apostles after our Lord's ascension, is not yet filled with the power." L Tyreman, *Wesley's Designated Successor* (London: Hodder and Stoughton, 1882) 411.

3. (Lanham, MD: Scarecrow, 2002).

4. Ibid., 40, 163–246.

have had a series of exchanges that have appeared in *Pneuma: The Journal of the Society for Pentecostal Studies*.[5] In reading through this exchange, it seems to me that Don and Larry speak past each other. I doubt that the issue will be settled until after both pass from the scene.

Don's dissertation has implications for the Evangelical movement as well. At first reading one might conclude that Don would question whether the Pentecostal movement and the Holiness movement should have joined forces with the Evangelical wing of the Reformed tradition to form the National Association of Evangelicals. However, that is not his conclusion at all. Rather he would argue that those Reformed groups that joined the Association have their roots in the nineteenth century theological trajectory of New Light Presbyterianism, Oberlin Perfectionism and the Keswick Movement. Far from being rooted in the Princeton theology that is reflected in the creed of the NAE, these groups actually sprung from a nineteenth century pietistic revivalism and all were the subject of the Hodge-Warfield critique. All of the groups in the NAE, Don would argue, have mistaken their desired teleology as the source of their origin. Their misplaced historiography, he would suggest, prevents them from making positive creative responses to the theological challenges they face today.

It is at this point that Don's frustration emerges at the current state of debate the thesis of his dissertation has created. By "quibbling" over details of his historiography, he feels, the leadership of the three movements discussed above is prevented from using resources within their respective traditions to address challenges they face today. The three he raises in the preceding essay: the oneness/Trinitarian challenge within Pentecostalism; the crisis/process issue within the Holiness Movement; and personal piety/social justice dilemma within Evangelicalism are suggestive of the issues which could be addressed from a new perspective should his understanding of origins be embraced.

---

5. *Pneuma: The Journal of the Society for Pentecostal Studies* 26:2 (Fall 2004) 355–61; 27:1 (Spring 2005) 63–172; 27:2 (Fall 2005) 367–75; 28:1 (Spring 2006) 120–30; 28:2 (Fall 2006) 265–70.

Response #2

Amos Yong

Wesley and Fletcher—Dayton and Wood: Appreciating Wesleyan-Holiness Tongues, Essaying Pentecostal-Charismatic Interpretations

Introduction: Dayton's Theological Roots of Pentecostalism

Don Dayton's *Theological Roots of Pentecostalism* may be one of a handful of books that helped put Pentecostalism on the map of the theological academy as a movement with its own theological voice.[1] Its major accomplishments toward this end were at least threefold. First, *Theological Roots* rescued Pentecostalism from the domain of sociologists and sociological analyses prevalent up to that point, even as it cautioned against explaining away the Pentecostal experience as a socio-psychological pathology. Central to success along the latter front was that glossolalia was only a minor chord in Dayton's analysis, subordinated to the major doctrines of Christ as savior, baptizer (in the Holy Spirit), healer, and coming king. This is not to belittle the socio-psychological research on Pentecostalism to that point; but it is to say that Dayton's work opened up the possibility of studying Pentecostalism as a theological movement, rather than only as a tongues-speaking one.

Second, and building on the first point, the roots of this "fourfold" gospel of Pentecostalism are located within the wider framework of American revivalism and nineteenth century Wesleyan, Holiness, and evangelical movements. While for intra-Pentecostal purposes the falling

---

1. Previous to Dayton's *Theological Roots of Pentecostalism* the work of Walter Hollenweger paved the way as well through his focus on the oral and narrative theological dispositions of Pentecostalism. But Dayton's work provided the needed kind of historical and diachonic analysis to complement Hollenweger's arguments.

of the Spirit "suddenly from heaven" makes for good testimonies, for academic purposes it is the identification of an historical genealogy which validates and legitimizes the theological pedigree of any movement. After *Theological Roots*, modern Pentecostalism ceased to be an inexplicable aberration in the history of Christianity; rather, it linked back to the history of Christian thought through its Wesleyan-Holiness ancestors in the North American context.

Not by accident then, thirdly, Dayton's *Theological Roots* inspired the emergence of a distinctively Pentecostal theological perspective in the academy. Whereas the 1970s saw the formation of the Society of Pentecostal Studies galvanized and organized primarily by historians of the movement who were achieving their PhDs at respectable institutions of higher education, and whereas the 1980s saw the first biblical scholars of the movement wrestling with issues of Spirit-baptism, subsequence, and conversion-initiation, the 1990s saw the first generation of Pentecostal theologians appear—e.g., Steven Land, Frank Macchia, Veli-Matti Kärkkainen—and these were in many ways dependent on Dayton's ground-breaking book.[2] *Theological Roots* opened up intellectual space that was previously nonexistent, and it was into this arena carved out by Dayton that others from within the Pentecostal movement have subsequently stepped and expanded the conversation.

Of course, Don Dayton's contribution to Pentecostal theology has far exceeded the publication of *Theological Roots* twenty plus years ago. Long before his book appeared, he had already contributed to *PNEUMA: The Journal of the Society for Pentecostal Studies* and in that way served as a stimulus to Pentecostal scholarship.[3] He has also been a faithful attendee of and participant in Society for Pentecostal Studies meetings over the years and even served as president of the society (1989). And more recently, in the last few issues of *PNEUMA*, there has been a vigorous exchange between Dayton and Laurence Wood on the theologies of Wesley and Fletcher and their implications for Pentecostal theology.[4]

---

2. I tell part of this story in my "Pentecostalism and the Theological Academy," *Theology Today* 64:2 (2007): forthcoming.

3. See, e.g., Donald W. Dayton, "Theological Roots of Pentecostalism," *PNEUMA* 2:1 (1980) 3–21, and "The Rise of the Evangelical Healing Movement in Nineteenth Century America," *PNEUMA* 4:1 (1982) 1–18.

4. See Donald W. Dayton, "John Fletcher as John Wesley's Vindicator and Designated Successor? A Response to Laurence W. Wood," *PNEUMA* 26:2 (2004) 355–61; Laurence W. Wood, "An Appreciative Reply to Donald W. Dayton's 'Review Essay,'" *PNEUMA* 27:1 (2005) 163–72; Donald W. Dayton, "Rejoinder to Laurence Wood," *PNEUMA* 27:2 (2005) 367–75; Larry Wood, "Can Pentecostals Be Wesleyans? My Reply to Don Dayton's

It is with such recognition of and gratitude for Don Dayton's contributions, then, that I wish to enter into what might otherwise be thought to be an "intra-Wesleyan-Holiness" scuffle. In the remainder of this essay, let me summarize the Dayton-Wood exchange and identify the main issues as I see them, and then attempt to provide what might be called some Pentecostal-charismatic interpretations of these Wesleyan-Holiness tongues in order to push the discussion forward, at least for those of us working in the area of Pentecostal theology. My goal is not necessarily to adjudicate between Dayton and Wood—although I'm optimistic that there is the possibility of identifying more common cause between them than the latest round of the exchange might suggest—but to pay tribute to Dayton's scholarship and do so precisely by engaging in the debate over the question opened up by his important book: regarding the theological roots of Pentecostalism.

Between Dayton and Wood: Speaking Wesleyan-Holiness Tongues

The recent debate between Dayton and Wood has brought to the surface underlying tensions in Wesleyan-Holiness scholarship that stretch back over three decades. Precipitating this airing of the issues was the appearance of Wood's *The Meaning of Pentecost in Early Methodism: Rediscovering John Fletcher as John Wesley's Vindicator and Designated Successor* in 2002.[5] Wood prosecuted the twofold hypothesis announced in the book's subtitle through a close reading of original Wesleyan sources—including the writings and other edited publications of Wesley and Fletcher—as well as a retrieving of nineteenth century American Methodist theological voices. In the process, Wood argues that the later Wesley agreed with Fletcher that the baptism of the Holy Spirit was a work (or dispensation) of grace subsequent to Christian initiation through which entire sanctification or Christian perfection in love is experienced in the hearts and lives of believers. The cash value of this theological argument, Wood suggests, is a reappropriation of the Anglican rite of confirmation which provides a sacramental moment during which the gift of the Spirit is imparted for

---

Rejoinder," *PNEUMA* 28:1 (2006) 120–30; and Donald W. Dayton, "A Final Round with Larry Wood," *PNEUMA* 28:2 (2006) 265–70.

5. Laurence W. Wood, *The Meaning of Pentecost in Early Methodism: Rediscovering John Fletcher as John Wesley's Vindicator and Designated Successor*, Pietist and Wesleyan Studies 15 (Lanham, MD, and Oxford: Scarecrow, 2002).

the purposes of transforming those justified by grace through faith (initial sanctification) into those fully perfected in love (Christian perfection).

Dayton's review of this book in the pages of *PNEUMA* brought forth Wood's response and the ensuing full-blown debate (see footnote 4 for the details). My own view is that there are a number of other broader issues that are animating the discussion. While readers of this essay who have not yet seen the original exchanges would be well-advised to do so and draw their own conclusions about what is being argued, Dayton himself has consistently called attention to these wider matters.[6] Allow me to put into my own words some of what is at stake, especially as articulated by Dayton.

There are six sets of issues as I see them—all of which are interrelated—and I will discuss them in no particular order. First, Dayton has long been concerned that Wesley's christocentric focus is threatened not necessarily by Fletcher's theology, but by post-Fletcherian developments which at the same time would legitimize their projects through appeal to Fletcher's writings. On this point, however, there is the irony to Dayton's worry that American Pentecostal theology—the roots of which are to be found in the American Wesleyan-Holiness movement inspired in part by Fletcherian insights linking baptism with the Holy Spirit to the Day of Pentecost—produced instead both a christocentric theology of Jesus as savior, baptizer, healer, and coming king, and a radicalized version of this in the "Jesus-only" or Oneness Pentecostal trajectory. This does not mean, of course, that there are no radical Pentecostal groups that have departed from this christocentrism, but it does mean that the theological stream opened up by Fletcher's theology of baptism with the Holy Spirit does not necessarily result in negligence of the person and work of Christ. Wood's retrieval of Fletcher, it appears to me, should mollify rather than exacerbate Dayton's anxieties here.

Second, Dayton seems to have been troubled, at least initially, by the turn in Fletcher's theology to Luke-Acts, in contrast to Wesley's more Johannine and Pauline focus. What is at stake on this issue is the eclipse of Wesley's emphases on perfect love and its replacement with Lukan themes of empowerment. Dayton is not necessarily rejecting Pentecostal readings

---

6. See, e.g., Donald W. Dayton, "Asa Mahan and the Development of American Holiness Theology," *Wesleyan Theological Journal* 9 (spring 1974): 60–69; "The Holiness Witness in the Ecumenical Church," *Wesleyan Theological Journal* 23 (1988): 92–106; *Theological Roots of Pentecostalism*, 51–54; and the essay printed in this volume—"Revisiting the 'Baptism with the Holy Spirit' Controversy: A Response to My Critics"—to which I am responding, at least in part.

of Luke and Acts—in fact he thinks that Pentecostals are better exegetes of the Lukan corpus, but for Pentecostal emphases on empowerment rather than for Wesleyan-Holiness purposes related to sanctification—yet he wants to guard against the quest for the Spirit's power eclipsing the traditional Holiness focus on the Spirit's sanctifying fruits. Further, since the Lukan narratives discuss the baptism with the Holy Spirit in terms of "crisis" experiences, a Lukan theology would sustain and perpetuate a more "crisis" interpretation of the doctrine of sanctification over and against the more "process" oriented understanding of Wesley's (as informed by John and Paul); and this shift, for Dayton, would be for the worse so far as the Holiness tradition is concerned. On these points, however, it is essential to remember first that Fletcher's original motivation for exploring the baptism with the Holy Spirit was to understand the Christian experience of full perfection through the sanctifying work of the divine Spirit. At the same time, Dayton is also right to note that in the hands of less astute Wesleyan-Holiness theologians in the nineteenth century, the nuance of Fletcher's theology of baptism with the Holy Spirit unraveled in the search for once-for-all evidences of the Spirit's sanctifying graces. So the question now may be whether or not (with Wood) to retrieve Fletcher as a corrective or (following Dayton) to return to Wesley.

The third issue builds on the second and concerns Wesley's insistence that the Holy Spirit is given at salvation (justification) rather than later on. Wood's research seems to indicate Fletcher and Wesley came into agreement finally that new believers did receive the Spirit at initial salvation, but that there remained also a post-conversion experience of the baptism with the fullness of the Holy Spirit in which the believer is transformed and sanctified by the outpouring of God's perfect love.[7] In this way, the initial "slight difference" identified by Wesley upon reading a draft of Fletcher's *Last Check to Antinomianism* appears to have been resolved. Yet the Dayton-Wood exchange does raise the question: was the resolution one in which Wesley came to see that Fletcher's position was at worst one to which Wesley did not object or at best one over which Wesley felt that Fletcher was entitled to his own opinion (Dayton's position) or did Wesley and Fletcher resolve their differences through Wesley's coming to agree with Fletcher that the second work of grace was to be equated with the baptism with the Holy Spirit (Wood's thesis)?

This historical and exegetical "intra-Wesleyan" question, however, opens up to the wider set of issues related not only to the theological roots

---

7. Wood, *The Meaning of Pentecost*, 66–68.

but also to the theological fruits of Pentecostalism. Put succinctly, there are important consequences for Pentecostalism precisely on this issue of whether or not there is an experience subsequent to Christian initiation and whether or not such an experience is what Fletcher called the baptism with the Holy Spirit. Undeniably, the doctrine of subsequence first defended by Fletcher was itself transformed during the nineteenth century Wesleyan-Holiness revivals, and when it was received by the early Pentecostals, the baptism with the Holy Spirit was no longer associated with perfection in love but with empowerment for Christian service and witness (except in Pentecostal Holiness circles when these two works of grace were expanded to three: salvation, sanctification, and empowerment). In this sense, Dayton's concerns are not misplaced since if left unchecked, what results at least in popular Pentecostal circles is a two-tiered Christianity: the "saved" at one level and those filled with the Holy Spirit at a higher level.

The fifth issue concerns Fletcher's doctrine of dispensations, the theological framework within which he understood the baptism with the Holy Spirit. Wood clearly explains that Fletcher understood there were four dispensations: that of the Gentiles, that of the Jews, that of the incarnate Christ (as represented by the "infant Christianity" of John the Baptist and the disciples during the life of Christ), and that of the Day of Pentecost representing the fullness of Christian faith. Wood also shows that Fletcher understood these dispensations to not only correlate with historical periods but also to apply as existential and experiential periods in the spiritual journey of individual lives. Dayton is distressed, however, by the implication that a covenant theological interpretation of human history divided by the incarnation, death, and resurrection of Christ will be displaced by a tri-partite interpretation of history in which the dispensation of the Father (in the Hebrew Bible) gives way to that of the Son (in the incarnation) and is later superseded by that of the Spirit (at Pentecost). Whereas Wesley clearly could be located within the former framework, Fletcher's doctrine of dispensations opened the door toward the latter, perhaps even inviting a Joachimite augmentation. The risks, Dayton suspects, outweigh the benefits.

This is especially the case when the final major issue at stake in this discussion is taken into consideration: whether or not Fletcherian dispensationalism might not only give way to but perhaps even inspire Darbyite dispensationalism and pre-millennialism on the one hand as well as pre-tribulational escapism on the other. For Dayton the major problem with the latter forms of dispensationalism is that they undercut the impetus toward social activism and social concern characteristic of Wesley's ministry and manifest clearly in nineteenth century Holiness abolition and other social reform movements. In the wrong dispensationalist hands, Christian perfection shifts so that social engagement is replaced by personal salvation (through the rapture of believers, for instance) and individualistically oriented sanctification (e.g., do not smoke, do not drink, and other such socially conventionalized mores). This is an anemic, subjectivistic, and inward-looking Christianity, and inasmuch as Fletcher's theology even provides any footholds for being co-opted by these kinds of dispensational emphases, all the more important (for Dayton) that we situate Fletcher in relationship to Wesley rather than the other way around. And insofar as Dayton thinks that Wood's argument about Fletcher being the vindicator and successor of Wesley takes us in the wrong direction, to that same extent Dayton continues to resist Wood's retrieval of Fletcher as Methodism's designated theologian.

I am very sympathetic to Dayton's enthusiasm; yet I can't help but think that these valid concerns have skewed his engagement with Wood in the process. At times, I've felt that both have been speaking past one another: Dayton being motivated by these larger issues related to modern Pentecostalism and its imagined and real excesses, and Wood being motivated by invigorating Wesleyan-Holiness and Methodist movements that have lost touch with the original vision of Christian perfection, purity, and power as understood by Wesley and Fletcher. In fact, from where I sit, it seems to me that Wood himself is just as concerned as Dayton that the Wesleyan-Holiness tradition does not lose its distinctive Christian witness, especially if that means being swallowed up and taken over by late twentieth-century Pentecostal-charismatic radicalism.[8] On the other side, Dayton's important insistence that Wesley remain a primary resource for Wesleyan-Holiness theology today could be read as having been maintained rather than undermined by Wood's rediscovery of Fletcher. Whither then this intra-mural Wesleyan-Holiness debate between Dayton and Wood on Wesley and Fletcher?

Between Dayton's Wesley and Wood's Fletcher: Toward Pentecostal-Charismatic Interpretations

I am interested in formulating some kind of response to this question in large part because in a recent book, *The Spirit Poured Out on All Flesh:*

---

8. E.g., Laurence W. Wood, "Third Wave of the Spirit and the Pentecostalization of American Christianity: A Wesleyan Critique," *Wesleyan Theological Journal* 31:1 (1996) 110–40.

Pentecostalism and the Possibility of Global Theology, I draw assistance from the Wesleyan tradition by recovering the work of both Wesley and Fletcher at key moments in my attempt to articulate a constructive Pentecostal theology.[9] At the time of my writing this book (the fall of 2003 through the winter of 2004), I had read Wood's *The Meaning of Pentecost*, but was not as privy to the extensiveness of the debate on this issue (as documented in part by Dayton's "Revisiting" essay in this volume). I now come to the discussion motivated by this latest round of exchanges between Dayton and Wood to go back through the debate especially as it evolved in the pages of the *Wesleyan Theological Journal*. While I do not presume in what follows to resolve the disagreements, especially as a relative "outsider" to the Wesleyan-Holiness tradition, let me suggest some Pentecostal-charismatic perspectives directed toward two objectives: to defend my own reading of Wesley and Fletcher for the purposes of doing the kind of constructive Pentecostal theology invited and even inspired by Dayton's lifelong work, and perhaps in the process bring Dayton and Wood, along with Wesley and Fletcher, back into a mutual conversation. To do so, let me argue three main points.

First, as a Pentecostal theologian, it is important to note that any retrieval of Fletcher for Pentecostal theological purposes was set up first by Dayton's *Theological Roots*. To be sure, Wood had published an earlier volume defending his basic theological thesis regarding Easter and Pentecost representing two stages of the Christian life.[10] However, this volume addressed first and foremost, if not only, Wood's fellow Wesleyan-Holiness scholars, and the retrieval of Fletcher only played a minor rather than major role in Wood's overall argument. On the other hand, it was Dayton who first called attention to the crucial role of Fletcher's more "pentecostal" perspectives for the emergence of the modern Pentecostal movement.[11] Without downplaying the potential for theological aberration in Fletcher's formulations (about which I will say more momentarily), I nevertheless think there is much more to be gained than lost from a Pentecostal reappropriation of Fletcher. From a historical perspective, I think that Dayton's argument in *Theological Roots*—about the lineage

---

9. See Yong, *The Spirit Poured Out on All Flesh: Pentecostalism and the Possibility of Global Theology* (Grand Rapids: Baker Academic, 2005) §§2.2.3 on Wesley's *via salutis* (with some reference to Fletcher) toward a dynamic soteriology, §6.2.1 on retrieving Fletcher's doctrine of dispensations toward a contemporary theology of religions, and §7.1.2 on Wesley the amateur scientist toward a contemporary Pentecostal theology of creation.

10. See Laurence W. Wood, *Pentecostal Grace* (Wilmore, KY: Francis Asbury, 1980).

11. Dayton, *Theological Roots*, 51–54, 92–94, and 149–53.

from Fletcher to modern Pentecostalism through the nineteenth century American Holiness movement—is unassailable. That being the case, one might as well do the best one can with one's genealogy (through Fletcher) rather than trying to leap over it (i.e., to go directly to Wesley).

But from a more theological point of view, I have elsewhere argued that Christian trinitarianism remains only rhetorical unless one moves from Nicea to Constantinople.[12] In other words, a christocentric theology without an equally robust pneumatology leaves us with a binitarian rather than fully Trinitarian Christian faith. Put in terms of the current intra-Wesleyan debate, might I suggest that Wesley's christocentrism (to use Dayton's terminology) without Fletcher's pneumatological and Pentecostal theology (Wood's reading) similarly leaves the Wesleyan-Holiness movement with the purity (the sinlessness of Christ) but without the power (the anointing of the Spirit). Now of course Dayton in no way wishes to separate the Spirit from the Son, and I am not suggesting for a moment that this is what he is insisting on. However, I am also both making the historical observation of the link between Wesley and Fletcher (which connections Wood has argued in detail), and the theological point that the "Pentecostal theology" of Fletcher flows forth at least logically from Wesley's christocentrism. Put alternatively, I am suggesting that Pentecostalism is a valid "grandchild" or "great-grandchild" (depending on how one is counting) of Wesley and Wesleyanism rather than either a bastardized or adopted offspring. With Pentecostalism, Wesleyanism's theology of experience—e.g., as identified in the Wesleyan quadrilateral—comes to fruition through the emergence of what could be called a theology of the Third Article of the creed (pneumatological theology). In this sense, Wood's argument is at least theologically sound—about Fletcher's "Pentecostal theology" as a logical extension of Wesley's theology—even if it might be contested at the historical level (by Dayton or others).

But having defended Wood's reading of Fletcher at least at the theological level, I now wish, second, to once again acknowledge Dayton's own explicitly theological cautions. As vital as is Fletcher's work for a full-orbed Trinitarian theology for both Wesleyans and Pentecostals, Dayton's repeated reminder of Wesley's christocentrism is just as important for protecting Pentecostalism from veering off the theological edge. The dangers of experiential theologies derived from an unchecked pneumatocentrism are well documented in the history of Christian thought. In my own

---

12. See Yong, *Spirit-Word-Community: Theological Hermeneutics in Trinitarian Perspective* (Aldershot, UK, and Burlington, VT: Ashgate, 2002; reprint edition, Eugene, OR: Wipf & Stock, 2006) ch. 2.

work, I have wrestled with the tension of on the one hand pushing for a robust pneumatology that is related but not subordinated to christology or defined exclusively in christological terms, and of on the other hand having to identify the theological content of any pneumatology apart from christological terms.[13] More recently, I have come to see that my own primary theological intuitions work best only when sustained in two directions: that, yes, Christian Trinitarian theology requires a fully developed pneumatology, but also that, yes, this in turn assumes not only a "high" christology of some sort but also an inseparable relationship between pneumatology and christology.[14]

This christological check on pneumatology, which we might call a "Daytonian reserve," can be seen in effect in my book where I draw on both Wesley and Fletcher, among others, to articulate what I there called a dynamic soteriology.[15] In that place, I presented an argument for the baptism with the Holy Spirit as a metaphor for salvation featuring crisis moments (first, second, and even later moments of gracious experiences) without denying the salvific process (I was saved, I am being saved, I will be saved).[16] The point I made there was to emphasize sanctification as part of salvation, rather than merely as the fruits of salvation. In this context, with regard to the Dayton-Wood debate, I wrote: "I remain unconvinced that the evidence demands the later Wesley to be understood solely in Fletcherian terms."[17] Re-reading these matters in light of the Dayton-Wood exchange confirms my initial theological intuition: that while Wesley clearly agreed enough with Fletcher to reprint the latter's works, even to the point of placing his imprimatur on these publications (here granting Wood's basic point), yet Wesley's own theological positions,

---

13. My working through these tensions are clearly documented in *Discerning the Spirit(s): A Pentecostal-Charismatic Contribution to Christian Theology of Religions*, Journal of Pentecostal Theology Supplement series 20 (Sheffield: Sheffield Academic, 2000) chs. 3–4, and *Beyond the Impasse: Toward a Pneumatological Theology of Religions* (Grand Rapids: Baker Academic, 2003) ch. 4.

14. I develop this argument in the arena of theology of religions in my forthcoming *The Spirit of Hospitality: Pentecost and Christian Practices in a World of Many Faiths* (Maryknoll: Orbis, 2008).

15. Yong, *Spirit Poured Out on All Flesh*, ch. 2, esp. §2.2.

16. Here I believe I am in the mainstream of Wesley scholarship; for example, David L. Cubie, "Perfection in Wesley and Fletcher: Inaugural or Teleological?" *Wesleyan Theological Journal* 11 (1976): 22–37, esp. 22, and Mildred Bangs Wynkoop, "Theological Roots of Wesleyanism's Understanding of the Holy Spirit," *Wesleyan Theological Journal* 14:1 (1979) 77–98, esp. 95, have made similar observations.

17. Yong, *Spirit Poured Out on All Flesh*, 105n63.

even later in his life, need not be seen as being identical to that of his designated successor. Put in Dayton's terms, Wesley could have endorsed in the main Fletcher's dispensational and Pentecostal pneumatology without relinquishing his own christological commitments. In fact, it was precisely such a christocentric framework, I suggest, that allowed Wesley to accept Fletcher's theological formulations and contributions toward early Methodist theology. Similarly, my own project in Pentecostal and pneumatological theology assumes rather than seeks to supplant the main lines of christological developments in the history of Christian thought. In short, pneumatology fills out Trinitarian theology not by discarding or neglecting christology, but by filling out, expanding, and even deepening the ongoing reception of the Christian confession of Jesus Christ as Lord.[18]

In the end, then, whither the Dayton-Wood debate about Wesley and Fletcher? Let me close with this observation. From one angle into the historical issues (and remember that I write as a Pentecostal theologian rather than as a Wesleyan historian!), I think Wood is right about Fletcher, but Dayton is right about Wesley. Wood is right to suggest that Fletcher was more important for Wesley and Methodist theology than Dayton is willing to grant (and this perhaps for theological rather than historical reasons), but Dayton is also right that this does not mean Wesley agreed with every detail of Fletcher's works that were reprinted. With regard to other historical claims, I am unsure that there can be any final adjudication of the Dayton-Wood debate, even among Wesleyan historians.[19]

But at the theological level, the Wesleyan-Holiness movement and Pentecostalism needs both Wesley and Fletcher, and Dayton and Wood. The latter pair seems to be speaking in tongues drastically different from the former two. However, if the Pentecostal gift of interpretation of tongues can be discerned at all in the foregoing, then perhaps we might conclude that these various languages—of Wesley and Fletcher, of Dayton and Wood—have all sounded forth in their own ways the wondrous works of God, even as happened on the Day of Pentecost two millennia ago (Acts 2:11). And if readers of this essay are even open to the possibility that such interpretation of tongues might be an ongoing gift of the Holy

18. This is the outworking of what I call the eschatological hermeneutic of Pentecostalism; see my "Performing Global Pentecostal Theology: A Response to Wolfgang Vondey," *PNEUMA: The Journal of the Society for Pentecostal Studies* 28:2 (2006) 313–21, esp. 318–20.

19. Here, the field of Wesley scholarship is divided, with individuals like Maddox and Grider seemingly supporting the points registered by Dayton, but others like Turner and Dieter weighing in on the side of Wood's reading of Fletcher. There are other scholars involved, who Dayton discusses in his essay on this matter in this volume.

Spirit, that is itself not only attributable to the emergence of modern day Pentecostalism, but is also due, at least in part, to the legitimization of this movement through Don Dayton's superb telling of the story of its theological roots. In this way and in many others, Dayton's legacy for Pentecostal scholarship in general and Pentecostal theology in particular is secured.[20]

---

20. My thanks to Christian T. Collins Winn for inviting my contribution to this festschrift.

7

The Pietist Impulse

A common theme highlighted in Dayton's work is the widespread neglect of Pietism in the Anglo-American world. This theme recurs in multiple settings, but none is perhaps as important to his theological and historical project as the question of the decisive influence of Pietism on 19th century evangelicalism and the later phenomenon of 20th century neo-evangelicalism. In fact, for Dayton, much of the theological and historical confusion that he detects in contemporary neo-evangelicalism can be traced to the widespread suppression of and ignorance over the historical and theological dynamics of Pietism, both as it arose in Germany and as it was later mediated to the Anglo-American context via Wesley and others.

In April 2001, Dayton presented the following essay at the Wheaton Theology Conference. The essay was later published in the Bacote, Miguélez, and Okholm edited volume, *Evangelicals & Scripture: Tradition, Authority and Hermeneutics* (Downers Grove: InterVarsity, 2004). In it, Dayton seeks to show that if contemporary neo-evangelicals are going to take their own history seriously, this will have serious implications in the contemporary debates over what "the" evangelical doctrine of Scripture is or should be. The essay also includes the essential elements of Dayton's Society for Pentecostal Studies Presidential Address, given in 1989, which Dayton was unable to fully commit to writing due to a family illness.

The Pietist Theological Critique of Biblical Inerrancy

Donald W. Dayton

In the 1940s there emerged a party from fundamentalism that came to be called "neo-evangelicalism," though the "neo-" was soon dropped. Within this party, a key role was played by those who came to be known as the "Harvard evangelicals"—a group of young scholars who had studied in Cambridge (and at Boston University). Many of them were under the influence of Harold John Ockenga, the pastor of Park Street Church in Boston, a major figure in the founding of the National Association of Evangelicals, later the president of both Fuller and Gordon-Conwell seminaries, and the major architect of the neo-evangelical platform. In a speech printed in *The Spire*, the Park Street Church's newsletter, he spelled out the platform's goals: to develop an intellectually respectable apologetic for Orthodox Christianity, to move beyond the separatism of fundamentalism and regain control of the mainline churches, and to recover an "evangelical social conscience" (a theme that was echoed in the 1948 *programmschrift* of neo-evangelicalism by Carl F. H. Henry, *The Uneasy Conscience of Modern Fundamentalism*).[1] In the face of fundamentalist reaction to this revisionist agenda, its defenders insisted on their "orthodoxy" by appeal to their continuing adherence to the doctrine of "the inerrancy of Scripture in the original autographs." They made it the litmus test of evangelical authenticity, most notably by making it the sole clause that one had to sign to become a member of the Evangelical Theological Society (ETS).

In their articulation of this doctrine, the neo-evangelicals appealed to the "old Princeton theology" of Charles Hodge and B. B. Warfield. Though anticipated earlier, this doctrine of "inerrancy in the original autographs" received its definitive statement in a famous article (and later book) in 1881 on "inspiration" authored by A. A. Hodge (son of Charles)

---

1. Carl F. H. Henry, *The Uneasy Conscience of Modern Fundamentalism* (Grand Rapids: Eerdmans, 1947).

and Warfield.[2] The phrase *original autographs* reflects the willingness of the Princeton theologians, and of especially Warfield himself, to engage in the task of "lower criticism" (the establishing of the original text of the Bible that had been corrupted through its history of transmission) while rejecting "higher criticism" as inconsistent with their understanding of biblical authority. The timing of this article is striking. It appeared about the same time as the Catholic declaration of papal infallibility appeared, and it represents a classic declaration of a Protestant counterpart of biblical infallibility in opposition to church and papal infallibility, both over against the relativity of modern thought and the "acids of modernity."

This Princeton doctrine is actually a complex mosaic of theological claims, though not all elements have been at the center of the discussion. It involved an exegetical argument: Warfield claimed to be defending the "biblical idea of inspiration." It involved an historical argument: Warfield claimed that his doctrine was "the church doctrine of inspiration" until the rise of modern biblical criticism. It also involved, at least implicitly, a series of what might be called "philosophical" claims, many of which became the increasing preoccupation of the International Council of Biblical Inerrancy statements: that language, history, scientific concepts and so forth could not be understood to be so enmeshed in cultural relativity as to preclude the "inerrant" character of Scripture.

This position also made a series of theological moves that have become increasingly seen as problematic, at least by some. Though Warfield and others were careful to distinguish between revelation and inspiration and to understand the latter as a process of "recording" the revelation, there was a tendency of those working in this tradition to use inspiration as the primary mode of revelation and to speak of "biblical revelation." This tradition's answer to the question of how we know about God is found in the claim that "God wrote a book." Inspiration is the fundamental axis of this position, and it is used to answer many questions, including the limits of the canon (consisting of those documents that can be demonstrated to be inspired). This leads to a reductionism that fails to grasp the complexity of scriptural patterns of revelation. I have always wondered (since my teenage years) why the first verses of Hebrews are not the *locus classicus* for answering how we know about God: that God has revealed God's self in "many and diverse ways," culminating in these last days in a Son who is the very image of God. I am not able to avoid the impression that the Princetonians and neo-evangelicals saw 2 Timothy 3:16 as the

---

2. A. A. Hodge and B. B. Warfield, "Inspiration," *Presbyterian Review* 2 (April 1881).

locus classicus, because they were already committed to the answer that "God wrote a book." The neo-evangelicals especially held firmly to the claim that "the Bible is the Word of God" in the face of a Barthian claim to a Christological center of revelation. I remember an article in *Moody Monthly* about three decades ago on "How to Tell If Your Pastor Is Going Neo-Orthodox," with the suggestion that one should be very worried if one's pastor were to speak of Christ as the "living Word."

By this time the neo-evangelical consensus based on the Princeton theology had begun to fall apart. Most notable was Fuller Seminary's tendency to move away from this formulation in a new statement of faith. Several faculty members left Fuller, some of whom went to Trinity Evangelical Divinity School, which claimed to be the carrier of the inerrancy tradition and the true evangelical tradition. In my tradition—which had reorganized its own institutions (the Christian Holiness Association and the Wesleyan Theological Society, founded because Wesleyan scholars did not feel entirely comfortable in the ETS) and in the process tended to adopt NAE and ETS "inerrancy" formulations—there was a movement away from these articulations to recover non-inerrancy traditions to be more inclusive of the variety of Wesleyan currents not accustomed to this language. In the midst of this ferment Harold Lindsell, former faculty member of Fuller and a board member of Wheaton College, published his book *The Battle for the Bible* and its sequel *The Bible in the Balance*.[3] In *The Battle for the Bible*, Lindsell painted a bleak picture of "decline" from the Princeton position, finding this "decline" where the position had never been held (at North Park Theological Seminary of the Evangelical Covenant) and also where it might more easily be documented (at Fuller, for example). I was caught in the middle of all this. I made Lindsell take out of later printings of *The Battle for the Bible* certain anonymous references to me, taken from unpublished correspondence, in his discussion of North Park. I was rewarded with a longer and friendlier discussion of my position in the sequel. In this period I was denied ordination in the Wesleyan church for my refusal to affirm the doctrine of inerrancy that had been written into our articles of religion only in the 1950s under the pressure of NAE affiliation.

The Battle for the Bible precipitated a debate about Warfield's historical claim that the Princeton articulation was the "church doctrine," a position he had defended in interchanges with Charles Briggs, who had been accused of heresy over his denial that the Westminster Confession

---

3. Harold Lindsell, *The Battle for the Bible* (Grand Rapids, Mich.: Zondervan, 1976), and *The Bible in the Balance* (Grand Rapids, Mich.: Zondervan, 1979).

had intended inerrancy. This debate was repeated as Fuller Seminary released Jack Rogers from teaching to write *The Nature and Authority of the Bible* and expand the argument of his doctoral dissertation at the Free University of Amsterdam. In the context of political struggles in the Presbyterian Church over the proposed "Confession of 1967," Rogers had originally intended to argue Warfield's position, but after spending months in the British Museum reading the writings of figures of the Westminster Assembly, he reversed his position. Lindsell was then defended against Rogers and Donald McKim by Trinity Professor John Woodbridge in *Biblical Authority*.[4] I merited one minor footnote in the Woodbridge book for my exploration of the position of the Pietist movement on the question, and it is to that position that we must now turn.

The Pietists on Scripture

Warfield claimed that his doctrine of "inspiration" (and thus his understanding of "biblical authority") was the "church doctrine" until modern times. This claim has, of course, been debated without much consensus. We will leave behind the question of whether, as Warfield claimed, this was the doctrine of the early church, both east and west, as well as of medieval Christianity. John Calvin, who is bent most easily to this position, is ambiguous, with the scholarship almost evenly divided about whether his thought moves in this direction. Fewer have tried to make the case for Martin Luther, though Robert Preus and John Warwick Montgomery have made the claim. It is clear, however, that there are antecedents to the Princeton position in post-Reformation Protestant orthodoxy. One thinks particularly of Genevan Francis Turretin (and parallel Lutheran figures), and Woodbridge makes much of Richard Simon who spoke of "original autographs."[5] It was, of course, the Latin edition of Turretin's *Institutes* that was used as a text for systematic theology in Princeton (until Hodge's three volumes replaced it), constituting the bridge to the American scene.

What has been little noticed in these historical debates is that Protestant orthodoxy, at least in the Lutheran context, precipitated a reaction in the Pietist movement that included a self-conscious rejection of the inerrancy articulation of the authority of Scripture. Fred Holmgren of North Park Theological Seminary and Jim Stein have argued that Pietism polemicized against the inerrancy formulation, and Pietist Philipp Jakob Spener ad-

---

4. John D. Woodbridge, *Biblical Authority: A Critique of the Rogers/McKim Proposal* (Grand Rapids, Mich.: Zondervan, 1982).

5. Woodbridge, *Biblical Authority*.

vised his followers not to defend it, especially with regard to concerns such as history, science and geography. This fact constitutes a direct challenge to Warfield's claim about the church doctrine. In fact, it is quite striking that the debates about whether inerrancy is the church doctrine make no reference to Pietism. Rogers and McKim ignore Pietism, for example, and Woodbridge makes only a minor reference to my work without exploring the fact that it constitutes a rejection of the inerrancy tradition.

We are not accustomed in the English-speaking world to taking Pietism seriously. The English connotations of the word *piety* imply an otherworldliness, which is surprising given Paul Tillich's comment that the two great gifts of Pietism to modern Protestantism are the modern missionary movement and the concern for the poor and the oppressed. Nor are we conditioned to take Pietism seriously as a distinct theological tradition. There has been a tendency to think of Pietism as a practical movement that assumed orthodoxy and applied it more enthusiastically and perhaps "subjectively" to the Christian life and the shaping of the church. This has also been the case with Wesleyanism and Pentecostalism—neither of which has always been taken seriously theologically when measured by the more abstract, philosophical and systematic theologies of the dominant Reformed and orthodox traditions. But it is becoming increasingly clear that these traditions constitute alternative theologies that must be taken seriously as theology, especially in the wake of the rise of the systematic discipline of "practical theology" and a renewed appreciation for those ethnic and minority traditions that have entered a protest against the dominant patterns of doing theology.

There is another way in which this claim about Pietism is counterintuitive. There is no doubt that Pietism was "biblicistic." Its rejection of philosophical theology in favor of biblical theology, its cultivation of the study of the Bible formally in the Canstein Institute at Halle University and informally in small groups, its founding of the first Bible society that distributed millions of copies of the Scriptures, and its cultivation of personal and family patterns of biblical devotion have led many to assume that this would be an unlikely movement to enter a protest against the "inerrancy of Scripture." But it is clear that a radical biblicism need not imply a particular doctrine of Scripture. For example, in his rejection of natural and philosophical theology, Karl Barth is more radically dependent on the Bible and therefore more "biblicistic" than his "evangelical" critics are, though he may not agree with them about the nature of Scripture.[6]

---

6. One even wonders whether Pietism might not be a neglected source of Barth's thought at this and related points— in light of the large collection of Pietist writings found

Many of us learned a similar lesson in the 1970s in the Sojourners experience: we claimed to take the Bible more seriously on questions of poverty and justice than the normative tradition of evangelicalism did, without accepting its doctrine of Scripture. In fact, for many of us this experience was what broke the hold of evangelicalism on us and drove us to drink at other wells. Especially influential for many of us was John Howard Yoder, who seemed in many ways to take the Bible more seriously, in both the "hard sayings of Jesus" and in his theological method, while being more open to biblical criticism.

With these comments in mind, let us turn to some of those aspects of the Pietist understanding of Scripture that contributed to the rejection of the orthodox and inerrantist tradition. Not all of these themes always appear in each figure, and often it takes time to work out the implications of slight shifts in language (shifts that, to some extent, continue in such Pietist traditions as Pentecostalism), but the following factors seem relevant.

First, figures like Spener and later Francke of Halle were self-conscious about their rejection of a view of inspiration that was text oriented, and they argued that inspiration was given to persons who then spoke more naturally out of their own experience. This allowed them to avoid several problems of the orthodox tradition, especially their uneasiness with differences of style and possible contradictions in the biblical texts. The orthodox were horrified, for example, by what they saw as the "blasphemous" claim of the Pietists that God could be speaking bad Greek.

Second, some would argue that this move would allow the Pietists at Halle to become the pioneers of biblical criticism. Their rejection of the historical subordination of the Scriptures to the creeds by the orthodox and a related tendency to deduce doctrine from small fragments of Scripture (Pietists argued for the use of large passages of Scripture to control this proof-text method) opened the way for a more historical and contextual method of studying Scripture. Pietists thus advocated the study of the original languages and cultivated some of the early forms of biblical criticism, especially textual criticism. Pietists were, therefore, more open to ideas of "progressive" revelation that implied historical development and to the idea of "degrees of inspiration." Our contemporary categories of thought make it hard to realize that at some points Pietists and Enlightenment figures were allied against orthodoxy.

---

in his library including three different editions of Bengel's *Gnomon*, the classic Pietist commentary on the New Testament.

Third, it is a commonplace of scholarship that the Pietists shifted in their soteriology from the forensic metaphors of the later Reformation and Protestant orthodoxy to "biological" images like *regeneration* or *new birth*. The point of Scripture was to communicate *life* in the first place rather than *truth*, though the latter was not ignored. But life can be communicated by imperfect instruments more easily than can truth, as is evidenced by effective preaching, the work of ministers, the witness of simple Christians and the life of the church. This position in a sense anticipated the critique of Warfield by contemporary James Orr in *Revelation and Inspiration*.[7]

Fourth, there is a sense in which the Pietists had a more complex doctrine of revelation that acknowledged the "many and diverse" ways in which God reveals God's self and that they saw a continuing process of revelation since biblical times. In a moderate sense the Pietists were more open than the orthodox to special experiences of revelation, dreams and Prophecies. At its core Pietism was an effort to recover the dynamic and power of the early church, a concern that opened them up to the recovery of gifts of the Spirit. They maintained an emphasis on the gift of healing, and Bengel comments on James 5 that this gift has continued to remind the church of its unfaithfulness, which had led to the cessation of other gifts.

Fifth, this effort to reconnect with New Testament Christianity was one of the deep structures of Pietist thought that flew in the face of the orthodox tendency to draw a sharp line at the end of the biblical period, arguing that God acted in different ways before and after that line—with regard to both gifts and revelation. This is especially clear in the exegesis of 2 Timothy 3:16. For Warfield, *theopneustos* is to be understood only in the past tense, as the production of the text, something that does not take place in the present; this position parallels his position on spiritual gifts, which are relegated to the apostolic age and do not continue in the church. Bengel explicitly rejects this position in the *Gnomon*, arguing that the Greek word also has a present tense in that the Scriptures are "God-breathed" in the present as the instrument of God continuing to speak. This tendency to collapse inspiration and illumination in the face of the orthodox concern to keep them separate is fundamental to Pietism. And John Wesley's *Notes on the New Testament* (basically a translation and paraphrase of the *Gnomon*) include this comment as a matter of course in his treatment of 2 Timothy 3:16.

---

7. James Orr, *Revelation and inspiration* (London: Duckworth, 1910).

Sixth, one wonders whether Pietism was not pushing in the direction of a logic that would be worked out in Pentecostalism, as I argued in my presidential address for the Society of Pentecostal Studies. If God continues to inspire in the present age (in, e.g., the gift of prophecy), then the understanding of the canon must be rethought; it becomes less the *depositum* of all inspired texts and more the canon or measuring rod by which one judges contemporary claims of revelation.[8] Al Sundberg (originally from the pietist Evangelical Covenant Church) argued along these lines at North Park Theological Seminary, reflecting a school of scholarship at Harvard under the guidance of Krister Stendahl.[9] He argues, citing a large number of patristic texts that the early church understood that the gift of inspiration was given to all Christians at Pentecost, that it continues in the church today and that it is not confined to the production of the biblical texts (contra Warfield).

Seventh, we should also notice the Pietist rejection of philosophical theology (a regular theme of Spener) in favor of practical and biblical theology. In fact, Leonard Woods, the president of Bowdoin College, translated in 1831 an early systematic of the Pietist tradition, Christian theology by George Christian Knapp, as illustrative of the "biblical theology" school of Halle—apparently as an illustration of a position that was both more biblical and more open to methods of biblical criticism than orthodoxy was.

Finally, we should notice that the Pietist practical and concrete use of the Bible is a more natural reading of 2 Timothy 3:16. I remember John Weborg of North Park Theological Seminary commenting a quarter of a century ago that the orthodox and the Pietist differ in the place in which they discuss Scripture in the organization of their theologies. For the orthodox the treatment of Scripture is located in the "philosophical prolegomena" to theology as the epistemological principle on which systematic theology is erected—as a sort of biblical "foundationalism" that ensures the truth of theology. Weborg argued that for the Pietists, Scripture found its place in ecclesiology as a sort of "church constitution" that regulated the life of the church and the individual Christian. It may well be that the Pietist way of working is more congenial to a modern, post-foundationalist way of doing theology.

---

8. This move seems to reclaim the original meaning of canon in the early church.

9. Al Sundberg (originally from the pietist Evangelical Covenant Church) argued along these lines at North Park Theological Seminary March, 28, 1973.

The Great Puzzle of Evangelical Historiography

If this analysis of Pietism is correct, it raises some very interesting questions, not only about Warfield's claims about the church doctrine of inspiration, but also about the very nature of contemporary evangelicalism. A substantial case can be made that contemporary evangelicalism—even in the neo-evangelical sense—is more a child of Pietism than of Protestant orthodoxy. This is becoming increasingly clear in recent scholarship. Mark Noll of Wheaton is now arguing (in *The Scandal of the Evangelical Mind*, for example) that evangelicalism in the modern sense did not exist before the eighteenth century, that it is a product of the post-Reformation "conversionism," which was born in Pietism and Puritanism and which came to its fruition in the Evangelical Revival in England and the Great Awakening in New England. Certainly the missionary movement, so central to evangelicalism, was carried by Anabaptism and Pietism—both seeing Christendom as a missionary field—and not by the magisterial Reformation with its commitment to national Christendoms. And the Bible societies and practices of piety that were born in Pietism would appear to be the heart and soul of modern evangelicalism. If this is so, we are left with a very great puzzle: how did modern evangelicals and even neo-evangelicals come to think of themselves as the children of orthodoxy and of the magisterial Reformation rather than of Pietism? I would like to conclude this paper with a few reflections on this issue.

On one level, successive generations of Pietists did not always work out the logic of their position. Pietism was often carried by currents outside the academic traditions and did not always maintain its self-conscious opposition to orthodoxy, and it even on occasion fell back from the apparent logic of its own biblicism and into the hands of the orthodox. Ulrich Zwingli scholar Robert Walton, one of the few Americans to be appointed to a German university, once pointed out to me in a walk around Munster that after the French Revolution, Pietism and Protestant orthodoxy were forced into a new coalition in response to the increasing radicalism of the enlightenment and biblical criticism. Some such alliance is clear in the *neu-Pietismus* of the nineteenth and twentieth centuries, which is more like modern American fundamentalism. And finally, the Anglo-Saxon world differs from the German in that these themes were often mediated through Puritanism and the English Presbyterian tradition, where the polarization of the German scene was not as strong. The direct mediation of German Pietism was often through marginal movements in ethnic and linguistic enclaves without wide cultural impact, and indirect influence was through Methodism, which was a carrier of this tradition but in a diluted and non self-conscious way.

But I would still argue that most forms of what we usually call "American evangelicalism" derive ultimately from Pietism. This became increasingly clear to me as I worked on the book *Theological Roots of Pentecostalism*, for almost all the themes of Pentecostalism (conversionism, perfectionist and higher-life themes, healing and eschatology) led me in that direction.[10] Pentecostalism is, of course, now the tail that demographically wags the dog of evangelicalism—by itself constituting worldwide a majority of evangelicals that clearly stands in the line of Pietism. When one adds other currents, like the various Wesleyan bodies of the Holiness traditions and other Scandinavian and European groups more directly rooted in Pietism, one could make a case that a vast majority of American evangelicalism may be seen in the Pietist line. My friends who count such things tell me that 75 to 80 percent of NAE membership would be in these lines; and, if anything, this is clearer when one looks at the evangelical culture of the Christian College Coalition.

But even more interesting is the extent to which other institutions that would identify themselves as in the line of the Protestant orthodoxy actually have roots that are more Pietist. This dynamic is perhaps clearest in the educational institutions of modern American evangelicalism. The most interesting case might be the institutions of A. J. Gordon: Gordon College and Gordon-Conwell Theological Seminary. Gordon was a Pietist/Holiness Baptist figure who was in many ways "proto-Pentecostal" in his advocacy of faith healing and other themes that shaped Pentecostalism. Gordon College has absorbed Barrington College, which has roots in Providence Bible College and ultimately in Faith College and other institutions of the New England Holiness movement. Even the leaders of New England evangelicalism associated with the Gordon institutions reveal this history: Harold John Ockenga came originally out of the Holiness movement in the Midwest, attended Taylor University, was a young Holiness preacher in college and died with a picture of John Wesley over his desk as a testimony to that abiding influence; J. Elwin Wright, of the New England Fellowship of Churches that birthed the NAE, came out of Pentecostalism. Gordon

---

10. Donald W. Dayton, *Theological Roots of Pentecostalism* (Peabody, MA: Hendrickson, 1991). When I finished this study, I discovered that I had an "alternative historiography" of evangelicalism that made more sense to me—a feeling that is often confirmed to me by German and Scandinavian scholars (living and working in countries where evangelicalism is still understood in the line of Pietism) who tell me that they find my work more useful than that of the neo-evangelical historians.

himself was a major target of the polemics of Warfield, who objected to the Pietistic shape of Gordon's spirituality and his claims of miracles of divine healing.[11] The irony is that today one cannot teach at Gordon-Conwell without standing in the line of Warfield, the old Princeton theology, and the Protestant orthodox doctrine of Scripture. The historiographical problem becomes how to explain this phenomenon—one of the great puzzles in understanding modern American evangelicalism.

The phenomenon is wider than the doctrine of Scripture and themes discussed above, which fed more directly into such Pietistic movements as Pentecostalism and the Holiness movement. One thinks of the claims that the evangelical doctrine of the atonement has always been the "penal substitutionary" view. I believe this is demonstrably false in a demographic sense. I would argue that the predominant view of American revivalism (and thus of modern evangelicalism) has been the "moral government" view of Grotius mediated through various traditions of "moral government" in the nineteenth century. It is little noticed that one of the most clearly Pietistic churches in the United States and Scandinavia, the Evangelical Covenant Church, was born precisely in a Pietist attack on the Protestant orthodox doctrine of the atonement. Yet such facts have been so suppressed in American evangelicalism that even candidates for the Covenant ministry are surprised to discover that the theological conditioning they have received at the hands of the neo-evangelicals makes them unfit for the Covenant ministry. Such phenomena scream for some explanation—one that is difficult to provide.

Any explanation must be multidimensional and complex. There is first of all the strong influence of the Presbyterian tradition on American evangelicalism. It has been a particular gift of that tradition to be a carrier of theological work that has had wide impact. The theological influence of Princeton (both old and new) has been profound and set the tone for groups that would not identify the tradition. Hodge's three volumes of theology have become the model for other traditions: the Baptists have to change the ecclesiology, and the Holiness folk have to change the soteriology, but the model shines through nonetheless. And historians of other traditions have flocked to Princeton (both old and new), where they have absorbed the narrative line of the struggles of Protestant orthodoxy and told their own stories within the categories of that narrative. And one must notice the influence of Westminster Seminary (founded to preserve

---

11. See Warfield's essays on perfectionism and his book *Counterfeit Miracles*.

the old "Princeton theology") in the shaping of the intellectual agenda of neo-evangelicalism.

Other levels point in this same direction. Claude Welch describes how "conservative revivalists" sought refuge in Princeton, as the only seaworthy craft in the storms of biblical criticism in the late nineteenth century.[12] They lived aboard this craft and became so accustomed to its luxurious intellectual staterooms that they forgot that they did not belong there. Such forces were given additional impetus by various sociological impulses. I believe that it is possible to trace a rising social mobility at places like Wheaton that has taken a correlated theological pilgrimage from Holiness and proto-Pentecostal piety, through a Baptist piety, then a Presbyterian piety and finally an Anglican-style piety. Historiography and theological interpretation have followed this trajectory by suppressing the actual theological history for traditions more serviceable in this sociological trajectory. Thus the kind of phenomenon that one finds at Gordon-Conwell.

I have become more and more convinced that the neo-evangelical theological self-understanding and its appeal to the Protestant orthodox doctrine of Scripture, for example, must be interpreted in the light of these dynamics. This is most obvious in Bernard Ramm's *The Evangelical Heritage*.[13] This book is perhaps the clearest expression of the (often implicit) self-understanding of neo-evangelicalism. It traces evangelicalism through a Pauline reading of the New Testament and Augustine into the (Calvinist) Reformation and Protestant orthodoxy, and it sees evangelicalism as the intellectual effort to preserve that tradition against the "acids of modernity" through Princeton and Westminster. I have not been able to make this perspective work in interpreting larger currents of evangelicalism whose actual roots (Anabaptism, Pietism, Methodism, Revivalism, etc.) are often not even mentioned in the book. It doesn't help me to explain either evangelicalism or the personal trajectory of Ramm himself, who is an "evangelical Baptist" who taught for a while at Christian and Missionary Alliance Simpson College. I was once helped by a student who commented that Ramm's book seemed more like a "prescription" for the ills of fundamentalism than a description of its history. It was what Ramm wanted fundamentalism to become. It was, in other words (taken from more modern conceptualities), a "constructed identity" adopted to support the theological and sociological aspirations of neo-evangelicalism.

12. Claude Welch, *Protestant Theology in the Nineteenth Century* (Hartford, CN: Yale University Press, 1999).

13. Bernard Ramm, *The Evangelical Heritage* (Grand Rapids, MI: Baker, 1986).

Wouldn't it be ironic if it should turn out that the despised and suppressed traditions of Pietism and its successors turned out to provide the clues one needs to escape the impasses of the orthodox doctrine of Scripture to find a better way to a more adequate doctrine of Scripture? I believe that to be a real possibility and commend to you the neglected tradition of Pietism and its suppressed doctrine of Scripture.

Response #1

Frank D. Macchia

B. B. Warfield and Karl Barth: Another Look at a Classic Evangelical Divide

Donald Dayton's essay, "The Pietist Theological Critique of Biblical Inerrancy,"[1] is vintage Dayton. He uses the Pietist, Wesleyan, and Pentecostal traditions to question Evangelicalism's commitment to the Old Princeton School of Theology, especially to what many regard as B. B. Warfield's effort to base Christian belief on the epistemological foundation of biblical inerrancy. In contradistinction to this Fundamentalist apologetic, Dayton prefers to restore Evangelicalism to its Pietist (which is also in this case Barthian) devotion to Jesus Christ as the central point of reference for the Christian understanding of divine revelation and to the Bible as Christ's living witness, "canonical" in the sense that it functions as the dynamic measure of all forms of Christian faithfulness. The Bible for Dayton is not a static deposit of infallible doctrines that speak with equal weight and relevance, because of a uniform doctrine of verbal inspiration that guarantees their infallibility. The Bible is rather a living witness to Christ and his liberating gospel, inspired in the function of this witness, so that the community of faith is bequeathed with the task of discerning in the Spirit the meaning and relevance of a given text in the light of the Scripture's central point of reference in Christ.

Dayton's trajectories are a helpful way of opening up an important discussion among Evangelicals, especially in the light of Gary Dorrien's insight into the emerging dissatisfaction among a growing number of Evangelicals with the Fundamentalist inerrancy doctrine and their increasing openness to a Barthian understanding of Scripture. Dorrien may be

1. Donald Dayton, "The Pietist Theological Critique of Biblical Inerrancy," in *Evangelicals & Scripture: Tradition, Authority and Hermeneutics* (Glen Ellyn, IL: Intervarsity Press, 2004) 76–92.

right that "the trend in evangelical theology is clearly away from a strict-inerrancy doctrine."[2] What complicates this discussion is that there have been various ways in which Evangelicals have defended biblical inerrancy. There are Evangelicals, especially within the Old Princeton School of Theology/Fundamentalist stream highlighted for us by Dayton (as well as Stanley Grenz[3]), that have elevated biblical inerrancy as vital to the entire spectrum of Christian doctrine. As article XIX of the *Chicago Statement on Biblical Inerrancy* (recently embraced by the Evangelical Theological Society) states, "We affirm that a confession of the full authority, infallibility and inerrancy of Scripture is vital to a sound understanding of the whole of the Christian faith." This expansive understanding of inerrancy is obviously crafted to meet the modernist demand for epistemological certainty. It implies that the whole of Christian doctrine rests in some way on the epistemological foundation of an inspired and inerrant biblical text, so that the loss of this belief at least threatens to place the entire Christian truth claim in jeopardy. Such is the position of Fundamentalist apologists, such as John Warwick Montgomery, who would readily name B. B. Warfield in support of his understanding of inerrancy.[4]

It is not so much the case that the Pietist-Wesleyan-Pentecostal stream has rejected biblical infallibility (or should do so to be consistent) but rather that their tendency has been to subordinate it as only one element of a broader view of biblical authority based on Christ as the central player of a sacred narrative. Unlike the Fundamentalist fixation on an inerrant text as the foundation for rationally-conceived doctrines, Pietists and (later) Pentecostals tended to subordinate biblical infallibility to the living Christ who stands at the heart of the canon's witness and to the Spirit who makes the canon's faithful witness to Christ a word absolutely binding in life. Biblical infallibility was not foundational; Christ was. Biblical infallibility, if made an issue, tended to function as an element of a broader biblical realism that assumed we can relate to God through Christ and in the Spirit today in exactly the same way as folks related to God in the pages of the

---

2. Gary Dorrien, *The Remaking of Evangelical Theology* (Louisville: Westminster John Knox, 1998) 205.

3. Stanley Grenz draws the lines from Presbyterianism through the Old Princeton School to Fundamentalism, which stresses the role of Scripture as a source of right doctrine, and the Puritan-Pietist line, which highlights the role of Scripture in nurturing spirituality; "Nurturing the Soul, Informing the Mind: The Genesis of the Evangelical Scripture Principle," *Evangelicals & Scripture*, 21–41.

4. John Warwick Montgomery, "Biblical Inerrancy: What Is at Stake?" in *God's Inerrant Word: An International Symposium on the Trustworthiness of Scripture* (Canadian Institute for Law, Theology, and Public Policy, 1974) 15–42.

biblical story. The Bible must be trustworthy in what it portrays if it is to provide the context for our interaction with God today. However, since God is the principle actor in the book, past and present, the authority of the book rests in the divine self-disclosure in Christ and in the Spirit and not in the book itself. Rather than function as the foundation for Christian doctrine, biblical infallibility becomes a component of a secondary witness that has its foundation in Christ (for there can be no other foundation than Christ, 1 Cor 3:8). This Pietist refusal to make biblical infallibility foundational to the entire structure of Christian faith explains why the Pietist who most influenced Karl Barth, Johann Blumhardt, wrote that there remained an "open table" of fellowship in his home for David Friedrich Strauss.[5] A Fundamentalist consistent with his or her understanding of biblical infallibility would have difficulty saying such a thing. And Gerald Sheppard showed convincingly that the authority of the Bible for Pentecostals was spiritually discerned in the context of experience and faithfulness rather than proved through scientific argumentation or rationally demonstrated as a philosophical (epistemological) necessity.[6] There is no question but that Pentecostal and charismatic scholarship has consequently been generally less concerned with issues of inerrancy than their Fundamentalist counterparts. One only need attend the Society for Pentecostal Studies or read its collected papers to discover this.

The tantalizing question for me in all of this, however, has to do with where to locate Warfield in Dayton's contrast between Pietism and Fundamentalism. Ever since I read David Kelsey's brief but provocative comments on Warfield's "experiential" hermeneutic, I had meant to read Warfield for myself to determine whether or not the later Fundamentalists can fully claim him as their own. Dayton's essay gave me the occasion to do this. I read Warfield's massive and dense *The Authority and Inspiration of the Bible*[7] with great anticipation of more than a few unexpected surprises, and I was not disappointed. I found a few significant insights that went beyond Kelsey's remarks in locating Warfield as in significant measure on the "Pietist" (even Barthian) side of the Pietist/Fundamentalist divide outlined by Dayton. Allow me to make my case.

---

5. See James Carroll Cox, *Johann Christoph Blumhardt and the Work of the Holy Spirit* (Assen: Van Gorcum, 1959) 39.

6. Gerald Sheppard, "Word and Spirit: Scripture in the Pentecostal Tradition," Pts. 1 & 2, *Agora* (Spring, Winter, 1980).

7. Benjamin Breckinridge Warfield, *The Authority and Inspiration of the Bible* (Philadelphia: Presbyterian & Reformed, 1938).

Warfield on Biblical Inspiration/Infallibility

Warfield assumes the verbal-plenary inspiration and infallibility of the Bible. This much must be stated from the beginning. He takes 2 Tim 3:16 as a description of the divine origin of the Bible and not technically the effects of Scripture as a channel of God's Word among us. Though he will not deny the significance of the latter (as we will note) he defined inspiration according to the divine guidance in the writing of Scripture.[8] Furthermore, Warfield described the process of biblical inspiration in ways that emphasized the role of the divine guidance. Though he admitted that the biblical authors brought their own unique humanity to their writing, he wrote further that this "contributed nothing" to the origin of the Bible as divine revelation.[9] The biblical authors were "elevated," "directed," "energized," and even "controlled" so that they would serve God's aim in producing an infallible text that functions as a veritable oracle of God.[10] The divine light of Scripture is thus pure and untainted. It shone through human authors as the sunlight shines through stained-glass windows to be sure, but in this case the divine architect designed these "windows" so that the colors would be of God's choosing.[11] In the light of these insights into Warfield's view of Scripture, it would seem that he was on a collision course with any effort to recognize the full humanity of the biblical witness or the need in this light to critically discern a scripture text's weight and meaning in the greater light of its central point of reference, namely, the person and work of Jesus Christ. His firm stance against Charles Briggs's use of "higher" criticism would grant some credence to this characterization of Warfield.

But there is more than meets the eye with Warfield. First, the inspiration/infallibility of Scripture for Warfield was one element of the church's faith among others based on *Christ* as the revelation of God. Scripture is thus dependent on Jesus Christ, who stands apart from Scripture and all else as *the* revelation of God. After seeking to describe the various ways by which the revelations "that underlie and give content to the religion of the Bible" may be categorized (e.g., "external manifestations" of God or "internal suggestions" by God), Warfield notes that such categories do not apply to the person of Christ as the revelation of all revelations. In clear reference to Col 2:9 and Heb 1:1–3, Warfield notes strikingly that,

---

8. Ibid., 296.
9. Ibid., 91.
10. Ibid., 95.
11. Ibid., 156.

in His Person, in which dwells all the fullness of the Godhead bodily, He rises above all classification and is *sui generes*; so that revelation accumulated in Him stands outside all the divers portions and divers manners in which otherwise revelation has been given and sums up in itself all that has been and can be known of God and of His redemption. He does not so much make a revelation of God as Himself is the revelation of God; He does not merely disclose God's purpose of redemption; He is unto us wisdom from God, and righteousness, and sanctification and redemption.[12]

Making the revelation of God on which the Bible is dependent a living person is more typical of the Pietist/Barthian understanding of Scripture than the one assumed among many of Warfield's Fundamentalist heirs. Warfield even refused to posit an analogy between the hypostatic union of the divine/human Christ and the role of the Bible as both a divine and a human word, as though the divine/human involvement in Christ and Scripture are in any way comparable.[13] Warfield's position implicitly undercuts the removal of any distinction between Christ and Scripture in our understanding of biblical authority/infallibility and opens up the possibility that the Christ of Scripture provides the broader biblical witness with the hermeneutical criterion for what the church spiritually discerns from a text as the Word of God for a given time and place.

Warfield did accept the reliability of the testimony of Jesus and the authors of the New Testament concerning God. He even went so far as to argue that this reliability can be reasonably proved. But, interestingly, he does not base this reliability upon Scripture as a divinely-given (i.e., inspired) and inerrant text, but rather on the trustworthiness of tradition under the providential care of God! Warfield wrote concerning his notion of inspiration as the divine origin of an infallible text: "Were there no such thing as inspiration, Christianity would still be true, and its essential doctrines would be credibly witnessed to us in the *generally trustworthy* reports of the teaching of our Lord and of His agents in founding the church, preserved in the writings of the apostles and their first followers and in the historical witness of the living church" (emphasis mine).[14] His guarded language concerning the "generally trustworthy reports" in Scripture should not be missed.[15] Warfield obviously wanted to make the case that even if

---

12. Ibid., 96.

13. Ibid., 162. Warfield felt that a comparison between the divine and the human elements of Christ and the Bible denigrates Christ, implying an adoptionist Christology.

14. Ibid., 210.

15. See also ibid., 211, 212.

there were no such thing as a doctrine of biblical inspiration that would guarantee biblical infallibility, there would still be enough reason from the reliability of tradition to assume that the Scripture's witness and the witness of the church through the ages concerning Christ and his gospel are "generally" trustworthy. It is from this general trustworthiness of Scripture that we can take seriously the Bible's own assumptions about its inspiration (i.e., divine origin) and absolute truthfulness. In other words, the Bible is inspired and infallible for Warfield in the final analysis because the Bible says so.

Warfield finds this biblical trustworthiness confirmed, however, not in the epistemological necessity of a divinely-given and inerrant text but rather in the *experience* of the church in relation to the role of Scripture in daily life. Warfield writes movingly about how,

> our memory will easily recall those happier days when we stood as a child at our mother's knee, with lisping lips following the words which her slow finger traced upon this open page, with words which were her support in every trial, and, as she fondly trusted, were to be our guide throughout life. Mother church was speaking to us in that maternal voice, commending to us her vital faith in the Word of God.[16]

What thus drove Warfield's exalted claims concerning the trustworthiness of Scripture as the historic teaching of mother church was not so much the epistemological demands of modernity as the demands of the historic *experience* of the church in relation to this Scripture as a living witness to Christ that proves itself faithful again and again in life. David Kelsey could thus write that the truthfulness of Scripture for Warfield is verified "in the corporate experience of the Christian community" where "the Bible is received as an awful and holy object."[17]

Though Warfield stresses the role of the Bible as a sure guide to doctrine, the Bible is no static deposit of infallible truths for him. He noted that the books of the Bible "become not only the words of godly men, but the immediate Word of God Himself, speaking directly as such to the hearts and minds of every reader."[18] Scripture does not just record redemptive acts for Warfield but is itself a redemptive act as it is read in the

---

16. Ibid., 107.

17. David Kelsey, *The Uses of Scripture in Recent Theology* (Philadelphia: Fortress, 1975) 18.

18. B. B. Warfield, *The Authority and Inspiration of the Bible*, 158.

church.[19] Warfield dreaded a "dead Bible" as a mere deposit of revealed statements for those seeking God's will. Rather, "from the 'In the beginning' of Genesis to the 'Amen' of the Apocalypse," the Bible is the living voice of God to us today.[20] It seems clear that the divine origin and infallibility of the Bible is for Warfield a conclusion drawn from the role of the historic Christ in laying claim to this Bible as his authoritative witness, a truth known first from both a tradition and an experience bequeathed to and confirmed within the church as a faithful body. It is only on these Christological and pneumatological foundations that the divine origin and infallibility of Scripture may be surmised as an important element of Christian faith.

It is in the light of the above discussion that we can understand Warfield's emphatic refusal to make biblical inspiration/infallibility vital to the legitimacy of the whole system of Christian truth. Warfield's denial is clear and strong: "Let it not be said that we found the whole system of Christian doctrine upon the doctrine of plenary inspiration. We found the whole Christian system on the doctrine of plenary inspiration as little as we found it upon the doctrine of angelic existences."[21] The actual foundation is elsewhere: ". . . the incarnate Word sets his seal upon the written Word."[22] Warfield added concerning the divine origin of Scripture: "were there no such as inspiration, Christianity would still be true and all its essential doctrines would be credibly witnessed to us . . ."[23] He rejected the thesis that "the infallibility of the Bible is the ground of the whole Christian faith," responding that "such a misapprehension, if it is anywhere current, should be corrected."[24] Warfield concludes: "What we are presenting is something entirely different from this overstrained view . . . and something which has no connection with it."[25] For Warfield, biblical inspiration/infallibility is an element of Christian doctrine but not in anyway foundational to it. In sharp distinction to article XIX of the *Chicago Statement on Biblical Inerrancy*, biblical infallibility for Warfield is clearly not "vital to a sound understanding of the whole of the Christian faith."

---

19. Ibid., 81.
20. Ibid., 125.
21. Ibid., 210.
22. Ibid., 213. He quotes a Bishop Wordsworth approvingly.
23. Ibid.
24. Ibid., 211. He notes this in agreement with Marcus Dods.
25. Ibid.

Warfield and Barth: A Constructive Proposal

It seems that Warfield doesn't quite fit the stereotype in which he has been cast by at least some of his Fundamentalist heirs. This complexity keeps Warfield in the conversation as a worthy dialogue partner for Evangelicals today who look to Karl Barth (and other voices) for a fresh approach to the authority of the Bible that respects both its humanity and its function in the church as the Word of God. Many are attracted to Barth's understanding of biblical authority as derivative from Christ and as a dynamic, functional characteristic of Scripture in the context of its role as witness. On the other hand, the more conservative wing of the Evangelical movement has tried to point out that a Barthian understanding of the authority of Scripture stands in danger of "subjectivism" or of shifting the weight of authority from the objective witness of Scripture to the inner judgments of the individual or the church. If the Bible only functions as God's Word as it bears witness to Christ in the hearts of believers, isn't the Bible truthful only when we recognize it as such?

Part of the problem here is the anthropocentric understanding of the Spirit bequeathed to Evangelicalism from its Western theological heritage. Typical of this heritage is to make all of the objective revelational categories Christological and all of the subjective (or intersubjective) categories pneumatological. If the Bible is God's Word only in its witness to our hearts by the Spirit, then within this objective (Christological) and subjective (pneumatological) polarity revelation collapses into the subjectivity of the believer or the church. The Bible loses its "otherness" or objectivity as a witness for God over against our often-twisted religious judgments. It was the desire to safeguard the canon from such devastation that Warfield and others sought to base the Bible's authority on the historic Jesus Christ and the witness that he handed down to the church and, secondarily, on the self-description of the Scripture as a revelation in its own right, a revelation that is experienced to be sure but that is also a characteristic of the text itself as an oracle of God.

At least some Evangelicals might be surprised to discover that Barth wanted to safeguard the Scripture from the control of human ideology as well, but he did not do so as Warfield did by making Scripture identical with divine revelation, but by allowing Scripture through the objective act of God to function as the living witness to revelation (continuously and miraculously "becoming" this revelation by grace in the process of this witness).[26] In other words, Barth secures the objectivity of the Scripture's

---

26. E.g., Karl Barth, *Church Dogmatics*, Vol. I, pt.1 (Edinburgh: T & T Clark, 1975)

witness to revelation through what may be termed an "objective pneumatology." Barth can thus constantly place the Scripture's witness over against the distortions of human subjectivity. The first article of the *Barmen Declaration* that he penned against the "nazified" Jesus of the *Deutsche Christen* read, "Jesus Christ, *as he is attested for us in Holy Scripture*, is the one Word of God which we have to hear and which we have to trust and obey in life and in death" (emphasis mine).

Barth clearly advocated the objective authority and inspiration of Scripture through what may be termed the "objective" work of the Spirit. The authority and inspiration of Scripture are thus not for Barth dependent on human experience for their validity. We will let Barth speak for himself:

> The statement that the Bible is God's Word is a confession of faith, a statement of the faith that hears God speak through the biblical word of man. To be sure it is a statement which, when venturing it in faith, we accept as true even apart from our faith and beyond all our faith and even in the face of our lack of faith. We do not accept it as a description of our experience of the Bible. We accept it as a description of God's action in the Bible, whatever may be the experiences we have or do not have in this connection.[27]

Barth is clear that the Bible is God's Word not by our experience of it but by God's action through it. We do justice to the role of the Bible as God's inspired Word "by believing and resting on the fact that the action of God in the founding and maintaining of His church, with which we have to do in the inspiration of the Bible, is objective enough to emerge victorious from all the inbreaks and outbreaks of man's subjectivity."[28] The Scripture thus has an objective witness to make through the Spirit that is valid whatever the church may or may not hear or experience at the moment.

The objectivity of the Spirit's voice through the text does not for Barth leave out the particularity of the Scripture as a human language with humanly-discernible content. Barth notes:

> Thus Scripture imposes itself in virtue of this content. In distinction from all other scripture, the Scripture with this content—really this!—is the Holy Scripture. When the church heard this word—and it heard it only in the prophets and apostles and

---

110; see also Vol. I, pt.1, 117–21.

27. Ibid., 117.

28. Karl Barth, *Church Dogmatics*, Vol.1, pt. 2 (Edinburgh: T & T Clark, 1956, 1978), 534.

> nowhere else—it heard a magisterial and ultimate word which it cannot ever again confuse or place on a level with any other word.[29]

Barth not only focused on the content of Scripture in describing the particularity of its witness, he also recognized that revelation involves the particularity of the Bible's verbal witness. The following quote is to the point:

> Thus God does reveal himself in statements, through the medium of speech, and indeed of human speech. His word is always this or that word spoken by the prophets and apostles and proclaimed in the church. The personal character of God's Word is not, then, to be played off against its verbal or spiritual character. It is not at all true that this second aspect under which we must understand it implies its irrationality and thus cancels out the first aspect under which we must understand it.[30]

Barth's agreement with "verbal-plenary" inspiration cannot be clearer than it is in the following quote concerning the biblical authors:

> If in their concrete existence and therefore in their concrete speaking and writing the witnesses of revelation belong to revelation, if they spoke by the Spirit what they knew by the Spirit, and if we really have to hear them and therefore their words—then self-evidently we have to hear all their words with the same measure of respect. It would be arbitrary to relate their inspiration only to such parts of their witness as perhaps appear important to us, or not to their words as such but only to the views and thoughts which evoke them.[31]

Barth goes on to say that this inspiration is by grace as the text bears witness to God's own self-disclosure.[32] Of course, Barth also maintained that the Bible is to be read according to its own internal witness, from which certain texts speak louder than others or by which texts in general should be interpreted. The human words of the Bible are to be "expounded rightly, i.e., in relation to its subject-matter" which is Jesus Christ.[33] Barth's concern in his doctrine of verbal-plenary inspiration was to resist the

---

29. Karl Barth, *Church Dogmatics*, Vol. I, pt.1, 108.
30. Ibid., 137.
31. Karl Barth, *Church Dogmatics*, Vol.1, pt. 2, 517–18.
32. Ibid., 518.
33. Ibid., 472.

church's attempt to twist revelation in service to its own self-interests or self-serving ideologies. Barth wrote forcefully that: "the personal character of God's Word means, not its deverbalizing, but the posing of an absolute barrier against reducing its wording to a human system."[34] Thus, Barth did not secure the otherness of Scripture by detaching revelation from the verbal witness of Scripture as many Fundamentalists have superficially characterized his position. Barth understood the otherness of Scripture under his broader understanding of the Bible as a *free text*. The meaning of this text for Barth is discernable through both exegesis (a "preparation" or *Vorbereitung* for hearing) and the hearing of the church through the witness of the Spirit, the combination of which can never be wholly predicted or controlled by the church.

Even a brief description of Barth's understanding of biblical authority such as I have just given begs for some kind of fruitful comparison with Warfield. Though a full comparison would not be possible within the limited confines of this brief essay, a few remarks would be in order. First, both Warfield and Barth based revelation principally on Christ and refused to make Christ and the Scripture equivalent sources of revelation. Scripture is subordinate to Christ and dependent on him for both its legitimacy and principle content. As Barth noted of Christ: "Jesus Christ was no less true man than the prophets and the apostles. But in virtue of his unity with God He stood absolutely over against them as a master over against his slaves."[35] Implicit here is that the church discerns the meaning of all Scripture in the light of its central witness to Jesus Christ and his liberating gospel.[36] Second, both regarded all theological statements about Scripture as valuable elements of Christian doctrine but not as something with which the entirety of Christian truth will either rise or fall. Warfield would not grant biblical infallibility the same expansively foundational role in legitimizing the entirety of Christian truth as Fundamentalists would who claim loyalty to his theology. Third, both regarded the witness of Scripture as objective or as given through the particularity of the text's

---

34. Karl Barth, *Church Dogmatics*, Vol. I, pt.1, 139.

35. Ibid., 145. See also *Church Dogmatics*, Vol.1, pt. 2, 500, 513, where Barth denies an analogy between the divine and human in Christ and the divine and human participation in Scripture. But he does allow for a very limited analogy between them only in the sense that in both there is no mixture of God and creature so that either God or the creature is obliterated. See Vol. 1, pt.2, 501.

36. I don't mean to say that Warfield understood this implication, only that it is there from what he says of Christ and Scripture.

content and verbal witness. Fourth, both found the authority of Scripture to be something that is spiritually discerned in the hearing of the church.

Of course, there are differences as well. Warfield undoubtedly regarded inspiration and infallibility to be characteristics or adjectives of the biblical text given through its divine origin. The text is thus identical ontologically with revelation. Barth ascribed such things as belong to divine revelation to the Word of God (God's self-disclosure in Jesus Christ actualized by the Spirit), which the Scripture as a fallible word "becomes" miraculously in living witness. The lofty descriptions of revelation are applied to Scripture as adverbs rather than as adjectives, descriptive of the function of Scripture in living witness.[37] My question is as follows: If truth is performative, can we really draw a dichotomy between adjective and adverb when it comes to biblical inspiration and infallibility? In other words, as Barth himself implied, if the Scripture consistently and faithfully functions as God's inspired Word in witness to Christ can we not say that this is characteristic of Scripture itself in all of its particularity and even weakness as a finite word of human beings from real cultural contexts? Are not all of the words of Scripture ordained by God to bear the burden of the central task of the biblical canon, namely, to reveal and to lift up the one who is the exact representation of the very being and glory of the Father (Heb 1:3)? Are not these words exposed in both their weakness and their strength as they bear up under this task in the proclamation and worship of the church? Is not the particularity of their human expression involved in this witness and discerned in the light of this witness as to how they speak to us today? In discerning the Word that comes to us through these particular human words, are we really in any position to argue? Do we have any other choice but to say that this is the Word of God, absolutely truthful and trustworthy? As Barth asked, "If the biblical text in its literalness as a text does not force itself upon us, or if we have the freedom word by word to shake ourselves loose from it, what meaning is there in our protestation that the Bible is inspired and the Word of God?"[38]

However one answers such questions, it seems clear that both Warfield and Barth can indeed be quoted on both sides of the Pietist/Fundamentalist divide in ways that are bound to make both feel uneasy. It is my view that neither Barth nor Warfield have always been read carefully enough on the issue of biblical inspiration and infallibility. Once this is done, I think the two of them together might help us all in various

---

37. *Church Dogmatics*, Vol.1, pt. 2, 528–33.
38. Ibid., 533.

streams of the Evangelical movement to work together in dialogue toward theologies of Scripture that neither collapse Scripture into the subjectivity of the church nor remove Scripture from its function as the Word of God among us.[39] I believe that if we embrace the best of what Warfield taught, we will tolerate one another despite some very real differences over how we negotiate the myriad issues we will confront toward this end.

---

39. I regard the work of Kevin Vanhoozer as forging an interesting way forward toward this constructive task. See, *Is There Meaning in This Text* (Grand Rapids, MI: Zondervan, 1998), and, especially, *The Drama of Doctrine: A Canonical-Linguistic Approach to Christian Theology* (Louisville, KY: Westminster/John Knox Press, 2005).

Response #2

Scott Kisker

WRITING family history is complicated. Such histories are usually either full of half-truths or are too embarrassing to be read to the grandchildren. In American families especially, many of the stories that are passed down about relations have little basis in historical reality or at least do not tell the whole truth. There are noble ancestors who never actually existed and members of the family whose stories are simply omitted. There is a story in my own family about an ancestor who emigrated from Germany. According to family lore, a nobleman's horse killed his father who had been forced to hold the reins of the horse while the nobleman beat it. This story may be true. However, the fact that the last name of these relatives (Klaudt) bears a strong resemblance to the German word "klauen" (to steal) makes one wonder if some parts of the story may have been left out.

In his article "The Pietist Critique of Biblical Inerrancy," Donald Dayton takes the conventional family history of American neo-evangelicalism and the self-professed cornerstone of its identity (the inerrancy of Scripture) and does what he does very well; he picks it apart. To this endeavor Dayton brings not the sterile scientific eye of a modern social historian but that of the family genealogist (granted, a black sheep) who knows the stories from the inside and yet delights in opening at least a few of the closets. In this article Dayton reminds the family, his family, of their history, especially of those parts and members they seem regularly to pass over. He points out those historically prominent members who seem to have been posthumously adopted, and thus invites the evangelical family to reevaluate their story and rethink the cornerstone of their identity.

Dayton has real sympathy with parts of the neo-evangelical project as it developed after the Second World War. The desires "to develop an intellectually respectable apologetic for orthodox Christianity, to move beyond the separatism of fundamentalism, . . . and to recover an 'evangelical social conscience'" are not far from Dayton's own hopes. What he is uncomfortable with is the appeal by neo-evangelicals to "the inerrancy of Scripture" as the defining mark of the evangelical family. This devotion to "inerrancy" is not simply theologically problematic from Dayton's perspective. It is also a betrayal of the ancestors.

Dayton traces the history of the neo-evangelical doctrine of inerrancy through the "Old Princeton Theology." Though he is careful not to caricature the doctrine (articulated by Charles Hodge, B.B. Warfield, et al.) as it became prominent in fundamentalist and neo-evangelical circles, it is clear his sympathies lie elsewhere. Understanding scriptural inspiration through the doctrine of biblical inerrancy in the original autographs is problematic for Dayton intellectually and theologically. At times he can't resist a Barthian (and scriptural) ribbing of his evangelical siblings along the lines of Heb 1:1–2. However, it is not the Barthian critique of inerrancy which engages him but the Pietist.

Tracing the history of the "Princeton doctrine" Dayton shows how the so-called "Church's position" on inspiration, including inerrancy in the original autographs, was more significantly the position of one party within the continental state churches of seventeenth-century Europe. Ironically, that party (Orthodox) is not the party most closely identified with evangelicalism. The other party (Pietist) was a renewal movement, opposed to the sterility of the establishment "Orthodox Party." While remaining part of the state church, Pietists wanted to reinvigorate the dead letter in the lives of living saints. Pietists were known for their Biblicism, spiritual vitality, and conversionist soteriology. Far from playing loose with the Bible, the name "Pietist" comes from a poem describing the Bible studies at the University of Halle under the leadership of August Hermann Franke where the students actually lived what the Bible says. And yet Pietists expressly opposed a doctrine of inspiration focused on the text itself.

Despite his iconoclastic reputation, Dayton's historical analysis is not simply an exercise in deconstruction. His purpose is constructive. Dayton returns to Pietism to retrieve the historical source of evangelical identity and recover a biblical and evangelical understanding of scriptural authority and inspiration. Far from trying to weaken evangelicalism's strong engagement with the scriptures, he longs to see the scriptures lived.

Dayton makes eight points about Pietism that bear repeating:

1) They rejected a text-oriented doctrine of inspiration. God, they argued, inspires people.

2) They were open to lower biblical criticism through close readings of the text.

3) They preferred biological to forensic metaphors for soteriology.

4) They had a more complex understanding of continuing revelation.

5) They had an intense desire to connect with New Testament Christianity.

6) They pushed in the direction of Pentecostalism to "open the cannon," believing the gift of inspiration is given to all Christians and scripture judges contemporary claims to revelation.

7) They rejected philosophical theology, opting instead for biblical theology.

8) They placed the doctrine of scripture within ecclesiology, rather than as the foundation for a systematic theology.

Dayton argues that most forms of what is called "American Evangelicalism" derive from the conversionism of Pietism continuing to and through Pentecostalism. So why has the Pietist tradition been "despised and suppressed" within evangelical circles? Here Dayton tells the story behind the stories we evangelicals tell about our history. In the face of liberalism, conservative revivalists in America and their neo-evangelical ancestors saw Princeton Orthodoxy as the only security for their Biblicism, the only "sea-worthy craft." Thus conversionist revivalism came to see itself as part of the establishment. "They lived aboard this craft and became so accustomed to its luxurious intellectual state rooms that they forgot that they did not belong there." That many of the leaders of neo-evangelicalism had been formed academically at Harvard probably did little to remind them of the sawdust in their bloodlines.

The identification of neo-evangelicalism with the "Princeton doctrine" and thus the "Orthodox" party of the seventeenth-century State Churches is related to that part of their agenda, quoted by Dayton at the beginning of the beginning of his article: "to move beyond the separatism of fundamentalism and regain control over the mainline churches." This desire to be accepted, in control, "mainline," one could argue, formed the movement from its inception in ways quite contrary to a simple "Biblicist" reading of the Scriptures.

As his student, I learned from Donald Dayton always to ask the historiographical question; why is this story being told in this way? This is especially true if the telling is connected to social class and respectability. Under his mentorship I began my second conversion to what I now think of as Methodism. I began to try to identify with what he sometimes called the "underbelly of Methodism"—the Holiness Movement and early Pentecostalism, Robert Strawbridge and Julia Foote, Francis Asbury and even John Wesley—people who cared much less about what the world thought of them than they did about the Kingdom of God. I also found a love for the Pietist roots of Methodism which has shaped my work ever since.

In this article one can sense the way Dayton's mind makes connections that historians brought up and educated within the religious establishment generally miss. One becomes aware of his vast and eclectic knowledge of Pietism and of his own Wesleyan tradition. One sees how his time at North Park Seminary in Chicago, and his sympathy with Pentecostalism have shaped him. Finally, one encounters his unique ability to critique and provide a more helpful context for the conundrum of American evangelicalism.

8

American Popular Religious Culture

Dayton's work is characterized by the suspicion of the unquestioned interpretive categories of academic culture. In general his concern has been with the elitist assumptions inherent in academic culture that pushes most scholars to look to the "leading lights" or "establishment" figures to understand a given phenomena. Across of a number of fields of study, Dayton has offered alternative categories and narratives to help explain different aspects of religious phenomena. These alternative categories are often provocative and tend to move from the grass-roots level up, rather than the other way round.

The following previously unpublished essay, presented to the Evangelical Theology and Popular Culture Sections at the American Academy of Religion in 1998, represents just such an attempt to provide an alternative reading of American neo-evangelicalism. The essay proved to be both controversial and illustrative of Dayton's idiosyncratic approach to some of the historigraphical questions surrounding American neo-evangelicalism. In it, Dayton uses the famous actor and 1960's icon, James Dean, as a case study for understanding the dynamics of American neo-evangelicalism. The essay also reflects Dayton's fascination with Dean, which began when he learned that the actor was reared in the Wesleyan Church, Dayton's own ecclesial family.

James Dean, Popular Culture and Popular Religion

With Implications for the Study of American Evangelicalism

Donald W. Dayton

"*Without Jimmy Dean, the Beatles never would have existed.*"
  —John Lennon

"*I want to be the James Dean of Rock and Roll.*"
  —Elvis Presley

"*Jim Dean and Elvis were the spokesmen for an entire generation. When I was in acting school in New York, years ago, there was a saying that if Marlon Brando changed the way people acted, then James Dean changed the way people lived. He was the greatest actor who ever lived. He was simply a genius.*"

  —Actor Martin Sheen (at the twenty-fifth memorial service [1980] held in the Wesleyan campground tabernacle, Fairmount, IN)

Introduction

SOMEWHERE about mid-century there was a sea-change in American religious history. As in the middle of the last century populist religious movements (Methodists and Baptists) began to swarm into the middle class and challenge the cultural dominance of the more established Presbyterians, Episcopalians, and Congregationalists, so too in this century a wave of new populist religious movements experienced *embourgeoisement*, bringing into the cultural mainstream religious traditions not well understood either by the traditional churches or centers of the academic study of religion conditioned by their own social location.

On occasion this has produced some delicious ironies, especially in the political arena. Thus Messiah College of the minuscule pacifist denomination of the Brethren in Christ has luxurious athletic facilities named after the Eisenhower family to commemorate the childhood brush with a Sunday school of that denomination of the great military president of our century. The disgraced Richard Nixon was reared at the confluence of two religious traditions stressing above all else themes of moral integrity—the revivalistic Quakers and the Holiness movement. Gary Hartpence left the Church of the Nazarene to go to Yale Divinity School, shorten his last name to Hart, and leave us the image of another disgraced presidential candidate with Donna Rice sitting on his lap. Only persons like George McGovern, reared among the Dakota Wesleyan Methodists (a source of his "plains radicalism"?) and Jimmy Carter (Georgian Southern Baptist who continued to teach his simple Sunday school lessons) seem to have escaped such fate—only to be largely rejected by their religious compatriots!

Perhaps even more striking and influential because of their impact on popular culture have been a number of figures who have arisen from such religious traditions to profoundly shape the way in which we view the world. One is tempted to pause to explore the roots of Elvis Presley in the Assemblies of God variety of Pentecostalism—and his continuing relationship with that church. He is reported to have said to his Pentecostal pastor, for example, at his mother's funeral, "I need to talk to you. I have done many of the things you told me not to do and have not done many of the things you told me to do." But for the purposes of this paper, we will turn to actor James Dean, whose short life and three movies have left a cultural icon and perhaps even a cult that continues to grow in power: his memorial services still draw thousands of people to a bewildered Fairmount, Indiana, that hardly knows how to handle the mix of academic, biker, drag racer, and teenage fans from around the world; I have collected six 1998 pictorial calendars—as well as innumerable assorted kitsch, from Dean cookie jars and plates to Jimmy Dean cologne, ties, and watches; the biographies continue to pour off the presses in increasing numbers—the last decade has seen probably as many substantial books as the whole preceding period since his tragic death in California in 1955; and of all places, the Jimmy Dean cult seems especially alive in Japan (where many of the picture books are now printed and whose business man, Seita Ohnishi, paid for the memorial at Cholame, CA).

Only recently did I discover how closely intertwined my own life was with the institutions that shaped the life of James Dean—as I happened to pick up a remaindered copy of *James Dean, Little Boy Lost: an Intimate Biography* by Hollywood columnist, author, and screenwriter Joe Hyams with his son Jay Hyams. It was about a decade after Dean's birth in Marion, Indiana, that my father took a position in charge of training Wesleyan Methodist ministers at Marion College, where studied Dean's two major mentors: his drama teacher, Adeline Brookshire Nall (who prepared Dean for speaking competitions at the WCTU—the Women's Christian Temperance Union), and a Wesleyan general evangelist, James DeWeerd (whose exact, and life-long, relationship to Dean is still a matter of controversy—Hyams claims that it was DeWeerd who initiated Dean into his first homosexual relationship). I was to attend the junior high school where Adeline Brookshire taught before moving to Fairmount and would spend my summers at youth camp, conference and revival meetings at the Wesleyan Campground in Fairmount, Indiana, in the town where Dean was raised by his aunt and uncle after his mother's death when he was nine. The tabernacle on this campground (where my family still maintains a family cottage) is still used for Dean's memorial services when thousands of fans overflow the capacity of other facilities in Fairmount. I was in my first year of junior high school when Dean's body was brought back to Fairmount for the funeral (at which DeWeerd would preach); yet I was hardly aware of Dean. My church could barely handle television, let alone the "decadent" culture of Hollywood from which we were carefully shielded.

Upon finding Hyams' book, I became intrigued with the discussions of Dean's religious background in Marion and Fairmount. The descriptions did not ring true, and I have yet to find in the vast range of Dean literature and memorabilia anyone who seems to have the story straight. This is particularly true of the Hyams book. On the one hand I suppose we can hardly expect Hollywood columnists to understand the details of small town religious life in Middle America; but the problem is also one of understanding the new religious movements spawned in the last century as they come into their own. I would like to use the case of James Dean to explore certain dynamics of populist religious movements (and the study thereof!). I will do this by first exploring the character of the dominant form of religious life in the northeast quadrant of Indiana, then, by using this description to correct and clarify the precise nature of the religious background of Dean—and to ask if this clarification helps us to understand Dean in new ways, and finally to extend this discussion into a revisionist vision of what constitutes the character of the "American evangelicalism" whose emergence in our time has become a cottage industry for so many scholars.

Dean Country—the Distinctive Religious Character of NE Indiana

Grant County lies a little southwest of the center of the northeast quadrant of Indiana (see the map on the next page). For a variety of reasons, the religious ethos of this area seems not to be well understood—as is characteristic of most populist religious movements. For a variety of sociological and cultural reasons the elite traditions in a culture provide the categories of analysis and understanding of those movements that are often outside the cultural experience of academics. This is often true even within such movements as the first generation of scholars attempt to interpret itself in the borrowed, culturally respectable categories of the dominant culture learned in the academic centers of traditions based in earlier and alien forms of religious experience. Thus, in part because of the academic influence of the Presbyterian tradition, categories derived from that experience are often used to interpret phenomena that do not yield to those categories.

This dynamic seems particularly true in the case of Indiana where at least three dynamics need to be discerned. The Northwest Territory was deeply influenced by those religious movements which were most vital when this territory was being settled—notably such movements as Methodism and the Disciples of Christ. Several of us have been pointing out for years the strange neglect of the history and experience of Methodism as providing the interpretative keys for the understanding of the American religious experience in general; it was after all the demographically dominant form of Protestantism in the United States from the beginnings of its *embourgeoisement* before the Civil War until the 1960s when it began to falter and was eventually overtaken by the Southern Baptists. Not only were the Methodists the largest Protestant denomination, they convinced half of the rest of Protestantism to act like Methodists. Recently Nathan Hatch, in his presidential address before the American Society of Church History, reflected on the "puzzle of Methodism" and its neglect in the academic study of the American religious experience. One cannot understand American religion and nearly everything since without reference to Methodism. To see the cultural impact of Methodism in the Northwest Territory one only need look at the maps produced by the NCC in which colors identify the counties in which different religious traditions are influential. Yet, for a variety of reasons both sociological and academic this originally "populist" Methodist experience is hardly used to read the history and culture of places like Indiana where it comes close to being an informally "established" religion. This is the first point: the necessity of bringing the Methodist experience into focus.

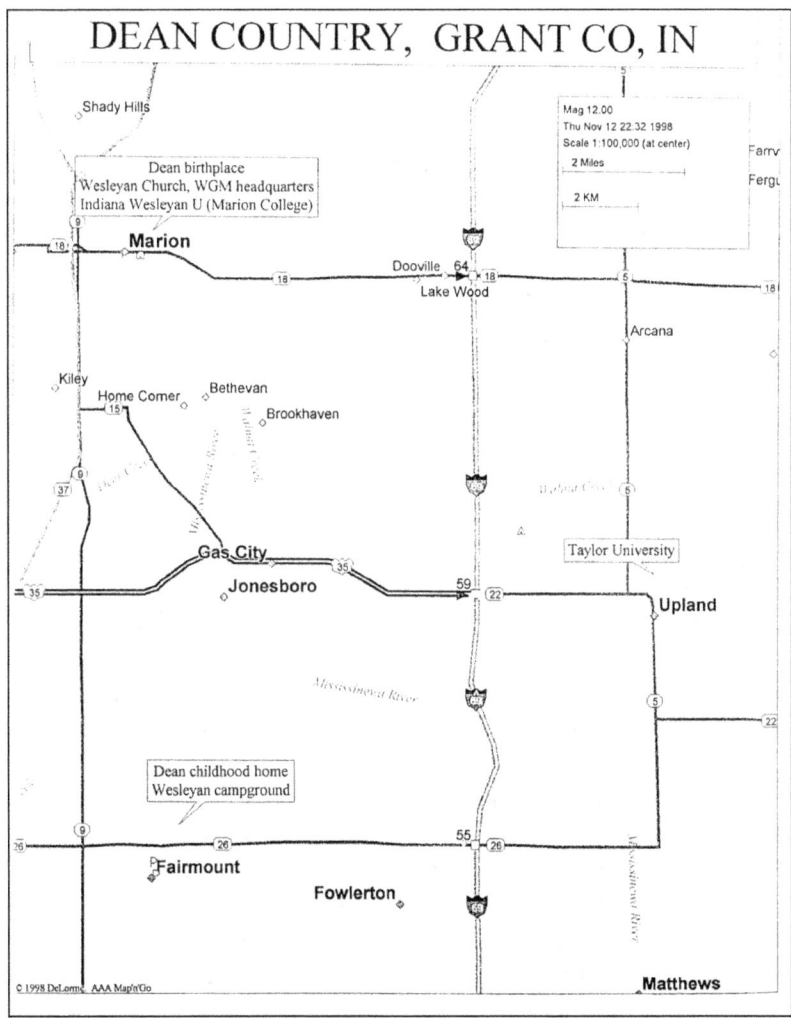

This focus is necessary if we are to understand the next wave of populist religious movements that arose in response to the *embourgeoisement* of Methodism. Long before (decades before!) the fundamentalist/modernist controversies that tore apart especially the Baptists and the Presbyterians in this century, Methodism had begun to fragment and produce a variety of radical movements that have come to identify themselves as the "Holiness movement"—the radicalization of which would later at the turn of the century produce Pentecostalism. These new movements cannot be interpreted in the logic of the later developments as the Wesleyan wing of fundamentalism or evangelicalism—as is usually done. Indeed, these movements provide the categories to better understand the emergence of currents usually interpreted by other cultural and religious experience. The point here is that there is probably no greater cluster of these Holiness currents than in this northeast quadrant of Indiana.

The most important of these movements for our story is the Wesleyan Methodist Church, which was born as the abolitionist party within the Methodist Episcopal Church in New England and the "burned-over district" of upstate New York—founded in response to the increasing compromise of Methodism on the slavery issue in its struggle to become a national church. This church would bring its headquarters eventually to Marion, Indiana, the site of one of its colleges, where it would merge with the turn of the century radical "Pilgrim Holiness" tradition that took shape in the culture of God's Bible School in Cincinnati. A sister church, the Free Methodist Church—also abolitionist and a protest against the *embourgeoisement* of western NY Methodism when the latter adopted pew rentals, paid choirs, and oyster suppers to finance church life—migrated to Winona Lake, NW of Marion, for its headquarters. Both the Wesleyans and Frees would eventually move to the Interstate beltline of Indianapolis. About thirty miles south of Marion is Anderson, the site of the headquarters of the Church of God (Anderson, Indiana—so named to distinguish itself from the many Pentecostal "Churches of God"). This interesting church combines the ecclesiology of the Campbellite (Disciples) tradition with the Wesleyan soteriology of the Holiness Movement. For a while the Christian Holiness Association was headquartered in Indianapolis, and both interdenominational mission societies in the Holiness tradition have their headquarters on this map (the Oriental Missionary Society so influential in Korea and Latin America is headquartered in Greenwood, just south of Indianapolis, and the World Gospel Mission is in Marion). In addition there are a variety of independent schools like Taylor University named for a maverick holiness Methodist bishop. This school in Upland is in Grant County just a few miles from Marion and Fairmount. If one would wish to attend college or university in that county one would have a choice of the denominationally Wesleyan Marion College (now Indiana Wesleyan University) or the independent holiness Taylor University (more recently evolved into "generic evangelicalism")—or Anderson University, one county to the south. Or if one wished to cross the state line, one would find a large number of similar schools in southern Michigan, western Ohio, eastern Illinois and so forth. There is probably no greater cluster of "Holiness" churches and institutions in any comparable geographical area.

But this is not the whole story; we must note another major dynamic that makes popular religious movements difficult to study. Just as Methodism's influence was felt far beyond the confines of the denomination strictly speaking—or the charismatic movement of our own time cannot be understood denominationally—so the influence of the Holiness movement set the tone for this area of Indiana in many ways. Ironically the Holiness impulse, which had a tendency to radicalize those in the mainline denominations and play a role in the formation of new denominational traditions, also caught up in its fervor a variety of more radical traditions and drew them back toward more traditional Protestantism by the mediation of the Sunday School, revival meetings, and among the Quakers more "programmed" worship. Thus, just north of Marion one finds Huntington College of the United Brethren (UBs that failed to merge with the Evangelical Association to form the EUBs that would merge into the Methodist Church in 1968), a denomination that reveals strong Holiness influence and is known largely for Bishop Wright, father of the Wright brothers of aviation fame. Among Mennonite-like churches a variety of mergers produced the United Missionary Church which has therefore both its colleges in this quadrant, Bethel College in Mishawaka, just south of South Bend and Fort Wayne Bible College. This church, also profoundly shaped by the Holiness movement, is best know through the work of Jasper Huffman, the major figure in the founding of the Winona Lake School of Theology (later taken up into Fuller Theological Seminary) and the father of John Huffman, prominent Presbyterian pastor in Florida. Also falling into this category would be the Brethren in Christ, headquartered in Nappanee, south of Goshen, a denomination known today primarily for the work of Ron Sider. But for our story, the most important development is the influence of the Holiness movement upon the Quakers in the area. A majority of Indiana Quakers were swept into the Holiness movement and would not identify fully with Earlham College in Richmond, Indiana, which represents the more mainstream Quakers. The holiness Union Bible Seminary in Westfield, Indiana, is supported by the Central Yearly Meeting of Friends. These Holiness Quaker currents would identify with a variety of yearly meetings around the country which would find expression through such schools as Malone College (Ohio), Friends University (Kansas), George Fox University (Oregon), and more distantly Whittier College (California—and thus Nixon, in a sense, whose pastor also had links with Marion and the Wesleyans in Indiana). Thus many religious traditions and churches cannot be understood in terms of their formal affiliation (as Friends, for example) without reference to the informal, populist movements that give them their real identity—just as a church may really be charismatic in identity while belonging to the Presbyterian or Methodist denominations. This issue is crucial in the interpretation of the religious background of James Dean.

The Religious Background of James Dean

Dean is generally interpreted in terms of his attendance at Back Creek Friends Church, located next to the Winslow Farm where he lived with his uncle and aunt on the edge of Fairmount. Most authors note this fact and then interpret the religious influence on Dean in terms of more generic understandings of Quakerism derived from some other source than observation of this particular congregation. Part of the problem is that the small Back Creek church is often confused (as in Hyams) with the much larger downtown Friends church which is more oriented to the Earlham tradition and takes on the character of the pastor of the moment (the Harley-riding "hippie pastor" of this church presided with James DeWeerd over the funeral which was held in the downtown church, presumably to handle the thousands of mourners—not in Back Creek as is often claimed). I began early on to be suspicious of many of the descriptions of Back Creek—and consequent extrapolations as to the nature of Dean's religious background. I have now attended services twice at Back Creek, and it is clear that this is a holiness Friends church. This was clear as soon as I drove into the parking lot from the Taylor University stickers—and later from the Taylor (rather than Earlham) propaganda on the literature table and bulletin board in the back of the church. The two pastors (husband and wife both ordained) were missionaries with the World Gospel Mission, the interdenominational Holiness missionary society headquartered in Marion just up the road. There is a Sunday school and "programmed" worship indistinguishable from any small mid-Western Holiness church. The sermon and its illustrations were based on Holiness themes and culture (the Salvation Army, China Inland Mission, and Oswald Chambers, etc.). The Back Creek Friends Meeting is Quaker in name but Holiness in style and content—as has been confirmed by the archivist/historian Paul Hamm at Earlham. The significance of this will emerge in a moment.

HOLINESS COUNTRY--NE INDIANA

The second major religious influence on Dean comes from the Wesleyan Church and especially the influence of James DeWeerd, Dean's mentor in high school and later, a figure that plays a prominent role in any biography of Dean. Again, most of the biographers fail totally to grasp who this figure was. Hyams, for example, describes him as pastor of the local Wesleyan church (Hyams says of the "Wesleyan Baptist Church"—whatever that might be!) and repeats this and other errors in his book even after DeWeerd corrected him in response to a much earlier *Redbook* article. I can find no reference to DeWeerd ever having been the pastor of this church. He *was* a member of the church and grew up in Fairmount after his Pilgrim Holiness parents (Fred and Leila, again *both* ordained) returned from missionary service in Sierra Leone. James lived with his widowed mother in Fairmount (again, his hometown) and served the church as a "general evangelist." DeWeerd became a major figure in the Holiness movement. He had served as a chaplain and was critically wounded in France, leaving him disfigured with a deep indentation in his chest. He claimed to have known Churchill and to have been invited to his funeral by the Queen. He was a little more flamboyant and eloquent than the usual Wesleyan evangelist—as evidenced by his interest in convertibles and other "hot cars" and the Indy races, his love of travel (especially bullfights in Mexico) and so on. He was also unusual as a Wesleyan pastor for his membership in the Masonic lodge (a strong taboo in the denomination). Despite these issues, he went on to have major roles in the Holiness movement as pastor of Cadle Tabernacle (an independent Holiness church in Indianapolis with the largest sanctuary in the city—DeWeerd flew to Dean's funeral in the Cadle Jet after his national radio broadcast), as president of holiness Kletzing College (Iowa—though only for a couple of years for some reason), as editor of *The Christian Witness*, a major holiness paper published from 1870 until it folded in 1959.

DeWeerd was probably the major influence on Dean. He took him to the Indy races, taught him to drive, entertained him at home with fancy meals accompanied with poetry and literature readings, plied him with maudlin and aphoristic spiritual advice, corresponded and visited him after Dean left Fairmont for Hollywood and New York City, staked him with several hundred dollars when Dean came through Indianapolis on the way to New York City to pursue his acting career there, awakened Dean's life-long interest in bullfighting with the home movies from his travels, preached at the funeral, and found his final resting place in Park Cemetery with his parents across the graveyard from Dean.

This is not the place to resolve the question of whether DeWeerd's relationship with Dean was sexual, either latently or manifestly, if indeed that question can be answered at this point. Dean was probably actively bisexual, both men and women have claimed to have had sex with him, though others describe him as strangely asexual. When asked if he was bisexual, he was reported to have answered indirectly that one could hardly expect him to go through life with one hand tied behind his back. Hyams describes in some detail a seduction scene in which DeWeerd invited Dean to explore the hole in his chest as a prelude to seduction into a sexual experience. Hyans claims to have based this report on a description by DeWeerd shortly after Dean's death in 1955—though the account was not published until 1992. But DeWeerd was pastor of Cadle Tabernacle at the time, and one wonders if he would so openly describe an incident the public knowledge of which would have almost certainly destroyed his career. On the other hand, rumors of his homosexuality followed DeWeerd throughout his life in spite of his late marriage. Older Wesleyan figures (including my father) confirm the existence of the rumors. And local folk in Fairmount played on his name, calling him "Dr. Weird" and wondered about the time he spent with the boys in town, including his practice of taking them to the YMCA in Anderson where he would apparently watch them swim in the nude. But whether he was homosexual or, if he were, whether he gave physical expression to this orientation with Dean, may never be known. And the conclusions that are drawn are often more dependent on what is brought to the question by the interpreters. Hollywood biographers have difficulty understanding an unexpressed orientation; while those from the Wesleyan church seem to understand easily the possibility of a sublimated but possibly homoerotic relationship that for religious and cultural reasons might not have found physical expression. In his recent book of Hollywood gossip *Laid Bare*, John Gilmore is frank about his own homosexual relationship with Dean, Dean's use of the male "casting couch" (claiming to have fellated "five of the biggest Hollywood moguls") in his efforts to get ahead and the possibility that Dean may have sold himself as a "hustler" on Santa Monica Boulevard, but he also insists that DeWeerd has been done a great disservice by Hyams and the controversies that ensued.

But no one seems to have noticed that the Dean family was much more intimately related to the Wesleyan Church in Fairmount than this relationship with DeWeerd. Among the stained glass windows in that church are the one donated by the DeWeerd family and another one donated by Cal Dean, the great grandfather of James. Cal Dean was a farmer, better known as an auctioneer, and apparently a long-time, faithful member of the church. By the time of Winton (Cal's grandson and James' father), however, there are indications that any religious commitment was more attenuated. But it seems significant that when James Dean's parents were married July 26, 1930, a woman minister by the name of Emma Payne presided. Rev. Payne *is* listed in Wesleyan yearbooks as being assigned to the Fairmount Wesleyan Church. I have not yet found out whether they were married in the church (the marriage was a bit of a shotgun wedding; James was born February 8, 1931), but it seems that the Wesleyan identification remained alive still in the early thirties, making the relationship with DeWeerd more natural. It may well be that the family religious tradition was actually Wesleyan, and that the Quaker relationship was more of an accident of the geographical proximity of the Winslow farm to Back Creek.

But the real point is that it makes little difference. The two streams are really one—the Holiness tradition that found slightly different nuances in the Wesleyan and Quaker local churches. It was common to move back and forth between the two cultures; my father, for example, moonlighted in Quaker churches in the area while directing the ministerial training program at Marion College. Any interpretation of Dean's religious background must be reoriented along these lines.

But Does It Matter?

From one angle it may seem an exercise in futility to attempt to correct this misunderstanding of Dean's religious background. On the most obvious level, the "rebel" Dean surely must be understood in terms of his rejection of religion. His sexuality, his constant use of the "f-word" and other characteristics would seem to be blatant violations of the holiness ethos that would have put him beyond the pale of the tradition. One member of Back Creek who starred in church plays with Dean lamented to me Dean's early death, which precluded the possibility of his return to the faith of his childhood. On the other hand, getting the story straight does seem to me to illumine several dimensions of Dean's life. Among these might be the following as starters.

(1) It certainly puts a different twist on the questions of Dean's sexuality. One academic suggested to me that the Quaker tradition would not have been troubled by Dean's sexuality (whether bisexual or homosexual), citing the famous study of the London Yearly Meeting of Friends that homosexuality has no more moral value than "left-handedness." But this

would be to completely misunderstand the character of the Holiness Quakerism that Dean was raised in. This perfectionist tradition would not even today allow expression to a homosexual orientation, expecting rather transformation and reorientation (through a strong doctrine of sanctification) or sexual abstinence—let alone the position that would have been assumed two thirds of a century ago in mid-western, rural Indiana under this religious influence. It may well be, in spite of Dean's apparent rejection of his childhood religion, that his life-long sense of guilt, his often described death-wish, and his sense of alienation may show unresolved questions with regard to his sexual orientation and behavior.

(2) Getting the story straight adds poignancy to the fact that this tradition produced a great Hollywood actor. As already indicated, major portions of the Wesleyan church could hardly handle the invention of television coming into prominence during this period. It was denounced as of the devil—perhaps with the fear that it might break down the strong taboos against the "decadence" of Hollywood and the theater. Stephen Paine, Wesleyan president of the denomination's Houghton College, wrote a book on *Why Christians do not go to the Movies*, and his college struggled with the issue. Christians might see a "film" but not a "movie" (a developed casuistry defined the latter as anything syndicated or distributed through Hollywood—though a reluctant exception was made for Disney "films" which were allowed, though occasionally censored by having the projector blocked when such "films" were shown on campus). I myself never entered a movie theater until living away from home on my way to college. And when I seduced my father into attending *The Sound of Music* when he visited me in seminary at Yale nearly a decade after Dean's movies, the experience was such a violation of his life-long conditioning that he vomited in the theater. It is entirely possible that some of Dean's self-loathing might be related to such issues. It is often reported that he hated Hollywood and its culture.

(3) But it seems to me that there might even be more significant connections to be drawn. There might even be correlations with some essential features of Dean's acting craft. Dean studied at the Actors Studio and was a devotee of its school of "method acting." This school, usually contrasted with a more "technical" style of acting, emphasized the need to master the full range of human emotion and act out of a genuine empathy with the character being portrayed rather than learning to portray all emotions artificially and technically without any emotional connection with the character. It is interesting that DeWeerd apparently encouraged Dean to explore the full range of human emotion and experience. It may also be

that the "sectarian" experience of being raised to see many forms of culture and art as inherently sinful may create by such cultural isolation a compulsion to compensate by embracing a range of experience that one feels deprived of by the "narrowness" of this cultural and religious experience. I certainly can testify to struggling with these issues, and efforts to test this perception among students reared in such traditions find a resonance with this struggle. Such dynamics may have led Dean in the direction of the "method" school of acting.

(4) We need more exploration of whether Dean carried into his twenties any genuine religious sensibility. He is reported to have been profoundly enamored of St. Exupery's *The Little Prince* which he described as his favorite book—and it has been suggested that his piety and religious life revolved around his dreaming of its themes. I have read only a little of the writings of DeWeerd, but they seem to me a naive mix of inherited Holiness theology and trivial spiritual aphorisms that sound more like Midwestern folk wisdom than reflective theology or religion—his doctoral degree was an honorary one from Taylor University, and his theological education was primarily undergraduate at Marion and Taylor. I find little evidence of genuine religious sensibility—other than what may lie behind his morbidity and sense of sin and self-loathing. All of this needs much more exploration.

Implications for the Study of American Evangelicalism

My study of James Dean has confirmed for me the inadequacies of the paradigms that we use to study American "fundamentalism" and "evangelicalism." We must remind ourselves that in dealing with this culture centered in northeastern Indiana we are dealing with the heart of what has emerged as the "neo-evangelical" movement that took shape as Dean was growing up. It was only a decade earlier that Harold John Ockenga would emerge from the Holiness culture of Indiana and Illinois to come to Taylor University, just up the road from Fairmount, to establish himself as a Holiness "boy preacher" around the state before moving on to Princeton Seminary, the pastorate of Park Street Church in Boston, the presidencies of Fuller and Gordon-Conwell Seminaries, and perhaps most significantly the major force behind the found of the National Association of Evangelicals. These currents are generally read through the experience of the fundamentalist movements among the Baptists and the Presbyterians, but a majority of early leaders were from churches with connections to this geographical area—Ockenga himself, Stephen Paine of the Wesleyans,

Bishop Marston of the Free Methodists, and so forth. The colleges we have mentioned and others associated with these churches are the core of the Christian College Coalition that so dominates the "neo-evangelical" subculture. Even Wheaton College, the symbol of the neo-evangelical movement, comes out of these traditions, having been founded by the Wesleyans, though their control was weakened after the Civil War by the decimation of their membership as pastors and congregants returned to the Methodist Church after the "resolution" of the slavery issue. The college continued until about 1890 as the seminary of the Wesleyans, and Presbyterian Jonathan Blanchard was a Holiness advocate of the Oberlin Perfectionist variety who circulated all his life through Holiness camps struggling with the issues of the movement—though the histories of the college never recognize these facts, usually transposing Blanchard into a Presbyterian of the later fundamentalist variety. But the facts that we have unearthed in the study of Dean will not yield to the analysis implicit in this paradigm. Let me end with a few examples.

(1) I have emphasized the role of women ministers through this history—James DeWeerd's mother, the Wesleyan pastor who married Dean's parents, the current pastors of Back Creek Friends Church. The Presbyterian paradigm tells us that such practices are a part of the "liberal" tradition, part of the capitulation to modernity that "fundamentalists" and "evangelicals" are called to oppose. As a matter of fact, just the opposite is true. The churches of the NAE ordained women long before the churches of the NCC, and in much greater numbers! The Wesleyans hosted the Women's Rights Convention of 1848 in Seneca Falls—the one celebrated this last summer as the beginning of the feminist call for women's suffrage. And it was a Wesleyan pastor who preached the ordination sermon for Antoinette Brown, the first woman to be ordained and a graduate of Oberlin during the period of Blanchard's identification with that school. Yet the paradigms we use to interpret the NAE and related movements will not allow these facts to surface—and actually suppresses them.

(2) The usual interpretations of "evangelicalism," especially those within the movement, emphasize the "orthodoxy" of "evangelicalism" with the implication that it lies at the center of classical Christianity while others have abandoned traditional Christianity. I have become increasingly impressed by the extent to which the evangelical tradition is a protest against the traditional church. The affinity of "evangelicalism" with the more radical traditions of the church is what becomes apparent to me in this study. The assimilation or homogenization of these forms of evangelicalism with or into forms of Quakerism, Mennonites, and other radical movements

makes this point indirectly. I am becoming increasingly convinced that the "Presbyterian" paradigm that is regularly used to interpret "evangelicalism" is a fantasy projected onto history out of the social aspirations of a populist movement trying to bring about its own *embourgeoisement*. The problem is that these fantasies are then used even outside the movement as supposedly value-free and obvious categories of interpretation. One of the most egregious illustrations of this dynamic may be seen in the book *Evangelicalism: The Coming Generation* by James Davison Hunter. Hunter assumes rather than proves his basic premise that "evangelicalism" is essentially a form of Reformation orthodoxy attempting to withstand the acids of modernity. Then his empirical work studies such institutions as Messiah College (Holiness/Anabaptist), Houghton College (Wesleyan), George Fox (Holiness/Quaker), and so on. By no stretch of the imagination can such schools be understood in the line of Reformation orthodoxy. They are radical versions of Christianity that cannot be assimilated into that tradition. An alternative paradigm would interpret the empirical data that Hunter adduces as evidence of the movement of these radical currents into the middle class and back toward the more traditional styles of church life—rather than the movement toward "liberalism" that Hunter discerns.

(3) Such revisionism would turn many accepted paradigms on their heads; it may be that we would do better to interpret the larger evangelicalism through these currents in northeast Indiana. Maybe, just maybe, these populist churches are the carriers of the emergence of the "neo-evangelical" impulse, which might be better seen as the *embourgeoisement* of those movements that originally took shape precisely as a protest against that process within earlier generations of Protestantism, especially Methodism.

Response #1

Woodrow W. Whidden II

THIS fascinating James Dean piece is just one of a number of salvos launched in one of the most sustained campaigns of Dayton's "illustrious" career.[1] The goal of this effort has been to bring to the consciousness of the academy, especially the Reformed/Presbyterian historiographic academy, the simple fact that they have just plain missed a whole lot of essential stuff by not fully acknowledging the presence of the Holiness/Pentecostal "riffraff" contingent at their Evangelical "party." The issue concerns not only the "location," but the agenda of this historiographic celebration.

For Dayton's instincts, the Evangelical party is not just a staid affair that has been organized in the banqueting halls of Fuller, Wheaton, Gordon-Conwell, and Notre Dame, but is more like a hippie "feast" (or "happening") thrown by the Holiness/Pentecostal student groups on the quads of these venerable places. The noise of the "event" is bad enough, but the Presbyterian/Reformed venues are not only scandalized by the noise, but also seem utterly put off by the odors emanating from what is being served up. It is not just that the layers have been peeled off Dayton's religious "onion," but that somebody has slung buckets full of chopped garlic at the doors of the banqueting halls. The whole messy thing is so revolting to the Calvin party that they not only refuse to stroll out and investigate the "doings," they simply stay in their banqueting halls, frantically plugging their ears and holding their collective intellectual and cultural noses.

Has Dayton succeeded in at least getting them to release their noses and open up their eyes and ears (and maybe their "hearts"?) to what is unfolding in the "riffraff" zone of world Evangelicalism? Most likely, no one can know for sure. Yet, in the final analysis, one senses that Dayton really doesn't care! That is, if by clearing the eyes, ears and noses, one has reference to the "anatomy" of the scholarship of the Reformed Evangelical

---

1. To my knowledge, the most seminal work in this campaign is Dayton's article entitled "Yet Another Layer of the Onion: Or Opening the Ecumenical Door to Let the Riffraff in," *The Ecumenical Review* 40:1 (1988) 87–110.

historians. I would suggest that, in one important sense, neither should Dayton's beloved "riffraff" really care if they get their due. The "happening" will continue to unfold and the question is whether the Reformed folks are going to come along and adventurously try a few fresh recipes at the "feasts."

If Dayton has succeeded in anything, he has been the main force for a younger generation of Wesleyan Holiness/Pentecostal scholars to simply come into their own and do their own unique historiographic and theological "thing" by making up some new recipes for the "feasts" that are going on all over the "quads" of the world (academic or otherwise). Just a few days ago, at a Thanksgiving "feast" thrown for expatriate American missionaries in the Philippines, I was chatting with a young missiologist/historian who shared with me the profound impact Dayton's scholarship has had on his own self-understanding and what courage it gave him to go ahead and "do" his more "radical" thing as an agent of Spirit-indicted missions and social reform. One senses that there are scores, if not hundreds who have shared the same experience. Yes, it is okay to be Holiness, Pentecostal, Charismatic, and a radical disciple of Jesus in the best sense of what these "riffraff" traditions have stood for and experienced.

Now, what about this James Dean piece? I would suggest that the main point of the whole thing could be best characterized this way: it is all a part of the Donald Dayton "Coming Home" Party. One always senses that the core of Dayton's life has swirled around a hate/love relationship with his Holiness "home." Whether it involved struggles with the mundane issue of not being able to wear a "class" ring with the rest of the graduates of his Wilmore High School senior class (no jewelry was a standard Holiness dress code for that era) or the more serious struggles with the expected second blessing, Dayton would rebel and try to walk away from the Holiness home farm—only to decide to "come back home." The James Dean piece is more particularly how Dayton has "come back home" to the Holiness sub-culture of North East Indiana and sought to make sense of those roots through the lens of the James Dean phenomenon.

The details of the Dean legend are fascinating and provide a classic revelation of Dayton's penchant for the "off-beat"—whether in his personal formation or his more formal scholarly agenda. Not only does he find a paradigm for his own struggles, but also the struggles of many who have come from these conservative, Holiness saturated venues. Yet, Dayton has always seemed to hear the siren call of an affective "radicalism" involved in the history and experience of his native "riffraff" zone.

Space does not permit an expansive treatment of this, but I would like to suggest that part of Dayton's "coming home" party might include a little visit to the archives in the house of "father" Wesley. I readily acknowledge that Dayton has instinctively appreciated that his home-base tradition has had very important contributions to make to theology, spiritual formation, social ethics, and mission. But could it be that "father" Wesley had a caution that all of us who revel in the Holiness/Pentecostal heritage need to hear—that is, if we would truly come all the way "back home" to the best that our "riffraff" party has to celebrate? Here I have reference to Wesley's little caveat that there was but "a hair's breadth" which distinguished his Soteriological accents from those of the Calvin party.[2]

In all of our celebration, would it not be profitable for the Dayton "party" to also "come home" for an occasional tutorial from the other "John" of our Protestant heritage? Maybe the whole thing could be framed with a couple of key questions: What is it that lies at the core of the Wesleyan fountainhead that the Holiness/Pentecostal offspring have legitimately carried forward? And what cautions could they most benefit from with a renewed, sustained listening to both of the key, founding mentors of Twentieth and Twenty-First Century evangelical Protestantism—the "Johns" Calvin and Wesley?

I would suggest that what lies at the core of the Wesleyan heritage is the whole notion of a graced, free will experience of Love Divine. Yes, an experience that was freely open to a direct experience with the Holy Spirit. Furthermore, this experience was full of optimism that the Spirit would not only bring moral transformation and power for witnessing, but that this power would include all of the gifts of the Spirit—not just the more formal and less spectacular. They wanted the gift package, including those that were the most spectacular—tongues, healing and prophecy. The "hair's breadth" of separation between Wesley and Calvin seemingly resides right at this experiential juncture.

Wesley could not stomach the ungracious "determinism" of Calvin, but he did pick up on the profound element of Calvin's practical soteriology and its notable accent on the subjective appropriations of the Spirit's

---

2. This terminology is found in the "Question and Answer" format of the minutes of "The Second Annual Conference" held at Bristol, Thursday, August 1, 1745: "Q.22: Does not the truth of the gospel lie very near both to Calvinism and antinomianism? A. Indeed it does; as it were, within *a hair's breadth* (emphasis supplied). So that 'tis altogether foolish and sinful, because we do not quite agree either with one or the other, to run from them as far as ever we can" (cited from Albert Outler, ed., *John Wesley* [New York: Oxford University Press, 1964] 151).

working to lure sinners into "mystical" union with the Lord of both justifying and sanctifying grace. Yet this experience of the "testimonium" of the Spirit was, for both Calvin and Wesley, always to be judged by the sobering testimony of the Spirit-inspired, written Word of God.

Furthermore, I would offer the proposition that Wesley was the first "free-will" theist who was willing to strongly restore the direct "witness of the Spirit" to our "spirits" as absolutely essential grist for not only Christian ethical and spiritual formation, but also theological reflection. And this theme has been greatly celebrated and exploited by the Holiness/Pentecostal heirs of Wesley. Yet, Wesley was always reminding his children that there was also the testing, indirect "witness" of the Spirit through the testimony of the written, canonical Word.

Now, while not wanting to unduly "rain on" this celebratory, homecoming parade, there are a few cautionary pauses which the Holiness/Pentecostals need to ponder in regards to our Spirit-induced "radicalism." Yes, Christian experience, both personal and corporate, can be very scary and messy affairs. But we need not fear "experience" if it is a robust, optimistic experience of sanctifying, gifting grace that is always undergirded with the primacy of the rich understandings of profound human depravity and justifying grace—themes which both Johns so strongly up-held. Thus, if any expression of Holiness/Pentecostal "radicalism" of the Spirit moves too far in a semi-Pelagian and subjective direction (especially to mindless emotionalism), I say let's "come back home" to the archives of our "fathers" John.

I will seek to put the issue in very practical terms: if our radical experience of the Spirit frees us to speak in tongues without a powerful theological and ethical (both personal and social) interpretation, the gift is false. If our gifting from the Spirit degenerates into a "health and wealth" gospel, our wealth needs to be channeled as a portion for the poor and disinherited—which is where most of our Wesleyan, Holiness and Pentecostal fore-parents came from anyhow. If our gift of healing has led us to say that physical healing (this side of glory) is unconditionally in the atonement, such presumption needs to be rebuked by the Spirit of God. If our doctrine of the Spirit has led to the house of Sabellianism, we need to go back to the Trinitarianism of Calvin and Wesley. If our eschatology has been overwhelmed by dispensationalism, we are now flirting with the "bondwoman" side of Calvinistic determinism, not the true eschatology of Scripture. If our concerns are with fundamentalistic inerrancy, the solid core of substantive Biblical truth will carry the day if we will major in the majors of redeeming grace and the solidity of biblical ethics. The substantive claims of Scripture are very much vindicated in the experience of the revealed Word and do not need any Uzziah hands from rationalistic modernity to steady its progress as the standard of the rising Kingdom of God. Yes, just maybe the Holiness/Pentecostal children of "father Wesley" need some sage counsel from "father Calvin."

I do celebrate all of the "home-comings" of Donald Dayton. I especially affirm his valiant efforts to bring needed historiographic and theological correctives to modern, Reformed "evangelicalism's" somewhat overweening hubris. The reminders of Evangelicalism's profound debts to the "riffraff" are desperately needed. But this gives no license to the "radical" children of John Wesley to ignore the sober counsels of Father Wesley and their other "father"—John Calvin. Again, let's be reminded that the legitimate lineage of paternity is only questioned as a cousin who is a "hair's breadth" removed. One senses that the "riffraff" do still need the steadying correctives of both our eighteenth-century English Arminian and sixteenth-century Reformed mentors. I simply pray that the "Reformed" partners will be willing to repent of their pretensions at the same altar that Wesley's children do penance for the vestiges of their subjectivist extremism.

When Dayton and his "riffraff" revelers come home to Fairmount, Indiana, for the next James Dean commemorative, I would urge the following: forget the James Dean memorabilia hustlers; in good Dayton style, spend some quality time making a pilgrimage to the Dean's home Church—the Back Creek Holiness/Friends Meeting House; but I would also urge that the pilgrimage include at least one respectful side-trip to the best Reformed evangelical fellowship in town; take a little time to compare the archival treasures that both houses of faith have to hold and celebrate. Maybe the archive metaphor is much too formal: to all of Donald Dayton's reveling rabblers I offer this suggestion: have a good time rummaging around in the residential attics of Fairmount's religious "riffraff." And finally, one more little caveat: the James Dean cult at Fairmount can be gently reminded, in loving Wesleyan fashion, that Dean would have been infinitely better served if he had become a "disciple with a mission," buried in an unmarked grave in some far-off Holiness mission station, than to have been adored as a "rebel without a cause!"

Response #2

William Kostlevy

Donald W. Dayton on James Dean

IN American popular culture one of the most common figures is the misunderstood post-adolescent male in rebellion against a narrow, foreign imposed conformity. It is Billy the Kid, Huck Finn or later Jay Gatsby, figures often from an ill-defined Midwest who in the perfect scenario die tragically, leaving an unfulfilled promise. As cultural icons such figures remain eternally young, free from physical decay, adult responsibility or the inevitable compromises that time forces upon the living. In its 1950s variant, the quintessential examples remain James Dean and, as a less common female illustration of the same phenomenon, Marilyn Monroe.[1]

It goes without saying that such figures have as little past as they do future. It is in fact remarkable how little is known about the real roots of most of America's most prominent iconic figures. We commonly remember that the "Wright brothers" operated a bicycle shop. We rarely recognize that they were printers, publishing the radical proto-feminist anti-Masonic gospel of their father Bishop Milton Wright of the United Brethren Church. While it has become common to note the religious roots of Elvis Presley, an eternal teenager of the highest order, the Pentecostal faith he inherited (with his neighbor Jerry Lee Lewis) and which profoundly shaped his music remains unknown to most of his fans and to the interpreters of popular American culture.

Donald Dayton's interest in James Dean is not without roots in his own life and history. Both Indiana and the Holiness tradition that are essential to Don's roots, have similar traditions of the death of young iconic figures that pre-date Dean. Sammy Morris (1873–1893) a native West African who in death, not in life, is often credited with saving Taylor

---

1. Monroe might have turned an almost unimaginable 80 in June of 2006, if she had not died in 1962 at the age of 36. Dean would be a mere 75.

University from bankruptcy and who remains a central figure in evangelical hagiography. Morris is the perfect example of the Victorian era's celebration of dying to self as a means of living for others and God; Dean, at least in the roles he played, stands as the quintessential illustration of the 1950s variant of the rebellion against the Victorian ideal exemplified by Morris.

It goes without saying that Don Dayton shares much with the James Dean legend. In the same way that Dayton has brilliantly noted in the Prologue to *Discovering an Evangelical Heritage*, material that will become a standard primary source for future scholars struggling to provide a context for the Evangelical revolt of the last quarter of the twentieth century, his own life has also been a life of resistance to a kind of Victorianism. In fact, Dayton's discussion of "prudentials," the personal behavior standards expected of Evangelicals, is one of the rare looks at a subculture as foreign to early twenty-first century Evangelicals as it is to their cultural warrior critics. In his saga of the Houghton yearbook, in which he published photographs of backs of the Houghton coed cheerleader's knees carefully placed in the backgrounds of other photographs Don boldly challenged the politically nuanced conformity of Houghton president Stephen Paine. Fittingly, Donald Dayton has spent a lifetime pressing students to explore the limits of inherited faith.

In one key way Dayton's life differs from Dean's and many other iconic figures. In spite of training at Columbia University, the Yale Divinity School and at the University of Chicago, institutions that provided Don with his primary intellectual and teaching mentors including the great medievalist Norman Cantor, Biblical scholar Brevard Childs and Martin E. Marty, the impact of these scholars was overshadowed by two other, perhaps less well-known but no less captivating figures which Don encountered: Sue Schultz, Asbury Theological Seminary Library (ATS) director, and Gilbert M. James, professor of Church and Society at ATS. Schultz and James helped Don discover the shocking reality that the counterculture/radical movements he gravitated toward, such as the Civil Rights Movement and the Women's Movement, had historical antecedents in the very tradition that observation and common sense had told him was completely barren. In fact, the heroes of evangelicalism, John Wesley, and to an even greater extent Charles G. Finney, were as much champions of the social causes of the 1960s as they were icons of American revivalism. Turning to popular journalism, Dayton published landmark articles in the *Post American*, later *Sojourners*, and wrote *Discovering an Evangelical Heritage*, both a tract for the times and a serious exploration of the roots not only of modern evangelicalism but of American society itself.

In perhaps Dayton's most significant contribution to the study of American culture, he discovered a world populated by radicals, often women and often very Victorian in their own way, who in fascinating ways provided radical alternatives to the stifling conformity of the 1950s. What separates Don from many of his disciples is that he keenly realizes that this legacy, like all legacies, is a mixed blessing. Even enlightened radical movements, such as the Woman's Christian Temperance Union, become narrow and conformist over time. The daughters of Victorian radicals had as great a need to rebel against an inherited ethos as their mothers had to rebel against earlier expressions of social conformity. Ironically, in rebellion they prove themselves to be heirs of a tradition and a history they cannot escape.

This brings us to James Dean, a personification of the rebellion against the conformities of the 1950s that would ferment in the 1960s context in which Don was raised. The central figure in Dayton's reconstruction of Dean and his world is holiness evangelist James DeWeerd whose discovery and proper cultural location by Dayton is perhaps his most significant contribution to James Dean studies. Don's dismissal of DeWeerd's thought as a "naïve mix of inherited holiness theology and trivial spiritual aphorisms that sound more like Midwestern folk wisdom than reflective theology," is, I believe, condescending and unfair. It is the least satisfactory portion of the paper. A child prodigy who served as a pastor at seventeen—DeWeerd published his first book at twenty-four, and had become president of Kletzing (IA) College by his early 30s—DeWeerd merits serious study. While I too have only sampled the fairly large DeWeerd literary corpus, which includes ten years of editorials in the *Christian Witness*, my tentative assessment is very different from Don's. To reduce DeWeerd's significance to speculation about his sexual orientation does not help us understand DeWeerd, Dean, or the holiness culture of the 1950s. As editor of the *Christian Witness*, pastor of Indianapolis' famed Candle Tabernacle and a frequent speaker on the one of the nation's most listened to radio stations, Cincinnati's WLW, DeWeerd was, in my estimation, not only the most important holiness evangelist of the 1950s but a figure of national significance. Unlike many of the holiness figures of his generation (I am thinking here of people like Richard S. Taylor and the founding generation of the Wesleyan Theological Society), DeWeerd, like his hero Salvation Army evangelist Samuel Logan Brengle, was a mystic uncomfortable with the growing literalism that characterized the emerging academic Wesleyanism of Bible Colleges and Seminaries. In the words of Paul Bassett, Deweerd was resisting the "fundamentalist leavening" of holiness spirituality. In spite of the fact that he was well read and articulate, with a cosmopolitan flair, DeWeerd was suspicious of reducing Christian spirituality to neo-Evangelical doctrinal formulations. In effect, DeWeerd's spirituality owes more to the traditions of personal testimony, edifying narratives and dramatic expressions of divine action than reasoned apologetics. DeWeerd's success as an evangelist and popular speaker suggests that the old spirituality had enduring power. As I am suggesting, traditional holiness spirituality was more deeply rooted in American culture than academic neo-evangelicalism either in its Wesleyan or Fundamentalist garb.

As someone nurtured and inspired by Don I do appreciate his ambivalence concerning both the subjectivism of traditional holiness spirituality and wooden scholasticism that commonly emerged among the first generation of holiness heirs to attain advanced academic degrees. He understands that holiness spirituality is a two-edged sword, which while capable of providing liberation is equally capable of leaving death and despair in its wake. In the words of E. P. Thompson, a person very much like Don in his insights and passions, Dayton knows that Methodist chapels can be "dark prisons for the human soul." In part, this insight and Dayton's insistence that it not be ignored has led to his marginalization within the movement he loves, seeks to understand, and has served for over three decades.

Returning to James Dean, Americans have always preferred heroes without past baggage, or even pasts. Don Dayton has spent his life insisting that his own people accept their past in its full complexity; as good, as bad and as capable of more fully fulfilling its highest ideals. Prophets are seldom honored in their own country. Don is no exception. This festschrift honors a scholar of remarkable insight and compassion whose work will shape American scholarship more in the twenty-first century then it did in the twentieth.

9

Re-Thinking Evangelicalism

Perhaps one of the most important contributions that Dayton has made to contemporary scholarship regards the historical and historiographical questions surrounding neo-evangelicalism. Questions about the actual historical and theological lineage of contemporary neo-evangelicalism are almost ubiquitous in Dayton's writings. The following essay represents Dayton's most sustained critique of the widespread historical account of contemporary neo-evangelicalism that was dominant from the emergence of neo-evangelicalism in the mid-1950's and up to the present day. The essay was originally published in *Christian Scholar's Review* 23:1 (1993) 12–33, with a series of responses by George Marsden and Clark Pinnock among others.

"The Search for the Historical Evangelicalism"

George Marsden's History of Fuller Seminary as a Case Study

Donald W. Dayton

"Any analysis of Fundamentalism must necessarily take the Pentecostal movement into consideration, but this has hardly been the case. When this is done, however, the inadequacies of existing historical interpretations will be readily apparent."

—Robert Mapes Anderson, Introduction, *The Vision of the Disinherited*[1]

"It [this book] is written by a Presbyterian who is filled with subtle Presbyterian prejudices, which readers should feel free to uncover and, if they wish, discount."

—George Marsden, Preface, *The Evangelical Mind and the New School Presbyterian Experience*[2]

Introduction

My title is a "take-off" on the one chosen by George Marsden some fifteen years ago when we dialogued in these pages about my *Discovering an Evangelical Heritage* under the title "Demythologizing Evangelicalism."[3] In the spirit of his use of the theological platform of

---

1. (New York: Oxford University Press, 1979) 5.
2. (New Haven: Yale University Press, 1970) xii.
3. My book was originally published by Harper and Row in 1976, but has been reissued more recently with a new preface by Hendrickson, 1988. Our exchange was in the *Christian Scholar's Review*, 7 (1977) 203–11.

Rudolf Bultmann to describe my book, I would like to respond by appropriating the title of Albert Schweitzer's famous book—and theological platform—to examine the very un-German phenomenon of American Evangelicalism in a review essay on Marsden's *Reforming Fundamentalism: Fuller Seminary and the New Evangelicalism*.[4]

A good book like this deserves careful analysis and reflection. And though it is now over five years old, I would like to respond in the good tone of dialogue that Marsden set fifteen years ago. I will attempt to make clear what I find increasingly troubling in his continuing project for the interpretation of American "evangelicalism"—and hopefully, in the process, clarify the differences in our approaches to that subject. This effort has developed into a more complicated sidetrack than I had once anticipated, and one that I hope will soon eventuate in a book.[5] I need to thank the Wesleyan Holiness Study Project (funded by the Pew Charitable Trusts) of Asbury Theological Seminary for a travel grant that enabled me to visit archives, interview principals in the discussion, and undertake a preliminary comparative study of the development of several "evangelical" seminaries. A research fellowship from the Association of Theological Schools later allowed me to spend a research term at Drew University, where as a "visiting professor" I taught my way through the material in a graduate seminar working toward something of a "reinterpretation" of the categories for the study of American "evangelicalism." It is now time to set forth in a preliminary way some of the results of that investigation and rethinking in the hope of engaging George Marsden in friendly dialogue about his book—and perhaps to open up a wider discussion.

Since the publication of this book, much historiographical water has flowed over the dam. Leonard Sweet has called attention to the "new evangelical historiography" and chided its practitioners for their neglect of the Methodistic and Wesleyan strands of American evangelicalism.[6] Kenneth Collins has complained in the pages of this journal of the neglect of the Methodist traditions.[7] And perhaps most interestingly, Douglas Sweeney, now a doctoral student at Vanderbilt, has published the results

---

4. (Grand Rapids: Eerdmans, 1987).

5. This would be a general critique of the "new evangelical" historiography—to be followed by reinterpretation of American evangelicalism according to my own categories of analysis.

6. "Wise as Serpents, Innocent as Doves: The New Evangelical Historiography," *Journal of the American Academy of Religion*, 56 (1988) 397–415.

7. "Children of Neglect: American Methodist Evangelicals," *Christian Scholar's Review* 20 (1990) 7–16.

of his Trinity Evangelical Divinity School M. A. thesis, which attempted a comparison of my perspective with that of George as two fundamentally different paradigms for the interpretation of American evangelicalism.[8]

I would, therefore, in view of this broader discussion, like to attempt two things in this review essay: (1) to clarify, as much as possible from my perspective, what seems to be at stake in the differences between myself and Marsden, and why we are driven to such different paradigms to understand the American evangelical experience; and (2) to illustrate the results of these differences in an analysis of *Reforming Fundamentalism*, his history of Fuller Theological Seminary, itself a case study of the development of "neo-evangelicalism" and something of a sequel to his earlier and much celebrated *Fundamentalism and American Culture*.[9]

Two Divergent Perspectives

I have spent a great deal of time reflecting on and attempting to discern the shape of the differences between Marsden and myself. I am still not sure that I fully understand all that is at stake, but I would like to attempt to describe as accurately as possible as much as I now understand in a series of contrasts. The contrasts are not meant to be "absolute" in the sense the two of us are always at opposite ends of a spectrum. I am sure that from a distance many of these squabbles look like minor territorial disputes. But they are significant divergences—and among them would be:

(1) We tend to use different source material in our research, and those differences in sources have profound implications for our historiography. I tend to work with Methodist sources, while George tends to focus on Presbyterian and Baptist literature. George's is the traditional pattern and reflects the dominant intellectual influence of the Reformed traditions in providing the categories of analysis and the determinative paradigms in much American theology and church history. I defend my use of source materials by pointing out that Methodism has been dominant (in size and influence—until overtaken by the Southern Baptists) in American

---

8. See especially "The Essential Evangelicalism Dialectic: The Historiography of the Early Neo-Evangelical Movement and the Observer-Participant Dilemma,' *Church History* 60 (March, 1991) 70–84, and "The 'Strange Schizophrenia' of Neo-Evangelicalism: A Bibliography," *Evangelical Studies Bulletin* 8 (Spring, 1991) 6–8.

9. (New York: Oxford University Press, 1980). Careful readers of the footnotes of this book will realize that we had occasion to dialogue while it was being written—and I had the privilege of being the one to draw the book to the attention of Oxford University Press while it was still in manuscript.

Protestantism, and that the "age of Methodism" in American life (usually the century from 1820 to World War I) is roughly equivalent to the "age of Evangelicalism." I would argue that what happens in Methodism is thus determinative for our interpretation of *American evangelicalism* as a whole.

(2) This difference in source material directs each of us toward different chronological periods when we seek to understand the dynamics and issues at stake in the formation of what Martin Marty calls "the two-party" system in American Protestantism—the party we usually call "evangelical" and the "other party" called variously "liberal" or "mainstream" or whatever. Marsden is more drawn to the twentieth-century "fundamentalist/modernist conflict" of the 1920s and 1930s—and especially to the split at Princeton Theological Seminary that produced the Westminster Theological Seminary. I am drawn to the fragmentation of Methodism in the mid and late nineteenth century, especially the formation at that time of the various branches of the "Holiness movement," and later, early in this century, of Pentecostalism. I defend this perspective by arguing that the vast majority of the membership of the National Association of Evangelicals is drawn from these Methodist derivatives, and that a similar pattern obtains in such other aspects of the evangelical subculture as the cluster of colleges that constitute the Christian College Consortium.

(3) These differences also lead us to see the phenomenon of "evangelicalism" in quite different terms. Here I am a little uncertain of what Marsden means by the term. Much of his use of the word "evangelical" is in reference to the twentieth-century phenomenon—the emergence in the 1940s from "fundamentalism" of a "neo-evangelical" party that later dropped the "neo-" to travel under the label "evangelical." I am more inclined to keep the "neo-" for the twentieth-century party and be more concerned about the "classical evangelicalism" from which "fundamentalism" developed. This difference between pre- and post-fundamentalist evangelicalism is real, and from my perspective it is a key issue. It seems to me important to become quite clear about what we mean by "evangelicalism" in its classical sense. When I use the term "classical evangelicalism," I generally refer to those currents that have their roots in the "conversionist" piety of Puritanism and Pietism in the seventeenth century, that flowered in the "Great Awakenings" in this country and in the "Evangelical Revival" in Britain in the eighteenth century, and that had their greatest cultural impact in the nineteenth century as they declined somewhat into a more mechanistic "revivalism." In addition to their "convertive" piety, these currents were distinguished by their evangelistic and missionary activity, their

social involvement, and their transdenominational or "parachurch" agencies (thus the roots of "ecumenism," etc.). I am less clear what Marsden means by the term "evangelicalism" in its more classical sense. Sometimes he seems to me to use the term along the lines I have just suggested;[10] at other times he seems to me to be referring to any "traditional" form of Protestantism—the way of using the word "evangelical" in nineteenth-century North America that would apply it to any form of Protestantism that was "orthodox," excluding primarily Roman Catholics on one side and Unitarians and Universalists on the other.

(4) These differences are crucial, if I understand things correctly. It seems to me that Marsden tends to see these classical evangelical traditions in continuity with the Reformation traditions. I, on the other hand, see them as a *corrective* (in their emphasis on "sanctification"—both personally and socially) to the Reformation over-emphasis on "justification" as the organizing principle of Christian life and theology. From the strictly Reformational stand-point such "evangelical" traditions have often seemed to be "semi-heretical"—in their perfectionist tendencies, in a sometimes perceived Pelagianism in their ethical "activism" that sometimes appears to be a form of "works-righteousness," and so on. Indeed, I would largely accept this "Reformed" judgment and be inclined to see in this line a rather consistent pattern of the rejection of "orthodox Protestant" forms of thinking (especially if one means technically the post-Reformation orthodoxy, whether Lutheran or Reformed). This pattern can be seen in the protest of Pietism against Lutheran Orthodoxy in the seventeenth and eighteenth centuries, in the rise of Methodism against Calvinism in the eighteenth century, in the emergence of "New School" Presbyterianism against the orthodox Calvinism of, for example, Princeton Theological Seminary in the nineteenth century, and so on. Theologically this has generally involved a movement away from "forensic" categories of justification to more organic and realistic soteriological categories that bring sanctification to the fore, a shift away from the "penal substitutionary" doctrine of the atonement toward "moral government" and other alternative articulations, a greater openness to doctrines of freewill and "human ability," less commitment to "inerrantist" views of Scripture, and so forth—themes which are all generally anathema to strict "orthodoxy," especially "Reformed orthodoxy." I know that this way of speaking flies in the face of most tendencies to speak of "evangelicalism" as a form of "orthodoxy," but I am increasingly

10. Cf., for example, *Understanding Fundamentalism and Evangelicalism* (Grand Rapids: Eerdmans, 1991) 2.

convinced that such patterns of thinking overlook an important "anti-orthodox" dimension of most forms of "evangelicalism."

(5) Such questions lead to a difficult and somewhat technical point about the nature of the "New School" Presbyterian experience in "evangelical" historiography. George's Yale doctoral dissertation on this subject is cited in one of the epigraphs with which I began this paper. Generally, I agree with this book and feel that George should have followed out more consistently the historiographical suggestions he makes there. "New School" Presbyterianism is a much more logical candidate for the antecedent (and roots) of both modern "Reformed" "fundamentalism" and "evangelicalism" than the "Old School" Presbyterianism of, for example, the "old" Princeton Theological Seminary. The "New School" was revivalistic, moved toward Arminianism on such questions as "free-will," utilized more freely the para-church organizations of the "evangelical empire" of the nineteenth century, and so on. But we are often inclined to forget the extent to which it was seen as "heterodox" by the "Old School" of Princeton. Albert Barnes, whose *Notes* on the New Testament have become a regularly reprinted resource by fundamentalist publishers in Grand Rapids, was tried for heresy in the nineteenth century. This illustrates the extent to which the roots of fundamentalism are "unorthodox" rather than "orthodox." My own reading of the significance of this "New School" party in the nineteenth century is that it reveals the significance of the Methodist impact—that for all practical purposes, the "New School" was the "Methodistic" party of Presbyterianism. This is perhaps most clearly seen in evangelist Charles Grandison Finney, who started out Presbyterian but ended up in Congregationalism. The "new measures" ("protracted meetings," the use of women, the "anxious bench," extemporaneous prayer and preaching, etc.) of his revivalism were largely derived from antecedent Methodist practices; they became controversial when imported into proper "Reformed" church circles. Finney went so far as to adopt the perfectionism of the Wesleyan tradition and wrote books and preached sermons on "entire sanctification" that led to his theology being labeled "Oberlin Perfectionism"—a theology that became a major source of both the theology of the Holiness movement and Pentecostalism. I believe that Finney is the best candidate for the fountainhead of modern "evangelicalism," though because of his perfectionism and Methodist tendencies he is usually rejected by Reformed historiography. The most egregious example of such rejection occurred in an essay on "The Theological Boundaries of Evangelical Faith" by John Gerstner, himself an interesting mix of "Old School" Princeton and revivalism in the tradition of Edwards. Gerstner

indicates the wide impact of Finney in the nineteenth century "in spreading what went by the name of evangelicalism"—but because Gerstner rejects Finneyite theology and accepts instead the Hodge-Warfield tradition of Princeton, he concludes that "Finney, the greatest of the nineteenth-century evangelists, became the greatest of nineteenth- century foes of evangelicalism."[11] I do not attribute this position to Marsden; he is much more balanced and sophisticated. But this question, and the "Reformed" theological rejection of Finney, is perhaps the Achilles heel of much Reformed "historiography" of "American evangelicalism." And it gets to the heart of the differences between Marsden and myself. Even though Marsden has moved on these questions, he still appears to me to be operating with "Reformed" theological categories that prevent him from seeing patterns and connections that seem essential to me—at least in part because his approach seems unwilling to grant the basically "unorthodox" roots of modern fundamentalism and evangelicalism.

(6) Let me attempt another way of speaking of this issue. If I am not mistaken, Marsden has been misled by his interest in the modem twentieth-century Presbyterian conflicts to adopt something that I would call a theologically oriented "conservative/liberal" paradigm in which "evangelicalism" is seen primarily as a "conservative" or "traditional" reaction against "liberalism." Evangelicalism becomes, in the line of most neo-evangelical interpreters from Bernard Ramm to Richard Quebedeaux, a theological position just to the left of "fundamentalism" and just to the right of "neo-orthodoxy" on a scale that measures accommodation to liberalism and the "Enlightenment." When I use the lens of Methodism, I see in the Holiness movement and Pentecostalism especially, but also in the larger mass of "evangelicals" (those descending from the "New School" experience?) a quite different phenomenon characterized by its distance from "traditional" or "conservative" Protestantism. The Holiness churches, for example, are not so much a conservative movement as a radicalization of the Methodist pull away from Anglicanism in the direction of revivalism and "low church" piety. Marsden regularly calls "evangelicals" "conservative" and "orthodox" in his writings. I would prefer some such

11. This essay was published in David F. Wells and John O. Woodbridge, *The Evangelicals: What They Believe, Who They Am Where They Are Going* (Nashville: Abingdon, 1975). The quotes are from page 27. The historiographical orientation of this book was deemed so strong and egregiously prejudicial—as pointed out by myself (in *Sojourners*) and Timothy Smith (in the *Christian Century*)—that the paperback edition by Baker Book House added a chapter by Pentecostal J. Vinson Synan to balance out the essay by Gerstner.

label as "radical"—and would point to the revivalistic marginalization of sacramental life and classical patterns of church order as evidence for my side of the discussion.

(7) Another difference is that Marsden tends to focus on the tensions within the mainline denominations, and to take as his base line the continuing "evangelical" presence in such groups. This seems to me to reinforce his commitment to a "conservative/liberal" paradigm. I am a little more inclined to take as paradigmatic the actual splits—and so am more inclined to use categories of "sectarianism." Marsden seems to think that he can interpret the formation of the new denominations as "conservative" reactions to the rise of "liberalism." I, on the other hand, am inclined to read the conflicts within the mainline denominations (especially those conflicts during the height of the fundamentalist/modernist controversy) in the categories of sectarianism. I see the continuing presence within Methodism of a less radical strand of Holiness piety that functions as an internal critique of Methodism, but one that comes from a radical rather than a "conservative" standpoint. I am also inclined to see the rise of dispensationalism as creating within the mainstream churches a "sect-like" mentality that fits my categories—not to mention the formation of new churches (sects?) out of the Presbyterian context, like the Christian and Missionary Alliance, which is (was?) essentially a "Holiness church" reflecting the dynamics of the Methodist fragmentation.

(8) This difference has profound implications for a number of issues. Marsden is fascinated in all his work, or so it seems to me, with a nineteenth-century process of "secularization," to which "evangelicalism" is a "conservative" response—and this period provides the grid from which everything else is read. My emphasis on the sectarian dynamic minimizes the influence of secularization, liberalism, the Enlightenment, and so on, and suggests that the difference between "evangelicalism" and the "mainstream" is more like the difference between the radical wing of the Reformation and the magisterial Reformers; or the Baptists and the Puritans and Congregationalists in the seventeenth century; or between Methodism and Anglicanism in England in the eighteenth century; or between Methodist revivalists and Presbyterians in the nineteenth century; or between Pentecostals/Charismatics and the traditional churches in the twentieth century. This type of conflict has always been in the church and is not primarily a product of the nineteenth century or a reaction to liberalism, though it occasionally looks like it.

(9) Thus I sometimes contrast my "Pentecostal" paradigm to Marsden's "Presbyterian" paradigm. By this I mean that "evangelicalism" is related to

the rest of Christianity more as the Pentecostal or Charismatic movements—that is as a specific and modern form of Christianity that disrupts the "traditional" and "conservative" churches—and less as the "orthodoxy" from which the "main stream churches" have departed in their supposed rush to "liberalism."

(10) My perspective puts greater weight on the factors of "class" that were very prominent in the formation of the Holiness movement and Pentecostalism. I believe that I can discern this same factor as well in fundamentalism and evangelicalism. Marsden does not seem to me to deny this factor, but he doesn't place great weight on it. I am inclined to follow the analysis of Robert Anderson in seeing what we largely call the "evangelical" world as having, historically at least, three levels: the Pentecostals on the bottom, the more moderate Holiness movement on the next layer up, and the culturally determinative and more middle class (and largely committed to the most moderate Holiness theology— that of the "Keswick" variety) on the top.

(11) Such class analysis brings to the fore the importance of the sociological dynamic that I often call *embourgeoisement* in which new religious movements are formed in the lower classes and gradually move up the social ladder into the middle classes. My own study of the Methodist tradition inclines me to see there a pattern of movement toward the poor classes followed by a period of upward social mobility and *embourgeoisement* followed by another reaction toward the poor and so forth. I see such patterns in eighteenth-century Britain and in nineteenth-century North America, where the Holiness movement was a clear reaction against the *embourgeoisement* of mainstream Methodism. The Holiness movement has since the mid-twentieth century been undergoing its own *embourgeoisement*—and I find that this pattern explains much more of contemporary "evangelicalism" to me than the more static "conservative/liberal" paradigm. I would like very much to see some longitudinal studies done of the student body of Wheaton College. I have the feeling that early classes were largely first- generation college students, and that students now are much more second- and third-generation college-educated and children of professionals. I would expect that my own impressionistic reading that Wheaton has successively gone through Holiness, Baptistic, Presbyterian, and more recently incipiently Anglican phases in religious tone would be confirmed and correlated somewhat with rising social location of student families.

(12) Much of what Marsden seems to me to interpret as the struggle between "conservative" and "liberal" I am more inclined to see as the

struggle of moving from forms of religious life more natural to the lower classes to a more "middle class" style of life. I'm not sure if we have the studies that we need, but from my study of Pentecostalism, I have the impression that lower class forms of church life are more "totalistic" (life is centered around the church and its multiple meetings) while the middle class fights to have the space for a more complex and diverse life style with a greater variety of cultural pursuits; that lower class churches see truth in firmer contrasts of truth and error; that lower class religion is more emotional while middle class church life is more softly "relativistic" and cooler and more rational in orientation; that lower class forms of religion are more radical in their rejection of the dominant culture but gradually come to terms with it in later generations. Much that Marsden would see as the move toward "liberalism" I would like to describe as a process of *embourgeoisement*, though we have been trained by neo-evangelical self-consciousness in theology and historiography to see it as "liberalization." This is not to deny that the processes may be related and share some of the same trajectories, but I suggest that "liberalization" is not the most helpful way of describing what is going on, and may fundamentally mislead us at times. Thus, the "pre-critical" stance of Pentecostalism (on biblical studies, for example) may look like the "anti-critical" stance of certain bourgeois fundamentalists, but we cannot be sure yet (until the *embourgeoisement* of Pentecostalism) whether this is accident (that is, a part of the lower class rejection of dominant culture that will be "outgrown") or essence of Pentecostalism. I expect Pentecostalism to move beyond such "pre-critical" perspectives, and tend to read the movement of "evangelicalism" toward more tolerance of criticism in similar categories.

(13) The focus on class and *embourgeoisement* serves to heighten my interest in the phenomenon of "dispensationalism." When Ernest Sandeen's book, *The Roots of Fundamentalism*, was first published, Marsden found overstated Sandeen's thesis that fundamentalism was essentially "millenarianism." I have always felt that Sandeen's work has been under-utilized, especially theologically. I have been inclined to think that many features of fundamentalism (its separatism, its rejection of social concern, its polemic against biblical criticism, its anti-cultural attitudes, its baptistic ecclesiology, its distinctive missiology, its anti-ecumenical polemic, and so forth) are better analyzed as implications of a basic dispensationalism than as a function of "orthodoxy" or "conservativism." It is interesting to me that Marsden tries regularly to incorporate dispensationalism into *his* framework as an archetypally "anti-modern" movement. I have always been inclined to see it in a longer line of eschatologically oriented movements

that antedate modernity—with the qualification that "dispensationalism" is a peculiarly *modern* version of this line. And again, much that Marsden attributes to a process of "liberalization" I would see as a natural product of *embourgeoisement*, as religious traditions move from the lower classes and the fringe of society up and toward the center. In the process, they progressively shed the "dispensationalist" categories that functioned well on the circumference, but which are increasingly counter-productive to a religious tradition trying to find its way to the center and closer to the levers of political power. How else can one understand the theological development of Jerry Falwell on these questions—or the emergence of political "reconstructionism" at the center of Pat Robertson's Regent University (formerly CBN University)?

(14) In all of this I think that I am more interested than Marsden in the *changes* in the history of "evangelicalism." I am especially troubled by the so-called "great reversal" that prompted my book *Discovering an Evangelical Heritage*—the puzzle of what happened to the radical social reform efforts of antebellum revivalism after the Civil War. I read Marsden as more interested in the continuity of the line from classical evangelicalism through fundamentalism to "neo-evangelicalism." But I can't get such perspectives to explain to me, for example, the history of women in ministry—a practice that was widely accepted in many nineteenth-century "evangelical" circles, but which became highly diluted in the twentieth century (whether in the A. J. Gordon tradition of New England, the Evangelical Free Church tradition associated with Trinity Evangelical Divinity School, or the more strictly Holiness and Pentecostal cultivations of this practice). But such dynamics fit well into my patterns of seeing the "evangelical" currents as movements that centrifugally move down the social ladder and toward the margins of society and then move centripetally back toward the center. Historically, in the nineteenth century such movement provided the space at the edges of the society for experimentation with the ministry of women and other "disreputable" practices that have been abandoned in the *embourgeoisement* of the twentieth century. Ironically, of course, the mainstream culture has moved toward such practices just as the "evangelicals" have been abandoning them – thus, the profound "culture wars" in "evangelicalism" over the possibility of a "Christian feminism." It seems to me that reflection on such dynamics would push Marsden more in my direction.

(15) Such revisioning of my framework has given me quite a different perspective on historiographical questions. I have become much more conscious of the theological and social purposes that historiographies often

serve. Thus I often use Bernard Ramm's book, *The Evangelical Heritage*, in my classes because it illustrates precisely, I believe, the process of *embourgeoisement* and its implications for historiography. I see that book as an illustration of the "presbyterianization" of "evangelical" historiography (reflecting the theological and social agenda of "neo-evangelicalism"). Ramm, a populist "evangelical" Baptist who taught at a Christian and Missionary Alliance college as well as American Baptist seminaries, offers a highly improbable "high Calvinist" and "Presbyterian" reading of the lineage of "evangelicalism." I began to understand this book when a student suggested that Ramm was not offering an historically valid *description* of "evangelical" history as much as a "neo-evangelical" *prescription* to cure the ills of fundamentalism. In this process there is a confusion of "teleology" with "genealogy," and the goal is used as a grid to sanitize history by suppressing inappropriate and "disreputable" elements so as to tell a story that is actually a reflection of a subliminal agenda rather than an appropriate reading of history. Ramm's book is a particularly egregious example of this process and the resulting distortions of historiography, and I do not wish to portray Marsden's work entirely in this light. His analysis is much more nuanced and subtle, but I am convinced that his work is shaped by such dynamics—as I hope to demonstrate below. And one way to counteract the distortions of such an agenda is to read the history from below rather than from above; thus I counterpose my "Pentecostal" paradigm for the reading of "evangelical" history over against the "Presbyterian" paradigm that I think Marsden is inclined toward.

(16) Such perspectives as one might guess, provide me with a different conceptual framework from which to study the history of the "evangelical" seminaries. I see two quite different lines of development. I see the founding of Westminster Theological Seminary as, in the line of Marsden's thinking, an effort to preserve the nineteenth-century Princeton theology from dilution by the "acids of modernity." But I also see the founding of many "evangelical" seminaries (the Nazarene Seminary, the Alliance Theological Seminary, Trinity Evangelical Divinity School, Gordon Divinity School—now Gordon-Conwell—and so on) that are better described in terms of the *embourgeoisement* of their constituencies, who are now entering the middle classes and calling for a more sophisticated and educated ministry. It seems to me that these are two fundamentally different base lines from which to tell the story—but here I am beginning to anticipate my critique of Marsden's history of Fuller!

But before moving on to that critique, I need to make a final comment. Some are inclined, I am sure, to describe our differences in terms of our own backgrounds. There is obviously some truth to that. My father was the first theological doctorate in the history of my church (the Wesleyan Church, originally founded about 1843 as the Wesleyan Methodist Connection—an abolitionist branch of Methodism and the original founder of Wheaton College). My father founded theological education for this church by moving to Asbury Theological Seminary in 1957 to establish a foundation that marked one of the clearest signs of the *embourgeoisement* of our denomination. If I understand correctly, Marsden's father was a staff member and field representative at Westminster Theological Seminary during a comparable period. No doubt each of us tends to reflect the history in which we were reared.

I'm reminded of the famous image that I associate with Albert Schweitzer's book, *The Quest of the Historical Jesus*, but was not able to find there—how each author of a biography of Jesus has looked down through the centuries, as down a deep well, to see the historical Jesus, but has only seen reflected back the image of the author. There is surely some truth to this tendency. We are conditioned to see that which our own experience and categories of thought allow us to see. But surely there must be more; there must be a way to break out of our own experience historiographically. Unless we are willing to accept a pure relativism, we must attempt to escape such solipsism by asking which history provides a better analysis of the phenomenon of "evangelicalism"—and of its seminaries. Which "base line" gives us insight into the motors that actually drive evangelicalism—sociologically and psychologically, as well as theologically? With these questions in mind, then, let us turn to the history of Fuller Theology Seminary as a test case for discerning the relative values of these divergent perspectives.

A Critique of Reforming Fundamentalism

I have great respect for Marsden's several books, and think that he deserves in many ways his reputation as the *doyen* of "evangelical studies" in our time. I especially enjoy his ability to write narrative history and his sure instinct for the illuminating incident that clarifies an age or a movement. I regularly use his books in my classes with high praise and the insistence that students read them with care. But at the same time, as I have indicated, I have become increasingly dissatisfied with many features of his work—and especially with his basic categories of interpretation. As I work through the literature and source material with my lenses, I see fundamentally different patterns that confirm my categories and cause me to question his interpretations. I think that the best way to get at the basic questions is to provide a series of illustrations of my concerns about the way Marsden tells the history of Fuller Seminary, to indicate how I see different patterns, and invite the reader to make his or her own judgments about how the story should be read and interpreted.

(1) One of the key issues in Marsden's book is the pervasive role of Princeton Seminary. Several pages are devoted to the experience of Dan Fuller (son of founder Charles Fuller and later Dean of the seminary) at Princeton (21–23). Much of the planning of Fuller is described in terms of a desire to found a "new Princeton" (24 et passim) that would have the prestige of Princeton but from an "orthodox" perspective. Chapter two ("The History Before the History") is largely about the conflicts at Princeton that led to the founding of Westminster Theological Seminary through the departure of J. Gresham Machen and others. Early Fuller faculty member Charles Woodbridge is pictured at his desk with a Princeton banner draped over the front (121). And so on. The effort to found a seminary in the line of the "old Princeton" is a key organizing principle of Marsden's history of Fuller.

To gain an independent reading of the role of Princeton Seminary in the life of Fuller, I decided to look closely at Harold J. Ockenga as a test case. Ockenga is a (the?) key player in the Fuller history—a major strategizer about the new seminary and its first president, though a commuter from the distance of Boston and Park Street Church. Ockenga coined the term neo-evangelical, was the major articulator of the movement's platform, and played a key role in the founding of the National Association of Evangelicals. Though he does not make it entirely clear, one gets the impression from the book that Marsden sees Ockenga as representing a slightly more "classically protestant" side of Fuller's origins over against the more populist, dispensationalist fundamentalist, revivalist Charles Fuller—though he says they shared a common passion for evangelism and missions.

But in what sense may Ockenga be said to be representative of the "old Princeton" theology that is said to be shaping the "new Princeton" of Fuller? My investigations of Ockenga reveal someone quite different from the picture that one gets in Marsden's book—one that fits my own categories as well or better than it does Marsden's and reveals Marsden's strong tendency to suppress any Methodistic elements in the story.

Harold Lindsell wrote a popular (and populist!) biography of Harold J. Ockenga under the title *Park Street Prophet*.[12] From that we learn that Ockenga grew up in Chicago, spent his childhood alternating between the Sunday Schools of a Presbyterian and Methodist Church before opting for membership in the latter, had an early conversion experience in an "old-fashioned Methodist camp meeting," reaffirmed this commitment later in a call to ministry that led him to Taylor University (a "Holiness" Methodist school—much more so then before its more recent drift toward "generic" evangelicalism). In college he was active in gospel teams and the holiness evangelism of the Holiness League on campus—though growing doubts toward the end of his college career led him away from the more radical "eradication of original sin" doctrines of the Holiness movement and toward the more moderate holiness teachings of the Keswick movement. Upon graduation Ockenga went to Princeton and was caught up in the conflicts that led to the founding of Westminster Theological Seminary, from which he finally graduated.

This experience would be the basis, I assume, of claiming that Ockenga shifted to stand in this tradition. Certainly it appears that way to Lindsell, who argues that there Ockenga "became a Calvinist"—his "theological training steeped him in the Reformed tradition from which he has not departed since his student days" (31). But one wonders. This is not the impression that I get from reading the literature and digging around in his life. Ockenga continued pastoring Methodist churches before moving to a Presbyterian context for a few years prior to his call to Park Street Church. Garth Rosell, director of the Ockenga institute at Gordon-Conwell and working on a biography of Ockenga, has lectured to the Wesleyan Holiness Study Project at Asbury on his own reading of Ockenga's theology, which Rosell is convinced remained basically "Wesleyan" in its shape until his death—a fact which he supported by showing copies of the manuscript sermons on which Ockenga not only scrupulously recorded when and where he preached but also the result, typically in the "holiness" pattern of reporting "conversions" and "sanctifications!" I am also told that the picture over Ockenga's desk (in his home office) at the time of his death was of Wesley. And my own impression of reading his sermons (especially those on themes of power, Pentecost, and the Holy Spirit) is that they reveal a late-nineteenth-century "Holiness" or near-Pentecostal theology of Spirit-baptism, though often expressed in the more moderate terms of "consecration" and "anointing of the Spirit"—still, however, rather more

12. (Wheaton: Van Kampen, 1951).

characteristic of Methodistic traditions than Reformed ones. And in a sermon on "The Church's Doctrine of Sanctification"[13] Ockenga sketches "Reformed" and "Wesleyan" views before going on to affirm the biblical evidence for "a subsequent experience" while denying the extreme Holiness view of "eradication" of the sinful nature, preferring "Keswickian" language of the "inhabiting" of the Holy Spirit.

There are other themes (his regular sermonic efforts, for example, to reconcile divine election and human freedom) that might allow Ockenga to be a moderate or "modified" Calvinist—but hardly of the classical Princetonian variety, though perhaps in the line of "New School" Presbyterianism. In the first place, he was clearly a revivalist, a conversionist, in a sense that would not be well-received in the old Princeton theology with its strong commitments to raising children in the "covenant" after infant baptism—a theme that discouraged "conversionism" as Charles Hodge's receptivity to the Horace Bushnell anti-revivalist polemic amply demonstrates. Secondly, he was probably a "moderate" dispensationalist (to use the words of Dan Fuller, who has made a specialty of classifying people on this question). He certainly was "kosher" enough to lecture at Dallas Seminary; he also preached on prophetic themes at Park Street (seeing the modern state of Israel as a fulfillment of prophecy—and discerning the role of Russia in prophetic texts). The one time I heard him speak he delivered a "jeremiad" about the decadence of the age that sounded pessimistically premillennial, if not dispensational, and somewhat at odds with his social agenda. Thirdly, the missions conferences, for which Park Street Church was known, were largely rooted, I am told, in the "faith mission" tradition that would have been anathema to the Princeton theologians on ecclesiological grounds.

After confirming the above points in an interview with Dan Fuller, I asked if there was any way in which he could see Ockenga standing in the line of the old Princeton theology. His immediate (and only!) answer was that Ockenga had great respect for Robert Dick Wilson, who defended Mosaic authorship of the Pentateuch, the early date of Daniel, and the unity of Isaiah. If this is so, then Ockenga's major point of contact with the old Princeton theology would be a traditional doctrine of Scripture (i.e., probably inerrancy)—hardly a firm basis on which to place him solidly in the Reformed tradition of the old Princeton theology! I am inclined to think that Ockenga is "Reformed" primarily in the sense that the Assemblies of God sometimes claim to be the "Reformed" wing of

13. *The Church in God* (Westwood, NJ: Revell, 1956) 221–22.

Pentecostalism—a claim that makes sense to me only if it is "Reformed" to deny the Wesleyan doctrine of "eradication" or "Christian Perfection." (One has a similar intellectual problem with some Baptists who affirm "eternal security" while denying the other four propositions of TULIP high Calvinism that lead to this conclusion. From a genuinely "Reformed" position such traditions look more "Arminian" and "Methodistic.")

These suspicions are confirmed from Ockenga's own writings. One collection of sermons celebrated *Our Protestant Heritage*. In a sermon about Wycliffe that is focused on the question of freedom and independency, Ockenga provides a list of the successors of Wycliffe in Anglo-American Protestantism—a list that I think gives a good clue to Ockenga's own sense of the lineage of "evangelicalism": "Oliver Cromwell, William III, Prince of Orange, John Wesley, General Booth, Charles Finney, and D. L. Moody."[14] After the Puritan age such a list is more Methodistic than Princetonian (or even Presbyterian)—and raises fundamental questions about whether Ockenga should be placed even in the "classical Protestant" category, even apart from the question of whether he is fundamentally "Reformed" or "Princetonian" in his theology. Even the non-Methodist figures in this list (especially Finney, whose revival ministry at Park Street Church in the nineteenth century Ockenga was often inclined to celebrate) were so infused with Methodistic themes as to be anathema to "old Princeton."

It seems to me that Ockenga (somewhat to my own surprise!) is almost an archetypal illustration of what I have sketched above—a populist, revivalist, holiness (!) figure "on the make" in his own upward social mobility. Marsden himself indicates that Ockenga was "keenly aware of status" (16)—perhaps in the style of those for whom such status is recently achieved. But of the rootage of Ockenga in the Methodist and Holiness streams—and of the "methodistic" orientation of his theology and self-understanding to the end—we get no hint in the presentation of Ockenga in *Reforming Fundamentalism*. For whatever reason, such themes are severely suppressed.

(2) I have been as surprised as anyone in the results of some of my research. I was especially astonished to discover that what I found to be true of Ockenga is also true of the larger life of New England "evangelicalism"—out of which came the New England Fellowship, J. Elwin Wright, who played a key role with Ockenga in the founding of the National Association of Evangelicals, and the various "evangelical" colleges and

14. (Grand Rapids: Zondervan, 1938) 129.

educational institutions that have been so prominent in the life of neo-evangelicalism in New England.

It has long been clear to me that A. J. Gordon, the founder of what has come to be Gordon College and Gordon-Conwell Theological Seminary, is best understood as representative of a baptistic wing of the "Holiness movement." And I have often complained that any valid interpretation of the history of "evangelicalism" must be able to explain to me how one gets historically from the baptistic, populist, missionary oriented, abolitionist, feminist A. J. Gordon (who was committed to a "ministry of healing," a doctrine of the "second blessing," and an eschatology that was not quite dispensationalist but comfortable enough with such currents to share the platform with leaders of the late-nineteenth-century "prophecy conference" movement) to modern day Gordon-Conwell with its Presbyterian ethos and drive to become, like Fuller, a center for the training of more Presbyterian ministers than Princeton. It is a great historical irony that A. J. Gordon was one of the objects of the fiercest polemics of B. B. Warfield of Princeton for his perfectionist tendencies and his commitment to "faith healing" and "modern miracles of healing" ("counterfeit miracles," in the title of one of Warfield's books)—but today one cannot really teach in the theology department of Gordon-Conwell without being in the line of Warfield. It is the contemplation of such developments that has led me to the categories that I have sketched above—ones that I think help me understand better institutions like Gordon-Conwell, where Ockenga finished his career as President.

Without full investigation, I would have been inclined earlier to grant the adequacy of the more usual categories of interpretation to other branches of New England "evangelicalism." My perception of such currents was revolutionized when I happened to read the manuscript of a new popular history of the New England Fellowship[15] that gives much attention to J. Elwin Wright, a figure with whom Ockenga was closely associated and, very significantly, the author of the exceedingly widely distributed celebration of "Old Fashioned Revival Hour" of Charles Fuller.[16] Joel Adams Wright, the father of J. Elwin, grew up a Free Will Baptist, but under the influence of Wesley's writings moved toward Free

---

15. Elizabeth Evans, *The Wright Vision: The Story of the New England Fellowship*. I have seen only the manuscript version of this book, which is, I believe, now privately published.

16. J. Elwin Wight, *The Old Fashioned Revival Hour and the Broadcasters* (Boston: Fellowship, 1940).

Methodism, which he joined in 1892, before going independent (under Pentecostal influence). He then founded the "First Fruit Harvesters' Association," a form of tent meeting evangelism that developed into the "Rumney Bible Conference," which sounds very much like a "Holiness campground" or an early Pentecostal communitarian movement (like several others in New England at the time). At the end of his career Joel asked his son Elwin, in typical Pentecostal dynastic fashion, to take over the leadership of the movement. At first Elwin refused because he thought that the First Fruit Harvesters' Association had become little more than another Pentecostal denomination, but he later accepted leadership on the condition that he be allowed to move toward a more open stance that would welcome Christians from other denominations—in effect moving toward a more "generic" form of "evangelicalism." Thus the New England Fellowship took its modern form in the late 1920s as a broadening of a *Pentecostal* movement! Speakers at Rumney were a "who's who" of the Holiness and Keswick movements, self-conscious fundamentalists, those from broader circles, and so on. Lists of speakers give a remarkable sense of the mix that constituted that generation just before the emergence of the "neo-evangelicals." And this Holiness/Pentecostal camp at Rumney was apparently a key arena for the formation of the network that coalesced in Fuller Seminary. Among speakers (besides Ockenga) were such later Fuller faculty as G. Eldon Ladd, Clarence Roddy, Gleason Archer, and Charles Woodbridge.

The New England Fellowship was then the womb of the National Association of Evangelicals—and Ockenga was something of a midwife and first President of the new organization. Yet there is not a hint of the Pentecostal character of the New England Fellowship in Marsden's book. But if the facts are as I have recorded them above, they revolutionize our understanding of the origins and character of "neo-evangelicalism." The usual interpretations of the founding of the NAE puzzle over why the Pentecostals and Holiness Churches were invited to participate. But this is much easier to understand if Ockenga is following a trajectory out of the Holiness movement and Wright is on a trajectory out of the Pentecostal movement. The real question is how the other "evangelicals" (Reformed, Baptistic, etc.) found themselves at home in this organization and movement. And the present character of the NAE (probably 75% or more Holiness and Pentecostal) is much more understandable. And the historiographical questions of the appropriate categories for the interpretation of "neo-evangelicalism" become all the more poignant.

But such revisionism can be extended to other institutions in the New England network of Evangelicalism. I had given little attention to the Providence Bible Institute that developed into Barrington College and eventually merged into Gordon College. I was willing to abandon this tradition to the more usual categories of the interpretation of fundamentalism until, during my sojourn at Drew, I had occasion to study the dissertation history of this line by Dale H. Simmons, a graduate of Oral Roberts University. His work reveals that this school arose under the leadership of E. W. Kenyon, generally considered the major figure in the articulation of the radical "name it and claim it" doctrines that have re-emerged in recent Pentecostalism and the Charismatic movement. Simmons traces the roots of the college to links with Faith College, founded in Boston by Methodist leaders of the nineteenth-century Holiness movement. Again the origins of another major circle of New England "neo-evangelical" influence are to be found in the Holiness/Pentecostal mix. Simmons goes on in his study to find roots of this movement in "new thought."[17] But enough has been said to raise fundamental questions about whether such currents should be read as expressions of "classical" or "traditional" Protestantism.

The importance of such revisionism is that, in turning to such currents, we are as close to the heart of the formation of "neo-evangelicalism" as we can get. But now, we find that these currents are rooted in a Pentecostal and Holiness ethos that has been radically suppressed in recent "evangelical" historiography. And significantly, we are dealing with New England, the location where we would least expect these traditions to be dominant. As Marsden puts it, Ockenga "played the role of the nineteenth-century New England gentleman clergyman"—his "style was as intellectualist as the Fullers' was folksy" (16).

(3) I would like to turn now to the "folksy" side of the tradition, and look at Charles Fuller to indicate how my "Pentecostal" paradigm highlights different dimensions in the life of Fuller than does Marsden's "Presbyterian" paradigm. Charles Fuller's father Henry (for whom Fuller Seminary is actually named) was, again, a Methodist, and so Charles was raised in that tradition. After a move, Charles Fuller transferred his membership from a Redlands Methodist Church to a Presbyterian Church in Placentia. Here he experienced a spiritual crisis under the influence of a Plymouth Brethren writer and other dispensationalists. Soon thereafter, he became notorious for his popular "Bible class" that outgrew the Presbyterian church and organized itself as "Calvary Church," which

---

17. See Dale H. Simmons, *E. W. Kenyon and the Postbellum Pursuit of Peace, Power, and Plenty* (Lanham, MD: Scarecrow, 1997).

then identified with a somewhat radical, dispensationalist wing of the Northern Baptists.

Sometime I would like to make a close study of the split that Fuller caused in the Placentia church with his Bible class. It would make a good test case to see whether the Fuller party was the "conservative" or "orthodox" party resisting a perceived "liberalism"—or whether the split was more like a "charismatic" group that left the "traditionalists" and "conservatives" behind in their classically Presbyterian church. I'm inclined to think—based especially on some quotes from the minutes of church meetings by son Daniel Fuller in a biography of his father—that it was of the latter sort.[18] Dan Fuller indicates that "there is no evidence that the Placentia Presbyterian Church was liberal," though there were some conflicts about social ministries. So far as I can tell, these were probably the result of Charles Fuller's dispensationalism rather than his "conservatism." Again, according to Dan Fuller, the issues with the Bible class included "aggressive evangelism, enthusiastic Bible teaching, and the hearty singing of Gospel songs"—to which would be added an emphasis on Bible prophecy and Zionism and a piety shaped (in part by his friendship with Charles Trumbull) by the Keswick piety of "victorious Christian living." Indeed, all that would seem to be missing for such a group to qualify as Pentecostal would be "speaking in tongues."

Interestingly, the issue of speaking in tongues was much closer to the center of Charles Fuller's spiritual struggle than one might guess. I was somewhat diffident in raising this question with Dan Fuller, fearing that I might offend him, and was astonished to hear that he considered this a central spiritual struggle of his father's life. The details of this are presented in his biography of his father, but apparently Charles Fuller struggled for some time with whether he should speak in tongues; moreover, he used to slip out of Placentia to hear the preaching at Bethel Temple, where a number of people spoke regularly in tongues. The issue was resolved for Charles Fuller when the pastor of Bethel Temple, a Dr. Eldredge, when invited to speak at Calvary Church, urged him to "seek the giver and not the gift." I also had the occasion to press Dan Fuller on his father's view of "divine healing." I was told that he had reservations about the Pentecostal doctrine of "healing in the atonement" but that he did believe in miraculous healing. I was astonished, however, that the base line that was used to describe his position was the classical Pentecostal doctrine, which seemed

---

18. Daniel P. Fuller, *Give the Winds a Mighty Voice: The Story of Charles E. Fuller* (Waco, TX: Word, 1972), especially 51ff.

to me to suggest that the issue was discussed in the Fuller home in terms of the Pentecostal claims.

I dwell on these issues for several reasons. One is to push the point that the split in Placentia is to my mind better described by my "Pentecostal" paradigm, one that repositions the players in a way different from the classical "Presbyterian" paradigm. It also highlights the importance of dispensationalism, a point to which I will return in a moment. It also raises questions about how we should read the conflicts that developed when early Fuller faculty members attempted to move their credentials into local presbyteries. Should such conflicts be understood as the resistance of "liberals" to the influx of "conservatives"—or should such conflicts be seen as the resistance to the influx of a near-charismatic piety and theology that was seen by the "conservatives" as the intrusion of something theologically foreign into the life of "traditional" Presbyterianism. After all, as Marsden himself indicates, the investigative teams of the local presbytery were generally looking for signs of "dispensationalism" and "Arminianism" in their visits to the Fuller campus.

But the fundamental point is that the life of Fuller was much closer to Pentecostalism than one would gather from Marsden's interpretation. If one reads the key figures from the bottom up, one finds these themes very close to the center of the life of Fuller. And it is no accident that while Marsden was writing his history the school was being led by a group of Pentecostals and ex-Pentecostals. If my facts are right, President David Hubbard grew up Pentecostal but moved toward the Baptists and the Evangelical Covenant Church. And School of Theology Dean Bob Meye also grew up Pentecostal and gravitated toward the American Baptists—again a classic pattern in the figures that we have studied (especially Ockenga and Wright). But it is also true that the two Associate Deans of the School of Theology at the time were ordained Assemblies of Cod clergymen—Russell Spittler and Mel Robeck. It seems to me that such facts provide a different context to the conflicts of the 1980s over the "signs and wonders" course of John Wimber and Peter Wagner. This and the "battle for the Bible" initiated by Harold Lindsell, though technically outside the chronological limits set by Marsden for his book, are so interesting that he cannot resist treating them in an epilogue. But it seems to me that the conflicts over Wimber lie much closer to the heart and soul of the Fuller experience. Such "Pentecostal" and "charismatic" themes are more at the center than a "Presbyterian" reading allows.

(4) Such Pentecostal themes raise the issue of the status of dispensationalism in Marsden's history of Fuller. The theme recurs often, but is

less often used in an explanatory manner. My own reading, based in large part on evidence that Marsden himself provides but does not fully utilize, is that the issue of dispensationalism was at the core of what was going on during the rise of neo-evangelicalism. It is probably not too strong to suggest that this was the crucial issue between the continuing fundamentalists and the emerging "neo-evangelicals." I have indicated above that Marsden and I have had rather opposite reactions to the significance of Ernest Sandeen's book, *The Roots of Fundamentalism*, which argues that fundamentalism was *essentially* dispensationalism. I was prompted to reflect on this theme by a comment of my major professor at Houghton College in the early 1960s. He had been a student of Carl Henry at Northern Baptist Theological Seminary in the 1940s, and he reflected once to me, long after graduation, that *the* intellectual task of his generation had been the repudiation of dispensationalism as a theological framework.

Whatever one makes of that comment, I am convinced that repudiating dispensationalism was at the center of the neo-evangelical agenda and was in many ways (perhaps on occasion implicitly) the fundamental issue in the first generation at Fuller. Perhaps my perception of this matter is shaped by my experience of teaching at Northern Baptist Theological Seminary, where Carl F. H. Henry wrote his "neo-evangelical" *programmschrift* entitled *The Uneasy Conscience of Modern Fundamentalism*.[19] The social agenda of that book is clearly dependent upon the repudiation of dispensationalism and the recovery of "kingdom preaching." It was also at Northern that Dan Fuller wrote his ThD dissertation refuting dispensationalist hermeneutics; Fuller's break with dispensationalism greatly disappointed his father, but seems to be a necessary step in the way to the sort of biblical perspective that Fuller later embraced in his studies in Basel.

The issue was central to many other figures at Fuller. Everett Harrison apparently moved to Fuller from Dallas in part to duck questions on some growing points of reservations about the dispensationalist scheme. The issue was clearly *the* fundamental question of the life work of George Eldon Ladd, who wrote several books on the question as he worked toward his own biblical theology of the Kingdom of God that emphasized the "already, but not yet" of an inaugurated but not consummated kingdom. I am inclined to think that Ladd's repudiation of dispensationalism was a precondition to his embracing of his "devout criticism" that led Fuller closer to "mainstream" biblical studies.

---

19. (Grand Rapids: Eerdmans, 1947).

But I think that there is a sense in which much of the recent agenda of Fuller is dependent upon the rejection of dispensationalism. It would seem to be essential to the recovery of a social vision, in the line of the work of Carl F. H. Henry and the articulation of "neo-evangelicalism" by Harold John Ockenga. It would seem to me to be behind the broadening ecclesiology of Fuller, its movement beyond separatism, and more recently its development of a self-conscious "ecumenical" agenda. I would argue that the development of a broader cultural agenda (again a part of Ockenga's platform) was also dependent upon moving beyond dispensationalism.

It seems to me that it is also possible to go beyond this general sort of analysis and suggest that at least one major crisis needs to be interpreted more explicitly in these terms. I notice that the faculty that left at the end of the sixties (persons like Wilbur Smith, Gleason Archer, Harold Lindsell, etc.) were dispensationalists who seemed not to be able to follow this trajectory of the repudiation of dispensationalism. Some of these faculty gravitated toward Trinity Evangelical Divinity School, which was rooted in the explicitly dispensationalist Evangelical Free Church. Trinity has tried to position itself as the carrier of the tradition of the "old Fuller," and the issue has been generally interpreted in terms of the battle over "inerrancy." But the more I ponder the situation, the more I am inclined to see the deeper issue to be dispensationalism—perhaps as a scheme of biblical interpretation that requires something like inerrancy to sustain itself. If so, it would appear that the question of dispensationalism might be much more central to the emergence of Fuller than Marsden implies—and that it can be used as a fundamental interpretive principle in analyzing key debates in the life of Fuller. Might it not just be possible that fundamentalism was essentially dispensationalism—and that the emergence of neo-evangelicalism is the story of the repudiation (albeit quietly and subtly at times) of that interpretive framework for the study of the Bible?

(5) Let us return then, finally, to some of the opening questions about the basic nature of Fuller Seminary and the role of Princeton in its emergence. I think that I have shown that many of the key figures in the founding and leadership of Fuller were on a trajectory *out* of Methodism (or its more extreme manifestations in the Holiness Movement or Pentecostalism). This suggests to me that we should use the founding of the Holiness seminaries after World War II (the Nazarene Theological Seminary, Western Evangelical Seminary, Anderson School of Theology, etc.) or the founding of the Pentecostal Seminaries in the 1970s and 1980s as the model for the emergence of Fuller Theological Seminary—rather

than either Princeton Theological Seminary or the Westminster Theological Seminary that split from Princeton.

I have the feeling that if Marsden had been asked to write the history of, for example, the School of Theology of Oral Roberts University, he would have told the story of the rise within the Pentecostal Holiness Church of the healing ministry and tent evangelism of Oral Roberts, who seized upon television and built on such use of the mass media a large ministry that drew him closer to the mainstream. I have no doubt that Marsden would have seen the social factors of class and would have traced the upward social mobility of Oral Roberts and his ministry toward a *university* and toward the "mainstream" United Methodist Church in a form of *embourgeoisement*.

But when I look at Fuller and its emergence, I see a very similar story. I see a man (Charles Fuller) moving out of a Methodistic, near-Pentecostal, and dispensationalist background to found a ministry that develops via the medium of radio and the "Old-Fashioned Revival Hour" into one of the first significant mass media ministries—in a style not unlike Roberts in a later generation with television. I also see a tradition qualifying its radicalism by moving *toward* the mainstream and the middle classes in a fierce *embourgeoisement*, though this time in the Presbyterian rather than the Methodist context. Such readings are confirmed when one turns to New England and finds similar, or even more radical, trajectories in the lives of J. Elwin Wright and Harold John Ockenga. Yet I don't really believe that this is the story that Marsden is telling.

Something of this is revealed in the structure of Marsden's book. After some basic facts about the founding of Fuller, Marsden turns in the second chapter to "the history behind the history." This history is not what I would expect. It is not the history of the "revivalism" (especially Finneyite revivalism) that would seem to lie behind Charles Fuller and the "Old Fashioned *Revival* Hour." It is not the history of the Holiness and Pentecostal Movements out of which Harold John Ockenga and J. Elwin Wright came. It is not even the story of the "New School" Presbyterianism that might be said to lie behind fundamentalism. The "history behind the history" in George's book is the history of the twentieth-century split at Princeton. I can't help avoid the impression that this history is really the "history in *front* of the history" of Fuller. It represents the "teleology" of Fuller in its aspiration to move out of fundamentalism to be a proper *Presbyterian* seminary—and not its "genealogy" in the sense of telling us where Fuller came from.

If this is the case, how might we better describe the story line that constitutes the background of Fuller? We might start the story with the refusal of Evangelist Charles Grandison Finney to attend Princeton Theological Seminary after his conversion and call to ministry. This refusal involved a repudiation of the (Old School) theology of Princeton, a turn to the lower classes (his churches in New York were known for their "free pews" that welcomed the poor), the embracing of a radical form of revivalism, and the adoption of a "populist" and "anti-hierarchical" social philosophy well-adapted to the emerging Jacksonian vision of democracy. We could trace the amalgamation of Finneyite revivalism with the emerging Holiness Movement and its further radicalization into Pentecostalism—and the parallel emergence of dispensationalism and the radicalization of "New School" Presbyterianism into a form of "Reformed" fundamentalism much like these other movements. In the twentieth century we could trace the upward social mobility of such traditions until their *embourgeoisement* required by mid-century the founding of seminaries like those they had rejected in their formative years. We would see a slightly more "Reformed" Fuller in this larger context of the founding of a number of seminaries that more clearly reveal the dynamics that I have been discussing. If this is true, then the basic story line of the emergence of Fuller would be something like the decision of the great grand-children of Finney deciding to go to Princeton after all. And it seems to me that this basic story line provides quite a different setting for the narrative history of Fuller, and raises fundamental questions about the recent historiography of American evangelicalism.

Response #1

Robert K. Johnston

Evangelical Studies

ROOTED in the Wesleyan, rather than the Reformed, tradition of American evangelicalism, Don Dayton has considered the category "evangelical" to be "an essentially contested concept" (the phrase is W. B. Gallie's, who writes in the British analytical tradition).[1] Rather than being *descriptive* in character, charting out the central core beliefs of a variety of Christian traditions, Dayton has understood the word "evangelical" to instead be *prescriptive* in nature. Having been politicized, it is for him an "equivocal" term, perhaps even "inaccurate in some of its fundamental connotations" as commonly used.[2]

Basing his conclusions in an historical analysis of the wider evangelical tradition, Dayton has disputed what he calls the "Presbyterian paradigm," seeking to substitute a "Pentecostal" one in its stead. In a series of insightful essays that have helped define the conversation, Don has drawn attention to three periods of Protestant history where the term "evangelical" has been used. During the sixteenth century Reformation, evangelicals were those who, in reaction to a corrupt Roman Catholicism, stressed a *biblical*, Christocentric understanding of salvation. In the eighteenth and nineteenth centuries, "evangelical" was used to describe those pietists and revivalists who reacted to a dead orthodoxy by emphasizing conversion, sanctification, and *experience*. More recently, in the twentieth century,

---

1. Cf. William Abraham, *The Coming Great Revival: Recovering the Full Evangelical Tradition* (San Francisco: Harper & Row, 1984) 72.

2. Donald Dayton, "Some Doubts about the Usefulness of the Category 'Evangelical,'" in *The Variety of American Evangelicalism*, eds. Donald W. Dayton and Robert K. Johnston (Knoxville: University of Tennessee Press, 1991 and Downers Grove, IL: InterVarsity, 1991) 246.

evangelicals, reacting to a secular modernism, sought to defend orthodoxy by appealing to *tradition*.³

It is this third expression of evangelicalism—that which developed out of fundamentalism, which has wrongly co-opted the term "evangelical" according to Dayton. Based in the power politics of the rise of neo-evangelicalism after WWII, what later became "establishment evangelicalism" (Fuller Seminary, *Christianity Today*, et al.) has wrongly sought to apply indiscriminately its particular understanding of "traditional" Christianity to the broad range of traditions that evangelicalism represents. Instead, Dayton believes it more accurate to use the term "evangelical" to describe "the newer and innovative edge of Christianity." He observes that Pentecostalism is not a "traditional form of Christianity"—nor is Adventism, the holiness movement, the black church, restorationism, or dispensationalism. It is in these movements, thinks Dayton, that the heart of the evangelical movement is found, a movement that shares "little more than a common alienation from the so-called 'mainstream' of American church life."⁴

As co-chairs of the Evangelical Theology Group of the American Academy of Religion for much of the 1980's, and later as co-editors of *The Variety of American Evangelicalism* (1991), Don and I had many friendly disagreements over these points. Where I stressed a larger overarching unity among evangelicals, one rooted in theology, Don stressed the movement's diversity and sectarian dynamics. Where he looked to the conflicting historical traditions for his cues, I turned to the polyglot character of the present and sought, nevertheless, to find an underlying unity. Fuller Seminary, for example, now has 130 denominations and 60 nations represented in its student body, with "Presbyterians" and "Pentecostals" of all stripes being more or less equally represented. There are different emphases among the multitude of evangelical sub-groups to be sure, but I argued that they also shared a theological center that might be described as three-fold:

> A dedication to the gospel that is expressed in a personal faith in Christ as Lord, an understanding of the gospel as defined authori-

---

3. Donald W. Dayton, "The Social and Political Conservatism of Modern American Evangelicalism: A Preliminary Search for the Reasons," *Union Seminary Quarterly Review* 32 (Winter 1977) 72-74; Donald W. Dayton, "Whither Evangelicalism?," in *Sanctification and Liberation*, ed. Theodore Runyon (Nashville: Abingdon, 1981), 143-47; Donald W. Dayton, "The Use of Scripture in the Wesleyan Tradition," in *The Use of the Bible in Theology: Evangelical Options*, ed. Robert K. Johnston (Atlanta: John Knox, 1985) 121-26.

4. Dayton, "Some Doubts," 247-48.

tatively by Scripture, and a desire to communicate the gospel both in evangelism and social reform. Evangelicals are those who believe the gospel is to be experienced personally, defined biblically, and communicated passionately.[5]

While I continue to believe in the usefulness of the term "evangelical" to describe those who share this common theological center, Don has continued to challenge my thinking. His emphasis on evangelicalism's discontinuities seems more appropriate each year as evangelical tensions become more apparent. Thus, I have come to believe that the term "evangelical" might best be thought of as an "adjective" rather than a "noun."[6] Evangelicalism is not a common movement (despite what the media or the "religious right" might think), but a descriptor of shared theological convictions within a variety of disparate ecclesial traditions. There are evangelical Baptists, evangelical reformed, evangelical holiness churches, and so on. Thus, though I share little else with a Falwell, a Robertson, a Dobson, an Osteen, or a James Kennedy, I nevertheless share a basic "evangelical" theology with them—I share the adjective "evangelical."

It is import to continue to hear Don's strong objection to any process that would flatten the variety of American evangelicalism(s). To the hard of hearing he has had to shout, and to the blind he has had to write large (to paraphrase Flannery O'Connor). As one of the few, leading non-Reformed scholars working on the history of American evangelicalism (one also thinks of Leonard Sweet, Tim Weber, and Grant Wacker), Don has come at the data with different "spectacles." In the process, he has helped us all recognize that evangelical theology can as easily traverse the Trinitarian path from Spirit to Word, as from Word to Spirit. Evangelical theology can begin with experience and seek its grounding in the Word (the Pentecostal paradigm), just as it can move from the Word to its embodiment in life (the Presbyterian paradigm).

Alister McGrath has commented that evangelicalism is "a set of corrective emphases." Dayton, using more colorful language, refers to the "'anti-orthodox' dimension of most forms of 'evangelicalism.'" And surely this is right. Whether challenging the excesses of Catholicism, scholasticism, or modernism, evangelicals have always sought renewal and reform for the church. It is perhaps in this same light that readers can best understand Don's important article in the *Christian Scholar's Review* (1992)

---

5. Robert K. Johnston, "'American Evangelicalism' An Extended Family," in Dayton and Johnston, eds., *Variety of American Evangelicalism*, 261.

6. It was Tim Weber who first suggested this modification in terminology to me.

on Fuller Seminary as a case study in American evangelicalism. Rather than view the traditions of evangelicalism, as Marsden does, as being in continuity with the Reformation, Don sees them as a corrective (Pietism, Methodism, "New School" Presbyterianism, and so on), with social roots (evangelicals have largely begun in the lower classes) that more easily permitted such "anti-orthodox" expressions as women in ministry.

Dayton's re-interpretation of Fuller's history perhaps suffers from his commitment to evangelicalism as "an essentially contested notion." It makes difficult the holding together of evangelicalism's conflicting strands. Wanting to substitute as his model for Fuller's beginnings the founding of holiness and Pentecostal seminaries after WWII rather than seeing Fuller's beginnings as an attempt to correct Princeton and Westminster (and one should add, Dallas), he has perhaps fallen into the same univocal trap as Marsden. Fuller's origins belie homogenization. Yet by arguing his case, Don has also pointed to something important—the plural character of Fuller Seminary's beginning and development. There is more than one "history behind its history." To the deaf, he has felt the need to shout!

All of us who describe ourselves as evangelicals owe a huge debt to Don for forcing us to take more seriously our pluralities. As evangelicals stumble forward into the twenty-first century, it is our multiple histories that offer us hope—hope that we will continue to be a corrective force in the church, hope that reform will once again take place, hope that we can again be "un-orthodox" for the sake of the Kingdom.

Response #2

Clark H. Pinnock

I welcome the opportunity to celebrate the work of Donald W. Dayton and to interact with him on important themes that are dear to his heart. Don is a friend who possesses extraordinary mental powers in realms of church history and evangelical historiography and who can stand proud in a select group of other exceptional scholars such as Mark Noll, George Marsden, Grant Wacker, Kenneth J. Collins, Joel Carpenter, and others (When they speak, we listen!). The debate here is one to which colleagues have contributed, particularly George Marsden. A wide-ranging essay, it concerns the meaning of the term evangelical in the context of the twentieth century and the significance of Fuller Theological Seminary.

No one actually deserves or can lay a unique claim to the title: evangelical. For who among us embodies the good news of Jesus Christ without flaws? This has not (of course) prevented people from grabbing the title—most recently and with spectacular success—the National Association of Evangelicals (founded in 1943) did so. But what did it mean? In the NAE were some who viewed evangelicalism as heir of the conservative Reformation and a bulwark in opposition to the Enlightenment—let's call this the Marsden model. Others were of the opinion that evangelicalism was successor to holiness, revivalist and pietist groups that (not incidentally) were not defenders of the status quo as represented by old Princeton—let's call this the Dayton model. They did not see themselves as conservative and were in fact critical of many conservative traditions. For instance, they were more radical in their political and social witness and less driven by rational and propositionalist theology. They supported women in ministry against conservatism. Holiness people love the Bible as much as the others but did not define the doctrine of Scripture like Warfield did which eventually led to a battle for the Bible.

Leaders of the neo-evangelicalism opted to include both Calvinists and Arminians in the movement, reminiscent of the Wesley/Whitefield evangelistic alliance. The decision created tensions and has not been easy. Deep differences exist in such an alliance, making it hard to identify who the "real" evangelicals are. I remember an early meeting with Don in Vancouver when I heard him say that he thought that the term evangelical was not very good at identifying believers with any precision. What sense does it make to call free Methodists and orthodox Presbyterians both evangelicals? They might not even want you to, preferring a clear sectarian label that people could grasp. I see Don's point more now than I did before.

Dayton is to be commended for making people aware of the richness and diversity of American evangelicalism. He has described the plurality of movements that have gone into it, with their different stories, traditions, and theological positions. He is conscious of the temptation to privilege one's own group's story, as having the best and most orthodox beliefs and interpretations. In our generation, it seems to be the conservative Presbyterians who like to present themselves as the most deserving of the title evangelical and a step above the others.

In summary, when I first responded to this essay in 1992, I was a little skeptical of Don's thesis and drawn more to Marsden's, partly because it commended itself to my experience with the Presbyterian camp. I had always been of the opinion by Ramm and others that the evangelical heritage could be and should be traced back to the conservative reformers through old Princeton. Now I realise that much of evangelicalism was born out of revival and reform and was far from being Calvinist.

How does Fuller Theological Seminary fit into this picture? Dayton finds evidence that some of the movers and shakers behind the founding of Fuller Seminary had backgrounds in pietist and Methodist contexts. This is true but it is hard to gauge their influence over the seminary as such. One reason for this might be the simple fact that they all wanted a first class seminary, a "Princeton of the West." But dangers lie in this territory. If they want the very best scholarship and if they want to beat liberals at their game, while putting down their own background in fundamentalism, I say good luck to them. It's a very tall order.

As a university student myself in the fifties, I looked to Fuller as an example. I poured excitedly over the Fuller catalogue and dreamed of studying Semitic languages with LaSor and Archer, dogmatic theology with Jewett and Henry, and apologetics with E. J. Carnell. Where else could one do such things under evangelical instructors? Nowhere else! Fuller was a beacon of light for many students, the ideal if not the reality.

Had I gone to Fuller Seminary (however) I would likely have been disappointed because the reality of actually bringing this off was not quite there. The first couple of decades were marred by a schism already rising from differences over biblical inerrancy, a decidedly Presbyterian issue. It wasn't easy for them to get beyond fundamentalism and answer the liberals appropriately. Just how difficult it would be, one has only to consider the troubled life of the first real president of Fuller, Edward J. Carnell, and witness his pain intellectually and politically as the faculty struggled for control of the institution. Fortunately, things turned out better for Fuller with subsequent presidents, David Hubbard and Rich Mouw, and better faculty. Later on, it did prove to be possible for Fuller to surmount the fundamentalist problematic and to become a truly top-flight post-conservative evangelical place to study. It was just harder and it took longer to get from the ideal to the ideal.

It is really easy for me to identify with the real history of Fuller Theological Seminary. I too bought into the Presbyterian model in the sixties and tried to do what Fuller has tried to do. I wanted to see a school with excellence and balance that would be a model of irenic and generous orthodoxy. Fuller with its living history does not fit neatly into any theoretical model whether it be Marsden's or Dayton's. Certain great issues had to play themselves out and things could have gone either way. Fuller was one thing when it began and something else when it found its footing and could be a seminary where students of the Presbyterian persuasion could work alongside those of Dayton's Pentecostal reformers. What wonderful unintended consequences! What serendipitous creativity belongs to our God!

10

Toward a More Inclusive Ecumenism

Perhaps one of the least known of Dayton's contributions to the contemporary church has been his participation in the Ecumenical movement. Dayton has served as a member of the Faith and Order Commission of the National Council of Churches since 1983 and has been an active member in the North American Academy of Ecumenists since 1986. He was also present at the Vancouver (1983), Canberra (1991), Harare (1998), and Porto Alegre (2006) assemblies of the World Council of Churches.

The following essay—originally published in *The Ecumenical Review* 40, no. 1 (1988), 87–110—is illustrative of Dayton's ecumenical work and has been one of the most widely read of his many articles, not in the least because of the provocative title. The essay was written subsequent to a sabbatical Dayton spent in Geneva in the spring and summer of 1987, and at the invitation of the American Theological Society.

Yet Another Layer of the Onion

Or, Opening the Ecumenical Door to Let the Riffraff in[1]

Donald W. Dayton

I received the invitation to make this presentation while I was on sabbatical at the World Council of Churches contemplating the question of the relationship of the ecumenical movement or the churches of the ecclesiastical "mainstream" to non-member churches and movements like my own, the Wesleyan Church. Thus when the request came to use, and I quote, my "knowledge of the Holiness, Pentecostal and Keswick movements" to share my "observations of the peculiar problems in the historiography of these movements and on the ways in which the recovery of these materials will impact theology in the United States," I could hardly with integrity decline the opportunity to apply to this particular strand of American-born but now worldwide Christianity the theories and perspectives that I was trying to develop and articulate in the context of the World Council of Churches. What follows is an effort to reflect on the historiographical and theological significance of these neglected movements.

My title and subtitle are perhaps not self-interpreting (and may finally be an incoherent jumble of images!), but they are an effort to indicate something of the angle from which I would like to approach these issues. The title is intended to indicate that with all the efforts that we have made in the last few years to incorporate the perspective of the poor, women, the third world, ethnic and racial minorities, and so forth into the historiography and theological reflection of the mainstream churches and cultural institutions, the task is far from completed. As I have lived through these developments over the last two or three decades since arriving at college in

---

1. Editor's note: The original article was preceded by the following comments: "This paper was written for a meeting of the American Theological Society, and it is focused on the American context. But the issues it raises are of wider ecumenical interest. It makes a well-reasoned plea to open up the ecumenical door to let the evangelicals in, and concludes that there is much of stake in such a move for life on both sides of the door."

the midst of the civil rights movement, it has gradually dawned on me that I and my cultural and ecclesiastical experience are not yet represented in the various "quota" systems that we use to ensure fair representation. I am a white male, but I have never felt myself to be a part of that WASP culture that was supposed to have held the cultural and economic power in the traditional American experience. It eventually became clear to me that my experience was in a cluster of largely white but lower-class churches that were for all practical purposes invisible (being distinguished neither by color nor language) in both the older cultural patterns and the new, more sophisticated "quota" grids of recent years. In this sense my title is meant to suggest both that we have yet another "layer" to explore and that like the onion (and unlike the banana or other fruits and vegetables where we peel away skins or other layers to get at the real thing) the whole consists precisely in the layers—without all the layers we have only fragments and not the whole.

The subtitle is an effort to call attention to another aspect of the problem. Reared as I was in a "Holiness" church deeply influenced by "fundamentalism," I was acutely aware of the provincialism and sectarianism of that experience. I was for a while led in reaction to idealize the critical theologies of the cultural mainstream and especially of the ecumenical movement which I understood to be principally committed to a "dialogue" rooted in the valuing of the other. That enthusiasm has been gradually eroded as I have learned to be much more realistic about the "provincialism" and "sectarianism" of the cultural mainstream and the ecumenical churches. Its scholarship, while supposedly more objective and critical, is shaped by implicit ideological commitments that place themselves at the center and rule out data that would challenge its assumptions. Dialogue with many of the movements outside, for example, the ecumenical movement, is often not pursued because these groups are actually culturally despised, and it is unthinkable that critical theology would learn anything from dialogue with such sources. It remains the case that most of us move more readily towards profound interaction with those movements which are more powerful, more prestigious, more culturally established, etc. We move more naturally up the cultural and economic ladder than down it. Thus my subtitle is an effort to pose the question in the way that it must at times appear to those of the cultural and theological mainstream. I mean to pursue the question of what sort of historiographical and theological reorientation would be required by opening the ecumenical door to the sort of "riffraff" that would be represented by the "Holiness, Pentecostal and Keswick movements."

The paper will proceed in several steps. In the first place I will attempt a more factual survey of these movements—in terms of both the process of historical emergence and something of the present reality and configurations. This step is required because the cultural biases of the education to which most of us have been subjected have not even made us aware of these movements, let alone prepared us to interpret them sympathetically. In the second place, I will discuss the general historiographical reorientations that the study of this material has forced upon me. In the third place, I will move towards more concrete illustrations of the changes of important historical and theological assumptions that taking this material seriously would require. And finally, by way of a conclusion, I will attempt to speak more directly to the strictly theological significance of this material.

The Emergence of the Holiness, Pentecostal, and Keswick Movements

One of the most powerful and yet most neglected of nineteenth-century religious movements was what has come to be called the "Holiness movement." From one angle this current was a product of the confluence of "modern revivalism" (to use the title of William McLoughlin's book that traces the tradition from Evangelist Charles Grandison Finney to today's practitioner Billy Graham) and Methodism, which had arrived on the American scene about the time of the American Revolution but by the time of the Civil War had become the most powerful of American Protestant denominations. In a strictly theological sense the movement was a reassertion of John Wesley's doctrine of "entire sanctification" or "Christian Perfection," not only within the Methodist tradition, which was beginning to neglect this aspect of the Wesleyan heritage, but much more widely among all American denominations where such themes found much resonance in the young, optimistic nation suffused with a form of enlightenment perfectionism. From a social and cultural perspective the movement was a protest against the *embourgeoisement* of Methodism in the mid-nineteenth century. Methodism, which had found its greatest strength in a form of a preferential option for the poor in eighteenth-century England, was by the mid-nineteenth century moving into the middle classes with a vengeance. Celibate circuit riders were abandoning that rigorous life for families and "location" in churches more like the traditional denominations. Methodist theological seminaries were being founded. More expensive and traditional churches were being built that required new forms of financing to support. And so forth. In this context the Holiness movement, especially in North

America, was a movement of those people who felt uncomfortable with these developments and attempted to maintain structures of church life "more in touch with the masses."

But however one understands these various levels, there began to emerge in the nineteenth century a variety of currents and new denominations. The vanguard of what would happen later in the century might be found in the formation of a few new denominations during the antebellum period. The Wesleyan Methodists (my own church) emerged in the early 1840s over the conflicts about slavery. Orange Scott and others were converted to abolitionist sentiments that they felt compelled to share with their fellow Methodists. The bishops thought them rabble-rousers and extremists—and assigned them to hard-scrabble parishes and made other efforts to suppress them. The Wesleyans finally decided that both slavery and the episcopacy were "unscriptural" and founded the congregationally oriented anti-slavery Wesleyan Methodist Connection. They called themselves *Wesleyan* Methodists to recall Wesley's anti-slavery convictions and named their church paper *The True Wesleyan*. Similarly in 1860 the Free Methodists emerged with the "free" in their name indicating their reassertion of Wesleyan Christian Perfection ("free from sin"), their anti-slavery convictions, their insistence on "free pews" that would welcome the poor in opposition to the "pew rentals" used to finance the new imposing Methodist churches, the "free" styles of worship that emphasized congregational singing in opposition to the emerging professionalization of church music, and so forth.

Similar concerns were finding expression under the ministry of Charles Grandison Finney of the Presbyterians (though Presbyterians and Congregationalists were experimenting with church union during this period—and Finney moved back and forth). His revivalistic churches in New York City in the 1830s clustered themselves into the "third presbytery" (the roots of some of the modern "evangelical" Presbyterian churches there) characterized by its opposition to the pew rental system. In this decade Finney became the professor of theology (and later president) of Oberlin College in the opening new frontier of the Western Reserve (the area of modern Cleveland, Ohio) and moved more fully towards the adoption of Methodist practices and theology, including the adoption of the Wesleyan doctrine of "Christian Perfection" which led to the elaboration of "Oberlin Perfectionism"—a form of the Holiness teaching that orthodox Presbyterians and Congregationalists sought desperately to suppress. Oberlin's theological faculty was to provide many of the leading Holiness theologians of the day (Finney himself, President Asa Mahan,

John Morgan, Henry Cowles, and others). In both New York's third presbytery and Oberlin there was the same "preferential option for the poor," the same anti-slavery sentiments, and the harboring of the more radical and reformist wings of the "Evangelical United Front" that dominated the ecumenical Protestantism of the time.

The Holiness movement proper within Methodism had its roots in Boston and New England amongst abolitionist Methodists (Timothy Merritt and Henry Degen) who founded in the same period a journal (*The Guide to Christian Perfection*) that was to become profoundly influential throughout the century. Later this paper was taken over by Phoebe Palmer (to be described by Thomas Oden in a forthcoming anthology of her writings in the Paulist Press series of "Sources in American Spirituality" as the most important woman theologian in the Protestant experience before our own time) and her husband Walter who changed its name to *The Guide to Holiness*. Phoebe Palmer came to prominence by the founding of the "Tuesday meeting" for the promotion of holiness. This was a parlor meeting, not unlike many modern charismatic meetings, that cultivated a search for a deeper spiritual experience and was a little less oriented to the poor and the anti-slavery controversies, though Phoebe Palmer was involved in the converting of "the Old Brewery" into a mission house that is often celebrated today as the beginning of the modern city mission movement in nineteenth-century urban North America. The Tuesday meeting grew in importance (gaining a couple of hundred imitators by later in the century) and became more and more interdenominational as the movement spread beyond the bounds of Methodism.

It was the famous "laymen's" or "prayer revival" of 1857–58 that brought the holiness message to the attention of many non-Methodists and those outside of the USA. Presbyterian William Boardman had great impact in both the USA and England with his immensely popular book on *The Higher Christian Life* that articulated the Holiness doctrines in language less offensive to non-Methodists. At the same time the doctrine was permeating many other denominations: the Baptists had evangelist A. B. Earle; the Episcopalians physician Charles Cullis with his interest in healing, various social ministries, publishing houses, etc.; and even Unitarians and others saw the influence of the Holiness revival.

And the movement very quickly jumped the Atlantic. Oberlin and Finney had had major impact in Britain already. Phoebe Palmer spent much of the Civil War period evangelizing in the British Isles, where among other spiritual influences Catherine Mumford (the future wife of William Booth of the Salvation Army) felt called to public ministry by this example of a female evangelist. (William Booth had earlier been converted under the ministry of Phoebe Palmer's pastor James Caughey—and the Salvation Army is best understood as a product of this movement, particularly in the United States where links are especially close). Another woman, Hannah Whitall Smith, author of *The Christian's Secret of a Happy Life*—one of the most widely distributed books of any sort in the whole nineteenth century—with her husband Robert Pearsall Smith began to speak in England. Their meetings on the Broadlands Estate led to meetings in Oxford and Brighton in 1874 and 1875 that had thousands in attendance, including influential representatives of several European churches. These meetings fed into the so-called Keswick Conventions that met in England's Lake District to advocate a more moderate form of the search for holiness without the distinctive features of Methodist theology and continue to the present day there and in imitations throughout the English-speaking world. The missionary movements founded in the late nineteenth century along the model of the China Inland Mission were closely associated with Keswick and carried this piety around the world. Robert Pearsall Smith made tours of Europe and had a major impact on the emergence of the *Heiligungsbewegung* and *Gemeinschaftsbewegungen* that emerged in German-speaking Europe and continue to dominate much of German popular "evangelicalism."

Back in North America the Holiness movement proper found its major expression after the Civil War in the National Campmeeting Association for the Promotion of Holiness (the antecedent of today's Christian Holiness Association, the international interdenominational ecumenical agency of the movement). As the century wore on there were founded innumerable regional, state, and local Holiness associations, Holiness colleges and universities, hundreds of local camp meetings both within and without Methodism, and so forth. Early leaders of the National Campmeeting Association attempted to control this proliferation and keep it confined to a more respectably Methodist style of operation. But the movement was in places radicalized and began to cultivate doctrines of divine healing and the expectation of the imminent return of Christ. Such developments led to increasing tension with Methodist and other denominational hierarchies and the gradual separation of much of the Holiness movement from Methodism. By the turn of the century the movement was spread throughout the country in a variety of fragments that have since begun by a sort of agglutinative process to merge into a number of denominations including such groups as The Church of God, The Pilgrim Holiness

Church (later to merge with the Wesleyan Methodists), The Church of the Nazarene, and many other groups of varying size and influence.

The final development took place at the turn of the century in the emergence of a new movement that was a further radicalization of the Holiness movement—a sort of "holiness heresy." In the last third of the nineteenth century the Wesleyan doctrine of "entire sanctification" was gradually transmuted into a doctrine of the "baptism of the Holy Spirit." At the turn of the century a wing of the movement began to suggest that this experience was to be "evidenced" by the practice of speaking in tongues. This split the movement into two parties, the Holiness movement proper that understood the "baptism of the Spirit" in Wesleyan terms with the emphasis on sanctification and "purity," and the Pentecostal movement which emphasized the "empowering" of the baptism of the Holy Spirit and the practice of speaking in tongues. In one of the holiness slogans of the time, the Holiness movement emphasized the "fruit" of the Spirit and the Pentecostals the "gifts" of the Spirit. These theological battles split the movement and churches down the middle (not only in the USA but around the world—as for example in the *Gemeinschaftsbewegungen* in Germany) and remain a most bitterly remembered theological split that is only beginning to he bridged today.

The evolution of Pentecostalism throughout the world is better known than its Holiness antecedents. The Pentecostal movement proper has split into several branches:

1. Those churches like the Church of God (Cleveland, Tennessee) and the Pentecostal Holiness Church (and many others) that maintain both the Holiness doctrines of sanctification and the Pentecostal themes of the baptism in the Holy Spirit.
2. Those churches like the Assemblies of God or the International Church of the Foursquare Gospel (as well as many others) that have suppressed the Holiness teachings (or advocate it only in the more moderate "Keswick" variety).
3. A radical split within the latter movement that advocates a form of Unitarianism of the second person of the Trinity known as Oneness Pentecostalism or "Jesus Only" Pentecostalism. This is the most sectarian form of Pentecostalism, but a part of the movement that has been very influential in the American Black culture and in the third world (being the largest Protestant body, for example, in Colombia).

4. As Pentecostalism has spread around the world and has distanced itself front the control of American Pentecostal missionaries it has had a profound impact in the emergence of various indigenous forms of Pentecostalism—and has played a part in the emergence of other indigenous movements like the African Independent churches.

5. Since the 1950s the Pentecostal themes began to suffuse the mainline denominations to produce the very large and powerful "charismatic movement" that has manifested itself in almost all denominations, and now dominates the "electronic church" around the world and so on.

It is impossible to generalize much about these churches and the various aspects of the movements involved, but it is important to note that the various denominations founded in the nineteenth century (largely the Holiness churches) and the denominations founded in the twentieth century (largely the Pentecostal churches) have grown and prospered in this century—in many cases developing through aggressive missionary work into world churches. At the same time they have been experiencing their own twentieth-century *embourgeoisement*, founding theological seminaries and establishing critical theological traditions, and are revealing a sort of cultural broadening and signs of evolution out of a more "sectarian" mentality into a more "churchly" style. As these churches move into the middle class and demand a greater role in traditional church circles we experience a fair amount of cultural conflict that needs critical and careful reflection because the problems will wax rather than wane.

It is also difficult to estimate the real significance and power of these movements. In the first place there are a number of cultural biases built into the way in which we collect and use church statistics. If we take only the smallest cluster of these churches, the Holiness movement proper, and look at only those churches that cluster in the National Holiness Association (ignoring for the moment those movements and churches outside this association), there are about two million members of such Holiness churches In the USA. The United Methodist Church, until overtaken by the Southern Baptists, was the largest and most influential of the American Protestant bodies. Membership of the UMC is now somewhat less than ten million, perhaps a little over nine million. But on a given Sunday only about a third of these are in church—about three million. But because of a variety of factors (strict membership requirements, aggressive Sunday schools, etc.) attendance in Holiness churches is often double the membership. So on a given Sunday there are as many Holiness folk in church as Methodists. To move on to other comparisons, there are as many folk in Holiness churches on a given Sunday as there are members of Presbyterian churches in the USA. There are about as many members of Holiness churches as there are Anglicans in the USA. And this analysis does not take into account the large pockets of Holiness people within Methodism (the centers around Asbury College and Asbury Theological Seminary—or the folks who identify primarily with the innumerable Holiness camp meetings scattered across the American landscape). The cluster of classical Pentecostal churches is larger than the Holiness cluster, and similar comparisons can be made.

And what is true in the USA is often more so in other parts of the world. It is estimated that Latin American Protestantism is between 50 and 75 percent Pentecostal. In many countries of Latin America the largest Protestant church is Pentecostal—and often the competitors for the title are also Pentecostal (thus the International Church of the Foursquare Gospel is the largest Protestant body in Panama; the United Pentecostals the largest Protestant body in Colombia, etc.). And this does not count the various Holiness bodies (especially the Salvation Army, the Church of the Nazarene, the Christian and Missionary Alliance, the Church of God/Anderson, the Wesleyans and Frees, and the various churches founded by such interdenominational Holiness missions as World Gospel Mission and OMS International) that have churches and Bible schools in many countries. In these countries it is the magisterial Protestant traditions that are marginalized. Thus in Argentina a friend of mine directs a Pentecostal seminary with 6,000–7,000 students that also finds space to serve Anglicans, Lutherans, and others. In Costa Rica the Methodists go to the Nazarene seminary. Much of this pattern is replicated in other parts of the world, though often without the same imbalance. But the largest Christian seminary in Asia is operated by the Holiness Church of Korea, a country that has seen great impact of Pentecostalism as well.

Nor does this strictly denominational analysis reflect the impact of the broader movement. It is hard to know where to draw the line. In many ways the broader Keswick piety is the semi-official piety of the various "evangelical" groups and may be seen in most forms of modern revivalism and the modern faith missions. The theology of Bill Bright's Campus Crusade, for example, is of this variety. I once asked theologian David Cairns of Scotland how he would define an Anglican evangelical. His response was immediate: an Anglican who goes to the Keswick conventions. Many would find this overstated, but there is much truth to the observation. One surprise to me in my Geneva sabbatical was to read the huge new biography of Frank Buchman by Garth Lean. I gained a new and different appreciation of the Moral Rearmament movement and was amazed to discover that Buchman's formative religious experience took place at Keswick. And as I began to read of the distinctive theological themes and practices of Moral Rearmament (absolute purity and truth, the practice of quiet time and getting direct guidance from God, the practice of spiritual discernment of moral failings and other problems; the vision of Christianity as a person- and world-transforming power that needs only to be let loose in the world, etc.), it was difficult not to understand this movement as a further ripple of the impact of the holiness vision "contextualized" (in a move opposite of that which we usually speak of) to the upper classes, the nobility, and the inhabitants of Oxford and Princeton that Buchman was often seen to be unduly fascinated with and given to.

And similarly with the Pentecostal movement. After one has considered the limits of the strictly Pentecostal churches, how does one weigh and measure the wider impact? One can speak of the millions of "charismatics" in the traditional churches. But one has to look as well at the suffusion of Pentecostal themes in a variety of indigenous movements in the ethnic and racial subcultures both in the USA and abroad. In a recent essay in *The International Review of Mission* (January 1986), Walter J. Hollenweger cites the predictions of David Barrett in his *World Christian Encyclopedia* that while these three strands (Classical Pentecostals, Charismatics, and Indigenous non-white movements) numbered 100 million in 1980, they will number 250 million in 2000—or almost half of all Protestantism. And this is not to take into account the difference in intensity. These statistics take at face value the church statistics of largely secularized cultures in Europe and elsewhere where many members of churches are only "nominally" so affiliated. I am personally a little sceptical about whether these growth patterns will continue unabated, but even if they do not, when we look at the evolution of this Holiness, Pentecostal and Keswick movement, we are looking at one of the major strands of Christianity, at least in terms of sheer numbers. Yet this tradition has only recently begun to be taken seriously—and then primarily only in its Pentecostal form. And for the most part we have yet to take it seriously theologically.

The General Historiographical Reorientations Required

The above description, when taken seriously, obviously leads to a different sense of the texture and the future of the Protestant experience than is usually assumed in the mainstream churches. I found this to be true especially in the ecumenical movement of Europe as it is represented in the World Council of Churches. There, Methodists and Baptists are so marginal to the ecclesiastical experience that it is almost impossible to imagine a religious situation dominated by movements on the far side theologically and culturally of "mainstream" Methodists and Baptists. But I want to turn now to the more academic questions of the implications of this material for the ways in which we understand church history and theology.

I am tempted to explore the peculiar historiographical problems of working with the sort of source material that one works with in this arena. There is a parallel here to the broader question of "people's history" over against the histories of "academic theologies" or culturally dominant institutions. There is the bewildering complexity of these movements and their ecclesiastical fragmentation. I took a sabbatical in Argentina a few years ago to explore Latin American Pentecostalism. My informant told me that there are about 1,200 separate incorporated Pentecostal bodies registered in Argentina (both denominations and separate groupings that in some cases may exist only in a single congregation). There are the problems of working with traditions that are in many cases oral rather than literary (as evidenced by the problems of attempting to trace the emergence of Black Pentecostalism and its relationship to White antecedents—or where I have had to guess at the connections and migrations within the Caribbean that have led for example to the emergence of the Black Holiness "Christian Mission of Panama" among the workers who came to work on the Panama canal). There is the problem of gathering the literary sources where they exist. In many cases the material is ephemeral and has been discarded—and is to be found more often in junk shops and Salvation Army stores than in the libraries or even the used bookstores. Some of the best collections of materials have been built up by a process of following personal networks and exploring the attics of descendants of figures whose work is not understood a generation or two later. There is the problem of working with a popular movement that is just now establishing its critical traditions of theology and finding the categories for interpreting its theology sympathetically and appropriately. There is also the problem of breaking open inherited categories so that one can read the material in terms of its own intentions without the cultural biases imposed on the material by forms of thinking and cultural experience developed in and for the interpretation of other materials. It is this last problem that will be the focus of our reflections here.

Before entering directly into that discussion, I wish to draw attention to the clear historiographical lacunae about these questions in the mainstream literature. Pentecostalism is now too numerous and visible to ignore, but it still gets short shrift in the standard literature. And the situation is much worse for the antecedent Holiness movement. Reflect on your own education or study of American church history: How much did you learn of this movement? If one looks at the many hundreds of pages in, for example, Sydney Ahlstrom's *A Religious History of the American People* or Winthrop Hudson's *Religion in America* (probably the most common texts), one will find only a few paragraphs about the Holiness movement—and little awareness of the larger configurations or issues involved.

Perhaps it is not inappropriate to report here a couple of anecdotes from my doctoral program. When I was working at the Divinity School of the University of Chicago on my dissertation just published this year as *Theological Roots of Pentecostalism*, it was difficult to find advisers for such a project. I was in the theology department and the most obvious figure was James Gustafson because he was an expert in Edwards and had read a little Finney and Bushnell in nineteenth-century America! Martin Marty became co-adviser because of his generally comprehensive knowledge of modern church history and the American scene—as well as a certain interest in Pentecostalism, expressed especially in *A Nation of Behavers*. In the process of writing the dissertation I put together a collection of about 6,000 books that I could use in tracing the intricacies of Holiness theology in the nineteenth century. When Martin Marty lectured on North Park's campus, I took him to my "holiness room" where these books were in bookcases from floor to ceiling, stacked on the floor and stuffed in every available space—in part in the hope of impressing him with the seriousness of my project. Perhaps it is not inappropriate to report here that he seemed to be astonished. He picked up various books—this one that had been published in over 50 editions, that one that had sold some 300,000 copies in the nineteenth century, this one that is still being sold in modern editions after having achieved sales of several million. He finally asked me why he—surely one of the most informed persons about the nooks and crannies of American religion—had never seen or heard of these books. Why was he virtually ignorant of one of the most massive religious propaganda campaigns in American religious history? He was apparently so impressed with the question that my friend Nancy Hardesty had to field questions in her doctoral exams from Marty about the historiographical reasons for his virtual ignorance of the materials in Don Dayton's holiness room. Yet we know the much smaller literature of the "social gospel"—and it has been explored from every angle.

This holiness literature, however, is now being collected and interpreted with a great deal of energy. As is often the case, the impulse for the study of this literature has come largely from within the movements themselves. But it is only in the last decade or so that most Holiness and Pentecostal churches have established historical archives. The Pentecostal seminaries are just being founded, and the Holiness seminaries are only a generation or two old. (My father founded seminary education in my denomination only in 1957—one hundred and fourteen years after the founding of the denomination; he claims to have the first theological doctorate in the history of the denomination.) We have had few sophisticated histories written from a critical perspective—but there is a phenomenal burst of scholarship in this decade. And Asbury Theological Seminary recently received a grant of almost a third of a million dollars for the collecting and interpreting of the source material involved—and for the rewriting of the history of "evangelicalism" that must follow when all this is brought to light.

What reorientations will follow from the study of this material? From one angle it is too early to say, but from another I am willing to hazard my own reading of the situation. In terms of more general questions, we will have to learn to move out from under the perspectives that we have learned from Yale (and perhaps Harvard) about how to read the American religious experience in general and out from under the perspectives that we have learned from Princeton about how to read the history of the "evangelical" sub-culture in particular. It is obviously a caricature to use the names of these schools in this way. And I have no desire to impugn my own theological alma mater (Yale), but I do wish to use these symbols for schools of interpretation whose influence I have had to escape in order to develop categories adequate to understanding the history of the Holiness movement. (Here and in what follows I will concentrate on the history and theology of the Holiness movement for two reasons: it is my own tradition so I know it best; and it is less well known in general than Pentecostalism—and perhaps the more interesting case study.)

When I use Yale as a symbol I am objecting to that reading of the American religious experience that suggests that New England and what happened east of the Hudson River provide the key to the interpretation of American religion. Puritanism itself had to be rescued from historiographical obscurity and caricature a couple of generations ago—and is now used, for example, by Yale church historian Sydney Ahlstrom in his *Religious History of the American People* (Yale University Press) as the controlling motif of his work. In this scheme the nineteenth century becomes the "post–Puritan" age and one traces the "decline" of Puritanism into American revivalism (this is his "technical" definition of "evangelicalism"). To understand the nineteenth century in general and the religious experience of the mid-west especially, I have had to move out from under this perspective and learn to think more positively of the nineteenth century as the "Age of Methodism" and to find my clues for the broader interpretation of the period within the experience of Methodism. Such a proposal goes back at least to Philip Schaff, and earlier in this century Methodist church historian William Warren Sweet made eloquent appeals for a "Methodistic" reading of American church history. But it has been such Baptists as C. C. Goen and Winthrop Hudson who have more recently developed this concept in describing the nineteenth century (here roughly 1820 to World War I) as the "Age of Methodism." This concept is useful not only because Methodism became the largest American Protestant denomination during this period but also because much of the rest of Protestantism (and some of Catholicism as well—see, for example the argument of Jay P. Dolan in *Catholic Revivalism*) began to act like Methodists. The sharpest illustration of this is, of course, the movement of Evangelist Finney towards Methodist theology and practices. In fact, one might even understand the emergence of "new-school" Presbyterianism in this period as the evidence of the "methodistizing" of Presbyterianism.

We are not accustomed to viewing the American religious experience through Methodism—for a variety of reasons, including theological prejudices against Methodism. But to understand the emergence of the Holiness movement and its progeny we have to bring the Methodist experience to the fore. Once we see there what the dynamics are (especially the protest against the *embourgeoisement* of Methodism), we can see parallel movements within other denominations—such as the emergence of Finney's "third presbytery" in New York City—and understand later developments like the emergence of the holiness-oriented Christian and Missionary Alliance among the Presbyterians or the work of A.J. Gordon in Boston among the Baptists. But to really grasp the dynamics of this period—and especially to understand the commonality of these movements that would later bring them into various forms of coalitions—the lens of the Methodist experience is absolutely essential.

But when we make this move, we are also required to move out from under the interpretations that we have learned from Princeton as well. For a variety of reasons that we shall soon explore, the experience of Princeton has provided the categories for the interpretation of what is known today as modern "evangelicalism." Princeton was the major intellectual center of Presbyterianism in the nineteenth century and there developed in this seminary the theologies of Archibald Alexander, Charles Hodge, Archibald Alexander Hodge, and Benjamin Breckinridge Warfield, which taken together constitute the old "Princeton theology" that was rooted in the seventeenth-century Protestant Orthodoxy of Genevan François Turretini and constituted the major defence of "old-school" Presbyterianism in nineteenth-century America. In the latter part of the century the rise of biblical criticism with its implications for the doctrine of the inerrancy of scripture led to a monumental struggle in which the Princetonians felt that the truth of Christianity and the preservation of orthodoxy were at stake. This led finally in the twentieth century to a split at Princeton in which Westminster Seminary of Philadelphia was founded to preserve the themes of the old "Princeton theology"—the paradigmatic event of the modern fundamentalist/modernist controversy that has been used far beyond its applicability to explain what is at issue in the emergence of modern American fundamentalism.

By a complicated process that we shall discuss this experience of Princeton has become the norm by which the whole "evangelical" experience has been understood. It is seen and sees itself to be an effort to maintain "orthodoxy" and "conservativism" over against the rise of "liberalism" and "modernity." Most of the interpretation of the "evangelical" subculture (both within and without) presupposes this Presbyterian history. Let me illustrate.

I regret the fact that Bernard Ramm's book, *The Evangelical Heritage*, has gone out of print. It was such a perfect foil for use in class that I shall be hard put to find another such perfect illustration of how not to do the history of the "evangelical" sub-culture. Ramm's is not the most sophisticated historical interpretation, but his categories underlie most of the historical work that is done. His interest is more theological (and thus perhaps more useful for our purposes), and he attempts to offer what I have called a theological "historical geography" of "evangelicalism" by drawing a family tree or pedigree of the "evangelical heritage." In doing this he argues that "evangelicalism" belongs to the Western Augustinian tradition rather than to the East and to the tradition of the Reformation rather than the Catholic tradition. After the Reformation he traces the "evangelical" experience through Protestant Orthodoxy. With the rise of the Enlightenment "evangelicalism" is the effort to sustain the tradition against the rise of Enlightenment liberalism. His illustration of this line flows through Princeton into the more sophisticated forms of fundamentalism and finally into modern "neo-evangelicalism," which he sees in this line. This book makes a fascinating study. In the first place it is astounding to me that a Baptist would so celebrate the magisterial Reformation experience (he relegates the Anabaptists to a footnote because they made no lasting theological contribution to the church, and fails to mention Puritanism, Pietism and other movements that feed into the Baptist experience in various ways). It is fascinating to watch him struggle with Pentecostalism and argue that Pentecostalism really fits what he discerns to be the crucial theological move of "orthodoxy"—a sort of "Barthian" attempt to make "truth" and the "word of God" prior to human experience. He shows absolutely no awareness of the absurdity of making Princeton the carrier of the "evangelical" tradition. Many people emphasize the significance of Horace Bushnell's book *Christian Nurture* in marking the nineteenth-century challenge to the dominant "conversionism" of the revivalism of the age. When Charles Hodge reviewed this book, he essentially agreed, arguing that the controversial book took basically the position that "old-school" Calvinists had always taken against the "conversionists." It is absurd to see this line of development as normative if by "evangelicalism" one has in mind the "born-again" traditions of revivalism and Pietism.

And as a pedigree of the Holiness movement that so permeates the modern evangelical "sub-culture," it is almost ludicrous. One could argue that the Holiness movement makes the opposite move at every point in Ramm's flow chart. While Augustinian in some ways, Wesley thought Pelagius a much-maligned saint and derived much of his distinctive teaching from the Eastern fathers, especially the Cappadocians. In fact one of the major causes of misunderstandings of Wesley's doctrine of Christian perfection is that Western categories of "perfection" are used to interpret what is derived more fundamentally from Eastern categories. And Wesley's thought is as Catholic as it is Protestant not only in the sense that it ultimately derives from the "via media" of Anglicanism but also in the fact that he self-consciously used Catholic sources and that the fundamental shape of his thought moves more in a Catholic than a magisterial Protestant direction. And while it is true that Wesley had his "heartwarming" Aldersgate experience listening to the reading of a preface to one of Luther's commentaries, it is also true that when he got around to reading that commentary, he was horrified by it and the fact that he had recommended it. And in the post-Reformation period it is Pietism (which shared much of the Enlightenment critique of Orthodoxy) that would have the best claim (along with Puritanism) to be a determinate influence. The structures of Wesleyan thought are not characteristically those of the tradition of "Protestant orthodoxy." And in the nineteenth century, it would be new-school Presbyterianism that would most share the theological affinities of Wesleyan theology. Indeed, two of the ten volumes in the original Oxford edition of Princetonian B. B. Warfield's collected works are devoted to the intense refutation of all sorts of contemporary "perfectionisms" from Ritschl through Methodism and Oberlin to the major popular "Holiness" teachers of the late nineteenth century. Yet Ramm's understanding is used to interpret the whole of the experience of, for example, the National Association of Evangelicals in spite of the fact that a third of its member denominations are "Holiness" and another third are "Pentecostal." A close reading of Ramm's book reveals, however, that he really understands that "evangelicalism" is a movement of Bible camps and conferences, radio preachers, Bible institutes and so forth that do not reflect the theological tradition that he describes. What he has described in the book is not so much the actuality of the movement, but his own theological agenda for it. He desperately wants "evangelicalism" to be properly "old-school" Presbyterian in theology and as a result his book is largely a projection of this agenda on the history.

The issue is illustrated perhaps more acutely in a new University of Chicago Press book by James Davison Hunter, who claims to come at the question purely sociologically, though he assumes the same theological framework as Ramm. In this book, *Evangelicalism: the Coming Generation*, Hunter does not argue but assumes that "evangelical" is equal to "conservative" or "orthodox" and that it is a word that describes the effort to preserve intact the theology of the magisterial Reformation over against its dilution under the impact of modernity. Thus on a number of themes (theology, work, the family, politics, etc.) we are treated to a survey of sixteenth-century thought on the question before being presented with statistics about the tendency of contemporary evangelical collegians to move away from such themes under the influence of modernity. Yet the nine colleges that he uses to represent "evangelicalism" are derived largely from the Holiness movement. Thus George Fox College represents that wing of Quakerism in the Northwest that fell under the influence of the Holiness movement. Messiah College is a Brethren in Christ school representing that branch of the radical "dunkers" that fell under the influence of the Holiness movement. Taylor University is named for William Taylor, the famous holiness Methodist bishop of the nineteenth century. Houghton College is the major college of the Wesleyan Church. Seattle Pacific University is the largest of the Free Methodist Colleges. And even the four colleges that are the most "evangelical" in character reveal the same history. Gordon College derives from the work of A. J. Gordon, a holiness Baptist figure who was one of the major objects of Warfield's polemics (for his faith healing doctrines and his perfectionist tendencies). Wheaton College was originally founded by the Wesleyan Methodists with Jonathan Blanchard, a follower of Finney who always regretted that he had not been asked to teach at Oberlin—thus representing a sort of Congregational "new-school" experience. Bethel College derives from the Swedish free-church traditions of Pietism—and reveals the profound influence of the piety of the Keswick tradition. Westmont College is the most recent of these colleges, being founded actually as a sort of Wheaton of the West out of the modern "neo-evangelical" consciousness, but it could be easily argued that its life has been shaped by the modern traditions of Keswick and that it also fits the patterns. These movements are not classical Protestantism but protest against it.

Hunter's book represents exactly the strange schizophrenia of modern "evangelicalism." Historically it is better understood in terms of the Holiness movement; yet, theologically, it claims to be in the line of Princeton. Here is the essential historiographical problem: are we to understand this sub-culture along the model of the Methodist experience as the pulling off of the "underchurch" of the mainline denominations in response to a wedding to the middle classes, or are we to understand it according to the paradigm of the Presbyterian experience as the effort to preserve Protestant orthodoxy against modernity? Obviously I think the former is a better description. But if we take that path we have to explain the strange phenomenon of the present schizophrenia of "evangelicalism." I think that this can be done by analyzing the phenomenon of the increasing "Presbyterianization" of "evangelicalism" and "evangelical" historiography. By the "Presbyterianization of evangelicalism" I mean the tendency to move in the direction of Presbyterian theology (thus one cannot teach theology at the school of populist, Holiness, Baptist A. J. Gordon now unless one advocates the theology of his opponent B. B. Warfield of Princeton—and one can trace similar developments at such seminaries as Fuller or Trinity). By the "Presbyterianization of evangelical historiography" I mean the tendency to interpret and even to rewrite "evangelical" history according to the categories of this tradition. Exploring the reasons behind this Presbyterianization reveals a great deal about the character of "evangelicalism" and the historiographical confusions that we have been pursuing.

There is first of all a general level of explanation. One of the great gifts of the Presbyterian tradition to the rest of the Christian church has been its intellectual work, both theological and historical. Thus the three-volume *Systematic Theology* of Charles Hodge set a standard towards which many traditions have looked for guidance on how to do proper theology. So Baptist theologian Augustus Strong tended to appropriate Hodge and rewrite the ecclesiology along free-church lines. Nazarene theologian H. Orton Wiley of the Holiness movement tended to take Hodge as a model and rewrite the soteriology along Holiness lines. And so on. Similarly, when one wanted to learn to do proper church history, there was a tendency to learn how to do that from the Presbyterians. It was natural in doing so that one implicitly bought into a foreign set of theological assumptions and that the experience at Princeton should become more widely accepted as the best explanation for the existence of many churches and movements that understood themselves over against the larger mainline churches.

There is also a more concrete reason that is rooted in the particularities of the history of the period. Claude Welch has commented in his history of Protestant thought in the nineteenth century that during the conflicts over biblical authority in the late nineteenth century many conservative revivalist groups were looking for a lifeboat and climbed aboard the Princeton theology to ride out the storm. They stayed on board this lifeboat so long that many forgot that they didn't really belong there and gradually took their own identity from this shared experience. Thus contrary to most interpreters of the history, many evangelical groups were not originally committed to "inerrancy" formulations of the doctrine of scripture but began to adopt them under this influence. Many of the same groups (as in the Holiness movement) have now begun to reject these same articulations as their theological and historical maturity has revealed that they are foreign to their own theological traditions. One wonders how to read this period—how to relate the Methodist dynamic and the Presbyterian one. What would have been the development of these churches if the acrimonious fights of the fundamentalist/modernist controversy had not intervened—or are the experiences more intimately intertwined? I am inclined to find this important difference between the Holiness churches and the fundamentalists: the Presbyterian fundamentalists were self-consciously anti-critical, while the Holiness folk like many popular movements (Black church, etc.) were more "pre-critical." The difference is important—it is easier to grow out of the latter, as many groups are doing today, finding that the fundamentalist experience was a passing movement in their history and not their real identity.

This movement towards Presbyterianism was given added impulse, especially in those wings of the Holiness movement (especially the "Keswick tradition") less committed to the strong articulations of Holiness theology.

Sociologists of the evolution of "sects" into "churches" have often noticed how the earliest generations of a movement often will have stronger ethical and experiential boundaries to the movement but that later generations shift the emphasis to doctrine and orthodoxy as boundaries to admit the cultural broadening that takes place in such evolution. Such a movement would be in the Presbyterian direction. Sociologists have also noticed the tendency to move up the ecclesiastical ladder as one moves up the social ladder. If we are correct in using the Methodist experience in explaining the emergence of lower-class churches in the nineteenth century in opposition to the middle-class churches of the mainstream, then we are led to see in these movements today the same pattern of *embourgeoisement* that they reacted against in the nineteenth century. This social evolution could also very easily lead people in a Presbyterian direction. Again, sociologists have called attention to the fact that the oppressed often try to imitate their oppressors. If so, then we can even understand what is otherwise puzzling: why should the theological descendants of an A. J. Gordon want to adopt the theology of the man who so viciously attacked their forebear? And finally the sociologists have taught us that beliefs contribute to the creation of social realities. The Presbyterian description of what "evangelicalism" is has become so strong that it creates its own reality—it serves to draw people in its own direction; so that even Pentecostals have in many contexts and ways come to understand themselves as proper "evangelicals" in the Presbyterian sense and have begun to act in accordance with that self-understanding, betraying in the process the distinctive witness of their own tradition.

If there is truth in these sociological observations, then they would be accentuated especially in those circles that Hunter studies—the college and seminary intelligentsia, and even more so in the emerging class of intellectuals offering the interpretations, both historically and theologically, of the "evangelical" experience. And from informal observations of the scholars writing the history and theology of evangelicalism I think that it is possible to discern this movement. Thus the fascination of the evangelical tradition with the Princeton theology and the Presbyterian experience is, like in the case of Ramm, a prescription for the ills of "evangelicalism" rather than a history or interpretation of its own actual experience—even when it is offered in terms of the latter. And in such dynamics is born the very strange intellectual schizophrenia of modern "evangelicalism"—and the attendant historiographical problems. The more I have worked with the literature of the Holiness movement the more I have become convinced that the categories that one develops to understand that movement have wider applicability that begin to unlock the actual history of the broader "evangelical" movements obscured by a false "Presbyterianization" of that history.

The matter is important and of some ecumenical significance beyond matters of historiographical nicety. Is the ecumenical contribution of the "evangelical' subculture to be found in its resistance to "modernity" and the brakes that it puts on the tendency of the mainstream to cultural adaptation to the modern Enlightenment experience? Or are the contributions of these traditions to be found in the distinctly "modern" dimensions of their experience over against the more traditional churches? I think that the latter is the more appropriate reading of the situation—and that the Princetonian reading of the "evangelical" experience, rooted as it is in the longing to be a part of the ecclesiastical mainstream, is not only historically misleading but also ecumenically pernicious in that it confuses the nature of the discussion and obscures precisely the very contributions that such experience brings to the wider church world. It is to these questions that we must now turn.

The Specific Historiographical and Theological Reorientations Required

The issues are not just that the historiography be clear and that the chronicle be accurate. At stake are how we understand many matters of great importance in our culture and how we resolve very important theological questions. It is to these questions that we move in this section as we approach the subtle interplay of theology and history. Historiographical perspectives are not just history but they express and articulate theological visions. Theological agenda and ideological commitments shape the reading of history, and most readings of history are developed to support theological agendas. My travels in Latin America have brought this issue more into my own consciousness. Latin America and the third world in general are struggling with the implications of their own experience for the writing of history—one of my tasks in Geneva was to read the reports of consultations, edited by Lukas Vischer, on the problem of writing ecumenical history both across confessional lines and across the lines that divide North from South. I have learned much from this literature about the parallel problems of writing history from the culturally dominant locations within the societies of the North. I have on occasion been amazed to read polemics against the ways of doing theology in the "West" only to find myself siding with the third world, the African Independent churches or other sources of polemics against the "West." When the material of the Holiness and Pentecostal movements is fully incorporated into the discussions similar reorientations will be required. The significance of the assimilation of this "non-Western" experience in the West could be illustrated in several ways. Here I would like to turn to two concrete issues of both historical and theological significance.

The formative moment of the Holiness movement was the antebellum period in the United States that was characterized by the various social reform movements of the time, including especially abolitionism, the peace movement, physical culture and health, and so on. The Holiness movement, profoundly shaped by these themes, was one of the most consistent carriers of that reform impulse, especially in its earlier years. Yet we have difficulty accepting this fact and build our historiographical interpretations of this period out of our own presuppositions drawn from our more recent experience. Over the last generation, however, there has been a consistent push to reread the period and to give a greater weight to the role of the antecedents of the modern "evangelical" culture. Thus in the early 1930s Gilbert Barnes published his book *The Anti-Slavery Impulse* in an effort to overthrow the usual interpretations of the rise of abolitionist sentiment which were centered on various New England activists from Unitarian and Quaker traditions. Barnes had found in an old trunk the correspondence of Theodore Weld with his wife Angelina Grimké and her Sister Sarah. In the preface to an edition of these letters he was to argue that the anti-slavery

> agitation was accomplished not so much by heroes of reform as by very numerous obscure persons, prompted by an impulse religious in character and evangelical in spirit, which began in the Great Revival in 1830, was translated for a time into anti-slavery organization, and then broadened into a Congressional movement against slavery and the south.

Weld of course was a convert of Finney, his assistant for a number of years and one who adapted Finney's revivalistic techniques to the task of social reform, especially the anti-slavery campaign. This material unearthed by Barnes brought attention to Finney, Oberlin College, and similar bands of anti-slavery groups that abolitionized the mid-west in the USA—and had claimed credit for the shift of sentiment at the time. But their contribution had been lost—for a number of reasons. Especially in the early years of his campaign Weld self-consciously avoided the cities and other culturally dominant centers for the small towns and other locations. Our interpretations of this period have been written by New England historians more oriented to figures in that area (Barnes taught at Ohio State University!). It is contrary to our contemporary experience to expect these traditions to have been so involved—and try as we might, it is very difficult to break out of the Troeltschian category of "analogy" when we do our historical work.

In 1957 Timothy Smith published his famous *Revivalism and Social Reform*, making much of the same case but drawing out more explicitly the Holiness themes of perfection and millennialism that lay behind the reform impulse and tracing the extent of consistent Holiness leadership in these issues. While this book has been well received in many circles, it has also met a great deal of resistance not only by those reluctant to give religious ideas a significant role in historical causation but also by those who are not anxious to grant that the "social gospel" for example might have its roots in such traditions. (The recent edition of Walter Rauschenbusch's writings by Winthrop Hudson in the Paulist Press series of "Sources in American Spirituality" confirms Smith's analysis and shows the determinative influence on Rauschenbusch of the holiness classic *The Tongue of Fire* by William Arthur). The reactions of the "evangelicals" have, of course, been ambivalent. Many, like my friends at Calvin College, have ignored the word "revivalism" in the title, being willing to say "we" in claiming the reform impulse for their "evangelical" tradition while disparaging what they have called "Anglo-American evangelicalism" and thus the theological themes that lay behind the reform—an effort to claim the "fruits" while denying the "roots."

But it is getting harder to deny these conclusions in the face of further research. In *The Politics of Benevolence* Philip Hammond has brought cliometrics to the questions with his careful analysis of towns in Ohio, statistically correlating newspaper announcements of revival meetings with changing voting patterns, to argue that the rise of anti-slavery sentiment was profoundly rooted in the perfectionist revivalism of the period. And Thomas Lesick has studied in *The Lane Rebels: Evangelicalism and Anti-slavery in Antebellum America* the details of biographies of the leaders of the anti-slavery sentiment in Lane seminary that lie behind the founding of Oberlin College—to document the impact of Finney behind the anti-slavery impulse. And there is some unpublished research to the effect that as one works down to the popular level in the Unitarianism of the era, for example, anti-slavery soon disappears while when one moves down to the popular level of perfectionist revivalism of the period, the anti-slavery sentiment is perhaps even stronger, thus helping to explain the fact that followers of Finney may have been more abolitionist than he was—a fact that has on occasion misled the historians to minimize the role of Finney in the anti-slavery controversies.

But what of the theological and contemporary significance of this material? It would be the tempting to explore in some depth this period and the abolitionist movement as a form of Christian social action, but we cannot do so. Let me, however, quickly indicate a few of the ways in which this material cuts across some of the commonplaces of thinking about these questions today.

1. We use "Pietism" as a dirty word today, implying especially that it is the rejection of social concern. This is a travesty of both historical Pietism, which gave birth to many of the social ministries of Protestantism and to the reform movement of the nineteenth century, where it was precisely the intensification of piety that led to social reform. The Wesleyans were especially proud of the conjunction in their lift of both a greater "piety" and a greater "radicalism" than characterized the mainstream churches of their time. These movements of social transformation were rooted not so much in social analysis and careful strategy as in a call to the "sanctification" of persons and society.

2. While the editor of *The Christian Century* regularly advises us to abandon in the public arena the categories of theology and morality for a more neutral vocabulary of political strategy, these nineteenth-century reformers moved in the opposite direction—and in that movement found the energies and motivations to undertake the campaign that would finally root out the "sin" of slavery. It may be that some "demons" are not cast out by "cool" policy deliberations—and the abolitionist movement has been recently taken up as a model by the "new abolitionists" looking for a handle on the struggle against nuclear armaments. I, too, find the abolitionists moralistic, but I am not able to dismiss them as easily as many.

3. The millennial and perfectionist themes of the period were essence and not accident of the whole mix in the reform impulse. We have been reminded of the significance of such utopianism by the liberation theologians of our time who have used a form of Marxist utopianism to gain a critical perspective from which to critique society—and in the process have had to confront directly the "realistic" thinking of a generation nurtured on the thought of Reinhold Niebuhr. In the nineteenth century it was the Princeton theologians

who used the themes of "Christian realism" to undermine the impact of the Christian abolitionists—so much so that their writings were printed in volumes defending the institution of slavery. As one who is personally temperamentally "realist" but was reared in a "perfectionist" home, I have struggled much with this issue, but I am not able to dismiss the Christian utopianism of these movements as easily as some do today.

4. The reform impulse was part and parcel of a broader set of social and ethical commitments that are not much in favor today. These movements were perhaps overly scrupulous, giving moral value to many things that now seem trivial to many—card-playing, dancing, etc. A classical theological debate was at issue—the extent of those matters that could be considered *adiaphora* or morally indifferent. The perfectionist revivalists minimized this category, putting a moral value on everything, including slavery. The Princeton theologians maximized the category, arguing explicitly that slavery and political despotism were morally indifferent from the perspective of Christian faith.

5. Some of the most objectionable theological features (to the dominant forms of theology at least) were right at the heart of the issue. To a certain extent the "arminianizing" of theology brought to the fore a vision of personal responsibility for sin that included personal responsibility for social sin as well. These ideas were at the very core of "immediate abolitionism" in which as soon as one came to an awareness of sin, one was bound to take responsibility for it—and put it behind one. We may find such theology naive, but it was a large part of the energy that led to the final overthrow of slavery. And again, I believe that such models deserve more serious attention than they receive in contemporary discussions.

Before leaving the slavery issue for the other illustration that I wish to bring to the fore, I cannot resist making another historiographical comment that reveals the foibles of much mainstream interpretation of this period and material. There has been much discussion of what happened to the reform impulse after the Civil War in the USA—and much speculation about the reasons for its decline. The fact of the matter is that the people who were carriers of the reform continued their activity but redirected it to other issues of less interest to the historians. Thus towards the end of the century one finds abolitionist William Lloyd Garrison, the Oberlin activists, and others in their old age on the platform of the "Purity Crusade."

This campaign continued the techniques and the rhetoric of the abolitionist movement in a campaign to "abolish" the "white slave trade." Others turned to the prohibition movement, which was less about personal virtue than it was about cleaning up a society where the consumption of alcohol was ruining lives and preventing many children from getting a good start in life. And it was the brilliance of Frances Willard (later sentimentalism about her has obscured the radical character of her involvement in labor issues and the peace movement) to link the temperance movement to the campaign for women's suffrage (encouraging women to seek the vote for "home protection") in such a way as to marshall the support of middle America for female suffrage. And the Wesleyans turned their reform energies to the struggle against the influence of Freemasonry in the United States. Much of the reform continued (as documented, for example, in *Salvation in the Slums* by Norris Magnuson, a student of Timothy Smith attempting to extend his thesis), but it was directed in channels that have been distasteful to many historians—and so has been invisible.

But perhaps of more contemporary relevance is the issue of the ordination of women. And here the facts are again not in accord with the ideologies and self-understandings that are dominant either in the mainstream or the "evangelical" subculture. In fact, it was the study of the history of the ministry of women that forced me to rethink many of the general historiographical perspectives described above. And it is on this question that perhaps the greatest revision of accepted historical perspectives must take place. There is almost no mainstream history of the question of the ministry of women that understands what was actually taking place—and a large part of the problem is that students of women's history and American religious historians do not know enough of the history of the Holiness movement to understand the number of incidents in the history of the emergence of women into the ministry of the church that are situated in that movement. One of the most controversial features of Finney's "new measure" revivalism was the role given to the public speaking and praying of women. This was the major issue that almost derailed the New Lebanon conference of 1827 called to meditate the differences between populist Finney from the Midwest and the more conservative theocratic revivalists of New England. Oberlin College was the first coeducational college in the USA and therefore educated many of the most important leaders of the feminist movement of the nineteenth century. It was a graduate of Oberlin, Antoinette Brown, from a family of Finneyites, who became the first woman to be ordained in the Congregational Church—though she is often identified by her later membership in the Universalist Church to which she turned in revulsion against high Calvinist teachings about the fate of infants. The preacher of her ordination sermon was Luther Lee, one of the founders of the Wesleyan Methodists who had defended the right of Antoinette Brown to vote in the meetings of the temperance movement. The Wesleyans began to ordain women in the 1850s. The women's rights movement that issued the public call for women's suffrage was born in the 1848 meeting in the Wesleyan chapel in Seneca Falls, but most historians of the period do not know enough of the movements in question to understand the significance of the location, assuming it to be merely another Methodist church. Phoebe Palmer defended the ministry of women in *The Promise of the Father* (1859). The Salvation Army became arguably the most consistently feminist Christian movement, especially for its time, and Catherine Booth stated her case in *Female Ministry*. B. T. Roberts stated a radical case for *Ordaining Women* (1894) but failed to convince the Free Methodists who became the major holdouts in the Holiness movement on the ordination of women. Agitation on the question by Frances Willard and others under the influence of the movement brought the issue to the fore within mainstream Methodism but failed to win acceptance for the practice. By the turn of the century the ordination of women was accepted virtually throughout the Holiness movement. And in the more radical wings of the movement it was most enthusiastically embraced. Thus Alma White of the Pillar of Fire for years published a magazine entitled *Women's Chains* that called for suffrage, the election of a woman to the presidency and all levels of government, and polemicized against high-heeled shoes and other fashions under which women suffered to become the sexual playthings of men. As the founder of her denomination, Alma White was consecrated bishop and claimed to be the first woman to hold that office in Christian history. And when Pentecostalism emerged at the turn of the century, it carried through this theme and was perhaps even more consistent in the practice of the ministry and the ordination of women.

Thus arose the ordination of women in Christianity. Mainstream Methodists and Baptists moved towards the practice in the mid-twentieth century, to be followed soon thereafter by the churches of the magisterial Reformation. Anglicans are now in the midst of the struggle, and the ancient churches (Catholicism and Orthodoxy) are still opposed to the ordination of women. The history above and this brief chronology of the spread of the practice to the rest of the churches (actual historical connection can be traced in some cases) confirm many of the historiographical and theological claims made throughout this paper. The phenomenon of "evangelicalism," especially as it finds expression in the Holiness churches, is not "traditional" Christianity but a distinctly modern phenomenon in the churches, theologically, culturally and ecclesiastically at some distance from "traditional" Christianity. And if we take the National Association of Evangelicals as normative for "evangelicalism" in the USA (and elsewhere, for that matter), then the same applies much more broadly—not only that the Holiness movement and Pentecostalism (constituting about two-thirds of the organization) ordained women, but these movements are reflected in other churches and institutions in the NAE (thus the Evangelical Free Church, a Scandinavian immigrant group, reveals the same history with women—as does A. J. Gordon of the movements in New England and many other facets of the modern "evangelical" experience more often interpreted through the Princeton paradigm). Again, the Methodistic paradigm and the emergence of the Holiness movement provide the categories most widely applicable in explaining and interpreting the wider phenomena that cannot be explained in the categories of the Princeton experience. And in the tendency of institutions and churches to back away from this practice (most intensely in the Evangelical Free Church) we see the "Presbyterianizing" trends of which we spoke earlier.

Again the theological issues behind this history call out for exploration—more than we can give them. One short way of seeing what was at issue is to survey a series of theological factors that may be positively correlated with the ministry of women in the church:

1. Probably the strongest factor giving rise to the ministry of women is an emphasis on the Holy Spirit—as may be seen in various movements from Montanism through Quakerism to Pentecostalism. This theme often produces "prophetesses" who become the very mouthpiece of God, while it often supports a form of feminism that does not necessarily move towards a full egalitarianism.

2. The related emphasis on experience often supports the impulse towards the ministry of women. When ministry becomes the task of nurturing people through the religious stages on life's way and less a matter of endorsement by hierarchy on the basis of education and other criteria, women often rise to the fore—as they did to some extent in Pietism, which encouraged women to use their gifts but usually not in the public assemblies, and in classical Methodism.

3. The radical or "low church" movements within Christianity that minimize the distinctions between clergy and laity also find that women are able to cross the line more easily because the "sacramental" and "priestly" concerns are not so prominent. Thus once Methodism

adopted the ministry of the laity and local preachers it had difficulty denying women the same access to roles of the ministry.

4. The perfectionist impulse often leads to a form of feminism and thus to the ministry of women. Most feminist theologies have found it necessary to affirm a strong doctrine of grace to get a leverage on the patriarchal patterns of the Old Testament—or at least to emphasize the contrast between Old and New Testaments. Most classical doctrines of the subordination of women depend in some sense on a doctrine of the fall. Those traditions that have an "optimism of grace" (often combined with a "pessimism of nature") are inclined to see the elevation of women to equality under grace. Thus the Princetonians in the nineteenth century with their fascination with the pervasive impact of sin were inclined to see the curse of Gen 3:16 as prescriptive for all of life this side of the grave, while the perfectionist revivalists saw the same text as merely descriptive of the awful mess out of which we are being redeemed.

5. The sectarian movements marginal to the central tradition of Christianity have more often found the space for such new practices as the ministry of women—and as often happens the marginal and new movements often specialize in precisely those themes and practices that have been suppressed by the mainstream. Thus the nineteenth century saw such extremes as the Shakers claiming a complementary incarnation in Mother Ann Lee, the Christian Science Movement celebrating founder Mary Baker Eddy, the Adventists recognizing Ellen White as a prophetess—in increasing degrees of proximity to the classical tradition. And within the circle of traditional Christianity one has such figures as Phoebe Palmer and the various women ministers of the Holiness and Pentecostal traditions.

6. There is also a modern "enlightenment" or "liberal" strand within Christianity that moves towards feminism and the ordination of women as a "right" to be claimed along the line of other rights. Thus the Unitarian/Universalist movement in the nineteenth century often accepted the ministry of women—and it is possible to discern a form of this in the popular evangelicalism of the nineteenth century which arose in the wake of the Enlightenment and was to a certain extent more contextualized to it than the classical pre-Enlightenment Christian traditions. And modern feminism, even in the churches, often seems to derive from this source.

But it was the Holiness movement that brought all these currents together with a cumulative effect—and it was in that context that women broke through the barriers of informal patterns of ministry to achieve their full ordination and recognition in the church. I hope the above historical and theological analysis is sufficient at least to make plausible my claim that the history of the emergence of the ordination of women in the church and the range of theological issues surrounding the practice will never be fully understood until the history and theology of the Holiness and Pentecostal traditions are more fully absorbed into mainstream discussions and historiography.

A More Strictly Theological Conclusion

I believe that the above analyses, while they have been focused on historiographical questions, do reveal some of the theological significance of the material under discussion. In that sense I have anticipated many of the issues that might well be treated under this heading. Instead of exploring a number of discrete themes at this point, I would like to suggest that the special theological significance of the Holiness tradition ought to be seen on two levels—one methodological and the other having more to do with content.

On the methodological level perhaps the contribution is less original; it is primarily a voice joining a chorus of other voices in our time (often from the third world and especially but not exclusively in the varieties of liberation theologies) that the traditional forms of theology are not necessarily normative nor the most useful. The magisterial Reformation traditions have left us a powerful inheritance of constructive theology (that has sometimes moved towards the speculative and abstract) and a great tradition of formal confessions of faith. The theology of Methodism and its descendents has been of another sort—one that has not been so speculative in character nor has it found natural expression in the articulation of creeds and confessions. The classical traditions have found this puzzling; and the newer traditions have often been put on the defensive in their efforts to articulate their own visions, succumbing sometimes to the expectations of their elders in the tradition. The great Methodist ecumenist Albert Outler has struggled over the years with how to articulate the ecumenical significance of the Methodistic traditions of theology. For a while he played with Wesley as "folk theologian," but more recently he has backed away from such an expression because it gives away too much. Now he is more inclined to emphasize the catholicity of Wesley's sources and the significance of the movement as a bridge tradition that includes elements from almost all the other traditions of Christian faith. These elements are woven together with a great deal of subtlety and even theological rigor, but they are bent to another purpose than speculative or systematic theology. They are brought to bear on Christian experience, upon the organization of the life of the church for the cultivation of that experience, and the support of Christian life and mission in the world. Instead of great confessions, Methodism leaves behind in its wake testimonies of Christian experience and acts of love, including great campaigns for social justice. In this sense the theology of the Methodist tradition is a "praxeological" or "practical" theology *par excellence* that, when it understands itself aright, can make a significant contribution to wider discussion and even call others to account to its own theological insights.

But in this discussion there is a range of definite theological contributions to be made. I am tempted to defend dimensions of the theology of the Holiness traditions at such points as its anthropology, its synergism, its understandings of grace, and even its perfectionism in certain qualified terms. But here I would like to make my point in another way. We have already hinted above that the new religious movements in the church often reflect back the deficiencies of the mainstream religious experience—often in caricature. They in many ways testify to the unpaid debts of the traditional churches. I have been inclined to see the Holiness tradition as a canonical correction to an unfortunate tendency of the magisterial Protestant churches. In their reaction to Catholicism they overstated their case and became one-sidedly fascinated with the themes of faith and justification. The Holiness movement is just one of the last of the testimonies against this that have arisen since the time of the Reformation to incarnate the themes of love and sanctification. The line of such critiques would include the Radical Reformation, Pietism, Methodism, Kierkegaard, the Holiness movement and Bonhoeffer among others.

The point that I am making can perhaps best be seen in the theology of Luther and his tendency to deprecate the contribution of the Epistle of James to Christian theology. To my thinking this tendency points to a failing often expressed to varying degrees in the theology and life of the Protestant mainstream. On the other hand, it is amazing to note the number of themes of the Holiness movement that come from James. One finds there the more down-to-earth vision of Christianity as a way of life in the "wisdom" tradition; the call to purity of heart and the shunning of double-mindedness; the polemic against "mere orthodoxy" (as Wesley comments in the interpretation of James "even the devil is orthodox"); the concern that "faith without works is dead"; and even the involvement with the poor (the pew rentals were battled with texts from James about honoring the wealthy more than the poor in church); and so forth. In this sense the Holiness movement is a massive canonical corrective to the weaknesses of magisterial Protestantism.

But if there is any truth to this audacious claim, our discussion appears now in a new light. Methodism (and the Holiness movement and even Pentecostalism) have always been "movements" for the renewal of Christianity rather than churches, though they have often had to lapse back into ecclesiastical structures—in part for their own failings but in part because of the unwillingness of the traditional churches to hear their witness to neglected facets of scripture and the Christian faith. In many ways this development has been unfortunate for both sides. For obvious reasons Søren Kierkegaard reflected much on the problem of the "corrective"—the pinch of salt or the touch of color that finds its proportions only in the whole. When the corrective isolates itself from that which it is intended to correct it can become demonically turned in upon itself—and as useless as the arrogance that refuses to be corrected because the voice comes from the disrespectable or perhaps even from the "riffraff." But can it not be argued that the corrective generally comes in precisely that way and that it is a measure of Christian grace to be able to hear and recognize the voice of God from such sources.

If there is any truth to this analysis, then it may serve as an argument for opening up the ecumenical door to let such riffraff in. Much is at stake in such a move for life on both sides of the door—as hopefully has been illustrated by the range of historiographical and theological issues discussed above. Many things will not be understood until the various separated pieces are brought together. One might even argue that the full range of Christian truth and experience is at stake—that the whole is found, like the onion, only when all the layers are present. There is not a kernel that is something other than the layers.

Response #1

Brother Jeff Gros, FSC

Pioneering Narrative and Reconciliation

Donald Dayton's contribution to historiography and ecumenism are difficult to document in a few words. He has mentored many scholars in searching out the theological roots of their own heritage and beyond. This will be a stimulus to more scientific historians, theologians, and ecumenists to give disciplined attention to the influence of Dayton to late twentieth-century reconstruction of the master narrative of American Protestant historiography, and consequently the future of international Christianity. Furthermore, the impact of the opening of the ecumenical movement to the "riffraff" can only be read back from centuries to come, and how ecumenical structures and theological texts will be shaped as these new Protestant voices begin to make their appropriate contribution to the future of the pilgrimage of Christians together in response to God's call in Christ to unity and mission in the world. This paper will deal with Dayton's contributions to historiography and ecumenism.

The master narrative of American evangelical Protestantism has privileged the divisions in the historic Protestant churches during the modernist fundamentalist debates of the early 20th century. The heritage of Reformed Orthodoxy provided the early leadership in the institutions, structures and therefore historiography of conservative American Protestantism. By developing a careful historical account of the rise of Holiness and Pentecostal theologies;[1] but more especially by cultivating the learned societies of these two traditions—the real ecumenical form in which "Faith and Order" type work is done for these churches; and by mentoring two generations of Pentecostal, Holiness and evangelical scholars especially, from Asia and Latin America; Dayton has supplied the resources for rewriting Protestant history in the United States and its mission influence across the globe.

1. Dayton, *Theological Roots of Pentecostalism*.

Given his ironist, Kierkegaardian style following Reinhold Niebuhr and his mentor Martin Marty, he is often recognized more for his critical acumen in destabilizing the various master narratives of church history, theological development and missiological analysis, than for the volume of his collected systematic theology and historical narratives. However, make no mistake, his erudition is legendary if occasionally infuriating, and he has liquidated more unique library collections than most American Protestant historians have been gifted to read in a lifetime.

We do not yet have an American Protestant master narrative which we can use credibly in an introductory seminary history course, much less one that is truly accurate to United States church history: that is one that Catholic, Native American, Orthodox and African American as well as Protestant Christians can claim as accurate. However, such a history will not be able to emerge without taking account of the research generated by Dayton and his students, or the historiographic methods to which his work gives witness.

Another historiographic contribution that has tremendous ecumenical significance is the hermeneutics of piety.[2] Of course, Wesleyan, Marian, African American, mystical, feminist, and much of revivalist research has followed the hymnody, spiritual journals and visions, devotional literature and narrative accounts as primary sources for understanding the faith of a people. However, it has only gradually become evident in the ecumenical movement that rituals, piety and institutions need to be seen as important for ecumenical reconciliation as interpretation of texts.[3] This dialogue of pieties will become increasingly important between US Hispanic Christians, Pentecostal and Catholic.[4]

I recall a summer at San José, Costa Rica's Biblical University, when Dayton would exegete the millennial charts and eschatology of the variety of Pentecostal and evangelical movements and their social and political implications, while I would share the variety of Marian devotions and their class and political correlates. As Christians move forward together, understanding how the faith operates in piety, worldview and social values

---

2. Jeffrey Gros, "Towards a Hermeneutics of Piety for the Ecumenical Movement," *Ecumenical Trends*, 22:1 (1993) 1–12.

3. Faith and Order Commission, *A Treasure in Earthen Vessels: An Instrument for an Ecumenical Reflection on Hermeneutics*, Paper No. 182 (Geneva: World Council of Churches, 1998): http://wcc-coe.org/wcc/what/faith/nature1.html.

4. Jeffrey Gros, "Reconciliation and Hope: The Contribution of the US Hispanic Community: Building a Common Future; Recovering a Reconciling Heritage," *Ecumenical Trends*, forthcoming.

will be as important as interpreting the formal confessions and liturgical texts which they have inherited from their divided pasts. This will be especially true in the US Hispanic community where alienation between Pentecostal and Catholic heritages are exacerbated by alienations of both of these communities from the English speaking Catholic and Protestant traditions that have formed the older master narratives and ecclesial and public pieties of the nation.

While historiography is one of the inescapable contributions of Dayton's career, I suspect I have been invited to contribute to this anthology because of my ecumenical association with his work. There are three points I would like to make in this section: 1) his opening of Faith and Order to new voices; 2) his consistent witness to a critical but not politically manipulative approach to ecumenical institutions; and 3) his creative conceptualization of how to build theological bridges among the churches.

First, he has been personally involved in the 1980s in linking a wide variety of Pentecostal, Holiness and evangelical scholars to World and National Council of Churches theological work serving the unity of Christians in the Faith and Order movement. Like the work of John Howard Yoder with the Peace Church witness in the 1950s and 60s, it was not easy to convince the classical Catholic, Orthodox, Confessional Protestant and Anglican voices that the theological concerns raised on the American frontier and in the various waves of revival were issues of church division and church unity that needed as clear attention as the tragic divisions of the first two millennia of Christian history.

However, he has been able to establish that Pentecostal and Holiness perspectives were as important as Cappadocian and Augustinian views in looking again at pneumatology, for example.[5] Work on the "Constantinian era" that dealt honestly with the American Protestant ethos in both historiography and reconciliation would have been impossible without the voices he brought into the conversation.[6] Issues that divided Holiness and Pentecostal churches from their fellow Christians are as theological as the historic issues of *filioque* or justification by grace through faith.

Secondly, he has been at the center of discussions in the "evangelical" caucuses of the World Council of Churches assemblies since Vancouver in

---

5. Dayton, "Pneumatological Issues in the Holiness Movement"; Gerald Sheppard, "The Nicean Creed, Filioque, and Pentecostal Movements in the United States," in Theodore Stylianopoulos and Mark Heim, eds., *Spirit of Truth: Ecumenical Perspectives on the Holy Spirit* (Brookline: Holy Cross Orthodox, 1986) 171–86.

6. S. Mark Heim, ed., *Faith to Creed*, (Grand Rapids: Eerdmans, 1991).

1983, where I first met him. The evangelical caucus at each of these assemblies has produced statements which both affirmed and provided critical gifts to the ecumenical discussions. Many of these constructive criticisms have enhanced the future assemblies of the World Council.[7] However, with the emergence of the religious right on the US political scene there have been certain corporate financial interests that have funded organizations designed to be critical of the churches and ecumenical agencies for their stances on issues as diverse as apartheid or economic justice for the global south. Needless to say, evangelicals from Africa, Asia and Latin America, for the most part, are not sympathetic with all of the agendas that their north Atlantic, politically oriented fellow Christians bring to these assemblies.

Dayton, and other Holiness, Pentecostal and evangelical leaders from the north Atlantic community have been successful in attempting to balance the concerns of certain political voices with the more religious, theological, and justice oriented voices from around the world.

Finally, the creativity and critical voice that Dayton brings to his scholarship and ecumenical leadership is often destabilizing. Faith and Order is about the task of bringing churches together in conversation to resolve historical differences and serving the churches with convergence texts which will enable them to build a platform for ecclesial reconciliation and church union.

One has to make distinctions in theology before systematic synthesis is possible. It is sometimes necessary to clarify the church-dividing differences before Faith and Order type theological reconciliation and common texts can be developed. Churches and their theologians have to have a clear and confident sense of identity before honest dialogue is possible around the ecumenical table.

Dayton has sometimes been more helpful in identifying the problems that need to be attended to than in drafting agreement on how to resolve them. New voices always change the nature of the conversation. The ecumenical trick is to help all of these voices contribute to the common research and reconciling mission of Faith and Order.

However, Dayton's contribution of identifying the type and form a study should take has made an important and irreversible contribution. By identifying the types of voices and research styles that need to be represented around the ecumenical table he has provided an invaluable service. He has been helpful in assisting classical ecumenists, for example, see

---

7. See, for example, World Council of Churches, *From Harare to Porto Alegre: 1998–2006* (Geneva: World Council of Churches, 2005) 24.

how those churches who do not utilize the Nicene Creed can be equally interested in the study of the Apostolic Faith.[8] He has helped to conceptualize how to stage voices from the margins into the mainstream of the discussion, and how to help those who have controlled the master ecumenical narrative in the past find pathways to new ecumenical routes on the common journey.

In ecumenical theological work, the question is often as important as the paper attempting to address the question or the text attempting to capture the wisdom of a consultation or report the findings of a set of papers. This gift for the question is as significant for reconciliation as the equally important gifts of drafting and claiming the consensus.

Dayton has contributed irreversibly to American Protestant historiography and to the world wide ecumenical pilgrimage toward reconciliation for which Christ prayed. May his own intellectual journey continue to deepen and his influence as a mentor, scholar, and provocateur ever expand as he trips lightly around the globe.

---

8. Thaddeus Horgan, ed., *Apostolic Faith in America* (Grand Rapids: Eerdmans, 1988). Jeffrey Gros, "Faith on the Frontier: Apostolicity and the American Born Churches," *One in Christ* 39, no. 2 (2004) 28–48. Ted Campbell, Ann Riggs, Gilbert Stafford, eds., *Ancient Faith and American Born Churches* (New York: Paulist, 2006).

Response #2

Cecil M. Robeck Jr.

Letting the Riffraff In

DONALD W. Dayton must be numbered among the riffraff. For that matter, so must I. Riffraff are, of course, people that one might associate with flotsam and jetsam, or possibly even with flimflam. None of these nouns are particularly flattering. They aren't intended to be so. But depending upon where you sit, they may be thought to be accurate descriptions of those *beneath you*.

I suppose the most positive spin one can give a term like "riffraff" might be *hoi polloi* or *'am ha 'aretz*, references to ordinary people as over against the extraordinary ones. But Dayton did not give this term a positive spin. He meant it for what it was, a derogatory term. "Riffraff" are, after all, the disreputable types, "rabble-rousers." Just as flotsam refers to floating debris, jetsam refers to that which is expendable, and flimflam refers to some sort of fraud or deceiver, so "riffraff" are those who are thought to be disposable, even despicable. They don't really matter. To label a person "riffraff" is to make a statement regarding that person's class. It is a term for the other that is used by those who look down their noses.

As a Pentecostal, I know what it is like to be numbered among the "riffraff." The terms "riffraff" and "Holy Roller" have often been used as synonyms. Even Webster includes in the definition of "Holy Roller," reference to our worship services. They are "characterized by frenzied excitement—often taken to be offensive."[1] Offensive! I suppose that Pentecostal worship is offensive to some, but it is not offensive to other Pentecostals, because they understand it. And because I am a Pentecostal, I suspect that I am viewed as being offensive because I advocate such worship practices as dancing, or singing, or speaking in tongues while "in the Spirit." Being denigrated by other Christians has been a fact of life since the beginning

1. *Webster's New Collegiate Dictionary* (Springfield, MA: G. & C. Merriam, 1973) 547.

of the Pentecostal Movement, a fact shared by participants in the Holiness Movement from the mid-nineteenth century.

I can illustrate this quite easily by quoting the words of Dr. R. J. Burdette, the pastor of an upscale Baptist Church in Los Angeles. In a September 1906 sermon he criticized the worship of the Azusa Street Mission, the fountainhead of the revival that placed Pentecostals on the ecclesial map. His sermon made the local news. "They rant and dance and roll in a disgusting amalgamation of African voodoo superstition and Caucasian insanity," he charged, "and will pass away like the hysterical nightmares that they are."[2] "Hysterical nightmares," "riffraff," "offensive," and "disposable"—kind of like pond scum.

Eighty years later, when Dayton penned his article "Yet Another Layer of the Onion: or, Opening the Ecumenical Door to Let the Riffraff in," he did so knowing full well that his choice of words would likely offend someone. It did. After all, there were those among the "riffraff" who had been trying to shed their skins in such a way as to move beyond the stereotypes. For Pentecostals especially, that meant leaving behind the skin labeled "Holy Roller" and embracing a new, more sophisticated skin, that of "Evangelical." Those who had been most successful at becoming "Evangelicals" didn't like being reminded of their roots among the Pentecostal "riffraff." For some within the "Ecumenical" crowd, the offense was just as pointed. They thought of themselves as eminently inclusive—both liberal and open. They refused to acknowledge that they viewed certain Christians outside the ecumenical fold as "riffraff." Dayton contended, however, that while the accusations might not be made as directly as Dr. Burdette had articulated them, the attitudes behind them were still very much in place. Pentecostals were fine if they wanted to work on evangelism or mission, but they were not allowed to work in the field of theology with other Christians.

In 1987, Dayton took a sabbatical in Geneva, Switzerland, where he studied among the staff of the World Council of Churches. While he was there, he became increasingly aware of just how deeply the divide between certain "ecumenical" types, representatives of historic mainline churches, and the "riffraff", ran. It was while he reflected upon the historiographical and theological significance of the Holiness, Pentecostal, and Keswick movements within that context that he wrote this article.

---

2. From a sermon by Dr. R. J. Burdette, preached at Temple Baptist Church, Sunday, September 23, 1906, and published in "New Religions Come, Then Go," *Los Angeles Herald* (September 24, 1906) 7; Cf. "Denounces New Denominations," *Los Angeles Express* (September 24, 1906) 5.

Dayton recounted the history of the Holiness, Pentecostal and Keswick movements, looked at the ways they were traditionally treated historiographically, illustrated his concerns through discussions of their contributions to (1) social reform and (2) the role of women, and concluded with an assessment of the theological significance of what he had described. In the remainder of this contribution, I want to concentrate my thoughts on two or three of Dayton's points from my vantage point as a Pentecostal.

Relying upon the work of David Barrett and Walter Hollenweger,[3] Dayton noted the "sheer numbers" of the Pentecostal and related movements and interpreted their size relative to global Christianity. If anything the trends he pointed out have continued more rapidly than anticipated at that time. According to the figures Barrett released in January 2007, the total number of Christians in the world is 2,195,529,000. The largest church is the Roman Catholic Church, with 1,142,968,000 members. In second place is that group that Barrett has called the Pentecostal/Charismatics. According to him, they number 602,792,000.[4] The remainder would include all other Protestant, Anglican, and Orthodox believers. While I am fully aware of the criticisms that can be raised regarding these statistics, Dayton's point still remains.[5] Pentecostal and related churches are growing, while many historic churches have declined, some of them precipitously, though these facts are often masked.[6] In light of these developments Dayton's call to the churches is even stronger in 2007. The Church cannot afford to continue to ignore these vital movements. That being said, it continues to do so in a number of ways.

Dayton's critique of contemporary historiography in Church history is a case in point. He noted that one could find little more than "a few paragraphs about the Holiness Movement" in the two primary texts on

---

3. Walter J. Hollenweger, "After Twenty Years' Research on Pentecostalism," *Theology* 87 (1984) 403–12, reprinted in *International Review of Mission* 75, no. 297 (January, 1986) 3–12. A longer version of this paper appears as "Pentecostal Research in Europe: Problems, Promises and People" in the *EPTA Bulletin* 4:4 (1985) 124–53.

4. David B. Barrett, "Missiometrics 2007: Creating Your Own Analysis of Global Data," *International Bulletin of Missionary Research* 31:1 (January 2007), "Global Table 5: Status of global mission, presence and activities, AD 1800–2025," 32.

5. Allan Anderson, *An Introduction to Pentecostalism* (Cambridge, England: Cambridge University Press, 2004), 9–15.

6. Exceptions to this would include Harvey Cox, *Fire From Heaven: The Rise of Pentecostal Spirituality and the Reshaping of Religion in the Twenty-First Century* (New York: Addison-Wesley Publishing Company, 1995) and Philip Jenkins, *The Next Christendom: The Coming of Global Christianity* (New York, NY: Oxford University Press, 2002) 270.

American Church History at that time, Sydney Ahlstrom's *A Religious History of the American People* and Winthrop Hudson's *Religion in America*. The same could be said regarding Pentecostalism. New texts such as Mark Noll's *A History of Christianity in the United States and Canada* have joined these in recent years, but little headway has been made regarding Dayton's basic critique. These movements are typically ignored or treated as though they were somehow non-essential to our understanding of American religious history.

The problem grows more pronounced when we consider texts for a global course on Modern Church History. Justo Gonzalez's two volumes on *The Story of Christianity* promised much in its title, but delivered virtually nothing on Pentecostalism. And Glenn T. Miller, *The Modern Church: From the Dawn of the Reformation to the Eve of the Third Millennium*, ironically published by Abingdon Press, a Methodist company, is focused heavily on Europe and North America with virtually no treatment of Pentecostalism or related movements. It will be interesting to see the extent to which Dale Irvin's second volume on the *History of the World Christian Movement* will go to provide a much needed corrective to these lacunae.

The continued rise of globalization, secularization, and the emptying of mainline pews have gotten the attention of some ecumenists but old habits die hard. Dayton's article raised the consciousness of some in the World Council of Churches regarding the need to look at the "riffraff". Shortly after its publication, I was asked to become a Pentecostal advisor to the World Council of Churches' Commission on Faith and Order. I have served in that capacity ever since. Others continued to ignore his plea, and continued to rearrange the chairs on what could be described as a sinking ship.

Ultimately, Dayton and I were invited to participate in the Canberra Assembly in 1991, where we found ourselves playing roles that neither of us had anticipated. We were recruited to help formulate a way forward, drafting a number of points that were nearly all adopted by that Assembly.[7] The most significant recommendation was not passed at the Assembly but it was implemented within six months. It was the appointment of Huibert van Beek to fill an Office of Church and Ecumenical Relations, whose primary task was to develop relationships with Pentecostal and other non-WCC churches.[8]

---

7. Michael Kinnamon, ed., *Signs of the Spirit: Official Report, Seventh Assembly Canberra, Australia, 7–20 February 1991* (Geneva: WCC Publications/Grand Rapids: Eerdmans, 1991) 107–8.

8. The results of much of van Beek's hard work may be seen in the recent publica-

Dr. Konrad Raiser was elected General Secretary of the World Council of Churches at the Canberra Assembly. He would lead the Council through the closing decade of the 20th Century. As he watched the Pentecostal Movement continue to grow while many of the constituent churches of the World Council continued to decline, forcing the World Council to undertake a series of belt-tightening exercises, he encouraged the Council to seek a new "Common Understanding and Vision."[9] It was a painful exercise at best and the Council did not accept all of Raiser's recommendations. Ultimately his call to provide greater space for the participation of Holiness, Pentecostal, and Evangelical voices at the ecumenical table had to be taken outside the Council. The result is a new initiative, the Global Christian Forum, which will make its debut in November 2007 in Nairobi, Kenya.

Through the years, Donald W. Dayton has been a scholar who has called things as he has seen, and at times, experienced them. He loves the Church, he understands the churches, and he knows what it is like to be considered "riffraff". But his willingness to assess the situation forthrightly as he did in this ground-breaking article, his eagerness to break down artificial walls between Christians, and his unselfish ability to link new conversation partners thereby opening up new opportunities to explore across previously foreign territory, have each contributed to his value as *the* pre-eminent Holiness ecumenist.[10]

---

tion, Huibert van Beek, ed., *A Handbook of Churches and Councils: Profiles of Ecumenical Relationships* (Geneva: WCC, 2006).

9. Cecil M. Robeck, Jr., "A Pentecostal Assessment of 'Towards a Common Understanding and Vision' of the WCC," *Midstream: The Ecumenical Movement* 37:1 (January 1998) 1–36.

10. Cecil M. Robeck, Jr. is Professor of Church History and Ecumenics and Director of the David du Plessis Center for Christian Spirituality at Fuller Theological Seminary in Pasadena, CA. An ordained minister in the Assemblies of God, he and Don have worked together on various historical and ecumenical projects for over 30 years.

11
Interpreting Karl Barth

Dayton has been a member of the executive committee and board of directors of the Karl Barth Society of North America since its founding in 1972. He has published several articles on Barth, one of which is reprinted here. This essay was originally given as a paper at a conference hosted by the Unification Church in its efforts to foster interfaith dialogue. The text was first published in Peter Phan, ed., *Christianity and the Wider Ecumenism* (New York: Paragon House, 1990) 181–89.

Karl Barth and the Wider Ecumenism

Donald W. Dayton

KARL Barth, it may be argued, towers above twentieth-century Protestant theology and has had a pervasive influence far beyond the boundaries of Protestantism. Even those who have sought to evade his influence and articulate alternative positions have quite often had to do that in direct dialogue with him. This is perhaps especially true with regard to Barth's position on the question of the relationship of Christianity to the other religions of the world—the issue of "the wider ecumenism." Barth's position is often interpreted through its popularization by Dutch missiologist Hendrick Kraemer in *The Christian Message in a Non-Christian World*, a volume prepared for the Tambaran Conference of what has since become the Commission on World Mission and Evangelism of the World Council of Churches.[1] In this volume, largely rooted in Barth but qualified by a slight dose of Emil Brunner, Kraemer stressed Barth's contrast between revelation and religion to argue that the "true religion" is to be found "only in God's revelation in Jesus Christ" and that other faiths are "all in error."

More recent treatments of this question have taken Barth as the primary illustration of an "exclusivist" position to be avoided in the search for a more positive Christian attitude toward the world's religions. Thus Alan Race, in *Christians and Religious Pluralism: Patterns in the Christian Theology of Religions*, develops a tripartite typology in terms of "exclusivism," "inclusivism," and "pluralism."[2] In elaborating this typology Race takes Barth's thought to represent "the most extreme form of the exclusive theory." Similarly Roman Catholic Paul F. Knitter in *No Other Names?* has taken Barth as his primary example of the "conservative evangelical" position of exclusivistic "Christocentrism" to be overcome by his own proposal of a "theocentric Christology" more amenable to dialogue with other reli-

---

1. Hendrick Kraemer, *The Christian Message in a Non-Christian World* (London: 1938).

2. Alan Race, *Christians and Religious Pluralism: Patterns in Christian Theology of Religions* (Maryknoll, NY: Orbis, 1982).

gions.³ Knitter offers a more extended analysis of Barth in his earlier (1972) doctoral dissertation at Marburg published as *Toward a Protestant Theology of Religions*, a study of the work of German Protestant theologian Paul Althaus on this question.⁴ In this volume Knitter follows Althaus in using Barth and Troeltsch to mark out the "Scylla and Charybdis for any Christian theology of the religions" (37). Knitter accepts the label of Althaus to describe Barth's position as "Christomonist"—a "narrow, restrictive, exclusive understanding of the reality of Christ, which bans all extra-Christian reality into the realm of meaninglessness and godlessness" (23).

I will make no effort to minimize the exclusivistic tendencies that follow from Barth's "Christocentric concentration" in both the method and the content of his theology, but I do think that these readings of Barth are remarkably unsympathetic to his fundamental intention and fail to grasp some of the countervailing themes in Barth that do provide some basis for a greater engagement with non-Christian religions than these interpretations imply. I am especially intrigued that Knitter would use Barth as an example of the "conservative evangelical" approach to the world religions because such "conservative evangelicals" have always been troubled by Barth's "universalistic tendencies" that have seemed to them to erode any real need for the revelation in Christ. Thus I will explore three themes in Barth that seem to me to qualify the reading given above: (1) the extent to which Barth's condemnation of "religion" includes the "Christian religion" and from one angle at least thereby puts all the world's religions on the same level—and that the resulting subtle dialectical character of Barth's thought on this question is often insufficiently grasped by his critics; (2) the extent to which Barth's Christology is revelationally "exclusivistic" but soteriologically "inclusivistic" and "universalistic"; and (3) Barth's late statement on the issue in his articulation of the relation of "the Light and the lights" in such a way as to allow something less than the total condemnation of all religious experience outside of Christ.

The Abolition of Religion

The key text that has been repeatedly used to understand Barth's attitude toward non-Christian religions is paragraph seventeen (eighty-one pages, but usually designated as a "paragraph" in the structure of Barth's work) in the *Church Dogmatics* entitled in the English translation "The Abolition of Religion." As Herbert Hartwell points out in *The Theology of Karl Barth: An*

---

3. Paul F. Knitter, *No Other Names* (Maryknoll, NY: Orbis, 1985).
4. Paul F. Knitter, *Towards a Protestant Theology of Religions* (Marburg: Elwert, 1974).

Intruduction,[5] this is in many ways an unfortunate translation that misses precisely the ambiguity and dialectic that is present in this section. The word translated as "abolition" is the German *Aufhebung*, a notoriously difficult word to render into English (as has been illustrated in Hegel studies and elsewhere). Hartwell suggests that the title should be rendered "The Abolition and the Exaltation of Religion" because both ideas are present in the section; and Barth is deliberately playing on the ambiguity in the German word.

Barth is notoriously difficult to interpret—among other reasons because of the dialectical character of his thought in which what appears to be stated absolutely at one point will be qualified later in a manner difficult to reconcile with the first point. This is especially true in this paragraph. The three subsections of the paragraph are entitled (1) "The Problem of Religion in Theology," (2) "Religion as Unbelief," and (3) "True Religion." Some interpreters, in addition to missing the dialectic of this paragraph, have also failed to grasp the precise nature of the contrast that Barth is making between "religion as unbelief" and "true religion." In the first place this contrast is not primarily between Christianity and the non-Christian religions. Barth is struggling with the nineteenth-century tendency to interpret *Christianity* in anthropocentric and naturalistic terms and in light of a common human "religious" orientation or *a priori*. Barth's answer to this tendency was to emphasize revelation and the movement from above to below in such a way as to block all movement from below to above. The contrast in this paragraph is thus first of all between "revelation" given from above by the Living God as active subject and "religion" as human achievement and self-justification.

Barth is quite explicit that his condemnation of religion includes from at least one angle Christianity as well as other forms of religious life and activity. At this point Barth is a good Calvinist, understanding the human mind, and even the Christian mind, as an active *fabrica idolorum*. Barth's primary concern is to attack self-justificatory and idolatrous forms of the Christian "religion" rather than the non-Christian religions, though it is true that for Barth they regularly fall under the same condemnation. When Barth takes up the discussion of "true religion," he is quite clear about this point:

> In our discussion of "religion as unbelief" we did not consider the distinction between Christian and non-Christian religion. Our

---

5. Herbert Hartwell, *The Theology of Karl Barth: An Introduction* (London: Duckworth, 1964).

> intention was that whatever we said about the other religions affected the Christian similarly. . . . Therefore the discussion cannot be understood as a preliminary polemic against the non-Christian religions, with a view to the ultimate assertion that the Christian Religion is the true religion.[6]
>
> On the contrary, it is our business as Christians to apply this judgment first and most acutely to ourselves: and to others, the non-Christians, only in so far as we recognize ourselves in them.[7]

Now of course it is true that when Barth turns to unfold the character of "revelation," it is seen primarily and perhaps even exclusively (carefully here—at least from one angle of the dialectic!) in Jesus Christ. It is here that the usual reading of Barth has its most validity. Christian "religion" can become "true religion" as it is grasped by grace and becomes subject to the revelation in Jesus Christ. Here Barth is "radicalizing" and "actualizing" the Reformation doctrine of justification by faith in response to Divine initiative in such a way as to undercut any form of human initiative or *analogia entis* that can move toward God "from below."

But this radical subjection to the revelation in Jesus Christ is not the whole story or, as we shall see, all that Barth has to say on these questions. This conceptual framework puts the religions (including in some sense the "Christian religion" as well) on the same level as all other forms of human insight, including philosophy, natural theology, culture in general, and so on. It is generally assumed that Barth has no place for any of these, but Barth clearly does not operate on this assumption—as is evidenced by his wide reading and use in his *Dogmatics* of philosophy, history, social science, etc. What Barth takes away with one hand he gives back with the other. The issue is at what point these human achievements are brought into play and whether they are ruled by revelation in Jesus Christ. Thus philosophy or natural theology are wrong as starting points or as a place from which to launch a human movement of self-justification toward God, but they may be caught up in the *Aufhebung* and find themselves (or at least fragments of their insights) in the service of revelation. Thus in theory, at least, there could be, I believe, some role in Barth for the insights of the other religions and their dialogue with Christianity—if they do not presume to replace "revelation" and are brought into subjection to the Living God as revealed in Jesus Christ. But we shall have to explore this theme further, later where Barth takes it up most explicitly.

---

6. Karl Barth, *Church Dogmatics* I/2 (Edinburgh: T. & T. Clark, 1958) 326.
7. Ibid., 327.

Barth's Soteriological Universalism

Those who interpret Barth through his particularism and revelational exclusivism sometimes fail to notice or give adequate weight to the countervailing "universalistic" themes that so often bother "traditionalists." In so doing, such interpreters miss one of the most innovative sides of Barth and the unusual dialectical relationship in his thought between the particular and the universal. While the usual tendency of the modern study of religion is to seek a "universal" perspective by the qualification and relativizing of the particular, Barth on the other hand moves to the universal through the particular. This move is especially clear in volume four of the *Church Dogmatics* where Barth develops a cosmic Christology and a soteriology that is strongly "universalistic."

It is beyond the limits of this essay to expound the full shape and originating motives of Barth's Christology. Suffice it to say that Barth is concerned to avoid the tendency of the "infralapsarian" theologies to make the incarnation a contingent response to human sin. His theology is radically "supralapsarian" in that he makes the incarnation and Christology part of the basic intention of God. This move binds creation intimately to redemption and makes Christ both the "Creator" and the "Redeemer" in a profound sense. Creation is the arena of redemption from the beginning, and redemption is not an after-thought in response to human sin. From this orientation many of the distinctive themes of Barth follow naturally—particularly those themes that make his a radically "inclusive" and "universal" Christology.

Thus in volume four of the *Church Dogmatics* Barth is concerned to argue that the covenant of God with Israel from the beginning has a universal dimension and intention that not only is revealed in Jesus Christ but includes the whole human family. In Barth's view the fundamental reality that defines all human life is the actual and effective justification, sanctification, and vocation of all humankind. Though not all live according to this reality none can escape it and fall out of the hand of God. The church in this context—and ontologically true for the whole human race—believes that God has bound himself to humankind in an everlasting covenant. When combined with other themes in Barth (especially in his doctrine of creation that the sexual bipolarity is a testimony that from the beginning humankind is created to be in fellowship and in his ecclesiology that the existence of the church takes precedence over the faith of the individual) these claims move toward a radical doctrine of human solidarity.

We sometimes forget that Barth's theology was forged in the midst of the Nazi threat and fail to see the extent to which the fundamental thrust of his theology is toward forms of human solidarity that were denied by Hitler. This is true especially in the more restricted sense that his theology so binds Jew and Christian together that any form of anti-Semitism, for example, must become self-denigration. Similarly his theology binds all humankind together in a radical solidarity. It is true that this solidarity is defined Christologically—again partially in response to the German Christians' tendency to give the state a certain autonomy rooted in creation outside the Christological determination. This Christocentric focus may be offensive to advocates of other religious, but it should be clearly recognized that it is an "inclusive" and "universal" Christology aiming for a radical human solidarity rather than an "exclusive" Christology that rules out non-Christians and divides the human race ultimately and finally into the "saved" and the "lost." Here, of course, is the offense to more traditional theologies and the major reason that Barth should not be classed as a representative of the "exclusive Christology" of the "conservative evangelicals."

The Light and the Lights

One of the more difficult questions in Barth is whether to discern a fundamental shift between his earlier and his later work. We cannot resolve this question fully here. Those that do find a major shift notice a change in metaphors from the early work (especially his controversial commentary on Paul's epistle to the Romans) where he tended to speak of God as the "wholly other" and revelation as the "tangent" to the circle which has no integral relationship to the world of human experience and can only create the crater left by its impact to a later, more incarnational vision that finds expression in the "inclusive" Christology that we have developed above. This vision is one in which all of reality seems to be lifted up into Christ in such a way that there is a fundamental affirmation of human reality, at least as it is determined by Christ. Barth himself reflected a little on this question of change in an essay entitled "The Humanity of God." There he suggested that he could only utter the "yes" after the "no" had been clearly established. This seems to support the reading that we have given above that much depends on when human experience is brought to bear and for what purposes. For Barth, such human effort can never be salvific, but once that issue is clear and efforts at self-justification are undercut, Barth can gather insights, metaphors, and visions from almost any source.

This issue of fundamental change in Barth has also been debated in terms of his attitude toward the non-Christian religions. Paul Knitter describes the debate up to the publication of his dissertation in an excursus on "Did Barth Change his Verdict on the Religions?" He sides with those who maintain that Barth's position on the religions remains fundamentally unchanged.[8] A few years after the publication in 1974 of Knitter's dissertation, the question was taken up in the annual "Leuenberg" (a retreat center outside Basel) meeting of Barth scholars. The lectures by Dutch theologians Hendrik Berkhof and Hans-Joachim Kraus, and an Old Testament scholar who has moved to occupy the chair of theology that Barth once held at Göttingen, were published in *Theologische Studien* under the title *Karl Barths Lichterlehre*.[9] Here the issue is whether by contrast with the position in paragraph seventeen of the *Church Dogmatics* on the "Abolition of Religion" the elaboration of the third Christological theme in paragraph sixty-nine on Jesus Christ as the "Light of the World" reveals a new openness to the non-Christian religions. This issue is often debated in terms of the relationship between the "Light and the Lights."

Paragraph sixty-nine is found in volume IV/3 of the *Church Dogmatics* where Barth deals with the "prophetic" office of Christ—one that brings to the fore the role of Christ as "revealer" or as "the Light of Life." Here we find parallels to many earlier points. Barth's use of rhetoric lends itself to "exclusivisitic" interpretations:

> Jesus Christ is *the* light of life. To underline the "the" is to say that He is the one and only light of life. Positively this means that he is the light of life in all its fullness, in perfect adequacy; and negatively it means that there is no other light of life outside or alongside His, outside or alongside the light which He is.[10]

Barth also makes the point quite clearly that we indicated above—that Christian experience and truth is also brought under judgment along with all other forms of truth:

> Thus the criticism expressed in the exclusiveness of the statement affects, limits, and relativizes the prophecy of Christians no less than the many other prophecies, lights, and words relativized and replaced by it. . . . What it says concerning the importance of all other prophecy which attempts to rival its own is valid only in

---

8. Knitter, *Towards a Protestant Theology of Religions*, 32–36.

9. Henrik Berkhof and Hans-Joachim Kraus, *Karl Barths' Lichterlehre*, Theologishe Studien 123 (Zürich: Theologischer Verlag, 1978).

10. *Church Dogmatics* IV/3, pt. 1 (Edinburgh: T&T Clark, 1961) 86.

> analogy to, and a consequence of, that fact that first and supremely it is true of the Christian sphere.[11]

But Barth also quite explicitly in this section affirms the other side of the dialectic to say quite clearly that there are other words to which we should attend:

> We recognize that the fact that Jesus Christ is the one Word of God does not mean that in the Bible, the Church and the world there are not other words which are quite notable in their way, other lights which are quite clear and other revelations which are quite real. . . . Nor does it follow from our statement that every word spoken outside the circle of the Bible and the Church is a word of false prophecy and therefore valueless, empty and corrupt, that all the lights which rise and shine in the outer sphere are misleading and all the revelations are necessarily untrue.[12]

Barth then goes on to say that the issue is whether these lights are to be put on the same level as the one Word of God in Christ. The "lights" must not displace, transcend, or attempt to encompass the one "Light." But in their proper place they may function as true and real lights. Barth can make this move in part because of the role of Christ in creation and the way in which Creation and Redemption are unified in Christ. But the result is that there are other "lights" in the world that can also be genuinely called "lights" and genuinely reveal and inform—as long as they do not replace the "Light." Here we see quite clearly the other side of the dialectic expressed in the difficult translation of *Aufhebung* cited above in the section on "The Abolition of Religion." Here Barth quite explicitly uses the positive language of "exaltation":

> . . . they are taken, lifted, assumed and integrated into the action of God's self-giving and self-declaring to man and therefore to the world made by him. And in the power of this integration they are instituted, installed, and ordained to the *ministerium Verbi Divini*.[13]

The genuine dialectic in Barth is expressed quite clearly in the final lines of the section:

> This . . . is the critical, but also, since it is genuinely critical, the positive relationship of the light of life to the lights which the God

---

11. Ibid., 91.
12. Ibid., 97.
13. Ibid., 164.

whose saving action is revealed by the one light does not withhold from his creatures as such but gives them in His eternal goodness.[14]

The results of this study are modest. We have not challenged directly Barth's own Christotogical exclusivism. We have merely argued that he is often misunderstood—that his thought is more subtle and dialectical than is often assumed. I am not sure that Barth himself would have developed his own thought in the direction of dialogue with other religions (indeed, there are signs and incidents that indicate that he did not have much personal interest in these questions), but I do think that it is possible on Barthian premises to have more engagement with other religions than is usually assumed. This is to be sure a modest place, but I believe it to be a valuable place nonetheless.

---

14. Ibid., 164–65.

Response #1

Christian T. Collins Winn

In December 1998, I was privileged to attend the eighth assembly of the World Council of Churches in Harare, Zimbabwe, as part of the WCC sponsored seminarians program. It was in this context that I first met Donald Dayton. I was concluding my final year of study at Gordon-Conwell Theological Seminary and preparing to enter the doctoral program at Boston University to study liturgical theology. My encounter with Dayton altered those plans.

For a student coming from an evangelical context, Harare would prove to be eye-opening. Though involved in the ecumenical work of the Boston Theological Institute for the previous year—it was BTI director Rodney Petersen who actually introduced me to Don—my experience in Harare forced me to take even more seriously the myriad forms of Christianity in all their diversity and complexity, both liturgical and theological. Dayton, present as a representative of the Wesleyan Theological Society and as an observer of the Evangelical Caucus at the Assembly, immediately took me under his wing, giving me the "inside scoop" on the ecclesiastical and theological politics at play at Harare. His guidance through the ecclesiastical and theological issues at play in the ecumenical setting was illuminating and in many respects decisive in shaping my understanding of the ecumenical movement.

Dayton and I spent a number of nights talking about the ecumenical movement, contemporary evangelicalism and especially theology. We took a couple of "field trips" out into the countryside around Harare to experience the phenomenon of an African Independent Church. These experiences were the highlight of my time in Harare. I can especially remember Dayton's insightful observation during one of the services that the Deaconess who prophesied while leading our worship was being empowered to lead the community, a role that would have been counter-cultural in the context of African patriarchy. Little did I know at the time, but the connection between religious belief and practice and social liberation were one of the consistent themes of Dayton's work.

It was, however, Dayton's knowledge and facility with the theology of Karl Barth that would prove to be the most captivating dimension of our discussions at Harare. I knew at the time that I wanted to do doctoral work on some aspect of Barth, but had not narrowed my focus. Dayton's penetrating questions and observations about Barth eventually led us to a discussion of the little known Württemberg Pietists, Johann Christoph and Christoph Friedrich Blumhardt, and their influence on Barth. Dayton suggested I explore the relationship as a topic and that I consider applying to Drew University for the doctoral program to work with him. Upon return to the United States I subsequently did both of those, writing my final seminary theology paper on the influence of the Blumhardts on Barth and applying to the Drew theology program. Under Dayton's careful tutelage I reconceived and expanded that short, poorly written and deeply naïve seminary paper into my doctoral dissertation.[1]

I recount my early history with Dayton because it highlights the fact that my introduction to his thought was not through his ground-breaking work on neo-evangelicalism, Pentecostalism or the Holiness movement. Nor did I come to know him first as an advocate of Pietism, Anabaptism or the thought of John Howard Yoder. Nor was it his work on radical politics and the social progressivism of nineteenth-century evangelicalism. I came to know and appreciate all of these elements after the fact. Rather, I came to know him initially, as it were, through a side door. That's not to suggest that Barth's theology is simply a side issue for Dayton. To the contrary, I have come to find that Dayton's own theological perspective is as deeply shaped by the thought of Barth and Kierkegaard as by Wesley, a fact that is of considerable consternation to some.

Despite the differences between the theology of Wesley and the Holiness movement and Karl Barth, an element of continuity in Dayton's approach to the former can be discerned in his interpretation of the latter. The element of continuity of which I speak is Dayton's characteristic way of offering alternative, even counter-intuitive ways of reading that turn out to be extraordinarily insightful. As in his reinterpretation of the historiography of modern evangelicalism, Dayton has also advocated alternative ways of reading Barth. The current essay, "Karl Barth and the Wider Ecumenism" is just one such example. That Barth's theology might provide a foundation for a genuinely dialogical theology of religions is indeed counter-intuitive yet filled with promise. Another alternative reading that Dayton has been advocating since the 1980's has been to suggest that

---

1. *"Jesus is Victor!" The Significance of the Blumhardts for the Theology of Karl Barth* (Eugene, OR: Pickwick, forthcoming 2007).

Barth's relationship to Pietism needs to be reexamined. The widespread assumption among Anglo-American scholars is that Barth viewed Pietism in almost wholly negative terms, placing it alongside Schleiermacher and other developments originating out of the Enlightenment, forming a kind of unholy trinity. Dayton, inspired by the work of Eberhard Busch and his own study of Barth's work, has argued against this reading, placing in its stead the argument that Barth's relationship to Pietism ought to be construed as not primarily adversarial, but rather as a dialectical relationship of criticism and appropriation.[2] One can see this thesis at work in his essay, "The Pietist Theological Critique of Biblical Inerrancy," included in this volume, where he identifies Barth as in the line of Pietistic "biblicism" over against the "inerrantist" tradition of Protestant Orthodoxy.

Dayton first shared this thesis with me as we traveled around Germany and Switzerland during a summer study tour in 2000. Dayton took me to Germany to do some initial reconnaissance work for my dissertation on the Blumhardts and Barth, but while we were there two events opened me up to Dayton's outrageous suggestion that Barth might actually be favorably disposed to aspects of Pietism. The first was when we met with Eberhard Busch at his home and discussed his work on Barth's early relationship to Pietism. As we talked Busch revealed that his important study on Barth's early reception and response to the *Gemeinschaftsbewegung*, *Karl Barth und die Pietisten*,[3] was supposed to be followed up by a second study, being pursued by another scholar, that would have traced Barth's relationship to Pietism as his thought and work matured. Unfortunately, this study was never completed, though Busch himself did write a lengthy essay, "Hoffnung auf Umkehr der Bekehrten: Karl Barth und der Pietismus," exploring the overall shifts in Barth's relationship to Pietism and its theological themes. Through our conversations with Busch, we were able to see to it that this essay was integrated into the English edition of *Karl Barth and the Pietists* as an epilogue.[4]

Our discussions with Busch were a revelation, because they not only confirmed the thesis that Dayton had been presenting to me, but they also revealed that Busch, one of the leading European Barth scholars,

---

2. See Donald W. Dayton, "Foreword," in Eberhard Busch, *Karl Barth and the Pietists: The Young Karl Barth's Critique of Pietism & Its Response* (Downers Grove, IL: InterVarsity, 2004), trans. by Daniel W. Bloesch, ix–xii.

3. Originally published in 1978, this book was recently published in English as *Karl Barth and the Pietists: The Young Karl Barth's Critique of Pietism & Its Response*. See note 2 above.

4. See *Karl Barth and the Pietists*, 286–316.

was convinced that Barth's conception of and relationship to Pietism had shifted over time, and that his later engagement with Pietists and with the theological themes of Pietism was far more positive than has normally been recognized. In his later essay, "Hoffnung auf Umkehr der Bekehrten: Karl Barth und der Pietismus," Busch went so far as to describe Barth as a "critical friend or friendly critic," of Pietism, rather than its outright enemy.[5]

The second event that further opened me to Dayton's thesis occurred during our visit to the Barth archives in Basel, Switzerland. While there, we were given a tour of Barth's library and to our great surprise, we found that Barth had an enormous collection of Pietist sources. Dayton himself was rather surprised at the size of Barth's collection. The sheer amount and range of sources in the library indicated that Barth was far more interested in the themes of Pietism than I had previously thought, further indicating that the arguments that Busch and Dayton were making were not only plausible but probable.

Neither of these events were a kind of smoking gun, proving Dayton's thesis beyond a shadow of a doubt. At the same time, however, they were certainly intriguing to me and during my own research I found the thesis that Barth's relationship to Pietism was more deeply positive than his criticisms seemed to imply, to be very illuminating for understanding many of the dynamics at work in Barth's appropriation of the eschatology of the Blumhardts. Furthermore, through my study of the Blumhardts and the Württemberg tradition of Pietism, I have come to have a far more positive understanding of the nature and promise of the themes and dynamics of Pietism. Through this new understanding, due in large measure to Dayton's guidance and influence, I have also begun to see a deeper connection between Dayton's arguments about Barth and Pietism and his concerns about contemporary evangelicalism, which raises very important questions about the importance of Barth's theology for contemporary evangelicalism.

A major element in Dayton's project of re-conceiving evangelicalism is his attempt to re-connect it with Pietism. For a variety of historical and theological reasons, it has becoming increasingly clear that the real roots of nineteenth-century evangelicalism do not lie in Protestant Orthodoxy, but rather in Pietism. If it can be shown that many of Barth's key theological concerns are rooted, to some extent, in the dynamics of certain forms of Pietism, then this means that contemporary evangelicals, whose own roots are to be found in Pietism, have far more in common with Barth and are of a different variety than has been traditionally thought.

---

5. Ibid., 286.

Dayton argued for this thesis in outline form in an important essay entitled, "Karl Barth and Evangelicalism: The Varieties of Sibling Rivalry,"[6] but it has largely been ignored both by evangelicals and Barth scholars.[7] Like his groundbreaking work on evangelicalism, the ideas that Dayton puts forward in this article may have to wait for a hearing in the larger academy. But just as recent interpreters of evangelicalism have finally begun to "catch up" by beginning to integrate Dayton's theses about the Pietist origins of evangelicalism into the historiography of evangelicalism I also believe that scholars interested in bringing Barth into a closer dialogue with evangelicalism will have to "catch up" with Dayton if they want to get at the very real and deep connections to be found there. I believe time will vindicate Dayton in this matter, just as he has been vindicated in a number of his other "crack-pot" theories and theses.

Dayton's scholarly work is under-girded by a deep and genuine conviction that the particular theological and ecclesial traditions he is either arguing for or against have unique contributions to make to the wider Christian community. This concern is incarnated in his willingness to rethink the long-held assumptions of the scholarly guild, in the hope of freeing up particular communities and traditions to witness to the living Christ through the gifts they have been given by the one Spirit. Underneath the polemics and critiques, therefore, is a commitment—shared with Barth, the Pietists before him, and many contemporary evangelicals—to critique the church for the sake of the church. In this we owe a debt of gratitude and should be profoundly thankful, celebrating his work as an exercise in faith, hope and love. As this volume attests, there are many who have come to the same conclusion.

---

6. See Dayton, "Karl Barth and Evangelicalism," in the select bibliography at the end of this volume.

7. The general ignorance of Dayton's thesis was recently highlighted by the Princeton Theological Seminary Center for Barth Studies second annual conference "Karl Barth and American Evangelicals: Friends or Foes?" The conference organizers show no knowledge either of Dayton's work on this question, nor of the broader line of inquiry that his thesis opens up for the relationship of Karl Barth and evangelicalism.

Response #2

James S. Nelson

Karl Barth and the Wider Ecumenism

DONALD Dayton has been active in Barth Studies and the Karl Barth Society for many years. It was reading Søren Kierkegaard and Karl Barth's theology that led him back to the Christian faith, showing that good theology is an effective way to the credibility and truth of the Christian faith. Of course, the reading of Christian theology has different effects on people. For Dayton, I believe, there were certain themes and emphases that had a convincing power relevant to him. Of primary emphasis is the power of revelation to transform reality and critique the religious aspirations and behavior of humans. Deliverance from the subjectivity of experience to the formation of life in its entirety brought the personal and the social together in intelligible and transforming power. Barth's vision was not only commanding but also rich in theological meaning for an evangelical faith not hidebound to a dead orthodoxy. The creative thrust of Barth's theology, fresh and lively, deep in profundity, universal in scope and centered in Jesus Christ, was needed to counteract the superficialities and aridities of the theological fare offered for much of the twentieth century.

The essay before us is concerned to show that Karl Barth's understanding of the Christian faith, while centered in Christ, is not narrow or exclusive so as to limit God to a Christological focus, thus limiting it in relation to other religions and truths. A careful reading of the multivolume *Church Dogmatics* will find that, as Dayton states, what Barth takes away with one hand he gives back with the other in certain areas of Christian truth. Though it is true to say that Barth's theology is centered in Jesus Christ, this does not take away from a universal emphasis that sees all reality in Christ and transformed. How this is accomplished is to see that God's humanity in Christ brings solidarity with the human and all creation, so as to bring Creation and Redemption together. This Christological universalism is contrary to a certain understanding of orthodoxy where God in Christ is united to humans by faith, so that without this participation humans are bereft of God and the redemption in Christ until they, so to speak, bring down Christ into one's life for the experience of salvation. For Barth it is not true to say that all persons will be saved through his understanding of the universality of Christ in solidarity with all humans, as this is to deny the freedom of God in his sovereignty and grace. Such is Barth's understanding of the atonement in Christ that the power of redemption is resident in all humans, as all are elect in Christ, as Christ is the elected one of God to be the savior of all peoples who have lived or will live. The agency of human choice, by faith, to appropriate the redemption in Christ is necessary for salvation. While this view is basic to the whole of Barth's theology, its application to the wider ecumenism as Dayton understands it has to be further explicated and developed.

In a subsection entitled "The Light of Life" in *Church Dogmatics*, IV/3, Barth speaks of other words or lights. Dayton quotes a passage, which follows:

> We recognize that the fact that Christ is the one Word of God does not mean that in the Bible, the Church and the world there are not other words which are quite notable in their way, other lights which are quite clear and other revelations which are quite real . . . Nor does it follow from our statement that every word spoken outside the circle of the Bible and the Church is a word of false prophecy and therefore valueless, empty and corrupt, that all the lights which rise and shine in the outer sphere are misleading and all the revelations are necessarily untrue.[1]

Dayton use quotes such as this and others to deny, as many would have it, that Barth's theology is exclusivist in regards to the knowledge of God, salvation, and the truth in other religions. While it is true that for Barth Jesus Christ is the one Word of God, it is not true that other words and lights are of no value in Christian theology and knowledge of God. Dayton even suggests that out of Barth's theology there can arise significant dialogue with other religions, which is partly what he means by the wider ecumenism. Though Barth does not develop this, except by a brief discussion of Pure Land Buddhism and grace, it is still difficult to know what to do with this aspect of Barth. Some even talk about a new natural theology coming out of God. A very suggestive statement, coming from Thomas F. Torrance, in an article, "My Interaction with Karl Barth," which is also

---

1. Karl Barth, *Church Dogmatics* IV/3.1 (Edinburgh: T. & T. Clark, 1961) 97.

a key to Torrance's theology, especially relating to Science and Religion is the following:

> Since it is within this universe of space and time that God has revealed himself to us, and his Word who is the creative Source of all rational order within it has become incarnate, I had to believe that there is a profound consonance between the intelligibilities of divine revelation and the intelligibilities of the created universe. Without taking that consonance into account I did not believe we could offer a faithful account of knowledge of God as he has actually made himself known to us.[2]

The implications of this statement have profound entailments for the religion and science integration and natural theology, at least as Torrance envisions them. While Barth does not develop these implications, there do seem materials here in Barth's theology for the possibility of relating secular knowledge and even religious truth and experience from other religions to Christian theology. In this sense, Dayton is right to project the thesis of a wider ecumenism out of Barth's theology relevant to the issues and problems on the agenda today regarding religious pluralism and discussion with the religions of the world. In this, Dayton's creative working with a tradition and its issues for Christian transformation and prophetic thrusts is of scholarly value and significant for Christian living. We can be thankful that he has done this in other areas of Christian thought and history, as this volume in appreciation will show.

---

2. In *Karl Barth: Biblical and Evangelical Theologian* (Edinburgh: T. & T. Clark, 1990) 125.

12

Re-Interpreting Christianity in Korea

In recent years Dayton has become more and more fascinated with the nature and development of Korean Christianity. Dayton has taught and lectured at several different institutions in Korea and has overseen the work of a number of Korean scholars. His fascination with Korean Christianity is due in part to the deep influence that Methodism and the Holiness Movement have had on Christianity in Korea. This essay was originally given in different forms in 2004 and 2005 and later published in Korean.

The Four–Fold Gospel
Key to Trans–Pacific Continuities

Donald W. Dayton

I am honored to be with you and have the chance to address you. Korea is becoming increasingly an important nation economically and politically and a leader in the Christian world as well. I admire the energy and devotion of Korean Christianity—and especially the increasing commitment to the work of theology. It seems that every day I discover a new theological journal, a new book of significance, or a new emerging scholar who deserves wider attention. I expect that in the next generation Koreans will have much greater influence in the global theological world. If so it becomes all the more important that we cultivate "transpacific" dialogue and explore the relationships between Christians on the "Pacific Rim." The health and vitality of Christianity may depend upon it—and am delighted to have the opportunity to participate in this emerging theological work.

Today I would like to explore the "fourfold gospel" as a key to understanding the relationship between Korean Christianity and American "evangelicalism." As you know, the "fourfold gospel" (a description of the Christian message that emphasizes the themes of Jesus as Savior, Sanctifier, Healer and Coming King) plays a crucial role in the Holiness churches in Korea (and Japan, for that matter). It is less dominant in the United States, where it is identified primarily with The Christian and Missionary Alliance whose founder A. B. Simpson is often credited with coining the expression. Those who have inherited this expression are sometimes puzzled by what to make of it. It is sometimes dismissed by such persons as an "evangelistic slogan" that is of little help in scholarly and academic work that emerges as such churches mature and enter wider theological worlds and ecumenical currents. I, on the other hand, am increasingly convinced it is more theologically useful than is usually assumed. It is that case that I would like to argue today.

The Origins of the "Four–Fold Gospel"

As I have suggested, the "four-fold gospel" is often associated with the work of A. B. Simpson, the founder of the Christian and Missionary Alliance. But actually the pattern of speaking is much wider and comes out of the heart of the Holiness movement itself. Classical Methodism and the "mainstream Holiness movement" that began to emerge in the 1830s under the influence of Phoebe Palmer had in effect a "two-fold gospel" that emphasized the puritan/pietist doctrine of the "new birth" and a subsequent experience of "entire sanctification" or "perfect love"—the notorious "second blessing" of the Wesleyan tradition. In the last third of the nineteenth century the Holiness movement was troubled by new currents that were controversial and tended to split the Holiness movement into parties depending on whether such doctrines were to be accepted. Two such doctrines are of particular importance: the rise of the "faith healing movement" and the increasing impact of "premillennialism" (and especially "dispensational premillennialism").

The former movement had its roots in Europe. A Boston physician Charles Cullis made a grand tour of Europe and put together the "faith work" principles that had their roots in the Halle Pietism of August Hermann Francke that had been mediated to England by the ministry of George Muller in his Bristol orphanage and the emerging discussions in the German-world of the interrelationship between faith and health that had taken place in the wake of an event of "exorcism" under the ministries of the Blumhardts, father and son. Episcopalian Cullis had fallen under the influence of the Holiness movement and after experiencing sanctification began to explore whether the grace of God which he felt had saved him from the "guilt of sin" (Jesus as Savior) and the "power of sin" (Jesus as Sanctifier) could save him from the "effects of sin," especially disease (Jesus as Healer). Cullis became the teacher of Simpson on this theme, and the emerging "faith healing" movement had great influence in the broader "evangelical" movement, especially in the Holiness movement where it had been birthed but also in the emerging Pentecostal movement where it became a pervasive theme.

At the same time another movement emerged under the influence of John Nelson Darby who had become disillusioned with the Christian culture of the British Isles and in the Church of England. Darby was a major figure in the founding of the Plymouth Brethren movement and a key articulator of a new form of eschatological thinking that we now call "dispensational premillennialism"—the scheme of eschatology that is contained in the notes of the Scofield Bible, was advocated in a series of "prophecy conferences" in the late nineteenth century, and had great influence through the "bible school" movement and the popular writings of Hal Lindsay in mid-twentieth century and the recent "Left Behind" series of our own time. This movement, even when its details were not adopted, drew the attention of the church to the return of Christ—and the final theme of the "four-fold gospel" was in place.

These two themes, "divine healing" and "dispensationalism" generated much controversy in the "evangelical" subculture of the late nineteenth century and in the Holiness movement they tended to split the movement into two parties. More conservative leaders of the Holiness movement, especially in the Eastern part of the United States, tended to resist these innovations. They wrote books against the "faith healing movement" and Daniel Steele of Boston and Syracuse Universities attacked dispensationalism as *Anti–nomianism Revised* and the intrusion of Calvinism into Methodist circles. These themes were so controversial that the National Campmeeting Association for the Promotion of Holiness (the major mainstream Holiness institution) forbad its speakers to mention the issues from the platform.

In the mid-west and the West of the United States, these themes found more fertile ground in which to prosper. The acceptance of these themes in such circles led to the emergence of a more "radical" party in the Holiness movement that took pride in the advocacy of these new themes. This was a widespread phenomenon that could be illustrated by developments at God's Bible School in Cincinnati, Ohio, where under the influence of Holiness Quaker Paul Rees and holiness Methodist Martin Wells Knapp there was also a relatively self-conscious articulation of the "four-fold gospel." This school was important for developments in Asia because it was here that the Oriental Missionary Society began to take shape under the leadership of three telegraphers that had transferred from Moody Bible Institute. This, of course, was the path by which the "four-fold gospel" found its way to Asia.

The Wider Influence of the "Four–Fold" Gospel in America

The "four-fold gospel" has often been viewed as something of an idiosyncrasy of A. B. Simpson, and the existence of the pattern more broadly in the Holiness movement has often been ignored. But even more striking is the extent to which these themes gave shape to the wider evangelical culture in the late nineteenth century. One finds the pattern implicitly in the work of Holiness Baptist A. J. Gordon who lies behind the major centers of New England Evangelicalism of Gordon College and Gordon-Conwell Divinity School. Gordon wrote books on all four of these themes and little else. Similarly with R. A. Torrey, the superintendent of Moody Bible Institute in Chicago. He wrote books on all four themes—and then moved west to California where he played a similar role at the Bible Institute of Los Angeles (now Biola University).

The point of all this is that the themes of the "four-fold gospel" are so pervasive in late nineteenth-century evangelicalism that one could almost speak of them as defining and indicating the boundaries of that subculture. This is increasingly being recognized in the secondary literature. Douglas Frank, for example, in his *Less Than Conquerors*, analyzes the period in terms of "revivalism," the "Higher Christian Life" movement (or "Victorious Christianity"), and dispensationalism—three of the four themes of the four-fold gospel. And Joel Carpenter, author of *Revive us Again*, in an essay contributed to *In Earthen Vessels* describes the late nineteenth century missionary culture in terms of the same three themes. It this is so, then the existence of the four-fold pattern in Asia becomes more understandable.

The Question of Evangelical Identity

Evangelical circles in the United States have struggled with what holds them together as a common movement. Since the emergence of the "neo-evangelicalism" in the mid-twentieth century, such currents as the National Association of Evangelicals (NAE) and the Evangelical Theological Society (ETS) tended to find that unity in a common commitment to the doctrine of the "inerrancy of Scripture," but this has proved to be very problematic. The Holiness churches that played a key role in the founding of these organizations did not use the expression until they fell under the influence of the "neo-evangelicals." And the Pentecostals, as a radical wing of the Holiness movement, were even more distant from this articulation. That is to say, a majority of the members of the NAE do not fit the definition of evangelicalism proposed by the "neo-evangelicals."

George Marsden once suggested, somewhat tongue-in-cheek, that an "evangelical" is anyone who likes Billy Graham, the great evangelist of our time. What at first appears to be a joke may have a deeper significance in pointing to the history of revivalism as defining. It may well be that the most formative traditions of "evangelicalism" are shaped by revivalism and that this is more central than the features highlighted by "neo-evangelicalism." This move does call attention to the four-fold gospel that becomes a more adequate definition.

A similar dynamic is discovered when we turn to the second point of the four-fold gospel—the teaching of a second experience. This is true most clearly of the Holiness movement proper, but it is also true of Pentecostalism which turns this second point into the doctrine of the "baptism of the Spirit" as found in the "four-square gospel" of Aimee Semple McPherson, as I discovered in the writing of my *Theological Roots of Pentecostalism*. What is not noticed is that this "second blessing" theology permeates much of evangelicalism in North America and even around the world. As described above, it may be found in such persons as A. J. Gordon, A. B. Simpson, and R. A. Torrey. It is significant that the Campus Crusade Ministry of Bill Bright passes out two pamphlets—one on conversion and another on "how to be filled with the Spirit." And such themes are pervasive in most forms of evangelicalism. And the same is true of the "evangelicalism" of Britain and Europe. I once asked a famous Scottish theologian how to describe an "Anglican evangelical." His answer was that an "Anglican Evangelical" is someone who goes to the Keswick summer conferences. This movement was an extension of the American Holiness movement into Britain, especially under the influence of Finney and other figures from Oberlin and the ministry of Hannah Whitall Smith (author of *The Christian's Secret of a Happy Life*) and her husband Robert. It is even less often noticed that Robert Pearsall Smith's great campaign through Europe in 1875 produced the *Gemeinschaftsbewegung* ("fellowship movement") in German-speaking areas that is often defining of "evangelicalism" in those contexts. There is a sense in which "evangelicalism" is little more than the Holiness movement around the world—and that we would have seen this fact more clearly if we had given more attention to the "four-fold gospel," which would have called more attention to this second of its themes.

But the same is true of the last theme, the return of Christ. One of the most profound continuities in the various branches of American evangelicalism is that they are dispensational or have had a brush with dispensationalism. This is clearly true of such groups as the Christian and Missionary Alliance, the Evangelical Free Church, many Holiness groups, almost all of Pentecostalism, and so on. Those groups that have been the most ambivalent about joining the NAE have lacked this history with dispensationalism (The Nazarene Church, the Evangelical Covenant Church, the Christian Reformed Church, the Salvation Army, the Church of God [Anderson], and so on). This fact alone should have drawn attention to this issue in the shaping of "evangelical" culture. And if more attention had been paid to the four-fold gospel, this would have been more obvious.

"Evangelicalism" likes to interpret itself according to the "conservative/liberal" paradigm in which it sees itself as the "conservative" pole. Over the years I have become increasingly skeptical about the usefulness of this paradigm to explain what is going on or to define what "evangelicalism" is. A generation ago, Earnest Sandeen argued in *The Roots of Fundamentalism* that what he had experienced at Wheaton College (the flagship college of "neo–evangelicalism") was the late stage of the development of dispensationalism. The "evangelicals" did not like this proposal and have paid little attention to it (though continuing fundamentalists often give it a great deal of credence). As I have reflected on what happened in the fundamentalist/modernist controversy at the beginning of the twentieth century, I have become increasingly convinced that at its core it was a fight about dispensationalism and its themes. I have long struggled with how to fit the decline of social concern in evangelical circles into the conservative/liberal paradigm. The struggles with dispensationalism provide a much more adequate explanation for this development—and other issues (biblical criticism, cultural engagement, ecumenical reserve, forms of missiology, and even bible school curricula and the rise of anti-evolutionism) also yield to this analysis. Perhaps we should have defined an "evangelical" as someone who reads the "Left Behind" series of novels. Though said somewhat tongue in cheek this comment is intended seriously. It is certainly more adequate than many other definitions—and if we had paid more attention to the "four-fold" gospel we would have seen this earlier and more clearly.

The Situation in Korea

With this analysis in the background, let us turn to the Korean situation. Korean Christianity is very complex denominationally, but four traditions are predominant: the Presbyterian, the Pentecostal, the Holiness and the Methodist. But from the outside, Korean Christianity appears much more homogeneous, and Korean Christians seem to move across denominational lines with ease. How shall we understand this situation? Here the "four-fold gospel" offers some help. It is clearly at the center of the formation of the Holiness tradition. In its "foursquare" version, it has shaped Pentecostalism (the Foursquare Church and the Assemblies of God), even when it has been altered into the five-fold gospel of the Church of God and the reshaping of it by Dr. Cho of Yoido as the "five-fold gospel and the three blessings." Could the "four-fold gospel" also have broader application in Korea?

I am increasingly convinced that it makes sense to analyze the commonalities of Korean Christianity in terms of the "four-fold gospel." I was somewhat surprised to discover this when teaching a course on my book *The Theological Roots of Pentecostalism* at Hoseo University a few years ago. The class of thirty students included twenty-five from the Holiness churches with only a smattering of Presbyterians and Methodists. Those in the Holiness churches, of course, immediately identified with the history in my book. But I was surprised by the extent to which others did as well. At each point, I would ask the Presbyterians: Are your churches revivalist? You know, don't you, that this is a particular stream of Presbyterianism (more "new school" than "old school")? Are your pastors dispensationalist? You know, don't you, that "old school" Presbyterianism would have rejected this position? Do you have healing services in your churches? You know, don't you, that B. B. Warfield of Princeton and author of *Counterfeit Miracles* would have been very nervous about this? Do you pray to be "filled with the spirit"? You know, don't you, that classical Presbyterians would have been very concerned about any doctrines of "subsequent experiences"? As the weeks went on, I became more and more convinced that Korean Presbyterians are more shaped by the "four-fold gospel" than by classical Presbyterianism.

I was fascinated to have this intuition confirmed later when I invited Professor Myung Soo Park of Seoul Theological University to Drew University to co-teach a seminar in Korean church history. He read papers to the class that showed how determinative the Holiness stream was in the Korean revivals of the first decade of the twentieth century. And he showed how even the Presbyterian culture had been shaped by Wesleyan doctrines of sanctification and the practices of divine healing.

Conclusion

All of this leads me to wonder if we ought not to pay more attention to the "four-fold gospel" as a key to understanding the whole of "evangelicalism" and especially those currents that crossed the Pacific Ocean. Those of us who work in the Holiness tradition are too often sufferers from a massive "theological inferiority complex" that causes us to doubt the validity and usefulness of our own theological traditions. We tend to defer to others (often Presbyterians) whose theological and historical work we instinctively trust more than our own.

Greater attention to the "four-fold gospel" would enable us to see more clearly the continuities not only in the various branches of evangelicalism but also global continuities across the Pacific and Atlantic Oceans. We might understand both the North American and Korean theological cultures more accurately—let alone transoceanic continuities. Is it not time for us to pay closer attention to our own traditions and to use them for the edification of the whole rather than hiding our light under a bushel so as not to embarrass ourselves?

Response #1

Myung Soo Park

I

Professor Donald Dayton has been in large measure responsible for introducing the Holiness movement to a wide array of academics. Additionally, he is one of the leading scholars to show that the root of the Pentecostal movement can be traced to the Holiness movement. The importance of Dr. Dayton, however, does not end with these achievements. He has also been especially important to Korean Holiness churches. He has not only contributed greatly to the academic community by delineating the historical and theological background of Korean Holiness churches but has also made many disciples among Korean Holiness Christians who will follow in his ground-breaking path. One may even say that Dr. Dayton's influence is stronger and more pervasive in Korea than in any other country.

I also have maintained a special friendship with Dr. Dayton. When I was doing research for my dissertation at Boston University, his bibliographical study on the Holiness movement and *Theological Roots of Pentecostalism* helped my research immensely. Later, I had the opportunity of making a presentation on the influence of the Holiness movement on the Great Revival Movement of 1907 in Korea at the World Methodist Historical Society held at Asbury Theological Seminary in 2000. There I had a personal meeting with Dr. Dayton, and this resulted in the privilege of lecturing with Dr. Dayton on the theme of a "Wesleyan Reading of Korean Church History" at the Graduate School of Drew University.

In 2005, American and Asia-Pacific theologians gathered for an academic conference sponsored jointly by the Korea Evangelical Holiness Church Historical Research Center of Seoul Theological University and the Wesleyan Theological Society on the theme of "Wesley, Holiness, and Culture: Trans-Pacific Perspectives for the 21st Century." It was at this conference that Dr. Dayton presented the paper, "The Four-Fold Gospel: Key to Trans-Pacific Continuities."

II

I had the opportunity to converse with Dr. Dayton on several occasions both in Korea and in the USA. Our common interest was the role of the fourfold gospel in modern church history. I believe that the fourfold gospel represents the essence of the gospel, found by common people as they read the Bible from their own perspectives. Although A. B. Simpson was the first one to call these four points of the gospel a "fourfold gospel," the four points of the gospel—namely, regeneration, holiness, divine healing, and the second coming of Jesus Christ—were already important themes to many Christians in North America.

The fourfold gospel expresses important matters of interest to common Christians. Regeneration deals with the question of how to obtain eternal life. Holiness asks what makes "true" Christians. Divine healing deals with the question of how Christians should solve the problem of sickness. Finally, the second coming asks what will become of the future for humanity. I also believe that these four questions represent perhaps the most fundamental problems confronted by all religions.

Up until now, Christian theology has focused on such topics as the Trinity, church structure, and the sacraments. However, these inquiries pertained to theologians or clergymen more than common Christians. Church leaders have expanded the boundaries of theology by focusing on themes of interest to them. However, common Christians inquire into more specific problems, which are directly related to their real life. That is what the fourfold gospel enshrines.

It is my conviction that the revival movements of the nineteenth century came out of populist understandings of Christianity. Modernization brought about a new mass culture, and, along with this social change, Christianity adapted to the culture of this mass society. This adaptation led to change not only in the external forms such as a worship style but also the content of the sermon. This changed and adapted content is the fourfold gospel. The common people wanted to hear a Biblical answer to their everyday problems more than sermons filled with difficult or esoteric theology.

Evangelical historians need to investigate the fourfold gospel as an important research theme from this perspective. Especially for the evangelicalism represented by the revival movement, the fourfold gospel was the central theme. This point becomes clearer as we look through the history of Korean churches. The central theme of Korean revivalists was this fourfold gospel. Of course, the Holiness churches emphasized the fourfold gospel as the official slogan of their denomination, and the Full Gospel churches stressed a fivefold gospel that was similar to the fourfold gospel. Even the Presbyterian churches, which constitute the largest denomination in Korea, were no exception. The central theme of the Great Revival Movement of 1907 was holiness through the baptism of the Holy Spirit, and the great revivalist of the Korean Presbyterian church, Pastor Gil, Sun Joo, stressed the second coming, while another great revivalist, Pastor Kim, Ick Doo, emphasized divine healing. These examples illustrate that the fourfold gospel was a central theme of evangelicalism as represented by the revival movement, transcending the Holiness churches or the Pentecostal churches. In this respect, I agree with Professor Dayton. I believe we all have to treat the fourfold gospel as a central theme of modern evangelicalism.

III

Nonetheless, I think evangelism for personal salvation and the absolute authority of the Bible became an important theme of evangelicalism from the beginning of the century. I know that the revival movement in the nineteenth century not only achieved personal salvation but also resulted in social reform. However, the social gospel of the early twentieth century interpreted the concept of salvation more broadly than it was intended, and it ended up ignoring personal salvation, stressing social reform only. Against this, evangelicalism makes individual salvation the first mission of the church. Evangelicalism does not oppose social reform, but it opposes the church treating personal salvation lightly.

The Holiness movement in Korea believes in divine healing and the second coming both of which are supernatural in nature. However, the higher criticism of modern liberalism tends to exclude the supernatural elements in the Bible and tries to find only moral lessons from the Bible. When Holiness movement activists learned of this higher criticism, they knew the fourfold gospel would be destroyed if higher criticism was introduced. The representatives of higher criticism understood divine healing and the second coming as mythological residue from the Near Eastern context of the biblical authors. Thus, most of the Holiness movement, which stressed the fourfold gospel, also emphasized the authority of the Bible. This is the reason why the Holiness movement participated in the evangelical movement of the twentieth century. Higher criticism was introduced into Korea in the mid-1920's and it began to have a powerful influence after World War II. The Holiness churches believed that this influence threatened the gospel. Thus, the revised constitutions of Holiness churches in Korea inserted a clause, which stated that it is the mission of the Holiness churches to keep and protect the authority of the Bible. This has become an important tradition of Korean Holiness churches.

The Korean Holiness churches stressed the fourfold gospel and at the same time emphasized personal salvation and the authority of the Bible. Of particular importance is that, while many mainstream endeavors in the early twentieth century connected missions with westernization, the Holiness missionaries believed the essence of mission was salvation through Jesus Christ. Holiness missionaries believed that personal salvation was more effective with the direct approach of testifying about Christ through words rather than with the indirect approach of building schools or hospitals.

IV

I express a sincere gratitude to Dr. Dayton for letting us know the true features of the Holiness movement in the nineteenth century and the root of the Korean Holiness churches thereby. Our present Holiness movement should strive to bring about a social reform along with a personal change just like the Holiness movement of the nineteenth century. This concern with social holiness is rooted in the Holiness tradition of spreading the full gospel that brings the salvation of body, soul, and society. The present Holiness churches must revive this great heritage.

However, we should not forget that the Holiness movement has fought against liberalism since the beginning of the twentieth century. Liberalism extended the concept of salvation so much that the content of salvation became obscure and weakened the authority of the Bible. In the process of fighting against this liberalism, the Holiness movement began to participate in the evangelical movement and became an important member.

I believe as Dr. Dayton suggested that the fourfold gospel is the center of evangelicalism and the revival movement. Especially, this point will be made clearer when the gospel reaches the third world leaving the speculative and dogmatic Western churches. Isn't it the message of salvation, holiness, divine healing, and the second coming, that the Christianity around the world stresses? In this respect, we should develop the subject of the fourfold gospel more than ever as a central theme of evangelicalism as Dr. Dayton has contended.

Response #2

Dawk-Mahn Bae

Who Is Dr. Dayton to Me and the Korean Churches?

Who Is Dr. Dayton to Me?

Though I started my doctoral program under his supervision at Drew in 1999, I had already met Dr. Dayton through his famous book, *Theological Roots of Pentecostalism*, during my S.T.M. program at Yale Divinity School (1997–1999). As is well known, in that volume he tried to prove that Pentecostalism is not only a spiritual movement, but also a profound theological tradition with a long and deep history. Before reading that book, I had regarded or even despised Pentecostalism as one of the many helpless sects. That was one of the main reasons that I made up my mind to study Jonathan Edwards and Puritanism at Yale as a more decent and recommendable alternative to the Pentecostalism predominant in Korea. But *Theological Roots of Pentecostalism* helped to reform my view of Pentecostalism, and even drove me to regard it with serious intellectual concern. Eventually, I came down to Drew for my doctoral program to focus on Pentecostalism under the guidance and influence of Dr. Dayton.

The second major impact that Dayton had on me came from his other influential book, *Discovering an Evangelical Heritage*. I attended his seminar on Evangelicalism, and chose the book for my presentation in that class. Preparing for the presentation, I was overwhelmed by the forgotten stories of the nineteenth-century evangelicalism that Dr. Dayton successfully excavated in his work. Actually, while reading the work I was encountered by the concerns that I had had during the 1980s as they were manifest in the concerns of Dr. Dayton in the 1960s: evangelicals who were wrestling with serious contemporary issues. Through this work I also discovered a significant heritage—i.e., the social responsibility of evangelicals—which Korean evangelicals must restore in the twenty-first century. Thanks to this book, I could correct my misunderstanding of evangelicalism as one of the conservative, reactionary, and pessimistic Protestant subcultures. Eventually, I could accept my own self-identity as an evangelical without any guilt-feelings, and I subsequently translated the book into Korean, which was published 2003.

Thirdly, Dr. Dayton provided me with two valuable academic lenses, eschatology and sociology, through which to look at theology or theological phenomena more deeply and more comprehensively. In my view, Dr. Dayton paid special attention to eschatology in his own theological work for he believes it makes a powerful impact on believers' view of history. At the same time, he also repeatedly emphasized the significance and efficacy of sociological perspectives or methodologies in his interpretation of history. In his exposition of the origin of Pentecostalism as well as in his well-known debate with George Marsden on the genesis of Fundamentalism, Dr. Dayton continued to draw on his sociological viewpoint. I was so fully persuaded by his approach which focused on eschatology and sociology that I determined to select the title, "'Kingdom Now': Social Implication of Eschatology in Pentecostal-Charismatic Movement in America" for my doctoral dissertation at Drew.

Finally, I discovered my own theological calling under his influence. He led seminars in Pietism and Anabaptism at Drew. I took both of them. In particular, he introduced John Howard Yoder to his students in his seminar on Anabaptism. Immediately, the great Mennonite ethicist mesmerized me. As a matter of fact, I grew up as a hardcore anticommunist in Korea, which has been divided into two parts since the Korean War (1950–53). My father was born in North Korea, and came down to South Korea as a refugee with some of his relatives during the Korean War. After his move south, he would never see again his close relatives including his mother and brother. In addition, my maternal grandfather was murdered by the hands of North Korean soldiers during the Korean War. Therefore, it is quite understandable that I was thoroughly brainwashed by the anticommunist education at school as well as at home. Reading *The Politics of Jesus* written by Yoder, however, I came to realize very clearly the political dimension of Jesus' teaching, life, and ministry, and why we Christians must stand for pacifism. In fact, Korean Christians have tended to read the Bible from their own ideological perspectives, instead of evaluating and criticizing political and economic ideologies on the basis of the Word of God. I was one of the representative examples of that approach. Absorbing Yoder's pacifistic message, however, I began to look at the political situation of Korea surrounded by a variety of difficulties such as reunification, nuclear weapons, and Zaytun Division in Iraq from the pacifistic viewpoint, struggling to overcome the ideological trauma in myself. From then on, I have been doing my best to study and introduce the pacifistic tradition of American churches to Korean Christians so that I may be able to make a small contribution to the peaceful reunification of Korea. Had I not met Dr. Dayton, it would have been impossible for me to discover my academic vocation in that way.

Who Is Dr. Dayton to the Korean Churches?

While teaching at Drew, Dr. Dayton met many Korean students. By way of those personal relationships with them, he could not only make an indelible impact upon them, but also gain a good deal of information on the churches in Korea churches. I am sure that he must be one of the few American theologians to have a strong connection with, and deep understanding of Korean churches. As a result, he had several opportunities to visit Korea to give public lectures at academic conferences, classes, and even churches. One of the significant results of such academic activities in Korea was his paper entitled "The Fourfold Gospel: Key to Trans-Pacific Continuities," which he read in a Joint Conference of the Wesleyan Theological Society and Seoul Theological University in 2005. In this paper, Dr. Dayton suggested the fourfold gospel as a hermeneutic tool for understanding the historical and theological identity of the Korea Evangelical Holiness Church. In many aspects, this paper was both significant and controversial.

First of all, this paper was highly insightful and meaningful in that Dr. Dayton pointed out the theological commonalities that tie together Korean churches, and in particular Korean evangelical churches. As in the United States, Korean churches are divided into several subcultures in accordance with their theological, ecclesiastical, or practical distinctions. Some churches are preoccupied with spiritual experience, but others are eager to preserve theological purity. Some aspire to set up their churches based on the Calvinistic tradition, but others advocate a Wesleyan-Arminian theology. In this context, Dr. Dayton suggested the fourfold gospel to Korean churches as an interpretative lens by which they can move towards a serious academic ecumenical discussion.

Secondly, Dr. Dayton clearly illuminated the right position of the Korea Evangelical Holiness Church in the web of global Christianity. For the past generation, there has been a strong voice in KEHC in favor of its indigenousness. Thus, it became a common sense to believe that KEHC came into being in Korea without any noticeable connection with or help from the West. Such a belief played a significant role in shaping the self-identity of the KEHC members. Some developed their groundless pride of their denominational identity as the only single indigenous mainline church in Korea. Others fell into the pit of an inferiority complex like fatherless children or isolated islands. In particular, in the Korean setting where Presbyterian churches are extremely predominant, the revival-centered KEHC has not been rightly evaluated by the mainliners in terms of theology. In this situation, Dr. Dayton helped the KEHC members to understand their theological, historical, and ecclesiastical status in the global evangelical circle more fully and holistically.

Along with these important contributions made in this paper, I cannot but indicate some limitations in it, which is due to its short length and his fourfold framework in itself. First, while Dr. Dayton proposed the fourfold gospel as the theological commonality in Korean churches by which they can be united, he did not pay sufficient attention to the fact that there exist diverse, even conflicting interpretations of it in Korean churches. Of course, almost every denomination cherishes the doctrine of regeneration. But the emphasis that each denomination places on it is quite different according to its theological tradition. One can easily identify the similar situation in the case of baptism with the Holy Spirit, divine healing, and eschatology in Korea. Though most Korean churches use these terms, each of them uses them with quite different meanings or implications. In general, Pentecostals love to pray for miraculous healing, but most evangelicals tend to depend more on medical doctors than on divine healers. Some conservative evangelicals including Holiness people are still waiting for Jesus' premillennial second coming, but many others already gave up such an apocalyptic eschatology. Thus, it is at least possible to argue that most Korean churches are involved with the fourfold gospel whether or not they use the term explicitly. If one probes into the reality of Korean churches in terms of the fourfold gospel, however, it is not as easy to believe that the fourfold gospel can play the pivotal role in uniting Korean churches theologically. In fact, since there are deep, serious interpretive gaps concerning the meaning of the fourfold gospel, it is hardly easy to expect a sort of theological unity or ecumenism by simply stressing the fourfold gospel. Rather, when the fourfold gospel is overemphasized, in my view, it is likely to lead to a more serious or even harmful theological controversy against Dr. Dayton's expectations. Thus, to persuade Korean evangelicals to accept his fourfold gospel paradigm, he needs to deal with these interpretive differences with regard to the fourfold gospel in Korea more thoroughly.

Finally, it is certain that Dr. Dayton's fourfold gospel paradigm can be usefully applied to Korean churches. Also, there is no doubt that it includes some essential elements of Korean theological tradition. Nevertheless, that is not the whole story that needs to be addressed and analyzed in this context. Regardless of denominational differences, most Korean churches cherish regeneration, baptism with the Holy Spirit, divine healing, and Jesus' second coming. Along with those four doctrines or practices, however, Korean churches also have developed or preserved other important ideas and practices to which theologians need to pay deeper attention. For example, Korean Christians have shown their special reverence for the Bible as the absolute Word of God. Thus, they believe that all faithful Christians must devote themselves to reading, studying, and even memorizing the Bible. In addition, Korean churches place a great emphasis on the significance of evangelism, offering, and sabbatarianism. But Dr. Dayton did not address these factors or aspects of Korean churches at all. Thus, I hope that he would further refine his thoughts on the fourfold gospel to embrace these unique elements in Korean churches. Only then am I sure that his fourfold paradigm can be applied to Korean churches more universally and persuasively.

Before finishing my writing, I must express my deepest gratitude and respect to Dr. Dayton. Without his love, concern, and teaching I could never dream of being who I have become. Under his instruction I discovered myself theologically, learned what theology is, and have realized what I must do for Korean churches. Thank you and I love you, Dr. Dayton, my *Doktorvater*.

13

Donald Dayton as Teacher

No celebration of the work of Donald Dayton would be complete without recognition of the profound personal influence he has had on generations of students. It could be argued that Dayton's investment in the lives and intellectual growth of students over the thirty plus years he has taught in theological education has been just as significant as his contributions to the academy through his vast scholarship.

In 1998, while teaching at Drew University, Dayton was honored with the Will Herberg Distinguished Professor Award that recognized his contributions as a teacher and a scholar. The following text, written by Dr. Joel Scandrett, was submitted for the award and read by Dr. Scandrett at the award presentation in 1998.

1998 Drew University Graduate School
Will Herberg Distinguished Professor Award

by Joel Scandrett

Theological and Religious Studies Nominee: Donald Dayton

IN the course of this academic year, a remarkable number of graduate students in Theological and Religious Studies (and Religion and Society) have come to deeply respect and value the passion, commitment, and scholarship of Professor Donald Dayton. In considering possible nominees for this year's Will Herberg award, Professor Dayton's unstinting service to Drew graduate students has distinguished him as a uniquely qualified candidate. As an expression of gratitude for his invaluable contribution to our development as scholars and teachers, we hereby present Professor Donald Dayton as the *unanimously* elected (no abstentions) Theological and Religious Studies nominee for the 1998 Will Herberg Distinguished Professor Award.

Criteria

Professor Dayton more than satisfies the criteria for this award, as can be seen upon examination. Professor Dayton is:

Passionately devoted to his disciplines. Professor Dayton's devotion to his academic disciplines is passionate, to say the least. That passion is perhaps most clearly demonstrated in the unending stream of academic texts that flows—and overflows—through his office door. He is constantly locating, purchasing, and sharing with his students new and old works on his favorite subjects. Ecclesiastes says, "Of the making of many books there is no end." Professor Dayton is living proof of this ancient wisdom.

Actively involved in teaching. It quickly becomes clear to any student of Professor Dayton that the classroom is only one of many venues in which he actively teaches. A hallway, lounge, snack bar, sidewalk, or

Chinese restaurant will serve just as well—and often better—as contexts in which he continues to communicate his learning and ideas to students. It is this continuous stream of dialogue with students that perhaps most distinguishes Professor Dayton as a teacher.

Able to communicate an enthusiasm for excellence. Professor Dayton's enthusiasm for excellence is clear, infectious, and at times frightening. Any student whose work comes under his scrutiny knows the rigor of his expectations for method, form, and content. While he rarely chides, he will gently and persistently push the student to reexamine questionable methodological or conceptual assumptions, as well as to rework the form and style of an argument. This commitment to and enthusiasm for excellence is yet another distinguishing feature of Professor Dayton's contribution to graduate students.

Deeply committed to the academic, professional, and personal advancement of students. Professor Dayton's deep commitment to the advancement of students is evinced by the many hours of private mentoring and advisement he has given, as well as by the large number of students in Theological and Religious Studies (and Religion and Society) who seek him out on a regular basis. He is accessible. On any given day, one can often find him in his unofficial "office"—the Drew snack bar—intent in conversation with a student over a cup of coffee. It is this dedication and accessibility to students that have established him as a mentor in the eyes of so many in such a relatively short period of time. And it is this same dedication and accessibility that have placed him upon an unusually large number of thesis and dissertation committees. In addition, Professor Dayton is continuously encouraging students to be strategizing concretely about their academic and professional future as scholars and teachers. Graduate students recognize in him a person who is deeply concerned about and committed to their academic, professional, and personal advancement.

Recognized as a serious contributor to his field of study. Professor Dayton is a senior scholar who is recognized as a serious contributor to at least three fields (and several sub-fields) of study: the history of Christianity in America, the theology of Karl Barth, and Christian ecumenism. He has published numerous books and journal articles in these fields and has served as an officer for several academic and ecclesiastical societies related to their study. Just a few of his recognized contributions are:

Books

The American Holiness Movement: A Bibliographic Introduction (Wilmore, KY: Asbury Theological Seminary, 1971).

The Coming Kingdom: Essays in American Millennialism & Eschatology, ed. (Barrytown, NY: Rose of Sharon, 1983).

Contemporary Perspectives on Pietism, ed. (Chicago: Covenant Press, 1976).

Discovering an Evangelical Heritage (Peabody, MA: Hendrickson Publishers, 1976, revised 1988, reprinted 1994).

Ecumenism and the Evangelical Traditions: Historical and Theological Perspectives [in progress: papers from AAR session to be published by Eerdmans].

Five Sermons and a Tract by Luther Lee, ed. (Chicago: Holrad House, 1975).

The Higher Christian Life: A Bibliographical Overview (New York: Garland Publishers, 1985).

Holiness Tracts Defending the Ministry of Women, ed. (New York: Garland Publishing, 1985).

In the Name of Jesus: The Harvard Symposium on Oneness Pentecostalism, ed. [in progress].

Reflections on Revival, by Charles Finney; compiled by D. Dayton (Minneapolis: Bethany Fellowship, 1979).

Resources for Research (Wilmore, KY: Asbury Theological Seminary, 1972).

The Spiritual Writings of Asa Mahan [to be published in the series "Sources in American Spirituality" by Paulist Press].

Theological Bibliography and Reference Resources (Wilmore, KY: Asbury Theological Seminary, 1970 and 1972).

Theological Roots of Pentecostalism (Metuchen, NJ: Scarecrow Press, 1987).

The Variety of American Evangelicalism, ed. (Knoxville: University of Tennessee Press, 1991).

Articles

Professor Dayton has *eighty-two separate article and essay entries (not including reviews) in the ATLA religion database* which treat such diverse topics as Pentecostalism, social transformation, Holiness movements, Latin

American Protestantism, American evangelicalism, Karl Barth, ecumenism, 19th-century feminism, pietism, racism, and Soren Kierkegaard.

Academic and Ecclesiastical Societies

President, Wesleyan Theological Society (past)

President, Society for Pentecostal Studies (past)

Vice-President, Karl Barth Society of North America (past)

Member, National Council of Churches—Faith and Order Commission (present)

Representative, World Council of Churches—Upcoming Harare WCC Convention (present)

Education

PhD University of Chicago Divinity School, 1983.

MS University of Kentucky, Library Science and Bibliography, 1969.

BD Yale Divinity School, 1969.

BA Houghton College, Philosophy and Math, 1963.

14

An Autobiographical Response

Donald W. Dayton

I have been deeply moved by this project and its antecedent. On my sixtieth birthday, students at Drew University, especially the Koreans, bid me farewell and celebrated my achievement of an age especially significant in Korean culture. They presented me (and all participants) with an informal collection of my writings prepared by Young Hoon Yoon, now back in Korea in the early stages of carving out his own career and interpreting my work in that context. Now, for my sixty-fifth birthday, the counterpart age in American culture, one of those students, Christian T. Collins Winn has elevated this work to a new level with this collection of my writings with critical and celebratory responses.

I have been overwhelmed and often moved to tears in reading the various responses and commentary. I thank the colleagues, students, friends, and co-conspirators who have taken the time to write. I am particularly gratified that Christian has conceived of this imaginative variation on the genre of festschrift and has undertaken the task of organizing this book. Since we first met at the World Council of Churches Assembly in Zimbabwe, he has become a close friend, confidant and collaborator. We have lived through a lot together, and he has taught me much about how a professor's legacy is often more through his students than his writings. I agree with Christian that my scholarly work has been rather diffuse (in a variety of scholarly disciplines and published in sometimes unusual locations) and often indirect in style and focus—often taking more the shape of academic guerilla warfare than the building of an establishment academic career. As a result, some interpretation is useful in unfolding both the diversity and unity of that work.

It is also appropriate that Christian and his collaborators would choose to present this collection to me formally at the fiftieth-anniversary celebration of the 1957 Oberlin meeting of Faith and Order. Oberlin is a very special place for me, both personally and theologically. It brings together the diverse strands of my work in remarkable ways and also symbolizes the underlying unity that is there. My own church tradition, the Wesleyan Methodist Church, had a special affinity with Oberlin abolitionism and feminism. My college (Houghton College) was modeled after Oberlin and used it as a finishing school before a full four-year program was in place (even the head of our music program was organist Charles Finney!). Oberlin is the primary exemplar of the conjunction of revivalism and social reform celebrated in my first major book, *Discovering an Evangelical Heritage*. Figures at Oberlin were key players in the trajectories that I traced in *Theological Roots of Pentecostalism*. And Oberlin is also a symbol of the ecumenical work of "Faith and Order" that has dominated the last quarter of a century of my work. It is hard to imagine a more appropriate location for this event, and I am deeply moved by these convergences.

It has been suggested that I respond to the commentaries in this volume. It has not been clear to me how best to do this. Most of what has been written needs no response. I might have nuanced certain themes and stories slightly differently, but not significantly so. I have been tempted a little to pick up two major controversies in my career: the debates with Larry Wood on the interpretation of the trajectories of Methodist theology toward Pentecostalism (with their antecedents in similar conflicts with Timothy Smith in 1970s and 1980s) and with George Marsden on the historiographical interpretation of the fundamentalist/evangelical tradition. Much, perhaps too much, ink has been spilt over these issues, but they have not been resolved. Amos Yong and Bill Faupel have taken up the former issue in this book. Amos provides the bibliographic information on the recent dialogue between Larry and myself in recent issues of *Pneuma* (five essays in response to his book). I really have little more to say about this issue and remain convinced about the positions that I have taken.

The discussion with George Marsden is a little more complicated. If anything, I have become more radical over the years in my claim that the history of Pentecostalism and the Holiness Movement provide better clues for the interpretation of whatever we might mean by "evangelicalism" than the history of the fundamentalist/modernist split at Princeton Seminary in the Presbyterian tradition. I remain convinced that George's reading (admittedly the dominant, and perhaps nearly universal, one) imposes a foreign paradigm on phenomena that will not yield to its categories of analysis. I am often misunderstood (even by my students!) on this issue. I am not advocating the recognition of the diversity (or "variety" of American "evangelicalism" as in the title of one of my books). I am advocating the *replacement* of George's paradigm by a more adequate and explanatory paradigm. If he may be said, as I suggest, to impose a "Presbyterian paradigm" on the whole, I suggest that we would be better served by using another paradigm and set of categories.

George's reading presupposes a conservative/liberal construal of the issues at stake between the "evangelical" world and the "mainstream" of Christianity. It privileges the Orthodox Presbyterian Church as the paradigm of "evangelicalism." My reading of the situation uses the Holiness Movement to interpret the history of Presbyterianism (!) and privileges the Christian and Missionary Alliance (founder A. B. Simpson was a Canadian Presbyterian) as the paradigmatic split within Presbyterianism. I think that most observers of the American scene would agree that the C&MA is more than the OPC at the center of what we usually mean by "evangelicalism" as in the National Association of Evangelicals.

But this simple move has radical implications. It shifts the focus of study from the 1920s to the 1880s and 1890s as the opening up of the "two party" system that dominates American Protestantism—decades before the fundamentalism/modernist controversy. It brings different issues to the fore and draws attention to Simpson's fourfold gospel: Jesus is Savior, Sanctifer, Healer and Coming King. This move underlines the "revivalistic" character of "evangelicalism" (as with Billy Graham), suggests that eschatology (rather than "orthodoxy") is at the center of the fundamentalist/modernist controversy (notice the continuing influence of the "Left Behind" novels), and suggests that the "Higher Christian Life" (or "second blessing") spirituality is the shared element of "evangelical" piety (even Bill Bright's Campus Crusade hands out two pamphlets, the second on "how to be filled with the Holy Spirit"). And the "healing" motif reminds us that "evangelicalism" is dominated demographically worldwide by Holiness, Pentecostal, and Charismatic currents that are in many ways a protest against the "orthodox" traditions of Protestantism (as may be seen in the volumes of attacks on such currents by Princeton theologian B. B. Warfield). I don't expect to win this battle in this generation (the conservative/liberal paradigm is too firmly entrenched), but there are already signs of a greater openness to my perspective among younger scholars for whom the fundamentalist/modernist controversy is a fading memory and a longer view is possible. I only hope that I live long enough to see this vindication.

Rather than engaging directly the "responses" in this volume, I would like to expand (perhaps excessively) the biographical comments of Christian in his introduction with some autobiographical reflections and use this material in certain musing on the title of this collection (chosen by Christian in consultation with me). This would seem to be congruent with the style of my own theological work. Many are confused about how to describe my disciplinary orientation. Many assume that I am a "church historian." My PhD, however, was in the department of Christian Theology at the University of Chicago, and I prefer the label "theologian," albeit one who does theology in an historical mode. With the rise of "practical theology" as a discipline and with the increasing acceptance of more popular (that is, less academic) forms of theology, this way of doing theology meets less condescension. It is also somewhat tradition specific. I have often reflected on the curricula of various theological seminaries and noted how they differ in the implicit commitment to various "norming disciplines." Baptist seminaries (I was two decades at one!) give special emphasis to New Testament studies, and presidents and deans are often great preachers and New Testament scholars. Presbyterians and Lutherans are more likely to give these positions to theologians. Some traditions, I think of the Church of the Brethren and the Evangelical Covenant Church, more often gravitate toward historians or theologians who think historically. I place my own tradition in this last category—significantly all are products of the pietist tradition that complained that theology was too often done in dialogue with philosophy. I think of theology as essentially an "exegetical" and "historical" discipline, and I would claim Barth for this methodological orientation as well.

Christian has mentioned that I tend to work very closely to history and biography. I have usually started classes by probing student biographies to discover the trajectories on which they are moving—in part because I have often used a sort of Socratic style of teaching that assumes that students know more than they realize. It is often possible to stage a very sophisticated theological debate out of the instincts of untutored students who are carriers of tradition and hermeneutics without realizing it. I also think it important to help students realize the sociological trajectories on which they are moving, often unconsciously, so that they can confirm or correct such trajectories on theological grounds. I have very little patience with Euclidean and deductive models of theology and prefer to jump into streams of history attempting to bring coherence and develop the implications of living streams of theology. This has on occasion put me at odds with my deans. At Northern Baptist I was often asked to teach a course in "basic Christian ethics." My response was that I had no idea how to do that. For me ethics is an extension of dogmatics and not an autonomous discipline. I think that I am skilled at guiding students in seeing the implications of their theology, but I haven't the foggiest idea how to teach a course in "basic Christian ethics." Another way of saying all this is that I have tended to work at the intersection of exegesis, history, theology and ethics in a sort of missiological mode.

With this in mind, I turn to my own life and the way in which my theological interests have been rooted in concrete issues of my own experience. Students and friends have often urged me to write an autobiography. I often wonder whether I will ever do this and so would like to write in some detail about the emergence of the concerns that have dominated my life (especially my intellectual trajectories). In doing this I would like to correct some misunderstandings of what I have been about.

I was born in Chicago in 1942 (in the first year of World War II) and spent my first year in a walk-in closet that served as my nursery at Northern Baptist Theological Seminary where my father was finishing his ThD in New Testament with Julius Mantey of the famous Dana and Mantey Greek grammar (Some have suggested that this closet may help explain a continuing case of "theological claustrophobia"!). My father claimed to be the first theological doctorate in the Wesleyan Methodist church, the abolitionist wing of the Methodist Episcopal Church that had been pushed out a century earlier for its agitation against slavery. Some have claimed that this church became the first to adopt an article on "entire sanctification." That is probably incorrect but does help explain why the denomination has generally identified with the "Holiness movement" of the nineteenth century. The Wesleyan Church was drawn even more into the orbit of the Holiness movement by a 1968 merger with the Pilgrim Holiness Church. Of all the major Holiness churches (Church of the Nazarene, Salvation Army, Free Methodist Church, Christian and Missionary Alliance, Church of God [Anderson, Indiana], Brethren in Christ, the "holiness" Quakers, and so on) it was the Wesleyan Church that fell most under the influence of fundamentalism, writing both premillennial dispensationalism and the "inerrancy" of Scripture into its articles of religion, the latter under the influence of the mid-century emergence of the "neo-evangelical" party that was taking shape at Northern during the 1940s. The church adopted in the 1950s the doctrine of the "inerrancy of the Scriptures"—the first appearance I believe of this word in the Wesleyan/Holiness stream of churches that had heretofore not been inclined to use this language. My father had been a major player with his mentor Stephen Paine (his predecessor as president of Houghton College) in effecting this change, in hopes of, I am convinced, currying the favor of the neo-evangelicals by bringing the Wesleyan doctrinal statement into accord with "neo-evangelical" concerns—in part choosing this path as a means of gaining cultural respectability as a part of the larger, emerging "evangelical" movement.

I grew up in Marion, Indiana, where my father became the "dean of the school of divinity" (basically the undergraduate religion department) of Marion College (now Indiana Wesleyan University and perhaps the largest of the "evangelical" universities) and trained a generation of Wesleyan ministers. My few memories of Marion are pleasant. It was only in later visits to this hometown that I realized how economically depressed this county seat had become due to factory closures. Likewise, only later did I understand the extent to which this was the heartland of "holiness country" (as described in the James Dean essay; Dean was from Fairmont, nine miles south of Marion). Anderson University was thirty miles to the south, Taylor University was a few miles to southeast, Huntington College was to the North, and not too far away were Bethel College and Fort Wayne Bible College—all in the Holiness stream. Only later did I begin to understand how socially conservative this area was, when I saw near Marion billboards that advocated withdrawal from the United Nations or joining the John Birch Society. The Klu Klux Klan had been founded in Elwood, half way between Marion and Indianapolis. Finally, only later did I understand the extent of Marion's racism. It was the site of one of the last famous cases of lynching in the twentieth century. I was a happy student at McCullough Elementary and Junior High School that bordered the Black section of town and enjoyed my friendships with Effie Brown and other Black students.

McCollough was very important to me educationally. I was in the "honors" track and wrote my graduation paper on ancient and archaic language in "The Rime of the Ancient Mariner," was the campus "Latin freak" (authoring the "Latin Play," a knock-off of the Pyramus and Thisbe story that lies behind the modern stage musical "The Fantastiks," and producing a multi-volume "Latin notebook" documenting the influence of Latin on modern English vocabulary), and otherwise enjoyed a certain academic precocity. I was looking forward to vindicating McCullough's Latin program and rising to greater heights at Marion High when my world caved in. My father decided to move to Wilmore, Kentucky to found the Wesleyan Seminary Foundation at Asbury Theological Seminary, an independent holiness seminary in the Methodist tradition that has since evolved more in the direction of "evangelical Methodism."

The family moved to Kentucky in 1957—an event that coincides with this celebration and will be similarly celebrated by a family reunion in early August. The Wesleyan Foundation at Asbury was, in effect, the founding of graduate theological education for the denomination. My father's move from Marion College marked, I am inclined to think, the transition from a "blue collar" to a "middle class" church that was beginning to require more than collegiate level ministerial education and preparation. I was very reluctant to leave my honors program in "junior high" to attend Nicholasville High School (merged while I was there to form Jessamine County High School), whose only attraction for me was the fact that in a sort of weird time lag it still taught Latin.

Jessamine County is nestled in the beautiful Bluegrass region of central Kentucky (known for its rolling hills and horse farms). I expect to be buried there with my parents in Bluegrass Memorial Gardens. But the county was quite segregated racially—and was known for its moonshine stills and the hemp and marijuana plants that grew naturally (sometimes hidden between rows of tobacco plants to shelter the plants from official eyes in helicopters). Its major tourist attractions were "High Bridge" (an early iron span over the Kentucky River designed by the man who did the Brooklyn Bridge; at the northern end was a radical Pentecostal campground of the anti-Trinitarian variety rumored also to be the site of snake handlers) and Shakertown (now a tourist park celebrating an early colony of the almost extinct religious movement, the "Shakers").

I was deeply shaken in high school by the launching of the Russian Sputnik, and by graduation I was rather committed to a career of helping the USA regain preeminence in the "space race," perhaps as an astrophysicist. This commitment to a scientific career was in part a response to the fact that the religious culture of the Wesleyan Church and Wilmore never took hold of me. I did respond once to an altar call under my father's ministry as an evangelist in the Watervliet, Michigan, Wesleyan Church, but was never able to internalize what was going on. I did have a short career as "Magíco, the Teenage Christian Magician and Hypnotist," but on an experiential level, I couldn't make holiness culture "compute" for me religiously. I often identify with a comment of David Tracy that he is a theologian, but religiously he is unmusical. No doubt this helps explain my attraction to Karl Barth whose "objectivism" was a response to the "subjectivism" of the pietistic tradition in which he was reared. People often assume from my advocacy of Pentecostalism and the Holiness movement that I am committed to a form of "experientialism." This is not at all true. My interpretation of Pentecostalism is "theological" in orientation and thus often at odds with such interpreters as Harvey Cox and Walter Hollenweger. The evangelist Finney was known for his lawyer-like rational arguments and the Holiness movement was pervaded by a sort of "forensic" doctrine of "sanctification" in the altar theology of Phoebe Palmer, in certain forms of Keswick theology, or even in themes of the "finished work" branch of Pentecostalism (the Assemblies of God, etc). These movements are often misinterpreted in the assumption that "emotionalism" is at the center.

Nor was I able to embrace what was increasingly the fundamentalist, or "neo-evangelical," rationalist reading of the tradition. I was fed a sort of "foundationalist" line that made inerrancy the "philosophical" basis of Christian certainty. I was told that if this epistemological doctrine were not true the Christian vision was unsustainable. I accepted this logic and decided to test it by reading as a high school student everything I could get my hands on about this doctrine. One of my family responsibilities was to travel with my father and operate the projector for slides of his holy land trips. As we traveled to various churches for the slides, I'm sure that I frustrated my father with questions about whether "inerrancy" could be sustained in light of the New Testament quotations of the Old or whether the doctrine required, for example, that "Enoch, the seventh from Adam" (in Jude) to be an historical personage or merely a quote from the pseudepigraphical book of Enoch, and so on. We debated the NIV version of the Bible (my father was one of the translators) versus the RSV (which I preferred, considering the NIV "fundamentalist" in its tendency to import dispensational themes into texts and to fudge translations of quotations of the OT in the NT to preserve the doctrine of "inerrancy" and perfect harmony, claiming that the Holy Spirit made the New Testament the definitive commentary on the meaning of the Old Testament). I came to the conclusion that inerrancy could not be sustained and thus that Christian faith could not be sustained. It took me several years to discover that it was possible to have a genuine doctrine of biblical authority without these fundamentalist assumptions. I kept these thoughts largely to myself, and was further alienated from Christian faith by the praise lavished on me in Wilmore as a marvelous Christian witness at the high school, secretly amused that my quiet rebellion was celebrated more than the genuine article. I quietly harbored a radically "scientistic" orientation and somewhat arrogantly considered myself above the myths that propped up the lives of lesser men.

I was graduated from high school in 1960, and, as Christian indicates, was irrevocably shaped by the decade of the 1960s. I am sometimes amazed at how much I managed to squeeze into those years. Much of my later thinking is little more that the sorting out of issues and experiences of that decade.

The first crisis for me was where to attend college. My mother, largely out of cultural aspiration I am convinced, wanted me to attend "evangelical icon" Wheaton College—an option I rejected out of hand. I found the school too pretentious and the students "snobs" (These intimations of the social class structure of the "evangelical" world were soon confirmed by the president of the junior class at Houghton College who greeted the incoming freshmen class with the words "welcome to Houghton, all you Wheaton rejects!"). I wanted to accept a place in the honors program of Transylvania University in Lexington, which I could afford by living at home—an option that would, however, unhappily delay my escape from the Wilmore culture. My parents opposed this after a visit to campus that found cigarette machines in abundance, evolution in the biology classes and ball room dancing in the physical education classes. They offered to sell the second car and subsidize me to the tune of fifty dollars a month if I would attend my father's *alma mater* (he would later become president) in upstate New York in the "burned-over district" (by the "fires" of repeated revivals): Houghton College, the most prestigious of the half-dozen Wesleyan colleges. I caved in under the pressure; Houghton was at least 750 miles away from Wilmore, though this option again delayed my escape from the broader holiness and "evangelical" culture.

Houghton was ironically at the same time the most sophisticated and prestigious of the Wesleyan colleges while also the most fundamentalist, and most embedded, precisely because of this openness, in the "neo-evangelical" culture (it was sometimes called the "Wheaton of the East"). I later came to prefer the culture of the other colleges as more authentic and representative of the tradition, even if more "provincial." My memories of Houghton are, perhaps unfairly, mostly negative. I finished in three years primarily because I didn't think I could endure a fourth. My math major was decent and I gravitated toward such topics as "abstract algebra" and "symbolic logic." I was moving, however, toward philosophy, largely in a search for a "world view" to replace the Christian faith in which I had been reared. I was Houghton's first philosophy major, but the major still consisted mostly of Christian apologetics and the like, especially the "neo-evangelical" debates between "presuppositonalism" (Gordon Clark and Cornelius van Til arguing from the "law of non-contradiction") and "evidentialism" (John Warwick Montgomery et al., arguing from the "evidence" for the Resurrection of Christ). I also had minors in classics and German.

I don't remember much intellectual stimulation in the curriculum. My most interesting professor, Ronald Nash, was fired (he was "amillennial" in eschatology and the author of the supposedly controversial *The New Evangelicals*, a defense of "neo-evangelicalism" that carried his Houghton College identification on the title page, supposedly without permission of the school). He was also the author of *The New Amsterdam Philosophy*, a defense of the Kuyperian and Dooeyweerdian traditions of Dutch Calvinism, and dreamed of creating a "Christian" department of philosophy along these lines in a secular university. The University of Rhode Island was his model, and he eventually did something along this line at the University of Western Kentucky. Another influential professor, Richard Troutman (an American historian and perhaps the only Democrat on the faculty) was also forced out. I had enrolled the fall of the Nixon/Kennedy election. It was clear that Nixon was favored (his roots were holiness Quaker and his pastor also served the Marion College Wesleyan Church).

My most positive memory of my time at Houghton was actually a trip off campus to Princeton to hear Karl Barth's lectures on "Evangelical Theology" on his American retirement tour. A religion professor and several students piled into a station wagon and slept on the floor of the home of a student from Philadelphia. We had one of the first requests for tickets and were mistakenly given alumni front row seats right in front of the lectern. As a result, I was standing next to Barth when a group from Westminster Seminary broke through the crowd to introduce Cornelius van Til, author of several books on Barth, including *Christianity and Barthianism* and another that called Barth the greatest heretic in Christian history. Van Til towered over Barth, but the more diminutive Barth merely looked up and with puckish humor responded "Ah yes, that naughty, naughty man from across the river."

The most influential intellectual stimulation came from reading that I did outside the curriculum. I was deeply influenced by a reading of Husserl's *Phenomenology* and have since been driven by a concern for an intellectual methodology that is constrained by a radical immersion in the object of study. I'm never sure whether to blame Husserl for the way in which I appropriated his book—perhaps it was an early exercise in "reader criticism." My affinity for Barth and my work on Pentecostalism are partially explained in terms of this exposure. I also did a lot of reading in analytical and language philosophy, exploring especially questions of epistemology and the "verification" of philosophical and theological convictions.

My real struggles with the College were with the culture of legalism that I found bizarre. I was college photographer for the PR department, yearbook and newspaper. A district of the church threatened to withdraw from the denomination unless one of my "pornographic" yearbooks was not cleaned up within a year (it did withdraw eventually over similar denominational compromises). At issue were pictures of the male swim team without T-shirts (perversely, I suppose I might admire the rejection of a double standard that found the exposure of male nipples as offensive as female ones!) and violations of the rule that skirts should cover female knees both standing and sitting (I embarrassed the president when the printer failed to crop as instructed a picture that included his daughter in all the glory of her knees!). Another picture was vetoed by the president as obscene because the folds in the back of the knees of cheerleaders were exposed (this photo I managed to smuggle into the yearbook about a dozen times, but not as the originally proposed two-page spread prominently introducing the section on athletics). A major crisis was precipitated by an issue of the campus newspaper in which I, professor Troutman, and a daughter of the editor of the denominational paper all called for a more open style of education. The college decreed that "opinion" could be expressed only in letters to the editor; we responded with an issue that consisted only of letters to the editor! I longed to escape from the culture.

I also found the school curriculum riddled with the quirks of the faculty, though through historical study I have since learned the wider roots of such. One could choose either Greek or mathematics as one curricular option—in part because of the spiritual struggle of the president who came to love mathematics so much that as a spiritual discipline he switched in graduate school to classical Greek. His brother, from whom I took "earth science," was such a biblical literalist that he made major life decisions by a "casting of lots" according to biblical precedent. The dean and chairman of the English department nearly committed suicide in graduate school and bargained with God that if he were enabled to finish the program he would never again read another novel. He taught only poetry and Shakespeare (I never grasped the casuistry that distinguished his bawdy plays from novels). The level of my "art appreciation" class seemed to be in line with the charter of the school to train pastors, evangelists, Sunday school superintendents, and "chalk talk artists" (The music program was quite sophisticated, however, and we used to joke about the marvelous musical "Bach-ground" that we gained there). Showing the influence of a stream of radical nineteenth Holiness thought, my English teacher claimed that she had not sinned in twenty-eight years (it seemed to me that the claim itself disproved it!). Nor did she convince me with her oft repeated claim that work that would get a student a "B" at Cornell was only worth a "C" at Houghton. When I tried to find Julius Wellhausen's *Prolegomena to the History of Ancient Israel* for a paper on the "documentary hypothesis" of the authorship of the Pentateuch, I was told that it was on "non-circulating reserve" (along with the Kinsey reports and the novel *Elmer Gantry*). These books could be read only with special permission from a professor and in presence of a librarian! *Elmer Gantry* ironically was on sale in the bookstore where it was being used in class by a young professor.

I graduated in 1963 as salutatorian; I was prevented from tying for valedictorian by a "B" in a one-hour phys-ed course as a freshman. I did receive "examination honors" in philosophy by scoring in the 99th percentile in the SAT disciplinary achievement test, but by a quirk in the testing program, on the exact same form of the test that I had taken in the fall for admission to graduate school. I dropped ten raw points between the beginning and the end of my major; that is, the work seemed to have had a negative effect on my understanding of the field. This led to an interesting exit interview with the dean to determine which elements of the curriculum had contributed to my high test scores!

These test scores were crucial, however, in my efforts to gain independence and move out on my own. Ever since high school, I had lusted after a Woodrow Wilson Fellowship (the foundation had written me when I had scored in the top half dozen students in Kentucky on a math test). When I became a finalist in the much more competitive Kent Fellowship program, I was convinced that I had the WWF and was devastated when I received my rejection. After I had made plans to study in the Institute of Liberal Arts at Emory University, I received a strange call from the Woodrow Wilson Foundation offering me a "pre-Woodrow Wilson Qualifying Fellowship" at Columbia University in New York. I was convinced someone had seen into my private lusts and was playing a cruel hoax on me, but the offer proved to be genuine. Only later did I discover that I was the token integration in an all African-American program of "affirmative action" designed to help reduce the drop-out rate of Black students in the program. Ivy League graduates serving as professors at Fiske, Morehouse, and so on had called the program racist and the Foundation scrambled to find a way to avoid the problem in public relations. I was their answer. They changed the name of the program to "culturally deprived" and in their file of rejects found me (a three year graduate of a rural, denominational college in upstate New York with straight 99th percentile rankings on all my SATs)—the prefect candidate to integrate their program under a new rubric.

My parents found the idea of Columbia even more frightening than Transylvania, but I was not going to turn down this opportunity. To keep family peace I agreed to a special course of preparation at Asbury Seminary designed to prepare me for the fearsome world of Columbia and New York City. So after my summer graduation at Houghton I returned to Wilmore for an inoculation against the disease of "liberalism." I had three study projects with Professor Harold Kuhn, the Asbury philosopher of religion (a holiness Quaker with deep commitment to the military culture but one of the "Harvard evangelicals" that dominated the first generation of "neo-evangelicalism"). He wanted me to study German idealism. I wanted to study Augustine and his commitment to Platonism. We compromised on an independent study in patristic refutations of heresies in Irenaeus and Augustine (I was fascinated by the struggle with gnosticism and remember Augustine's mock that Romans needed three gods and only one dog to protect their homes!). I was surprised that Christian ethics was taught by an extended exposition of the Ten Commandments (no distinctive NT or Christian themes were invoked) and was repeatedly told that the invention of the automobile (a "brothel on wheels") was the major cause of moral decline in twentieth century America. I suffered through what seemed to me a sort of "genre confusion" when I heard Aristotle critiqued for not laying a proper foundation for the "second coming" of Christ. But with such instruction I was deemed prepared for Columbia!

I loved New York City and Columbia. For many years I thought I would literally die if I did not find a way to return to New York and its cultural riches and bookstores (now mostly closed except for the Strand—as a poor graduate student I had to turn down a $5.00 signed copy of Dietrich Bonhoeffer's dissertation *Communio Sanctorm* from the library of Reinhold Niebuhr). To supplement my stipend I worked for Hannah Josephson (wife of Matthew, author of *The Robber Barons* and other such books) in the library of the American Academy of Arts and Letters. I served coffee to novelist John Updike, doled out a stipend to beat poet Gregory Corso a little at a time so that he would not waste it on his addictions (since then my contribution to "talent nights" has often been a bar stool reading of Corso and other "beatniks"), mounted a show of Jewish artist Ben Shahn and so on. I spent too much time in museums and off-Broadway theaters. I was determined to overcome my "cultural deprivation" in a few months!

It was an exciting time to be at Columbia. I attended "free speech" and SDS rallies at the sundial in the center of campus. Moving from Houghton to Columbia was like moving from one parochial school to another. Columbia was demographically and culturally Jewish, and the rabbinical students on the seventh floor of John Jay Hall were fascinated with me as a strange "culturally deprived" specimen from the hinterland. I was free to study what I wanted. I took a course on the history of the novel, studied the middle ages with medievalist Norman Cantor at Barnard College (for women) across the street, took Protestant Thought in America with Robert Handy at Union Seminary in the next block. But my major work was in philosophy. In a more classical vein I had one of the last philosophy of history classes of John Herman Randall, and in the more analytical tradition I studied theory of knowledge with Arthur Danto (a whole semester on whether all knowledge is known by inference from other knowledge or whether some is known directly) and metaphysics with Richard Taylor (a year long seminar on whether cause and effect could be contemporaneous). I loved the technical character of these latter courses, but I began to move away from philosophy because I was interested in the more classical patterns of the discipline. This I found eventually in my turn to theology. Mine has always been a more "liberal arts" interest in theology, and I have become convinced over the years that theology in our time has taken over many of the functions of classical philosophy for those seeking to think in a Christian manner and so understand human life.

It was at Columbia that I returned to the Christian faith. I had continued to read Karl Barth and Søren Kierkegaard and these became the instruments of my "reconversion" (My poor son is named Charles Soren for Kiekegaard, Barth, Charles Wesley, Charles Finney, and my favorite uncle Charles). A key to this was the fact that I had finally encountered a number of Christians whose faith I really admired. Many of these were a part of the Inter-Varsity Christian Fellowship on campus. A one-time Christian Nurses Fellowship staff member was loving prostitutes off the streets of New York in spite of being constantly ripped off, and bible studies were held in Greenwich Village artist lofts and included debates about modern art. I had finally found a form of Christian faith that was not "culturally provincial." My relationship to IVCF, however, was not unambiguous intellectually. Francis Schaeffer was the guru of the hour in such circles, and for him my heroes Barth and Kierkegaard marked the end of viable Christian theology. Thankfully, I had already been inoculated against his thought by my rejection of the doctrine of inerrancy. But I did find identity with this very diverse chapter of IVCF and participated in its efforts to "infiltrate" the Single Young Adults Fellowship at Riverside Church where we attempted to add bible studies and other programs to the usual tours of mid-town Manhattan architecture and the Museum of Modern Art.

During this year I decided that I wanted to go to seminary to find a theology for my newly found Christian faith, but the Woodrow Wilson

Foundation rules no longer allowed this; so, after being rejected by some of the finest universities on the east coast I finally settled on a PhD in the history of Christian Thought at Drew University. Drew said that I was the first student admitted to the PhD program without a seminary education, but that option didn't feel right. The WWF had become an albatross around my neck. I needed it to maintain my independence, but was not free to do what I thought I should do.

My experience in the program at Columbia was also profoundly influential as I struggled with racial issues with my classmates. I still have pictures from the campus newspaper of about a dozen Black students in a line with me on one end and a white dean on the other. I was shocked to discover the racism at Columbia—in ways that would have been unthinkable at Houghton. My whiteness gave me special privileges in the program and the dean clearly was not at all bothered by this. We students, of course, discussed all this together and I was commissioned to call the Foundation director to tell him about all this and insist we all be treated equally. It was quite an experience to have the racial situation reversed—for me to be the token integration for a program designed for African-Americans. Some relationships became quite close, and I roomed the next summer with two of the fellows in the program (one of them, Bob Allen, became an editor of the *Black Scholar* and the author with his wife of a book about the racism of the nineteenth century abolitionist movement). We lived on 118th street, and 1964 was the summer that the urban riots broke out on that street—the night my parents visited. This experience added urban questions to my struggles with racism and laid the foundations for a couple of decades of involvement in various forms of urban ministry.

Just as I was getting ready to move to Drew, my educational trajectory was radically altered in what I consider to be one of the most providential events in my life. A young Disciples minister, who had just graduated from Yale Divinity School and taken a job at the nearby Inter Church Center (the famous "475 Riverside Drive"), dropped in on the bible study in my apartment on a Wednesday night. I was so impressed with his Christ-like character (when his apartment was burglarized, rather than complain he rejoiced in the freedom from the worry over the safety of his possessions!). That first night I dumped all my struggles on him, and was stunned to discover that he had held a Woodrow Wilson fellowship at Yale Divinity School. Within ten days he had me admitted to Yale and against all odds and the new policy of the WW Foundation I convinced them to let me transfer my fellowship to YDS (I returned the favor when I dropped into his life years later and helped him with a struggle with drugs. He is now divorced and pastors a church, living with a same sex partner). I knew that my decision to go to Yale would create another family crisis. They would be delighted that I had opted for seminary, impressed that I would be studying at Yale, but horrified by the conjunction of the two. I was not surprised when prestige won out and the Christmas letter announced that "Don is pursuing further graduate study at Yale." As I left for Yale a Drew graduate student asked me why I wanted to study at that "fundamentalist school."

My Yale years were wonderful and could not have been better. They were the perfect solution for me—one that I had not known to reach for. It was the best time for me to be at Yale. It seemed (but was of course not literally true) that nearly every course began and ended with a volume of Barth's *Church Dogmatics*. I was in the teaching and research track, and after fulfilling a few distributional requirements, I divided my time between seminars in great figures in theology and work in biblical studies. I drank deeply at the wells of the emerging "Yale School" of biblical interpretation. I exorcised the demons of the Warfield (old Princeton theology) tradition in a seminar that laid the foundation for David Kelsey's book on Scripture. I had the seminar with Han Frei that became *The Eclipse of Biblical Narrative* (though I had "mono" that term and didn't absorb as much as I should have!). I was completely enamored with Brevard Childs, whose "canonical criticism" was still taking shape.

I consider Childs the greatest teacher that I have ever had, and I still think about Scripture in ways shaped by him. Over the years I have teased him that his project is essentially a Barthian agenda. He will grant this in private, but said that he would be laughed out of the Old Testament guild if he were to sail under those colors. YDS students were astounded when they asked what biblical commentary they should buy for their pastorates, expecting to hear something like *The Interpreter's Bible*. Childs and Sib Towner (who preached in my wedding) would recommend purchasing Barth's *Dogmatics* and using the Scripture indexes. The level of Childs' commitment to Barth was once revealed in his response to an article by Jerry Sheppard (his prize student and my close friend) in the *Union Seminary Quarterly Review*. Jerry offered a "gay positive" rereading of the Old Testament. Childs sent a postcard saying, "Jerry, you have betrayed Barth" (presumably because he had given too much credence to social science in guiding his reading of Scripture). But Childs was ever gracious—even when I stumbled through his advanced Hebrew seminar on the Psalms without ever having taken the summer elementary Hebrew intensive that had been cancelled for want of registrations. In exasperation

Childs exclaimed, "Don, you read Hebrew with what I can only describe as sort of a southern Egyptian accent!"

I had the last wonderful course on the History of Christian Thought offered by Robert Lowry Calhoun—one of the last of the great "liberals" now, as he said, "bloodied but unbowed." I was able to attend the weekly bible/prayer groups with Kenneth Scott Latourette, the great church historian. I had Paul Holmer on Kierkegaard and Wesley. That latter was a surprise to me. I enjoyed Holmer's chuckles over the wine bills in Wesley's papers and through his rather Kierkegaardian/Wittgensteinian reading of Wesley began to see that in many ways I was still a "Wesleyan" in theology at many key points. I took Augustine with Eugene TeSelle who would later write books on the saint and theologian—and had other similar experiences. I took a Barth seminar with Dean Robert Johnson—and modeled my popular Barth seminar over the years on his course. The students at Yale protested and demanded a course on Paul Tillich in a dean's office "sit-in." Johnson offered to teach one, commenting that he "had five faculty members who had written dissertations and books on Tillich but none of them now wanted to waste their time on such a minor bump on the theological log." I skipped this one; I had read Tillich's three volumes of systematic theology at Columbia on my own. My major academic regrets have been that I did not take work with ethicist James Gustafson (that was remedied at Chicago a few years later) and theologian George Lindbeck.

I can only remember one negative experience. I cut the whole second semester of systematic theology because I was unimpressed by the lectures, but passed the course by attending all the tutorials in which we read through Calvin's *Institutes*. I wound up writing very significant papers in my own development that rejected Calvin's model of divine human interaction and offered a Barthian critique of Calvin's Christology. I have several times since taught my way through the *Institutes*, and am always surprised by those who assume that my Wesleyanism should make me hostile to the Calvinistic tradition.

I was profoundly shaped as well by various co-curricular experiences. The first semester I joined other students on an election time trek to Mississippi to work with civil rights organizations like SNCC and COFO in gathering statistics for Fannie Lou Hamer and the Mississippi Freedom Democratic Party to challenge the seating in Congress of the regular Democrats. I have vivid memories of crawling in the mud through bushes to avoid the police in Gulfport and Biloxi and sleeping on the floor of the Civil Rights Office in Jackson with the White Citizens' Council prowling outside in pickup trucks. We feared that any moment we might bombed with Molotov cocktails. I worked in a black Disciples Church in the Black section of New Haven. One year I was buyer for the YDS book co-op, which helped propel me toward a career in librarianship (The manager that year was Charles Willard, later librarian at Princeton and Harvard). I graduated with double the required number of field work credits. Three of these were from my work as an orderly at Yale Psychiatric Institute. YPI specialized in male juvenile delinquents and sociopaths (which did wonders for my pool game) and highly alienated Yale schizophrenic dropouts. With the latter I remember many conversations sitting on the floor of padded cells in "solitary confinement" discussing whether neurosis and psychosis aided or blocked creative expression.

I was also a freshmen counselor for a year in Pierson College—in spite of the nervousness of the student personnel office that a divinity student might be too interested in converting the students. As I look back on this experience, it was more the opposite. I was trying to compensate for my "cultural deprivation" by playing "Yalie" for a year. I wore penny loafers with bright shiny pennies, Gant shirts with the little loop on the back from the Yale Co-op, preppy chino pants and tweedy sport coats—all in an effort to experience what my "cultural marginalization" had denied me. One element of my disappointment with the divinity school had been the discovery, after arriving supposedly at an elite Ivy League institution, that most of my classmates were graduates of Midwestern and Southern church colleges on a similar sociological trajectory. But the year was a good experience, and I eventually outgrew my tendencies to overcompensate with a compulsive desire to assimilate into mainstream culture. Novelist John Hersey was the master of Pierson College and my dorm was next to Battell Chapel. William Sloane Coffin was chaplain, and I came to admire this man very much (he was later pastor of Riverside Church in New York and very controversial for his anti-Vietnam War activities; I shall never forget the standing ovation he received after a lecture on sex ethics to 1500 horny teenagers as a part of the Yale freshmen orientation).

It was also at Yale that I first began to take Pentecostalism seriously. Shortly before my arrival Harald Bredesen of the Reformed Church of America had visited campus and brought "charismatic renewal" to the Yale Inter-Varsity (an event enshrined in most histories of the charismatic movement). The results had been mixed. When I arrived, some students were in a "burned out" post-charismatic stage, and the IVCF had split into a radical and somewhat sectarian "God Squad" that required the exercise of spiritual gifts and a more moderate group that tolerated them. The "God Squad" created great controversy on campus with their aggressive evangelism among Jewish students. I was about the only YDS student who knew these circles and so arranged a session of "YDS meets the God Squad" on campus. I became a friend of several members of the moderate group and ended up rooming at YDS with an Episcopalian who had been part of this renewal. All of this enlivened my interest in this Pentecostal/Charismatic tradition, but I have never embraced it experientially.

In the middle of 1966 I dropped out for two years to travel and add to my reservoir of experience, again packing an incredibly diverse range into a short period. I spent June in Brooklyn in an exposure course in urban ministry with Gilbert James, Professor of Church and Society at Asbury Seminary (he preferred the title "Professor of Worldliness!). Gilbert was the son of a socialist carnival worker, had attended God's Bible School in Cincinnati (a school in the "radical holiness" tradition) and had a PhD in urban sociology from Northwestern University. He became so influential a mentor that I dedicated the first edition of *Discovering an Evangelical Heritage* to him. It was also in this course that I first met Howard Snyder and formed a friendship that has lasted over the years. This experience was the first major step in a couple of decades of interest in urban ministry. I worked with Howard in his church in Chicago, his modernizing of the ministries of the Olive Branch rescue mission there, and with the Wesleyan Urban Coalition which he founded to bring college students to Chicago for immersion experiences.

The rest of the summer I spent in volunteer mission work in Medellin, Colombia. My whole family went down. I read the Tolkien trilogy while laid up with whatever the Colombian counterpart of Montezuma's revenge might be. The trip included a week on the Amazon in canoes. I was not terribly impressed by this experience. It seemed that the missionaries spent most of their time on the "Plantelle" holding silver tea receptions for visiting church groups. I was also turned off by the "colonial" style of relating to Colombians (not allowed to enter the houses, for example, lest they become too accustomed to such luxury and not return to their villages on the Amazon). This was, however, I believe, my first trip abroad. In a sense it was the beginning of my rather extensive foreign travel (I've visited at least sixty countries, studied on four continents, and lectured in two more—missing only Antarctica!). It was also the beginning of my interest in Latin America, where I have studied and taught for extended periods of time. For a decade or so I was the only outsider to participate in the international gatherings of Latin American indigenous Pentecostalism, and the Spanish edition of my *Theological Roots of Pentecostalism* has had a substantial influence there. I recently reaffirmed this interest by buying a half-interest in a condo in the center of Buenos Aires.

I returned to the USA for a fall term as a student ministry intern at Greenville College, a Free Methodist College in Illinois near St. Louis. This was a stunning experience. I still have close friends from this period and remember with nostalgia all-night conversations with students sitting in (yes, in!) the dryers at the village laundry-mat. It was fun to live in the dorm while the faculty debated dropping the ban on movies. The faculty seemed to live with the conceit that their decision would have an influence on student behavior. I assisted Professor Stanley Walters, who later taught OT in Toronto and served as best man in my wedding.

In January of 1967 I left for a term in Israel at the Institute of Holy Land Studies in Jerusalem. My father was serving on the board and arranged a scholarship for me. This school had in a sense been founded in Israel to be where the action would be in the "end times," though it advocated a "covenantal" rather than a more radical "dispensational" orientation. My classmates were an odd assortment of bible school and seminary students (including a future leader of the "Jews for Jesus" and future professors) who found intriguing my relative lack of interest in biblical prophecy. We had a stunning program of field trips that took us in the back of a truck over most of the roads in the country to visit every site of biblical interest. We also excavated with Bill Dever at tel Gezer attempting to confirm the hypothesis of Yigael Yadin that what had been identified as a Hellenistic warehouse in the early excavations of R. A. S. Macalister was actually a "Solomonic gate" that had parallels at Hazor and Megiddo. I was the one that unearthed our modest find (an Egyptian scarab) and my shovel first hit what did turn out to be a "Solomonic gate."

A couple of students left as war threatened, but most of us voted to stay in part in solidarity with the Jewish people (most foreigners and Christians were on foreign passports and left in times of danger, leaving the Israelis fearful and evoking memories of the holocaust). The head of the Evangelical Free Church amused me by scrambling home before the war to write a book on the six day war (he didn't need to stay as we had; he used biblical prophecy as his source material!). The war broke out in June (I write this autobiographical response on the fortieth anniversary of this war). My basement room in the school on the Street of the Prophets a few blocks from the border served as our bomb shelter for a couple of days (the Jordanians were trying to take out an Israeli command post across the street and often hit our building). After a couple of days we emerged to serve sandwiches to the Israeli soldiers, attempting unsuccessfully to snare them into revealing hatred for their enemies (I think this orientation has declined in the years since).

I was so caught up in all this that I postponed my return to Yale to live on a Kibbutz near Megiddo to take an "ulpan" (an intensive course in modern Hebrew) and live through the aftermath of the war. This kibbutz was radically socialist (so much so that children were not allowed to stay overnight in their parents home, but had to return to the "house of the children" to symbolize the fact that their rearing was a communal responsibility). It was also secular in orientation (deliberately fielding Sabbath work teams), but this allowed me to take Sunday off to attend an Episcopal church in Haifa. I was able to tour the occupied territories of Syrian Golan Heights and Jordan's West Bank. The latter almost made me regret that I had earlier sneaked across the border during Easter week, as I almost froze nights in a hammock in the gardener's shed at the "Garden Tomb" in old Jerusalem; it was the first time it had snowed and sleeted for a whole week in a century! I worked half a day in the kibbutz fruit crate factory to earn half a day of Hebrew instruction. This experience was deeply influential. Part of my intention had been to place myself in a context completely different from anything I had ever experienced in an effort to test whether I would sustain my emerging Christian convictions without the usual cultural props. And I continue to have concerns that most forms of Christianity have too strongly suppressed OT roots, and notice that sectarian protests against mainstream Christianity (Seventh-Day Adventism, Oneness Pentecostalism, the Jehovah's Witnesses, Mormonism, etc.) often attempt to redress this tendency. I tend to read the NT through the OT rather than vice versa and am convinced that these questions need further exploration. Rooted in this discussion are some of the reasons that I prefer the Wesleyan articulation of Christian faith to the Lutheran and classically Protestant ones.

I spent a couple of months on a "grand tour" of Europe on my way home. I squeezed every mile out of my return ticket and traveled on less than $5.00 a day by sleeping in bus and train stations. I visited several of the seven cities of the book of the Revelation in southwest Turkey, the classical sites of Greece, and the Christian spots in Rome, did my art tour of Italy, slipped behind the iron curtain in Germany and Czechoslovakia, did a Kierkegaard pilgrimage in Denmark, nervously wandered through German cities (sensitized by a year in Israel), did the low countries, and spent a couple of weeks in England on a Wesley pilgrimage.

I returned home to await the next academic year at Yale and put the time to use in studying New Testament at Asbury Seminary. I eventually completed all the classwork for a ThM, but never finished the thesis comparing Barth and Bultmann on Romans 5 (the accrediting association forced Asbury to end the program and I didn't make the deadline which came in the midst of my PhD studies). I was very aware of faculty politics. As I studied in the dining room, I often heard my father and Harold Kuhn in the living room plotting against my favorite faculty members, Gilbert James and NT professor Bob Lyon. Gil James wanted me to take notes, because he was sure that all this would result in legal action. As it happened, under the administration of President Frank Bateman Stanger, who had brought these faculty members to Asbury, a conservative wing of the faculty (inerrantists committed to the traditional campmeeting culture and theology) were pushed to the side and began to leave. Stanger was brought in to restore accreditation that had been lost in the 1950s so that Asbury could more easily serve mainstream Methodist students. My father did not leave until about 1970, but I have often teased my Asbury friends that my father left when Asbury "went liberal."

That summer I began an MS in library science. I did this very deliberately for several reasons. I was a natural bibliophile (some would say "biblioholic") and found this a natural career. I wanted to remain a theological generalist with an overview of the theological disciplines, and the library was a good location for this. I admired many of the great theological librarians like Charles Briggs and Adolph von Harnack. I needed a way to finance my doctoral studies (and my PhD expenses became tax deductible once I had achieved a faculty appointment!). And most importantly I was unsure about how I would fit into any of the theological locations that I knew. Most people will tolerate all kinds of idiosyncrasies in the librarian, and with certain resources in such an administrative position, it is a very good place from which to do "theology from the margins." The University of Kentucky gave me a scholarship. I specialized in the book trade, reference and bibliography, and so on. I continued my tendency toward academic socio-pathology by being enrolled in both Asbury and UK, even to the point of taking two courses that met at the same time.

I returned to Yale to finish my BD and had a whirlwind courtship that ended in a thanksgiving engagement. On June 9, 1969, I had University commencement in the morning, YDS services in the afternoon, and a wedding service in the evening. I was ready to begin my career. I had two offers. Chuck Willard of the YDS bookstore was now the librarian at Princeton and wanted me to become the reference librarian there. Asbury wanted me to be acquisitions librarian and offered a comparable salary in a much cheaper housing market. I went to Asbury on economic grounds and curious to see if I could function in that context before I began my doctoral studies where I would face larger questions of theological identity.

I spent three years at Asbury, in part so that my wife could do a degree in student personnel work at UK. I finished my MS in December and formally was appointed to the faculty. I overlapped with my father on the faculty for a year. Our votes often, but not always, cancelled each other out. My father was in the midst of a career crisis and, apparently on the losing end in the political struggle, returned to Marion College for a year or so before being elected the president of Houghton College. My responsibility, in addition to collection development, was to teach a course in "bibliography and research method" tailored to each program that required a thesis. This I did with enthusiasm, and students often said they learned more about theological method in these classes than in their theology classes.

I must give tribute to Sue Schultz the librarian. She ran the most progressive and forward-looking library that I have ever experienced. I left librarianship a little over a decade later in part because I could not find anything as congenial—and in part because librarianship became more a matter of computers than books. Our librarians were scholars in their own right and the library was a major center of the intellectual activity on campus (this tradition at Asbury has recently been decimated). We created some controversy by holding in the library a standing room only memorial service after the assassination of Martin Luther King, Jr.—and even more by inviting Vinson Synan of the Pentecostal Holiness Church to speak on continuities between the Holiness and Pentecostal Movements. This latter lecture confronted the official line of separation and distance. The Holiness movement has always been threatened by its more radical and successful offspring—Pentecostalism. Bill Faupel, David Bundy and I were committed to academic orientations that emphasized the continuities, and the three of us from this original triumvirate have carved out careers based on this assumption.

My major intellectual reorientation at Asbury came in response to an uncharacteristically direct order by Sue Schultz. The library association had a practice of inviting bibliographic papers on the theological tradition of the institutions at which it held its annual meeting—so that other libraries could be guided in collecting the basic literature of each tradition. We were going to meet at Pasadena College of the Church of the Nazarene, and Sue was committed to a paper on the Holiness movement. Delbert Rose, the official historian of the Christian Holiness Association, refused to spend his limited travel budget from Asbury on this project, and Sue in desperation turned to me. I protested, saying that I had no interest in such a project. I had no knowledge of the material and didn't want to get in to it. She insisted that I do it, releasing me for months from all but the essential library work to complete this project. This changed my life.

I was fascinated by the literature that broke many of my stereotypes. I gave the paper and the library published a pamphlet version of it—my first major publication. This in turn inspired Bill Faupel to do a counterpart on the Pentecostal tradition, which in turn inspired David Bundy to produce one on the Keswick movement, the more moderate holiness piety that dominates the "evangelical" world. These pamphlets became the defining basis of a project that over a decade later came to fruition in a reprint series of forty-eight volumes of source material for the study of "The Higher Christian Life." This project in many ways redefined the relationship between these movements and their connections to abolitionism, the ministry of women, and so forth. The publisher said that it was their bestselling reprint series. There is a sense in which scholarship is still catching up with many of the implications of this material (the history of the ministry of women, for example, or the historiography of American "fundamentalism" and "evangelicalism"). This bibliographic paper also sucked me into collecting this material while it was still available, resulting in a collection of perhaps 10,000 volumes, most of them now in the library of Fuller Theological Seminary under the care of David Bundy. It was the eventual sale of this material that paid for my son's undergraduate education at the University of Chicago.

It was at Asbury that I ran into a conflict with the denomination over ordination. I was pressured by Asbury to get ordained so that they could save a few hundred dollars on my social security taxes. I resisted this, not only because I found this a less than noble reason for ordination but also because I had a growing commitment to a "low church" ecclesiology that gave much less weight to ordination. My wife on the other hand, struggling for women's ordination, found it an important symbol. I finally relented and sought ordination in western New York based on my continuing membership in the Houghton Church. I had shifted in that direction because I was planning a double ring ceremony and Indiana had yet to ordain anyone whose spouse wore a wedding ring. In western New York a few spouses but no ministers wore wedding rings (All this in response to the biblical injunction to avoid the putting on of gold and silver!). I had not taken into account that it was this conference that had "memorialized" the General Conference to insert the word "inerrancy" into the article of religion on Scripture. My first question in the ordination interview was:

what word would I use to describe the "original autographs"? I was not quick enough on the uptake to say "lost" and refused to say the word "inerrant" while insisting that I was in the circle and could sign earlier and related statements. The interview was officially over, but the committee was embarrassed to have me walk out immediately. They used the time to have me reflect on "the drug culture of the modern university." I was relieved to have a good excuse not to pursue ordination.

On reflection, I think there was more at stake than meets the eye. My District Superintendent was probably as much offended by my civil rights work as by my theology. He was the only person I have ever known to wear a Spiro Agnew watch (whose hands move backward) out of genuine admiration for the man. I was surprised by my father's reaction. Blood *is* apparently thicker than theology. He thought that since I knew more about the subject than any of my questioners, I should have discerned the question behind the question and answered in words that spoke to that question and reassured them that I really believed in biblical authority. I was not about to compromise my hard fought conclusions about this doctrine and have never really regretted what happened. I have had more freedom not being under ecclesiastical authority and have handled the problem (in what I hope is a spirit of generosity) by remaining identified with the church as a "lay theologian" and perhaps the major articulator of the significance of the church to the outside world—though not always for the reasons that the church would wish.

This stance has had major implications for my positioning in the ecclesiastical world. "Inerrancy" was for a long time the single marker of "evangelical" identity, especially for the "neo-evangelical" tradition and the Evangelical Theological Society that for a long time required adherence only to this doctrine. I could not work in such arenas. The early confessions of the Wesleyan Theological Society and the Society for Pentecostal Studies tended to use the word in initial years of their development under the influence of the neo-evangelicals. Some of us petitioned the WTS in the late 1960s to eliminate this word as divisive and not characteristic of the original impulse of the tradition. In the late 1960s the word was changed after a tie vote was broken, and since then, in several steps, the neo-evangelical influence has been repudiated. Similar developments took place in the Pentecostal society. I have then done most of my theological work in these two arenas—and occasionally in the "evangelical studies" group of the American Academy of Religion, founded along with the Institute for Biblical Research in the Society for Biblical Literature to provide arenas for those who refused to make this subscription. I have been president of both WTS and SPS (the only non-Pentecostal, non-Charismatic to serve in this position). I have also chaired the "evangelical studies" section of the AAR.

Before I left Asbury I had the chance to tweak the editors of *Christianity Today* on this question. Harold Lindsell had editorialized about Hans Küng's rejection of papal infallibility and endorsed his book *Infallible?* In a letter to the editor, I couldn't help pointing out that the real thesis was found much later in the book than his quotations: that God alone is infallible and therefore neither the pope or church nor the Scriptures were to be so described. In private correspondence, Lindsell responded that it was the essence of good scholarship to take from a book that with which one agreed and leave behind that which one rejected. I couldn't help replying that it was not good scholarship to take the conclusion of an argument while rejecting the premises on which it is based. Lindsell went on to engage me in his polemics on these questions in *The Battle for the Bible* and *The Bible in the Balance*. With this act I shook the dust of inerrancy off my feet and never looked back. And I have become increasingly disenchanted with any use of the word "evangelical" presupposing the neo-evangelical stance on this question. This tendency has been increased in more recent years by the rise of the politics of the new religious right, and I now prefer the label "Holiness" to "evangelical"—to the point of puzzling people with the complaint, "why should I be called with the name of my theological enemies."

At Asbury I began to spend summers teaching with Gilbert James in the Lilly-funded Urban Ministry Program for Seminarians (UMPS). I became committed to that great "second city" Chicago and moved there in 1972 to begin graduate study at the Divinity School of the University of Chicago and to continue various urban ministry ventures in this area. I was twice diplomaed by the Urban Training Center with its "plunges" on the streets of Chicago (I slept in Pacific Garden Mission and behind a flying buttress of St. James Episcopal Cathedral). When the UMPS network was reconfigured as the nucleus of the Seminary Consortium for Urban Pastoral Education (SCUPE) I served on the board and faculty until I became disillusioned with SCUPE's drift toward a more psychological and CPE orientation leaving behind a more sociological and outward looking style. I regularly participated in a bible study of Chicago professors of urban ministry and worked with Howard Snyder on his various projects.

I loved my experience at the University of Chicago. Many students were unhappy, wanting the divinity school to be church and womb as well as university. I, on the other hand, loved the sheer intellectuality of the place. I was there in glory years. I had realized after leaving Yale that the person I wanted most to study with would have been ethicist James Gustafson, but I had decided to go to Chicago on other grounds. In another providential educational fluke, it was announced that summer that Gustafson was moving from Yale to Chicago. As I heard the story, Gustafson had been frustrated with moves to take the PhD program at Yale out of YDS to lodge it in the religion department and subject it to the social scientific and history of religion methodologies there, thus undercutting the great tradition of classical theology at Yale. By a fluke, the design of the curriculum at Chicago, the great center of empirical theology, had among seven disciplines retained the PhD in both the History of Christianity and Christian Theology while consigning the other five to a more social scientific and cultural orientation. Gustafson's arrival marked a sharp break in the life of Chicago. He had replaced the great process theologian Schubert Odgen. I still remember the gasps of the theology students who asked Gustafson about his relationship to process theology and he unapologetically replied, "That's one tradition that I have never managed to internalize." One could hear the theological gears stripping as Chicago made a major turn. I consider Gustafson another great teacher, though we had a few awkward moments when he realized that I was the one who had reviewed one of his books in the *Christian Century*, praising his great analytical skills but wondering if he would ever break through to a major synthetic statement.

I loved David Tracy as well. He tells me he still remembers my paper in a Lonergan seminar where I offered a sort of Barthian critique of Lonergan's tendency toward Catholic themes of natural theology. Gustafson offered with Tracy seminars on classical themes in theology (method, love, sin). I took them all. I also had a seminar that Tracy taught with Paul Ricoeur. I still remember a comment of Riceour to a student, "But you forget that theologically I am a Barthian." I studied contemporary theology with Langdon Gilkey, who was more Tillichian in orientation, and I was intimidated by his glancing at me whenever he referred to Barth, often critically. It took me a long time to tumble to the fact that he was a little threatened to have in class a member of the board of the Karl Barth Society of North America and was checking my reaction before he committed himself too fully to a line of interpretation. I studied revivalism with Jerald Brauer and unsettled him a bit by questioning his use of the history of religion categories of Mircea Eliade to interpret revival preaching as a call to an "initiatory rite" (his great contribution to church history after years of deaning). I argued on the other hand that the word "revival" had to be taken seriously as an exercise in the "reviving" of the already initiated. I liked Martin Marty a great deal; we read books in the same way (he once said, "that's about a half-hour book, isn't it, Don?"). I still chuckle over the campus joke about the student who called Marty, got the secretary, and was told that he was not available because he was writing a book. The student was reported to have replied, "That's all right; I'll hold." Another key experience was my work with Brian Gerrish, though we had some tensions over his agenda to overthrow the "Barthian revolution" and return to the unfinished tasks of nineteenth-century liberal theology. Ironically, because I was the only member of his history of Christian thought class that knew the names of figures in the tradition of scholastic Calvinism he kept putting me in the wrong box theologically.

My original intention was to write on Barth's doctrine of sanctification. Gustafson vetoed that and pulled down a dissertation from his shelf, plopped it on his desk and said, "Sorry, Stan Hauerwas has already done that." In a contextual with Marty on Oberlin Perfectionism, I encountered the writings of Asa Mahan, the first president of Oberlin College, and felt that I had fallen onto the keys to unlock "the theological roots of Pentecostalism." Tracy and Marty encouraged me to take on this topic, suggesting that everybody and his uncle in Europe was writing on Barth and probably understood him in their bones, while I would be one of only a handful working on this new topic. I did a quick market analysis based on the growth trajectories of Pentecostalism and concurred. Gustafson and Marty became co-directors and Brauer joined the committee. It took a few years (I was still collecting books), and I disciplined myself by volunteering chapters as conference papers. I finished in the early 1980s after more than a decade, still not bad by Chicago standards that averaged over a dozen years between collegiate degrees and the Ph.D—and I was working full-time! None of my committee had much of an idea what I was doing and left me alone to do my own thing. I wondered what I was paying my tuition for, but appreciated the freedom. The dissertation was accepted with little feedback (Gustafson thought, incorrectly actually, that he had detected four typos) and the oral defense was waived. Marty approved it with the comment, "It teaches well; I taught it this morning."

I was unprepared for the storm that would follow the dissertation. Much of the reaction is detailed in the essay in this book responding to my critics. An early report of my work won the SPS "student essay contest" and began to circulate. The Nazarenes were particularly threatened because it called into question their claim to be Wesleyan. I once infuriated Timothy Smith, the great Nazarene scholar, by suggesting that his theology was closer to Pentecostalism than to Wesley (and this only after his systematic attack on my original essay). He began a campaign to discredit my work. He for a decade or so proposed a paper attacking me for every WTS annual meeting. He published a least two books that he thought proved me wrong and spent many of the latter years of his life studying Wesley to prove his own interpretation. The Fuller seminary archives has the draft of the dissertation that he red-penciled. This issue has continued in dialogue with Larry Wood, as discussed in some of the responses in this book.

My book has been translated into Spanish and Korean (where it has gone through several printings, meaning that I am probably better known per capita in Korea than in the USA) and is being translated into Chinese. It needs yet a Portuguese translation. The book has been especially important in Latin America. It has been more or less the only sympathetic theological analysis of Pentecostalism in Spanish and has helped Pentecostalism to find its place in the larger Christian world. I am proud of the fact that my writings continue in print after two or three decades.

I supported myself at Chicago by serving as librarian at North Park Theological Seminary. I enjoyed my experience there very much, and it may have been a mistake to have left after seven years. North Park is supported by the Evangelical Covenant Church, sometimes jokingly called the "episcopalianism" of "evangelicalism" for its liturgical sensitivities and more advantaged middle class social location. It claims roots in Swedish Pietism, and while at North Park I came to appreciate the importance of Pietism for the interpretation of many things. Some of this work came to fruition when I edited for *The Covenant Quarterly* papers from an AAR session that we planned on Pietism. This was also published in book form as *Contemporary Perspectives on Pietism*.

A major area of scholarly work while at North Park was in "women's studies," especially the history of the ordination of women. I attempted to join the disciplinary group in the Chicago area theological consortium, but soon found that this was a gender specific support group in which I was not particularly welcome. I published a number of articles in this field but eventually backed away. I much later tried to harvest this work in the SBL plenary paper included it this volume. It contains most of my insights in this area.

My moving to Chicago brought me into contact with the emerging Sojourners community. I became the first book editor of *Sojourners* just as they moved to Washington, D. C. This distance did not work, but I remained a contributing editor for many years. I also became involved with most of the similar magazines of the era. I was a contributing editor to *The Other Side* with its roots in the Civil Rights movement. *Daughters of Sarah*, the Christian feminist magazine was an occupational therapy project to get my wife out of a bout with depression. I duplicated and mailed the early issues. I was a contributing editor with *The Epworth Pulpit*, a Nazarene equivalent (The title relies on the image of John Wesley standing on the grave of his father to preach to the Epworth congregation after being locked out of his father's church). I worked with the urban ministry oriented Boston magazine *Inside* and was involved with *Right On* (later *Radix*) out of Berkeley.

These currents came together in 1973 to produce "The Chicago Declaration of Evangelical Social Concern," an event that the *Chicago Sun Times* called the most important of the decade in the religious world. Burton Nelson and I hosted the planning committee at North Park when Ron Sider could fly in from Philadelphia, David Moberg could come down from Marquette, and Richard Pierard could drive up from Indiana State in Terre Haute. The meeting brought together these various groups of "young" and "post" evangelicals and a few of the older generation (especially Carl Henry, Rufus Jones, Paul Rees, and Vernon Grounds, as I remember) to confess "evangelical" neglect of social responsibility and issue a call for renewed engagement. This event has not received the attention it deserves; so I would like to offer some analysis of its importance.

It should be noted that this event harvested currents that had been circulating for as long as a decade or so and took place half a dozen years before the founding of Jerry Falwell's Moral Majority. That is, the first calls of this sort were more from the "left" (of the sixties), but were later overwhelmed by the rise of the "new religious right." Many have joked with us that we were too successful in calling the evangelical world into the social arena. Most analyses of the new religious right start the story too late and don't have the full picture. The history of this decade has yet to be fully written, though fragments exist.

Secondly, this event was based on trajectories that converged for a moment and then diverged. It was rooted in a variety of disaffections with the "evangelical" world. Bob Webber of Wheaton was on the "Canterbury trail" toward a reaffirmation of classical patristic theology and liturgy, for example, and social concern was less central to his vision. I was continuing my path out of "generic evangelicalism" to reaffirm my own tradition in its distinctiveness and to a recovering of its tradition of social engagement before it had become "evangelicalized." Some were coming out of the Jesus Movement of the 1960s and moving toward a more classical Christianity. Others were scandalized by either the conservatism or passivity of the "evangelical" world. Some, like *Sojourners*, were drinking at the wells of Anabaptism and the left wing of the reformation under the tutelage of John Howard Yoder, while others worked within the Reformed, more theocratic tradition. A couple were evangelicals at secular universities and had evolved into progressive Democrats. It was remarkable that we were able to make a common statement, something that might not have been possible a year or two later or earlier.

This was soon made clear in a follow up meeting at North Park. It was not possible to make a common positive statement of an agenda. We explored different models of Christian social engagement (Reformed, Anabaptist, revivalist in my case), and failed to find a unity that we could share. I have argued since that there is no such thing as a "generic" evangelical social ethic. As soon as one opens up the ethical questions, one is driven back to specific Christian traditions. One becomes a Lutheran, a Calvinist, a Catholic, and so forth, and these differences are more important than an undefinable vague "evangelical" identity. I argued in the 1970s and 1980s with David Gill and others that there is no such thing as an "evangelical" ethic in the modern "neo-evangelical" sense. More recently I have been arguing with Peter Heltzel of New York Theological that he cannot give coherence to his category of a "progressive evangelical social ethic."

Sojourners struggled in this era with its "evangelical" identity. Carl Henry reviewed in *Christianity Today* under the title "Revolt on the Evangelical Frontiers" an early book by Richard Quebedeaux on the "young evangelicals." Jim Wallis replied that he disagreed with Henry not on theology but only on the role of the US in the world in a "post-American" era. I responded in a lengthy memo that this was foolishness and that the Sojourners vision was as different a vision of Christianity as might be found between confessional traditions (I later forced Harold Lindsell to take out of *The Battle for the Bible* unauthorized and dishonestly used quotations from this memo). I argued that Sojourners was the carrier of a new vision and that "evangelicalism" was only one root of that vision. As important, or perhaps more important, were such roots as John Howard Yoder's articulation of the Anabaptist tradition, the socially radical (and gay!) Episcopalian lawyer Bill Stringfellow, Dan Berrigan and the (predominantly Catholic) Center for Creative Non-Violence, the 1960s charismatic communal movements (like the "Fisher Folk"), and so forth. I suggested Sojourners' significance was also "ecumenical" in that it was read with equal enthusiasm in Geneva and Wheaton, Fuller and Union—and that it would never fulfill its calling until it cut itself loose from its "evangelical" identity to serve the whole Christian world. In spite of its continuing breadth and positions that often could hardly be called "evangelical," the magazine is often called "progressive evangelical" and I am amused when Jim is introduced on television as an "evangelical minister." Such labels contribute to the misperception that Sojourners is little more than "enlightened evangelicalism."

Ron Sider and I began to pick up debates from classes together at Yale. In a course on the OT prophets with Sib Towner we had divided on how to interpret passages like Amos' call to "Return to the Lord; Establish justice in the gate." For him this text spoke of two moments: Return to God in a sort of Lutheran fashion apart from works and then as an act of discipleship seek justice. I argued that this was a Hebrew parallelism—the two phrases meant the same thing. One returns to God by establishing justice. In the wake of the "Chicago Declaration" we debated the theological health of the "evangelical" world. He thought it was essentially healthy and all that was needed was to add the fruit of social responsibility. I argued that there was no fruit because the roots were bad, that things needed to be rethought from the ground up and that the movement had discredited itself in its reaction to the civil rights movement and other issues.

I argued for the ecumenical significance of the "Chicago Declaration," especially when Dean Kelly, author of *Why Conservative Churches Are Growing* and head of the National Council Board of Church and Society, led his group in a parallel confession of the sins of the "mainstream." I considered this one of the most important ecumenical events in mid-twentieth century America and fought for the publication of the NCC statement. Ron resisted this because his narrow "evangelical" agenda was threatened. But we did have a secret meeting with the NCC in the Poconos to ponder the significance of the two statements—and we met in other dialogues in Washington and elsewhere. I argued at the time with Ron (who was then my brother-in-law!) that if he was willing to reconsider the neo-evangelical understanding of Scripture, as he had done at Yale, and to rethink the importance of the "social gospel," as in the "Chicago Declaration," then he lacked integrity if he was unwilling to open up the question of "ecumenical fellowship" that had been broken over the other two issues. We began to part ways, he to found "Evangelicals for Social Action" with a narrower agenda, while I moved toward ecumenical and church unity questions through a variety of channels.

I was driven by all this to explore my own traditions of social action (the abolitionist Wesleyan church and others). This movement was given more energy by our efforts to promote the "Chicago Declaration." Ron tried to get the National Association of Evangelicals to adopt it as a resolution, but the NAE (already on a trajectory toward the "new religious right") wouldn't touch it with a ten-foot pole. I took it to the executive committee of the Christian Holiness Association where it was resisted for completely different reasons. A Nazarene who had been arrested the previous decade for his civil rights work didn't identify with the statement, and a Salvation Army officer echoed his sentiments. But they agreed to propose it, especially if it might help their more benighted "evangelical" brethren and sisters. As I remember it, the resolution passed without a negative vote. This experience further pushed me out of the "evangelical" orbit and back toward the "Holiness" tradition as separate from and superior to "evangelicalism." I don't think I have been back to an NAE meeting since.

At the time I was studying nineteenth-century revivalist traditions and discovered the social witness of antebellum revivalism and related currents. I found there the closest parallel to the position that I had been working toward for a decade. I felt quite betrayed that all this had not been mediated to me by the modern manifestations of these currents. This work resulted in a series of articles in *The Post American* (later *Sojourners*). Bill Leslie, pastor of Lasalle Street Church, suggested I had a book. I submitted them to Harper and Row and within a week had a contract to produce *Discovering an Evangelical Heritage*. Wesley Theological Seminary last fall (2006) threw a party for me to celebrate its thirtieth anniversary. I am amazed that it is still in print. Harper and Row almost rejected it at the last minute because of critical comments about Billy Graham on the first page—and finally let it go out of print when I refused to rewrite it a decade later. It is now published by Hendrickson and has gone through several printings with them. The book is often misunderstood. I often hear it described as a demonstration that "evangelicals" have always been socially involved when I actually intended the opposite. My original title was "What Ever Happened to Good Old-Fashioned Evangelicalism?"—one that had more the edge of an attack. But the book continues to recycle and I am told that it is gaining popularity in "emerging church" circles. Convinced that it could be heard now in Korea, one of my students translated it into Korean. We shall see.

Much of the rest of my career works out the implications of seeds sown in these years. In 1979 I left North Park a little jaded by the Swedish culture and reserve that prevented it from projecting itself as a more graceful expression of the "evangelical" impulse. I was also concerned that David Larsen, from a part of the Covenant oriented more to the inerrantist Trinity Evangelical Divinity School, was beginning to raise concerns about my rejection of inerrancy. As a non-Covenanter, I did not want to cause trouble for North Park and jumped at the opportunity to move to Northern Baptist Seminary in the Chicago suburbs.

This move may have been a mistake, but at the time I was captured by a vision that several of us shared: to use Northern as the place to articulate the next generation's vision as the "neo-evangelicals" had done in the previous generation at Northern. Ray Bakke came in urban ministry, Bob Guelich in NT, Osvaldo Mottesi directed the Hispanic Program, and I came as librarian. We argued for a "post-evangelical" position that was critical in biblical studies, socially engaged (and open to dialogue with liberation theology), and ecumenical in spirit. We joked that we held, both geographically and theologically, a position midway between Wheaton College and Hyde Park (the location of the University of Chicago and its associated schools in protest to which Northern had originally been founded). This project never really took off. Bob left to get space for his writing. We went through two deans. The president had a heart attack, and the new president was less captivated by our vision. I was chair of a dean search committee that threw me into such major conflict with the president that I barely held on to my job and was forced to dismantle my 25,000 volume library (Fuller Seminary bought over 21,000 volumes of it). The rest of the faculty never completely bought into our vision either. I couldn't make the administration of a joint library (with Bethany Seminary) work and moved to full-time teaching. In the midst of this I suffered a divorce and a tragic automobile accident that left me partially handicapped. Such factors dissipated our energies.

I was also never completely at home in a Baptist theological culture. I could never get used to the idea of a momentary salvation that divided the world into the "saved" and the "unsaved." I viewed, in a more Wesleyan manner, "salvation" as a much more complex process from "prevenient grace" to "entire sanctification" with many stages and ambiguities along the way. I never really understood a culture that held reunions under the category of an "evangelism conference" no matter what the topic (small groups, renewal, homiletics, etc.). I did, however, have many good experiences with students. My signature courses were a Barth seminar, a course on "Protestant Evangelicalism" deconstructing the "neo-evangelical" vision and helping students to find historical alternatives, a course on "recent evangelical social thought" that attempted to sort out the issues that I had lived through in the 1970s, a course on Pentecostalism, and so on. I also worked in homiletics and with the supervision of the writing of graduation confessions of faith.

Northern had a good sabbatical program and some of my best experiences were on these breaks. In 1980 I went to Germany to study in Tübingen, where I worked with Jürgen Moltmann and Eberhard Jüngel (Hans Küng was on leave that term because of his conflicts with the Roman Catholic church). I failed in most of my efforts to catch Moltmann's eye (he had a thousand students in his basic lecture course and two hundred in a more "intimate" seminar on the trinity in Barth and Rahner!) Only latter did he become interested in my work on eschatology, especially the volume entitled *The Coming Kingdom*, based on a conference funded by the Unification Church of Rev. Moon. Much later one of my friends from North Park dropped in on a class in which Moltmann was translating various passages about early Oberlin College from *Discovering an Evangelical Heritage*. I also studied Pietism, fell into the German circles comparable to Sojourners, and scoured European bookstores. I began to develop some controversial theses about the relation of Barth to Pietism. Some of this is reported in my introduction to the English translation of Eberhard Busch's *Karl Barth & the Pietists* and much of this sabbatical was harvested in an article prepared for the Karl Barth Society, "Karl Barth and Evangelicalism: The Varieties of a Sibling Rivalry."

A second sabbatical took me to Buenos Aires to study at ISEDET. My Spanish had to improve rapidly. I wrote back that the good news was that I was studying in probably the most prominent Protestant Seminary in Latin America. The bad news was that it was so because the school was so dependent on European theology. I had courses on Marx, Ricoeur and other European figures. My course on Protestant theology from Kant to Bonhoeffer with José Míguez Bonino differed from my American course by the fact that we read Schleiermacher's *Ethics* rather than his *Hermeneutics*. My favorite course was Latin American church history (taught by an American Disciples missionary). We read unidentified snippets from various books. The students were brilliant in sniffing out the ideological orientation of each text. I remember it being obvious to students that an outline for the history of the church in Central America was written by a graduate of Fuller's School of World Mission. They made their judgment based on the periodization employed. I learned much about the "epistemological advantage of the marginalized and oppressed" through this experience. I spent much of this time with "indigenous" Pentecostal groups, exploring the relationship between liberation theologians advocating being a church of the poor and the leaders of churches of the poor (It is often said that in Latin America the liberation theologians have opted for the poor and the poor have opted for Pentecostalism). I finished this term off with a month in South Africa and an extended visit to Asia, ending up in Korea to attend the hundredth anniversary of Korean Protestantism.

A third sabbatical took me to the World Council of Churches in Geneva at the invitation of General Secretary Emilio Castro in the late 1980s. This experience shaped my understanding of the ecumenical movement in profound ways. I was expected to volunteer my time in an appropriate section of the Council. As a theologian I assumed this should be in "Faith and Order" and was astonished when my service was refused by the German Lutheran head of the commission. I was shunted over to "World Mission and Evangelism." I apparently had no *theological* contribution to make to the Council; my only apparent function was the energizing of evangelism. This experience revealed to me how condescending the Council can be and how much it presupposes the European situation where the issues are more a matter of negotiation of the relations of national churches. I am convinced that the Council will be able to cope with the rest of the world only when it can grow out of its Eurocentrism. I had little luck convincing the Council that as one moves to the periphery one must also make theological adjustments to the more radical ecclesiologies found there. Global Christianity is much more than European Christianity in local dress. And the shedding of Eurocentrism must take place on the theological as well as the social and cultural levels.

I also had the chance to address the Staff Executive Group on the self-defeating strategy of the WCC in attempting to address that "other" usually described monolithically as "evangelicalism." By the use of this category they empowered precisely those who most defined themselves in opposition to the ecumenical movement and made them the spokespersons of the whole, failing to recognize that many groups assumed to be in that category would be happy to engage the Council on their own terms rather than through the filters of the "evangelical" grid. These questions are quite different from the tired conservative/liberal categories that usually are employed to analyze such conflicts.

The experience at the Council gave me access to other meetings. I was invited as an observer to the Central Committee meetings in Moscow, Faith and Order in Norway, World Mission and Evangelism in San Antonio, Texas, and so forth. For a time I worked with the Council on several levels, but especially in relationships with the Pentecostal world in Latin America. One of my most significant contributions was to work with Mel Robeck in the Canberra Assembly to lay the foundation for what has become the Joint Working Group with Pentecostals, parallel with the one with Roman Catholicism. With these groups the Council has at least some formal connections with the two largest groups outside its predominantly Protestant/Orthodox constituency. Just after my time at the Council I wrote the essay included in this volume, originally as an address to the American Theological Society. It was published in *The Ecumenical Review*, and through the title alone it has become one of my most discussed articles.

During this period at Northern I also worked intensively with the Oxford Institute for Methodist Theological Studies. I served on the central core planning committee for a quarter of a century where my major function was to identify persons to be integrated into the discussions so that the full range of Wesleyan traditions could be represented, not just those connected with the mainstream traditions of British and American Methodism and their missionary churches. I generated the idea for a nineteenth-century working group by arguing that one could not just move from the eighteenth-century Wesley to the twentieth-century configurations without attention to the nineteenth-century mediation. I chaired this group for a while. I gave two plenary addresses over the years. The one included in this volume was one of the most discussed. In it I argued that splits in the Methodist tradition do not yield to theological analysis, but are best understood as conflicts over Wesley's "preferential option for the poor."

A final sabbatical took me back to Buenos Aires to teach a course on Pentecostalism at ISEDET. The course itself was a study in the complex relationships of Pentecostalism in Latin America. I had three generations of the Church of God (Cleveland) tradition in my class, at least one of which had to attend the class incognito because he was forbidden to enter the doors of ISEDET since two members of the church had lost their faith in miracles while students there. The politics were such that certain members of the class had to absent themselves when official representatives of the other churches spoke. But it was a great experience for me.

Two leaves from Northern took me to Drew University for my own study and research. I was drawn especially by the Methodist Archives on campus. These periods led to an invitation to join the faculty there for a few years. This was both a very rewarding and also a very frustrating time. The Theological School has a long history of internal conflict, going back at least to the 1950s and more recently manifesting itself in conflicts about the work of Thomas Oden. It has also had a hard time finding its natural niche in the academic world. The dominant ethos has been a very modern and post-modern ethos (remember my graduate student friend from Drew who wondered why I should want to study at fundamentalist Yale!). In many ways it has wanted to "out-Union Union" by having representatives of the latest developments in theology (liberationist, womanist, mujerista, and so on). The student body, however, has been drawn much more from traditional pockets of church life both here and abroad. This led to a very strange campus life. Black and Korean students often held prayer meetings for a "protective covering" as they entered some classes.

Some saw me as the emerging replacement for Tom Oden, including for a while Tom himself. But the political situation required that he advocate for me in secret. Public endorsement would have meant instant death for my candidacy. Few seemed to realize how different I was from Tom and the extent to which I resisted his anti-modernist agenda. On a stroll on the sand of the Asbury Park beach I once asked him how he reconciled his advocacy of the ministry of women with the demands of the Vincentian canon (to believe nothing that was not accepted in all times and in all places in the Church). He blustered for a minute before replying that at least he didn't argue for the practice on modern grounds. I, on the other hand, have always been impressed by the extent to which the "evangelical revival" was embedded very much in the enlightenment and modernity. But I was caught in many ways in Tom's struggle with the rest of the faculty at Drew—and often looked upon with suspicion.

I had a wonderful time with the graduate students there. Some faculty resented the fact that I received the Will Herberg teaching award from the students after a single term of teaching (In my thanks for the honor I asked the graduate students how I should understand an award named for a professor who had never finished college and had faked his whole educational career since!). That reward is represented in this volume. I was overwhelmed by requests to supervise dissertations and began to collapse from the workload (at one point I counted that I was involved with as many as fifty dissertations—far more than I could handle). I was especially welcomed by the Korean students and helped them organize a group they called Pneuma (a support group that consisted primarily of Pentecostal, Holiness and evangelical students from various countries in Asia). As far as I know, this group still functions and has been the source of sections for Asian studies in the WTS and SPS.

Drew has an incredible number of Korean PhD students in theology. The first Protestant missionary to Korea was from Drew, and in many ways a Drew degree is more prestigious than a Harvard one in Korea. My involvement with these Koreans coincided with an increasing interest in Asian Christianity. On a dozen trips to both Korea and Thailand (as well as to other countries) I have taught and lectured in a number of contexts with a special interest in the "indigenous" Holiness and Pentecostal churches in each context. I taught at Drew a course in Korean Church history with Myung Soo Park, represented in this volume. We questioned the usual interpretations of Korean Christianity and applied some of my rethinking of "evangelicalism" to the Korean context.

While I was at Drew another conflict broke out and the Dean was fired after the faculty rebelled against him. I was caught up in these struggles since I had been appointed on his own authority without faculty consultation. The situation was more complex, but this led to my leaving to accept a position at Azusa Pacific University near Los Angeles. There I lasted only a couple of years before retiring after thirty-five years of service on seminary faculties.

Azusa Pacific was not yet prepared intellectually and culturally for the PhD in theology that I was expected to found. It was also the embodiment of all that I feared for the Holiness movement. In spite of the confluence of seven rich streams from the Holiness tradition (from holiness Quakers to the Salvation Army), the school, again one of the largest of the "evangelical" universities, had been over taken by a fundamentalist/evangelical mindset. Rather than drawing on the rich heritage of feminism and social concern in the Holiness movement, the school used gender experts from Focus on the Family and was drawn into the themes of the new religious right, becoming fixated on such themes as gay marriage and abortion. Jaws dropped once when I commented to the Dean in a "chairs" meeting that one of my greatest shocks in coming to APU was to enter a culture where I was expected to take James Dobson seriously. I don't think I really believed in the existence of the new religious right until at APU I met a mathematics professor researching the "biblical worldviews" of the students and faculty. When I asked about themes of biblical worldviews, I was referred to the Federalist papers. Again, a number of conflicts emerged within the school of theology, and the Dean who had brought me on was fired. In the midst of this I gladly took the opportunity for an early retirement and have since then been hanging around Fuller seminary where I can work with many of my own books that are now housed in that library as I continue to write and teach in a variety of contexts.

But finally, should such a career be described as "theology from the margins"? Some might suggest that it represents more a struggle to leave the margins and find my way into the "center." I grant that to be true of certain stages, like my Yalie penny loafers and Gant shirts. Such impulses are almost universal in sectarian movements, whether of the right or of the left. These movements find it almost impossible to pass on a vision to a second generation when children grow up with a compulsion to belong to the wider culture. I remember the humiliation and resentment I felt when I was the only one to stay in a classroom while all the others went out to buy their high school class rings—or the times I was released from physical education classes when the curriculum turned to dancing. And on a more profound level I think of peers who grew up in a church that ordained women (sometimes their mothers) who longed to belong to a "proper middle class" church with male pastors.

Jim Hedstrom, a graduate student at Vanderbilt at the time, once commented about my profound ambivalence about sectarianism. I think he was on to something. I've never been able to fully embrace it and I've never been able to escape from it. I discovered in the 1960s and 1970s that I had a built-in "governor" that prevented me from being a 100% "true believer" in anything without being haunted by the truths that were carried by other partners to the debate. This became especially clear to me when I participated in discussions in Grand Rapids between representatives of *Sojourners* and *The Reformed Journal* after an extended dialogue (one still worth studying; I've often used the articles in classes) in the pages of these journals. I was caught in the middle. I embraced certain themes of the Reformed side (its "cosmic Christology and redemption"; a conviction that the "Kingdom of God" should not be too quickly reduced to the church, and so forth), and I was deeply appreciative on the other hand of the radicalism of the more Anabaptist tradition (a taking seriously of the teachings and especially the "hard sayings" of Jesus, its willingness to try to live in a stance of non-conformity to the "world," and so forth). I am convinced that this middle stance was due to the influence of Barth, and consider that this is one of the most important, but least appreciated, of his contributions. He may have been on a "free church trajectory," as John Howard Yoder argued at a Karl Barth Society meeting that I once organized, but if so, he did this without leaving behind important themes of the more magisterial traditions. I tend to think of myself as a more "catholic" or "synthetic" thinker who often starts with a typological analysis of the basic Christian options (something I learned from James Gustafson) and then tries to synthesize the valid themes of each position without lapsing into a single one. In this sense I would consider myself to be the very opposite of a sectarian.

I also worry about a sloppy use of the terms "margin," "center" and so forth. I found the 1960s very confusing as I tried to find my way between Asbury and Yale. I grew up with television to which I am still addicted, and my father allowed me to spend early paper route money in Marion on a family television set (in part to keep me at home and out from under the feet of the neighbors). But in Kentucky where the church tended to think very literally of television as an "instrument of the Devil," my father had his appearance at a ministers conference cancelled when the conference president saw my TV in the dining room on a courtesy visit after our move to Wilmore (my father at least had the integrity not to hide the TV in a cabinet, but he was relieved that the antenna got good reception in the attic so that he did not have to advertise its presence). But when I got to Columbia, I had to cope with a culture that often found television, at least metaphorically, an "instrument of the Devil" in its mediation of the worst of materialism and consumerism. All this was profoundly confusing to a poor "culturally deprived" student from the hinterland. Similarly, I came from a tradition that renounced "make-up" for women, and had to process the fact that I discovered similar attitudes in the SDS and my socialist kibbutz in Israel (though even there on my last visit I discovered that the generational sociological pressures had taken their toll). Such experiences have at least relativized such terms for me and often have helped free me from captivity to the sociological trajectories that determine the lives of many peers (I am still amazed at the arrogance and condescension of a Nazarene who opposed a WTS meeting at a radical holiness school that still maintained the old standards—he was not going to subject his [!] women to such disapproval!—thus revealing I thought his own insecurity in fleeing such patterns).

On the other hand, I do embrace the title in many ways. I have often worked from the "margins" as a deliberate strategy of change that avoids a direct attack on the center from the center. I have hinted earlier about the advantages of working from the library in theological institutions. I used a similar strategy in the Wesleyan Theological Society, where I served on the executive committee for a couple of decades as "promotional secretary." I could not have been as effective if I had aspired to the presidency as a location from which to effect change—though this was later granted me. I learned some of this from the model of early Oberlin in its struggle against slavery. Theodore Weld, in contrast to many of the more famous abolitionists on the East Coast, preferred to launch his campaign from small towns and local churches. Student evangelists from Oberlin fanned out over Ohio and after revival services founded anti-slavery societies that pushed voters to a new stance against slavery—as has been demonstrated by Phil Hammond in *The Politics of Benevolence* with his "cleometrics" studying voting statistics after newspaper reports of revivals in the county seat towns in Ohio. This fact has, of course, caused distortions in a historiography that has relied on mainstream and Eastern sources.

There is a theological parallel to this sociology. I suppose there are exceptions (Vatican II?), but my study of theology finds that change comes more often from the margin and slowly finds it way to the center. Pentecostalism started in the Azusa Street Mission (almost lost to history until the work of Mel Robeck and others rediscovered its location under the plaza of the Japanese-American cultural center in Los Angeles) among the African-Americans, and its themes are now being debated in the centers of theology. I have often made pilgrimages to centers in Europe that became the sources of major renewal currents. I think of the small town of Möttlingen near Stuttgart from which the Blumhardts, father and son, launched currents that produced religious socialism in Switzerland, the "healing movement" that has transformed the church in many locations, and shaped contemporary theology in profound ways (Tillich, Barth, Moltmann, Cullmann, and so on). Similarly, one should notice the holistic ministry of J. F. Oberlin in Waldheim near Strasbourg in the French counterpart to American Appalachia. This ministry was protected by Napoleon and gave the name to Oberlin College in Ohio. But in both cases these towns are so small that one can find them on maps only with great difficulty, and the churches in question are smaller than average-sized classrooms.

This counterintuitive fact is also well illustrated by the history of the ministry of women. Most people associate this practice with "liberal" churches (I'm reluctant to use the term; it does not get to the heart of the issue). But the fact is that the churches of the NAE (i.e., more marginal) ordained women a century before the churches of the NCC (i.e., more mainstream) and in much larger numbers until recently. Charlotte Allen, a conservative blogger and author, for example, suggested in a recent "op-ed" piece in the *Los Angeles Times* that the Episcopal Church is reaping the results of sowing "liberalism"; she praised "Evangelicals and Pentecostals" for resisting such. She has her history dead wrong, of course, but the assumption is common and reveals more about the way we think than the way things actually happened.

Charlie Cosgrove, my NT college at Northern, and I were once thinking of planning an AAR session on "Disreputable Sources of Now Reputable Ideas." His case study was going to be a study in Barth's dependence on E. F. Ströter, an apparently oxymoronic universalist dispensationalist, who influenced Barth's interpretation of the book of Romans, his doctrine of election and his "universalist" tendency. I was going to trace the ministry of women from Holiness sources to the mainstream (even the founder of the major association of women clergy in the United Church of Christ had been originally a Salvation Army evangelist!). We were thinking of using the comment of Max Weber that in the midst of otherwise "idle chatter" of academics their major function is the mediation to the center of the culture ideas forged in the passionate struggles of the poor and disenfranchised.

One might also offer a theological defense of this situation. In early Christianity the Apostle Paul suggested that the foolishness of the cross in opposition to Greek wisdom should be seen as a sign of the divine origin of the Gospel. Whatever one makes of all that, I should attribute some of these ideas to John Howard Yoder, who was a great influence on my thought over the years, at least since my *Sojourners* period and my reading of *The Politics of Jesus*. Some have argued that we are entering a post-Christian, or at least a post-Constantinian, era where Anabaptist models will come into their own again. I used to tease James Gustafson about his tenacious commitment to doing medical ethics from a distinctly Christian starting point in hospitals so populated by Asian medical personnel. He granted the struggle and admitted that he did his work always with the feeling that John Howard Yoder was looking over his shoulder. Both figures were extremely aware of the work of the other. When I asked them to participate in a Barth Society meeting, they agreed, but only on condition that they appear on separate days and not together—and each absented himself when the other appeared. But again this struggle has deeply conditioned my own thought.

I would like to make one final comment as an interpretation of my work. I have always been impressed how many of my theological mentors (Yoder, Wesley, Barth, the Holiness movement, liberation theology, Howard Snyder, William Booth of the Salvation Army, and so on) have each in their own way been passionate advocates of a "preferential option for the poor." Such concerns lay behind my deep involvement in urban ministry, but I have often struggled with more personal questions of how such a theme should find expression in my own life. For periods of time I have vowed to speak each day to a poor or homeless person to remind myself of this imperative (Wesley said that anyone who did not visit the poor on their own turf at least once a week was "in danger of losing his eternal salvation."). I have struggled with the model of St. Francis, also a major influence on Wesley, but without rejecting that tradition, I have fought more to find ways to put my scholarship at the service of the poor. I have learned much from this strategy, but it is not to be recommended to the faint of heart.

This concern has been a part of my decision to give myself in many ways to the advocacy of Pentecostalism. Robert Anderson in *The Vision of the Disinherited* suggests that the "evangelical" subculture has been sharply socially stratified, at least early in the twentieth century, with Pentecostals on the bottom, evangelicals on the top, and the holiness folk in between. In their social aspiration each has attempted to suppress those elements that might block their movement up the ladder (the Pentecostals fearing, for example, that they would be judged by the Black origins of Pentecostalism or the existence of anti-Trinitarian or "snake-handling" streams; the Holiness historiography attempting to distance the movement from Pentecostalism; the evangelical distortions of their historiography by suppressing relationships with the other two and constructing an identity in their desire to be viewed as "conservative Presbyterians"; and so forth). I know of no better way to grasp the ways in which scholarship serves social agendas than to throw oneself into this vortex with the agenda to move against the sociology. Even in the ecumenical movement it is clear than most wish to dialogue with those higher on the social ladder, better understood and studied, and more ancient and prestigious. I remember being in a room with a United Methodist ecumenist who would break out in a cold sweat at the suggestion that the UMC should pick up dialogue with the Holiness movement and Pentecostalism; he would desperately try to turn the conversation to Buddhist dialogue. I have even wondered if this issue might not lie behind the difficulty we have had in soliciting responses to my work on Methodist history.

The issue is also illustrated by an interchange that took place in Claremont a few years ago. A Dean of the graduate school circulated a memo suggesting that in the light of the changing demographics of American religion it was important to expand the faculty by addition of Jewish, Islamic, Buddhist, Hindu and other scholars. The president of the theological school, bless his heart, circulated a response that said, yes, it was important to reflect the American religious landscape and consideration should be given to hiring an evangelical, a Pentecostal, a Seventh-day Adventist, someone who identifies with the Holiness movement, a Mormon, and so on. There is the issue that I have struggled with and my work cannot be understood without reference to such themes.

This is more than enough at self-interpretation. And again my thanks to Christian and all those who have made this volume possible.

Select Bibliography

THE following select bibliography was partially compiled by Young-Hoon Yoon, PhD. Dr. Yoon studied with Dayton at Drew University and has served as bibliographer of Dayton's work, having compiled a nearly exhaustive two-volume collection of Dayton's works that was made available to friends and colleagues of Dayton at his 60th birthday in 2002. The sources were further documented and the list was filled out by Tyler Gerdin and Aaron Emery from Bethel University.

Books

The American Holiness Movement: A Bibliographic Introduction. Wilmore, KY: B. L. Fisher Library of Asbury Theological Seminary, 1971.
Discovering an Evangelical Heritage. New York: Harper & Row, 1976. Republished with new preface. Peabody: Hendrickson, 1988.
The Theological Roots of Pentecostalism. Metuchen: Scarecrow, 1987; Reprint, Peabody: Hendrickson, 1991. Spanish edition, *Racies Teologicas del Pentecostalismo*. Buenos Aires: Nueva Creacion and Grand Rapids: Eerdmans, 1991.

Selected Volumes from the Garland Series

"The Higher Christian Life": Sources for the Study of the Holiness, Pentecostal, and Keswick Movements

SERIES EDITOR, DONALD W. DAYTON

The Higher Christian Life: A Bibliographical Overview. Edited by Donald W. Dayton. New York: Garland, 1985.
Holiness Tracts Defending the Ministry of Women. Edited by Donald W. Dayton. New York: Garland, 1985.
Late Nineteenth Century Revivalist Teachings on the Holy Spirit. Edited by Donald W. Dayton. New York: Garland, 1985.
Seven "Jesus Only" Tracts. Edited by Donald W. Dayton. New York: Garland, 1985.
Three Early Pentecostal Tracts. Edited by Donald W. Dayton. New York: Garland, 1985.

Fundamentalism in American Religion, 1880–1950
SERIES EDITOR, JOEL CARPENTER

The Prophecy Conference Movement. 4 volumes. Edited by Donald W. Dayton. New York: Garland, 1988.

Other Edited Volumes

Five Sermons and a Tract by Luther Lee. Edited with an Introduction by Donald W. Dayton. Chicago: Holrad, 1975.

Contemporary Perspectives on Pietism. Edited with an Introduction by Donald W. Dayton. Chicago: Covenant, 1976.

Reflections on Revivals. By Charles Grandison Finney. Edited by Donald W. Dayton. Minneapolis: Bethany Fellowship, 1979.

The Coming Kingdom. Edited by M. D. Bryant and Donald W. Dayton. New York: Rose of Sharon, 1983.

The Variety of American Evangelicalism. Edited by Donald W. Dayton and Robert K. Johnston. Knoxville: University of Tennessee Press, 1991. Paperback edition, Downers Grove, IL: InterVarsity, 1991.

Chapters in Books

Co-authored with Nelson F. Burton. "The Theological Seminary and the City." In *Urban Missions*, edited by Craig Ellison. Grand Rapids: Eerdmans, 1974.

Co-authored with Lucille S. Dayton. "An Historical Survey of Attitudes toward War and Peace within the American Holiness Movement." In *Perfect Love and War: A Dialogue on Christian Holiness and the Issues of War and Peace*, edited by Paul Hostetler. Nappanee, IN: Evangel, 1974.

Co-authored with Nancy Hardesty, and Lucille S. Dayton. "Women in the Holiness Movement: Feminism in the Evangelical Tradition." In *Women of Spirit: Female Leadership in the Jewish and Christian Traditions*, edited by Rosemary Ruether and Eleanor McLaughlin. New York: Simon and Schuster, 1979.

"Wither Evangelicalism?" In *Liberation and Sanctification*, edited by Theodore Runyon. Nashville: Abingdon, 1981.

"Millennial Views and Social Reform in Nineteenth Century America." In *The Coming Kingdom: Essays in American Millennialism and Eschatology*, edited by Bryant M. Darrol and Donald W. Dayton. New York: Rose of Sharon, 1983.

"Protestant Christian Missions to Korea as a Source of Unification Thought." In *Religion in the Pacific Era*, edited by Frank Flinn and Tyler Hendricks. Harrisburg, PA: Paragon, 1985.

"The Use of Scripture in the Wesleyan Tradition." In *Use of the Bible in Theology: Evangelical Options*, edited by Robert K. Johnston. Atlanta: John Knox, 1985.

"The Radical Message of Evangelical Christianity." In *Churches in Struggle: Liberation Theologies and Social Change in North America*, edited by William K. Tabb. New York: Monthly Review, 1986.

"Pneumatological Issues in the Holiness Movement." In *Spirit of Truth: Ecumenical Perspectives on the Holy Spirit*, edited by Theodore Stylianopoulos and Mark Heim. Brookline, MA: Holy Cross Orthodox, 1986.

"The Emergence of Pentecostalism." In *American Christianity*, edited by Ronald C. White, Jr., Louis B. Weeks, and Garth M. Rosell. Grand Rapids: Eerdmans, 1986.

"Some Doubts about the Usefulness of the Category 'Evangelical.'" In *The Variety of American Evangelicalism*, edited by Donald W. Dayton and Robert K. Johnston. Knoxville, TN: University of Tennessee Press, 1991.

"The Limits of Evangelicalism: The Pentecostal Tradition." In *The Variety of American Evangelicalism*, edited by Donald W. Dayton and Robert K. Johnston. Knoxville, TN: University of Tennessee Press, 1991.

"Good News to the Poor: the Methodist Experience after Wesley." In *The Portion of the Poor: Good News to the Poor in Wesleyan Tradition*, edited by M. Douglas Meeks. Nashville, TN: Kingwood, 1995.

"The Global Impact of the Wesleyan Traditions and their Related Movements." In *The Global Impact of the Wesleyan Traditions and their Related Movements*, edited by Charles Yrigoyen, Jr. Lanham, MD: Scarecrow, 2002.

"The Pietist Theological Critique of Biblical Inerrancy." In *Evangelicals and Scripture: Tradition, Authority, and Hermeneutics*, edited by Vincent Bacote, Laura C. Miguelez, and Dennis L. Okholm. Downers Grove, IL: InterVarsity, 2004.

"Forward." In *Karl Barth and the Pietists*. By Eberhard Busch. Translated by Daniel W. Bloasch. Downers Grove, IL: InterVarsity, 2004.

Articles

"The American Holiness Movement: A Bibliographical Introduction." *American Theological Library Association Summary of Proceedings* 25 (1971) 71–97.

"Asa Mahan and the Development of American Holiness Theology." *Wesleyan Theological Journal* 9 (1974) 60–69.

"An American Revival of Karl Barth?" *Reformed Journal* 24, no. 8 (October and November, 1974), 17–20 and 24–26.

"Holiness Churches: A Significant Ethical Tradition." *Christian Century* 92 (February 1975) 197–201.

"Dialogue on Women, Hierarchy, and Equality: An Egalitarian View." *Post American* 4, (May 1975) 8–15.

Co-authored with Lucille Sider Dayton. "Women as Preachers: Evangelical Precedents." *Christianity Today* 19, no. 17 (1975) 4–7.

"Piety and Radicalism: Ante-Bellum Social Evangelicalism in the US." *Radical Religion* 3, no. 1 (1976) 36–40.

Co-authored with Lucille S. Dayton. "Your Daughters Shall Prophesy: Feminism in the Holiness Movement." *Methodist History* 14, no. 2 (1976) 67–92.

"Evangelical Roots of Feminism." *Covenant Quarterly* 34, no. 4 (1976) 41–56.

"Battle for the Bible: Renewing the Inerrancy Debate." *Christian Century* 93, (November 1976) 976–80.

"The Social Political Conservatism of Modern American Evangelicalism." *Union Seminary Quarterly Review* 32 (Winter 1977) 71–80.

"The Doctrine of the Baptism of the Holy Spirit: Its Emergence and Significance." *Wesleyan Theological Journal* 13 (Spring 1978) 114–26.

"Breaking Down the Barriers to Faith: Karl Barth's Determinative Influence on My Life." *Sojourners* 7 (December 1978) 25–26.

"The Holiness and Pentecostal Churches: Emerging from Cultural Isolation." *Christian Century* 96 (August 15–22, 1979) 786–92.

"The Church in the World: 'The Battle for the Bible' Rages On." *Theology Today* 37, (April 1980) 79–84.

"Some Perspectives on 'The New Christian Right.'" *Fides et Historia* 15, no. 1 (1982) 54–60.

"The Rise of the Evangelical Healing Movement in the 19th Century." *Pneuma* 4, no. 2 (1982) 1–18.

"Evangelicals and the World Council of Churches: A (Very) Personal Analysis." *Theological Students Fellowship Bulletin* 7, no. 1 (1983) 14–17.

"Engaging the World: The Evangelism of Charles Finney." *Sojourners* 13 (March 1984) 16–19.

"Karl Barth and Evangelicalism: The Varieties of Sibling Rivalry." *Theological Students Fellowship Bulletin* 8, no. 5 (May-June 1985) 18–23.

"Pneumatological Issues in the Holiness Movement." *Greek Orthodox Theological Review* 31, nos. 3–4 (1986) 361–87.

"The Emourgeoisement of a Vision: Lament of a Radical Evangelical." *Other Side* 23, no. 8 (1987) 19.

"Yet Another Layer of the Onion: Or Opening the Ecumenical Door to let the Riffraff In." *Ecumenical Review* 40, no. 1 (1988) 87–110.

"The Holiness Witness in the Ecumenical Church." *Wesleyan Theological Journal* 23, nos. 1, 2 (1988) 92–106.

"Pentecostal/Charismatic Renewal and Social Change." *Transformation* 5, no. 4 (1988) 7–13.

"The Holy Spirit and Christian Experience in the 20th Century." *Missiology* 16, no. 4 (Oct. 1988) 397–407.

"Presidential Address: The Wesleyan Option for the Poor." *Wesleyan Theological Journal* 26, no. 1 (1991) 7–22.

"Law and Gospel in the Wesleyan Tradition." *Grace Theological Journal* 12, no. 2 (1991) 233–43

"'The Search for the Historical Evangelicalism': George Marsden's History of Fuller Seminary as a Case Study." *Christian Scholar's Review* 23, no. 1 (1993) 12–33.

Miscellaneous

"Interview with Donald Dayton," *Modern Reformation* 1:10 (Mar/April 2001).

Contributors

WILLIAM J. ABRAHAM
Outler Professor of Wesley Studies and Altshuler Distinguished Teaching Professor
Perkins School of Theology
Southern Methodist University

DAWK-MAHN BAE
Professor of Historical Theology
Asia LIFE University

DAVID BUNDY
Associate Provost for Library Services and *Associate Professor of History*
Fuller Theological Seminary

CHRISTIAN T. COLLINS WINN
Assistant Professor of Historical and Systematic Theology
Bethel University

MELVIN EASTERDAY DIETER
Professor Emeritus of Church History and Historical Theology
Asbury Theological Seminary

BILL FAUPEL
Professor of Theological Research and *Director of the Library*
Wesley Theological Seminary

BROTHER JEFF GROS, FSC
Professor of Church History
Memphis Theological Seminary

NANCY A. HARDESTY
Professor of Religion
Clemson University

S. SUE HORNER
    Independent Writer and Scholar
    Boston, MA
    Recently *Associate Professor of Women's Studies*
    North Park University

ROBERT K. JOHNSTON
    Professor of Theology and Culture
    Fuller Theological Seminary

SCOTT KISKER
    James Cecil Logan Assistant Professor of Evangelism and Wesley Studies
    Wesley Theological Seminary

WILLIAM KOSTLEVY
    Professor of History and Political Science
    Tabor College

FRANK D. MACCHIA
    Professor of Theology
    School of Religion
    Vanguard University

JAMES S. NELSON
    Associate Professor of Biblical and Theological Studies
    North Park University

MYUNG SOO PARK
    Professor of Church History and *Director of Korea Evangelical Historical Research Center*
    Seoul Theological University

CLARK H. PINNOCK
    Professor Emeritus of Systematic Theology
    McMaster Divinity College

CECIL M. ROBECK JR.
    Professor of Church History and Ecumenics and *Director of the David du Plessis Center for Christian Spirituality*
    Fuller Theological Seminary

JOEL SCANDRETT
    Associate Academic and Reference Editor
    InterVarsity Press

HOWARD SNYDER
Professor of the History and Theology of Mission
E. Stanley Jones School of World Mission and Evangelism
Asbury Theological Seminary

DOUGLAS M. STRONG
Dean of the School of Theology
Seattle Pacific University

JIM WALLIS
President
Call to Renewal/Sojourners

WOODROW W. WHIDDEN II
Professor of Religion
Andrews University

AMOS YONG
Associate Research Professor of Theology
Regent University School of Divinity

www.ingramcontent.com/pod-product-compliance
Lightning Source LLC
Chambersburg PA
CBHW071234300426
44116CB00008B/1028